ENVIRONMENTAL QUALITY ANALYSIS
Theory and Method in the Social Sciences

ENVIRONMENTAL QUALITY ANALYSIS

Theory and Method in the Social Sciences

Papers from a Resources for the Future Conference
Edited by
ALLEN V. KNEESE AND BLAIR T. BOWER

Published for
Resources for the Future, Inc.
by
The Johns Hopkins Press, Baltimore and London

208575

Resources for the Future is a nonprofit corporation for research and education in the
development, conservation, and use of natural resources and the improvement of the
quality of the environment. It was established in 1952 with the cooperation of the Ford
Foundation. Part of the work of Resources for the Future is carried out by its resident
staff; part is supported by grants to universities and other nonprofit organizations.
Unless otherwise stated, interpretations and conclusions in RFF publications are those
of the authors; the organization takes responsibility for the selection of significant
subjects for study, the competence of the researchers, and their freedom of inquiry.

RFF editors: Henry Jarrett, Vera W. Dodds, Nora E. Roots, Tadd Fisher.

This book is one of RFF's studies on the quality of the environment, directed by Allen
V. Kneese. Blair T. Bower is associate director. The book is based on papers prepared
for the RFF conference on "Research on Environmental Quality: Theoretical and
Methodological Studies in the Social Sciences," held in June 1970 in Washington, D.C.

The manuscript was edited by Sheila Barrows. The charts were drawn by Clare and
Frank Ford. The index was prepared by L. Margaret Stanley.

Copyright © 1972 by The Johns Hopkins Press
All rights reserved
Manufactured in the United States of America

The Johns Hopkins Press, Baltimore, Maryland   21218
The Johns Hopkins Press Ltd., London

Library of Congress Catalog Card Number 78-181556
ISBN 0-8018-1332-8

Contents

Introduction.. 1
Allen V. Kneese and Blair T. Bower

I. THE ENVIRONMENT AND ECONOMIC GROWTH

1. Economic Growth and the Natural Environment............. 11
   Ralph C. d'Arge
2. A Materials-Process-Product Model........................ 35
   Robert U. Ayres
3. Observations on the Economics of Irreplaceable Assets........ 69
   John V. Krutilla, Charles J. Cicchetti, A. Myrick Freeman III, and Clifford S. Russell

II. DEVELOPING MANAGEMENT PROGRAMS

4. A Quantitative Framework for Residuals Management Decisions 115
   Clifford S. Russell and Walter O. Spofford, Jr.
5. Agricultural Pesticides: Productivity and Externalities........ 181
   Max R. Langham, Joseph C. Headley, and W. Frank Edwards
6. Air Pollution Damage: Some Difficulties in Estimating the Value
   of Abatement... 213
   Lester B. Lave
7. The Distribution of Environmental Quality.................. 243
   A. Myrick Freeman III

CONTENTS

III. DESIGNING POLITICAL AND LEGAL INSTITUTIONS

8. Environmental Quality as a Problem of Social Choice......... 281
   Edwin T. Haefele
9. Legal Strategies Applicable to Environmental Quality Management Decisions..................................... 333
   Joseph L. Sax
10. Power Structure Studies and Environmental Quality Management: The Study of Powerful Urban Problem-Oriented Leaders in Northeastern Megalopolis.......................... 345
    Delbert C. Miller

Index.. 397

Authors of Papers

Robert U. Ayres
Physicist, International Research and Technology Corporation

Charles J. Cicchetti
Economist, Resources for the Future, Inc.

Ralph C. d'Arge
Economist, University of California, Riverside

W. Frank Edwards
Economist, Wake Forest University

A. Myrick Freeman III
Economist, Bowdoin College

Edwin T. Haefele
Political Theorist, Resources for the Future, Inc.

Joseph C. Headley
Economist, University of Missouri

John V. Krutilla
Economist, Resources for the Future, Inc.

Max R. Langham
Economist, University of Florida

Lester B. Lave
Economist, Carnegie-Mellon University

Delbert C. Miller
Sociologist, University of Indiana

Clifford S. Russell
Economist, Resources for the Future, Inc.

Joseph L. Sax
Lawyer, University of Michigan

Walter O. Spofford, Jr.
Engineer, Resources for the Future, Inc.

Discussants

Blair T. Bower
Civil Engineer–Economist, Resources for the Future, Inc.

Gardner Brown, Jr.
Economist, University of Washington

Rufus P. Browning
Political Scientist, Michigan State University

Donald A. Chant
Ecologist, University of Toronto

Matthew A. Crenson
Political Scientist, Johns Hopkins University

Martin H. David
Economist, University of Wisconsin

Otto A. Davis
Economist, Carnegie-Mellon University

Robert Dorfman
Economist, Harvard University

John R. Goldsmith
Medical Doctor, California Department of Public Health

Robert H. Haveman
Economist, Resources for the Future, Inc.

Milton S. Heath, Jr.
Lawyer, University of North Carolina

Philip H. Hoff
Lawyer, Burlington, Vermont

Kent M. Jennings
Political Scientist, University of Michigan

Richard W. Judy
Economist, University of Toronto

George O. G. Löf
Chemical Engineer, Denver, Colorado

Daniel P. Loucks
Civil Engineer, Cornell University

Edwin S. Mills
Economist, Johns Hopkins University

DISCUSSANTS

Peter H. Rossi
Sociologist, Johns Hopkins University

Robert H. Strotz
Economist, Northwestern University

Azriel A. Teller
Economist, Temple University

Each paper presented at the conference was followed by one or two formal discussions. All of the discussants raised significant points and some of them were outstandingly penetrating. The main purpose of the formal discussions was to help the authors improve their papers, and in almost all cases the papers were substantially revised in light of them. Accordingly, the editors have decided not to publish the discussions themselves.

ENVIRONMENTAL QUALITY ANALYSIS
Theory and Method in the Social Sciences

Introduction

Allen V. Kneese and Blair T. Bower

BACKGROUND

By now it is certainly not necessary to point out that environmental quality is a matter of deep interest and concern to the citizenry, government, and the professions. But for the social sciences it is a new area of concern. With the exception of some theoretical inquiries in economics and some early work in social psychology, applied social science work on environmental questions is less than ten years old.

Resources for the Future ventured into the environmental field as a result of natural evolution in its research mission with respect to natural resources. When RFF came into existence about fifteen years ago, the United States was at the crest of a wave of concern about the scarcity of natural resources. This followed a period of rapid depletion of resource stocks and little new exploration or development during World War II. A period of quantitative study at RFF indicated that resources scarcity as such was unlikely to put a brake on economic development in the United States until at least the end of this century.

But it also became clear that consideration of resources problems could not stop with this comforting conclusion. It was already apparent in the late fifties and early sixties that the quality of some of our important, if neglected, resources—particularly air and water—was deteriorating. Moreover, projections of resources inputs implied that vastly larger quantities of fuels, foods, minerals, and forest products would be used in the future. Conservation of mass tells us that these materials do not disappear into the void after they are burned and processed, but that a residual mass about equal to that initially extracted from nature must eventually be ac-

1

commodated. Unless economical and carefully designed control of residuals generation and recycling processes is undertaken, the common "dumps" of air and water must suffer spectacular quality degradation with grave effects on ecology and in due course on man. Furthermore, as time passes it will be necessary to utilize lower grades of ore deposits that require more processing so that progressively more energy and residual "tailings" will be associated with each unit of resource recovered. Accordingly, residuals will tend to rise at an increasing ratio with the use of resources. Also there will be a tendency to reach further into remote places to obtain resource commodities and energy, thus destroying or threatening to damage rare ecological or geomorphological features.

For the last decade RFF has been developing a program of studies on environmental quality. The focus in this program remains on *natural* resources so at this stage it does not incorporate much work on some of the more strictly urban concerns that are often included under the broad, and usually ill-defined, term "environment." These concerns include such matters as the aesthetic aspects of buildings and urban patterns, bad housing, traffic congestion and accidents, and crime. Thus the large-scale problems of managing the quality of such natural resources as air, water, and ecological systems is a subset, but a very important subset, of what are often called environmental problems.

The papers brought together in this volume are an extensive, but by no means complete, sampling from the work of the RFF program on the quality of the environment, which falls naturally into three broad areas: (1) The Environment and Economic Growth. This includes both theoretical and empirical projects on the impact of growth on the natural environment. (2) Management Programs. This includes both formal mathematical modeling to aid in understanding the complex interrelationship between human activities and environmental systems and analysis of salient public policy alternatives. (3) Political and Legal Institutions. The environment presents society with the problem of making special kinds of collective choices; i.e., about how particular commonly owned natural resources are to be used. They are special because with respect to traditional resources like land and minerals we usually rely mostly on the market to make these choices. Questions of leadership and institution building are also deeply involved here.

Understandably, in view of its short history, social science research on most of these issues is still largely at an exploration or methodological stage. But work is now advancing rapidly as we hope the papers in this volume will show. Before turning explicitly to them, however, we will develop the conceptual basis for RFF work in this field a little further and make some comments on the background of social sciences research in it.

ALLEN V. KNEESE AND BLAIR T. BOWER

A USEFUL CONCEPT FROM ECONOMICS

To address a research problem effectively it is important to have a reasonably clear concept of its central character and preferably one to which the pertinent disciplines can relate their work. We cannot hope to find such a concept that would please everyone, even in the social sciences. But we do know that for it to be operationally useful for social science research it must pertain to society's decision making systems and institutions, and yet, to be useful in connection with natural resources problems it must also intersect in meaningful ways with the phenomena of the natural world.

It seems to us that the most nearly suitable concept is that of "common property resources." The common property terminology arose out of the contemplation by economists of a rather limited range of natural resources problems—although in a more general sense it grew out of the term "commons" applied to commonly held lands of medieval England. Problems such as those associated with the exploitation of petroleum pools, groundwater aquifers, and ocean fisheries came in economics to be called "common pool" or "common property" problems. This is because the physical circumstances of their occurrence made it difficult, if not impossible, to assign private property rights to clearly identifiable portions of them under prevailing social institutions. Mapping out holdings on the surface of the earth or water did not suffice because the valued resource was "migratory" or could be captured in disproportionate amounts by intensive exploitation at particular places. So long as the prices or values of these resources could not be established by private exchange, the market system failed in a most fundamental way to allocate them to their most productive uses or provide for a pattern of development or exploitation which would serve both present and future uses in an efficient manner.

While economic theory has long recognized the existence of such situations and worked out an elaborate explanation of the types of overuse and misuse of resources that must result, these cases were treated as rare and exceptional occurrences in the overall workings of the economy. In general the economic theory of resources use and allocation has developed on the presumption that virtually everything of value is suitable for private ownership with little or no "spillover" to other persons, households, and firms when the private property is put to use by its owner. If this were true, the competitive market could then be visualized as a mechanism through which all mutual gains from trade could be exhausted until no one could be made better off by further exchanges given his preferences, the resources available to society, and his ability to call on those resources (the distribution of income). These statements may be regarded as a loose

3

description of the fundamental theorem of modern welfare economics. Of course, it was realized that sometimes adjustments had to be made for "market failure," but these were implicitly, if not explicitly, regarded as minor with respect to the overall allocation.

But it has become more clear over the past few decades that the pure private property concept applies satisfactorily to a progressively narrowing range of natural resources and economic activities. As time has passed, common property natural resources have become rapidly more significant in our production and consumption activities and in the quality of life more generally. This has resulted both from their increasing scarcity and their declining quality as well as from the fact that they tend to be "superior goods," the demand for which rises more than in proportion to increases in income. The air mantle, watercourses and oceans, landscapes, the electromagnetic spectrum, complex ecosystems, climate, and rare geo-morphological features of the earth are becoming relatively more valuable than the goods and commodities whose production impinges upon these "superior goods." Private property and market exchange have but little applicability to their allocation, development, and conservation. Collective choice mechanisms and institutions are needed if they are to be used and conserved effectively and efficiently. Man is not only overusing and mis-using these resources in quite understandable ways, given our current institutional milieu, but actually is starting to affect the basic supply of some of them—for example, through inadvertent weather, climate, and biota modification. We are at but a primitive stage in our understanding of these resources, and of the problems of management, analytical meth-ods, policy, and institution building with which they present us—although it can be claimed that the papers in this book reflect progress in all these respects. In one way or another they all relate to the problem of managing that set of natural resources that are held in common by the society.

PREVIOUS WORK IN THE OTHER SOCIAL SCIENCES

If economics has been slow to adapt itself to the increasingly pervasive importance of common property natural resources, attention from other disciplines, with the exception of law, has been close to nonexistent. There was a phase in the development of sociology, social psychology, and social anthropology, extending into the twentieth century, when the influence of the natural environment on human behavior was regarded as important if not dominant. There were reasoned, if not necessarily correct, links from climate to physiology to personality and finally to war and politics. There were even some primitive efforts at the application of scientific

4

method to the propositions. For example, early in this century, Edwin Dexter correlated weather and behavior, including such things as deportment in New York public schools and murders and arrests for drunkenness in Denver. Theories like his fell into disrepute later in the twentieth century with the result that sociologists, social psychologists, and social anthropologists turned their attention almost entirely away from the natural world. Moreover, as American society became more urban, these fields came more and more to be populated by persons of urban origin and orientation. The result is that there is very little in the recent literature of these disciplines helpful in understanding basic attitudes toward, and preferences with respect to, common property natural resources or in devising collective management policies, strategies, and institutions with respect to them. A few good beginnings have been made but have not been followed up by the force of concentrated professional research. For example, Walter Firey in his *Land Use in Central Boston* (Harvard University Press, 1947) showed that the value of land in Boston was not so much a function of its location with respect to natural features or relative to the remainder of the city but was associated primarily with symbolic meanings. Interestingly, the most pertinent and successful work with a social psychological cast was done not by social scientists as such but by geographers—especially those associated with Gilbert White at the University of Chicago. In recent years there have been a few studies by sociologists and political scientists of the institutional aspects of watershed organizations and of decision making with respect to specific issues relating to water supply or water pollution at the local governmental level. Only a few sociological studies have been made of societal power structures with respect to environmental problems; perhaps the most ambitious of these is reported in this volume.

Political science research is equally undeveloped with respect to what is so centrally a problem of politics and government—the management of common property natural resources. Our political institutions face a number of hard challenges arising from the rapidly growing importance of common property resources. For example, the "problem sheds" in which these problems occur do not conform in areal extent to existing units of government. They are regional and international—rarely local, state, or national. Thus we face the difficult problem of designing government institutions to comport better with the spatial character of these problems and defining the relation of these institutions to governments of general jurisdiction. Furthermore, since the market does not assign values to common property natural resources, we must learn to understand what kind of political structures can accurately reflect the preferences of affected people. While political scientists and public administrators have con-

5

cerned themselves with natural resources—especially water resources—they have usually not addressed the problem of institutional design, and the existing literature as yet contains little of real help on this pressing problem. A small group of political theorists, economists, and legal scholars is now beginning to provide a structure for the analysis of these problems and to make some progress on them. A substantial part of this work is reflected in the final section of this book.

PLAN OF THE BOOK

This book, like the RFF program, is organized around the three main themes—understanding environment and economic growth, developing management programs, and designing political and legal institutions. For the most part the papers are theoretical and methodological in character as is fitting at this stage of social sciences work. But if this were the end of the matter little would have been gained, for empirical work based on carefully developed theory is badly needed. Several of the papers already report significant empirical results, and some of the others are at the take-off point for applied work. We feel that there can be found in this book at least modest encouragement that the social sciences will meet the challenge to help improve the management of our common property resources.

The first paper in the section on environment and economic growth is by Ralph d'Arge. He applies the concepts of modern economic growth theory to a situation where finite limits exist, both with respect to non-renewable natural resources that serve as inputs to production-consumption processes and to the ability of the common property environmental resources to accommodate the unrecycled residuals from these activities. This involves the application of a "materials balance" approach adopted from basic physics. Put simply, this means that the mass of residuals generated is equal to that embodied in the natural resources inputs used in production and consumption, except for that part that accumulates in the economic system. The residuals generated can be disposed of ultimately in only two ways: recycled back into production and consumption activities or discharged into the environment—air, land, water. A portion, and often all, of the residuals generated is discharged to common property resources. Such discharge is therefore unpriced in the ordinary course of market exchange, even though the waste disposal services rendered by the environment conflict with other valuable uses of the common property natural resources. The second paper in this section (by Robert Ayres) uses a similar approach, but at a much more detailed and therefore less comprehensive level, to examine how the quantity of residuals is influenced by the nature of the production activities and the character of the products produced. Some illustrative applications to specific manufacturing processes and operations are presented and some suggestions made as to how this approach could be used to project residuals generation and discharge into the future. The final paper in this section (by John Krutilla, Charles Cicchetti, Myrick Freeman, and Clifford Russell) deals with the special problem of natural assets—valuable in their natural state—that cannot be restored once their natural state is altered. A case situation is considered in detail—Hells Canyon of the Snake River, which contains irreplaceable ecological and geomorphological features. Methodology for analysis of these types of situations is developed and applied. The analysis is also pertinent to irreplaceable cultural assets.

The second section of the book deals with management programs. The initial paper (by Clifford Russell and Walter Spofford) is the first rather full report on a major project aimed at building a regional model for the analysis of residuals management in a region. The master model contains submodels of production and consumption activities, modification of residuals after generation in such activities, discharge of residuals (with locations preserved), dispersion and degradation of residuals in the environment, effects on receptors, and mechanisms for feeding back information for decisions in the production-consumption-residuals modification segment. The next phase of this project will be to apply the model to a regional case study. The second paper (by Max Langham, Joseph Headley, and Frank Edwards) discusses a pair of studies analyzing the benefits and costs of pesticide usage in American agriculture. A technique is developed for estimating the trade-off between pesticide and other production inputs, and a case study of the benefits and costs of pesticide usage in Dade County, Florida, is presented. The third paper (by Lester Lave) addresses the general question of how social damages from deteriorating common property resources can be evaluated and develops a measure of the health damages from deteriorated air quality. The final paper (by Myrick Freeman) deals with the questions of how damages of environmental quality deterioration tend to get distributed among income classes who in one way or another use these common property resources and the relevance of such information to policy decisions.

The final section of the book deals with designing political and legal institutions. The first paper (by Edwin Haefele) reviews recent developments, including the author's own, in the analysis of public choice mechanisms. In particular, several methodological tools for evaluating the results of collective choice mechanisms are discussed and applied to some actual cases of existing or proposed regional environmental quality management

7

institutions. The second paper (by Joseph Sax) provides insight concerning how legal processes may play a role in the allocation of common property resources—especially by forcing a fuller examination of alternatives than would otherwise occur. The paper also points out very clearly the limitations of the government agencies that are supposed to protect "the public interest." The final paper (by Delbert Miller) describes the methodology and results of an application of community power-structure research techniques to a much larger and more complex area than any previously studied in this way—the northeastern U.S. megalopolis. In it an effort is made to identify those people and organizations who could provide leadership in effectively addressing the environmental quality problems of this region. He also comments on a parallel study of a subregion—the Delaware River Basin.

We hope that other scholars working on environmental problems will be interested in and stimulated by this book.

PART I

THE ENVIRONMENT AND
ECONOMIC GROWTH

1. Economic Growth and the Natural Environment

Ralph C. d'Arge

I. INTRODUCTION

Perhaps one of the most enlightening ideas to emerge in the twentieth century with respect to scarcity of natural resources is the realization that man lives in a virtually closed resource system—a natural environment with essentially fixed dimensions in terms of mass-energy and assimilative-regenerative capacity (Ayres and Kneese 1969; Boulding 1966; Daly 1968). Barring consideration of economically feasible extraterrestrial transportation systems, inputs of solar energy or meteorites, or destruction of matter by symmetrical antimatter, whatever is produced, consumed, *and discarded* within the resource system is still here and will continue to be. Of course, in the very long run man may be able to colonize other planets and/or import relatively cheap raw materials and energy from and export wastes to locations outside this planet—science fiction has an uncanny and unpredictable knack of becoming nonfiction. But what is of pressing concern if we accept the premise of a closed resource system is the quantitative and qualitative characteristics of the system in relation to: (a) man's health, material, and aesthetic demands, and (b) population growth and clustering. The question is whether the size and regenerative capability of the natural environment is large enough to allow sustained economic growth and population expansion without seriously impinging on health and aesthetic demands. This question in a general sense is as yet un-

The author is indebted to A. V. Kneese, R. Strotz, R. Dorfman, K. C. Kogiku, J. S. Earley, and E. Brook for comments and discussion on an earlier draft. A substantial portion of the research reported on here was funded by a grant from Resources for the Future, Inc.

11

answered, but there is evidence that at least in a number of metropolitan-urban population clusters, the answer is a resounding no.

As a rather striking example, Leighton (1964), using data from the Los Angeles air basin, has calculated that tonnages of air-polluting emissions increase according to the following formula:

$$E_t/E_{t-1} = (P_t/P_{t-1})^n, \tag{1}$$

where E_t and P_t denote tonnage of emissions and population in period t, respectively; and n is a constant. Leighton estimates n as equaling 1.6 for total oxides of nitrogen emissions and 1.5 for gasoline emissions. Clearly, emissions increase more than proportionately to population growth if these calculations are correct. In addition, Leighton and McMullen (Leighton 1964), using the same data, have calculated that a doubling of population density *and* city land area results in a twentyfold increase in the area in which visibility is reduced by air-pollutant emissions.[1] These results taken together are only one rather limited example of the observation of Scitovsky, Kneese, Barnett and Morse, and others, that externalities, particularly external diseconomies, grow increasingly pervasive with expanding population and economic growth if left unregulated (Scitovsky 1966; Ayres and Kneese 1969; Barnett and Morse 1963).

The natural environment or resource system essentially provides four important roles or services for man: (a) source of raw materials; (b) space for waste accumulation and storage; (c) assimilation-regenerative capability for chemically or biologically active wastes; and (d) determinant of health level and life style, and of aesthetic satisfactions. But as ecologists have known for a long time, these services are not separable but highly interdependent. Relatively large amounts of wastes dumped into a river may alter significantly, and irreversibly, its natural ecology and thus destroy the river's ability to assimilate even much lower waste loads. This waste flow may also markedly raise downriver water costs, even if the river's assimilative capability is not damaged, and influence the location of housing and industry downriver. The list of external diseconomies induced by waste emissions to airsheds and waterways can conceptually be endlessly cataloged. For example, if there are M points of emission,

---

[1] Using the Leighton-McMullen estimates, I have calculated that distance between the center of a city and farthest point of reduced visibility increases approximately fourfold with a doubling of population density and area. Thus, if Los Angeles were to increase sevenfold in area and population, with *assumed* wind direction and velocity, overhead inversion layer constant, and *assuming* the United States is a horizontal plane, Boston would be a recipient of Los Angeles' smog. However, Bostonians need not worry since these idealized assumptions are pure fiction, and almost everyone residing in the lower coastal California valleys would have died of asphyxiation long before such a New England catastrophe!

N directions of emissions, and S potential types of damages for each emission, without consideration of interaction of emissions or potential combinations of damages, there will be NMS possible damage functions to be estimated. Even in terms of a medium-sized city, NMS may well exceed 50,000 for just major stationary sources of pollutant emissions. Of course, with sufficient and reasonably consistent aggregation this immense task might become feasible.

Elsewhere, Kneese and I have attempted to demonstrate, using a highly simplified static model, that Paretian conditions throughout the economy including the economy's interaction with the natural environment and optimal utilization of this environment could be achieved through a tax (or set of taxes and subsidies) applied to each type of consumer product (d'Arge and Kneese 1969). Given several very restrictive assumptions on waste technology, such a tax would be proportional to the amount of waste embodied in each product including both wastes generated by production and wastes from the product's ultimate disposal. The proportional tax embodied components for qualitative aspects of the assumed scarce natural environment, and for the interaction of waste storage on availability of raw materials and the effect of raw materials extraction on assimilative capacity. The model analyzed, however, contained two rather limiting ancillary assumptions; the first of linearity of production processes, and additivity of waste flows and assimilative capability of the natural environment; the second of an essentially static economy exhibiting no growth in population or change in output over time. This paper will explore some of the connections between the economy and natural environment when the assumption of a static economy is removed. However, in most instances the assumptions regarding linearity and additivity in production activities and waste generation will be retained.

II. THE MATERIALS-BALANCE APPROACH

The materials-balance view of a closed resource system indicates that tonnages of raw materials extraction utilized by an economy is approximately equal to waste products generated by the economy in the long run (Ayres and Kneese 1969). Figure 1.1 is a simplified diagram depicting material and waste flows between the natural environment and economy. Specifically, let it be assumed that flows of matter-energy can be aggregated in a meaningful way so that we are able to analyze such a closed resource system with only a few variables. It is also assumed initially that nothing is temporarily stored or saved within the economy and no recycling exists within or between production and consumption sectors. Then a basic

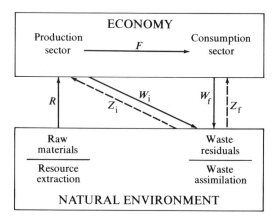

Figure 1.1. Material flow depiction of the economy and natural environment.

identity derivable from the principle of conservation of matter-energy, given the depictions of material flows in figure 1.1, is:

$$R = W_i + W_f = W, \qquad \text{with } Z_i, Z_f = 0; \\ F = W_f, \tag{2}$$

where R, F, Z, and W denote material extraction and fixation, final consumption, recycled materials, and total waste flows, respectively. W_i and W_f are the amounts of waste flow originating in, and Z_i and Z_f the amounts of recycled residuals returning to, the production and consumption sectors.

Given these fundamental identities and assumptions, it is possible to write an additional identity provided the flow F of material is assumed homogeneous and a flow S of services in the economy embodying no material goods is also homogeneous. Basically, I assume that there are only two types of consumer goods, one containing material and the other purely nonmaterial:

$$P_f \cdot F + P_s \cdot S = Y \cdot N, \tag{3}$$

where P_f and P_s denote unit prices of F and S, and Y and N denote money income per capita and population. For this discussion, assume that $P_s \cdot S$ equals zero and money income is only counted in units of material.[2]

---

[2] This assumption may appear to be Marxian in orientation—pure services do not create value. However, whether Marx did embrace such an extreme view is currently disputed (Coontz 1966). In any case, I hope to alter the structure of what follows so that services can be explicitly included. For now, suffice it to say that as the economy grows, if the effects of increasing waste densities are to be ameliorated, a significant shift toward "pure" service types of industries becomes almost imperative.

Then

$$P_f \cdot F = Y \cdot N$$

and   (4)

$$F = y \cdot N,$$

where y is per capita income in units of material flow per capita. Finally, following our previous assumptions of linearity, let it be assumed that total waste flows are proportional to final product in each period t (Ayres and Kneese 1969; d'Arge and Kneese 1969):

$$W_t = gF_t. \tag{5}$$

Then, by assuming that each variable previously defined refers to one time interval, t, waste flows are linearly related to total income measured in material units:

$$W_t = g \cdot y_t \cdot N_t. \tag{6}$$

Thus a relation is obtained between waste flows and output per capita. Actually the assumption of proportionality is even more restrictive than one might at first assume, since it also completely specifies an implicit technology relating output to raw materials. By definitions, $W_t = R_t$, so $W_t = gy_t \cdot N_t$ yields $y_t = (1/g)(R_t/N_t)$. Thus, in this most simple case, production results only from the magnitude of raw materials and there is, by implication, no substitution between labor and raw materials in the production process. In what follows, the assumption of linearity, while simplifying the discussion, also restricts the generality of the conclusions in this section. In terms of empirical units, the number $g \cdot y_t$ for the final sector—i.e., W_{ft}/N_t—is estimated to be greater than 1 ton per capita, per year, for the United States at current levels of production, but is projected to exceed 1½ tons per capita by 1980.

The next task is to "model" the environment in some semirealistic and yet manageable way. Environmental pollution, at least in its quantitative dimensions, is usually expressed in terms of concentrations—i.e., parts per million of dissolved solids or DDT, parts per million (suitably indexed) of carbon monoxide or reactive hydrocarbon concentrations in air, or tons per cubic acre of solid wastes. Thus, a natural unit of waste concentration appears to be density. Of course, concern only with densities may be misleading—particularly when considering such pollutants as methane gas generated from solid wastes. Also, density per se is undoubtedly an unrealistic single measure to be associated with long-run health effects of persistent pollutants; for example, relatively low concentrations of carbon monoxide causing a rise of carboxy-hemoglobin in humans. How-

15

ever, for the moment it will be assumed that density is a reasonable, abstract measure of waste concentrations.

Let D_t denote waste density at the beginning of time interval t and V denote total environmental waste holding capacity. Thus, in effect the closed resource system has been identified by a simple fixed volumetric magnitude, V. Then

$$D_t \cdot V = \sum_{j=0}^{t-1} W_j + VD_0, \tag{7}$$

since by definition waste divided by volume equals average waste density. By substitution of (6) into (7),

$$D_t = \frac{g}{V} \sum_{j=0}^{t-1} y_j N_j + D_0, \tag{8}$$

given exogenously determined percentage rates of growth in population $(\theta - 1)100$ and material flow per capita $(\beta - 1)100$ such that

$$y_j = \beta y_{j-1} \qquad \beta \geq 1 \tag{9.1}$$

and

$$N_j = \theta N_{j-1} \qquad \theta \geq 1. \tag{9.2}$$

Waste density can be related easily to initial levels of population and material flow per capita

$$D_t = \frac{g}{V} y_0 N_0 \left(\frac{\beta \theta^t - 1}{\beta \theta - 1} \right) + D_0. \tag{10}$$

From equation (10) it is clear that if population and material flow per capita are increasing, waste densities are increasing even more rapidly. This is true even though I have assumed linearity between waste flows generated and products consumed. Increasing density of wastes within the closed resource system is not necessarily bad per se. However, if the resource system (natural environment) is relatively small compared with current and expected future sums of waste flows, people may suffer health, psychic, or other damages. Thus, for each individual a monotonic, continuous increasing function relating per capita damages and waste densities could be presumed where aggregate damages are measured in terms of some common unit such as dollars or utils:

$$\mu_{it} = \mu_D(D_t) \qquad i = 1, \ldots, N; \tag{11}$$

where μ_{it} equals damages to the ith individual during period t. Then total environmental waste damage costs, if all individuals have identical tastes, preferences, and incomes, and there is no locational variation in waste densities, equal

16

$$\mu_t = N_t \cdot \mu_D(D_t). \tag{12}$$

By substitution of (10) into (12):

$$\mu_t = N_t \cdot \mu_D \left[\frac{g}{V} y_0 N_0 \left(\frac{\beta \theta^t - 1}{\beta \theta - 1} \right) + D_0 \right]. \tag{13}$$

Since waste density is increasing more rapidly than either population or material flow per capita, damage costs per capita must also be increasing. If μ_D is linear with a positive coefficient between density and damage costs, then per capita damage costs increase at the same rate as waste density. Finally, since total damage costs are equal by definition to population multiplied by damage costs per capita, total damage costs due to waste accumulation must be increasing at an even faster rate than damage costs per capita. Thus, a spiraling rise in damage costs associated with waste accumulation is obtained, resulting from an ever increasing population and rising material flow per capita. Each individual's waste from production and consumption activities effects a toll of damages on himself and all other individuals, including future generations.

Rothenberg (1970) differentiated "congestion" and pollution externalities as special cases of "generic congestion" phenomena. However, he defines the case of "pure" pollution externalities as one where "some users generate very high rates of interference [polluters] while others generate zero rates." The paradigm discussed here in Rothenberg's terminology is one of "generic congestion" where all individuals both generate pollution and share the resulting damages.

Without controls, this simplified depiction of an extraction-consumption-waste economy yields a Malthusian type of scenario—population and material flow per capita increase until some threshold waste density for viable human populations is reached. At that point, instead of subsistence level existence, material output per capita must become zero so that the population is decimated.[3] Presumably, damage costs approach

[3] There might be other biological thresholds before catastrophic decimation is reached. For example, increasing concentrations of waste may adversely affect reproduction rates so that population growth is reduced as waste density builds up. Potentially, then, we may have an "iron law" of pollution such that the "natural" negative rate of growth in population is just sufficient to offset the positive rate of growth in density of wastes necessary to support the population at some minimal subsistence level. Alternatively, if the natural environment could assimilate a certain amount of wastes, population may reach some steady state where wastes generated are exactly offset by environmental assimilation or regeneration and material flow per capita is at some minimum subsistence level. The dynamics (or even possibility) of such macro-ecological connectives are as yet far from being understood. Yet it is interesting to note in a practical vein that the Los Angeles County Health Association recently reported that approximately 10,000 individuals were leaving that county per year on physicians' advice because of respiratory ailments. At an earlier time, Los Angeles suburbs were described as an asthmatic's panacea.

(or equal) infinity at that point if some portion of the population desires to continue to exist. Alternatively, other variants of this scenario may be contemplated; i.e., where population for the most part is decimated but a viable few continue to survive. If the natural environment over long periods of time is able to regenerate and assimilate these wastes, then a cyclical pattern is obtained for the human species, characterized by periods of rapid growth in population and consumption, decimation thresholds, and then very small populations at minimum subsistence consumption until environmental regeneration allows another phase of economic development to proceed. Clearly, from the biologist's viewpoint, this population-material flow paradigm suggests an almost continuous interspecies-disequilibrium (Lotka 1956). Of course, such a potential state of affairs seems impossible if not pure nonsense unless one recalls that current estimates indicate that for each dollar of GNP generated in the United States economy in 1967, possibly 9 lb. of waste materials (6 lb. of biologically active materials) were also generated (Ayres and Kneese 1969).

III. OPTIMIZATION OVER TIME

The foregoing simplified model of the economy's interaction with the natural environment casts man in the role of a rabbit (or lemming). Growth rates of population and material flow were assumed to be exogenously determined, and the natural environment was viewed as an unregenerative, nonassimilative volume. In addition, the possibilities of recycling or technical progress toward reducing waste flow per unit product, reduction in rates of material flow through saving and by increasing durability, and altering rates of growth in material flow and population were not considered. Here I shall start by analyzing a hypothetical economy for which all of the previous paradigm's assumptions are retained except for exogenously determined material flow per capita. Thus, I wish to inquire into the possibilities for and behavior of an economy characterized as a purely extraction-consumption-waste process.

In order to examine a time-related optimization within such an economy, in addition to equations (2), (4), (5), (8), and (11) a time-related utility (or felicity) function relating material flow per capita to utility per capita must be specified along with the previously given disutility function for increasing waste densities. For expositional purposes, we shall also assume that the time intervals are discrete, and that the optimization planning interval is finite.[4]

---

[4] Possibly a reminder that another glacial age may occur in 2×10^5 or 3×10^5 years if glaciation is periodic (or sooner according to some "doomsday" ecologists),

18

The following per capita utility function will be assumed:

$$\mu(y_t, D_t) = \mu_y(y_t) - \mu_D(D_t), \qquad (14)$$

such that identical utility functions prevail for each member of society. Thus, total utility during period t is:

$$\mu(y_t, D_t) \cdot N_t, \qquad (15)$$

with N_t as previously defined. Several conditions are presumed with regard to the form of μ_y and μ_D in addition to separability which side-steps the problem of interpreting cross partial derivatives of $\mu(y_t, D_t)$:

$$\begin{array}{ll} \mu'_{y_t} > 0 & \mu''_{y_t} < 0 \\ \mu'_{D_t} > 0 & \mu''_{D_t} > 0. \end{array} \qquad (16)$$

In essence, these conditions stipulate that per capita marginal utility of material flow is increasing but at a decreasing rate during each time interval. In addition, per capita disutility generated by increasing waste densities is increasing at an increasing rate. This assumption appears to be realistic in that it implies rising marginal costs associated with increasing waste densities.

While the assumption of identical utility functions may appear to be vacuous, it greatly simplifies our exposition and has become almost a tradition in modern growth theory (Shell 1967). So far, I have not mentioned the problem of crowding and congestion within the context of this model, yet the fixed volume concept of a closed resource system is strongly indicative that crowding and congestion externalities may, at some level of population, appear. In this case, we should make N_t a separate argument of the per capita utility function. However, for the present the analysis of congestion externalities phenomena will be omitted.

From equation (7), a recursive relation between waste flow and waste densities can be written:

$$D_{t+1} - D_t = \frac{1}{V} W_t \qquad (17.1)$$

or

$$D_{t+1} - D_t = \frac{g}{V} y_t N_t. \qquad (17.2)$$

and that the "earth's life" according to some geologists is 4×10^7 years or thereabout, should cool some of the dissent against the idea of a finite planning interval. See C. Schushert and C. Dunbar, *A Textbook of Geology*, 4th ed. (New York: John Wiley, 1941), and C. R. Longwell and R. F. Flint, *Introduction to Physical Geology* (New York: John Wiley, 1959).

Equation (17.2) is in effect a description of the changing state of the natural environment as a result of the amount of consumption in period t. Note that it has been assumed that material flow per capita equals consumption per capita and that the appropriate point in time to measure the disutility of waste densities is at the beginning of interval t. Relations (16) and (17.2) yield the "pollution process" model except for specification of initial and terminal conditions and inclusion of a social rate of time preference factor.

The terminal period τ is conceptualized to be that period in which waste density for the beginning of the next period reaches a threshold level that decimates the population. Given a presumed decimation density level (2,000–4,000 parts per million of carbon monoxide for example), $\bar{K}$, then $D_t \geq \bar{K}$ with $t - 1 = \tau$. Thus, I am implicitly assuming some finite, though unspecified, time interval—$t = 1, \ldots, \tau$—in which the period $\tau + 1$ is presumed to be that period at which decimation occurs, applying an optimal policy with regard to the flow of wastes. In so doing, implications cannot be deduced about the optimal period of survival, but only about the conditions of optimal consumption and waste generation during the survival period.[5]

To complete this exposition, the initial waste density is specified as $D_1 = \underline{K}$, and population at period t as $N_t = \theta N_{t-1}$. Also, if the utility function is dated by a t subscript, I will presume it contains a discount factor (embodying a social rate of time preference ω) equal to $1/(1 + \omega)^{t-1}$ for each period t.[6] Given the above definitions, a Lagrangian function can be formed:

[5] A finite planning interval coupled with a finite environmental capacity for wastes is an extremely rigid assumption. Of course, infinite planning intervals in conjunction with an unlimited natural environmental assimilative capacity reduce to a trivial nonexistent scarcity case. Alternatively, an infinite planning interval in conjunction with a finite environmental waste assimilative capability appears to be philosophically inconsistent, provided population is increasing over time, material flow per capita has a positive lower bound, rates of environmental waste assimilation are very low or zero, waste generating technology is completely static in character, and wastes at some level of concentration become lethal to the human species. These conditions quite obviously ensure that at some moment in the finite future, decimation will occur. The alternative case of a finite planning interval and infinite waste assimilative capability is also philosophically inconsistent. Specifying an infinite planning interval for mankind, of course, implies the imposition of a constraint on the decision process, namely that regardless of how degraded man's habitat becomes, he must continue to exist. A more general and encompassing decision process would stipulate that the survival period be optimally chosen with infinity as one possible choice. I have chosen the course of specifying a finite planning interval, thinking that finite numbers can be very large. However, such a decision precludes consideration of an infinite time horizon.

[6] Although a discount factor will be applied that reflects a positive or zero rate of time preference for material-consumption flows, several potentially explosive ethical questions are brushed aside. If the human race faces the possibility of extinction by

$$L = \sum_{t=1}^{\tau} \mu_t(y_t, D_t)N_t + \sum_{t=1}^{\tau} \lambda_t\left(D_t + \frac{g}{V}y_t N_t - D_{t+1}\right)$$
$$+ \lambda_o(\underline{K} - D_1) + \psi_{\tau+1}(D_{\tau+1} - \bar{K}),$$

(18)

with

$$y_t \text{ and } D_t > 0;$$

where λ_t and $\psi_{\tau+1}$ are Lagrange multipliers for constraint-equalities between waste densities and material flow. The problem is to select y_t such that a maximum of discounted total utility is achieved over the interval $1 \le t \le \tau$. Taking derivatives and specifying signs according to (14):

$$\frac{\partial L}{\partial y_t} = \mu'_{yt} N_t + \lambda_t \frac{g}{V} N_t = 0 \qquad t = 1, \ldots, \tau \tag{19.1}$$

$$\frac{\partial L}{\partial D_t} = -\mu'_{Dt} N_t + \lambda_t - \lambda_{t-1} = 0 \quad t = 1, \ldots. \tau \tag{19.2}$$

$$\frac{\partial L}{\partial D_{\tau+1}} = \psi_{\tau-1} - \lambda_\tau = 0; \tag{19.3}$$

with prime superscripts denoting partial derivative taken with respect to the subscripted variable. Also N_t is written in place of $N_0\theta^t$, since population in each period is determined outside of the presumed decision process. Interpretation of these first-order conditions is relatively easy. The first set of conditions, (19.1), merely indicates that discounted per capita marginal utility of consumption each period be equated with a "cost" of utilizing an increment of waste density resulting from consumption, where the cost implicitly reflects a negative value associated with waste density or a positive value for increased waste-holding capacity. From (17.2), (4), and (19.1) the term g/V can be interpreted such that:

$$\lambda_t \frac{g}{V} = \lambda_t\left(\frac{D_{t+1} - D_t}{F_t}\right). \tag{20}$$

---

pollution (or other means) over a finite interval, are intergenerational utility comparisons defensible? Dasgupta (1969) suggested that a "small positive discount of the future" may be accepted as "ethical." However, if we assume that each generation can be exactly separated from another, so that distinct generations are identifiable, current generations with higher rates of time preference may eliminate the existence of some distant future generation. The faster we consume in a closed resource system, the more rapidly extinction occurs. While the utility of distant generations may seem valueless now, if we were that distant generation, we probably would value our continued existence at, or approaching, infinity. Even very high rates of time preference over a finite interval would not make it worthwhile to consume currently above some basic subsistence level, provided the last future generation's utilities were considered. In any case, I shall assume that such intergenerational utility comparisons can be contrived so that each generation would be equitably considered.

The second set of conditions (19.2) indicates that the shadow price or value of waste density is changing according to the marginal disutility of the entire population due to the increment in waste density during the current period. Equation (19.2) adjusted for sign can be rewritten as:

$$\mu_{Dt} = -(\lambda_t - \lambda_{t-1}). \tag{21}$$

Thus, as waste densities increase over time, the shadow price (negative) of waste density may increase or decline (in absolute value). If the discount rate ω is zero then this shadow price must decrease in absolute value. With a positive discount rate the shadow price may at first increase in absolute value, but as waste densities increase and the undiscounted magnitude of marginal disutility increases, at some point it will decline. At first glance, this result may appear incorrect since with increasing population and, by implication, increasing total waste flows over time, a greater degree of "control" (compared with no regulation) on pollution loads would seem imperative. Note, however, that the first-order conditions (19.2) refer to optimal utilization of waste storage over time and not to unregulated utilization patterns. Accordingly, optimal utilization over time commencing from an unregulated state generally requires that in the initial period a substantial shadow price should be applied to waste density. Following the initial large-scale shift, the shadow price will be decreased in each period which follows.

From (19.1) and our conclusion with regard to changes in λ_t over time:

$$(\mu'_{yt} - \mu'_{yt-1}) = \frac{g}{V}(\lambda_t - \lambda_{t-1}). \tag{22}$$

Substituting (21) into (22):

$$\mu'_{yt} - \mu'_{yt-1} = -\frac{g}{V}\mu' Dt\, N_t. \tag{23}$$

The implications of (23) are straightforward in that discounted per capita marginal utility of consumption is decreasing at a rate determined by the discounted marginal disutility of waste flows for the entire population.[7] Letting $\bar{\mu}$ denote undiscounted marginal utility or disutility:

---

[7] Since waste density in any period is strictly determined by past decisions with regard to material flow per capita, an alternative method of obtaining first-order conditions is available. From (17.2) and initial conditions, $\underline{K} = D_1$:

$$D_t = \underline{K} + \frac{g}{V}\sum_{j=1}^{t-1} y_j N_j \qquad t = 1, \ldots, \tau. \tag{a}$$

Substituting this expression into the per capita utility function, multiplying by N_t, and summing over τ, one obtains:

22

$$\frac{1}{(1+\omega)^{t-1}} \hat{\mu}'_{yt} - \frac{1}{(1+\omega)^{t-2}} \hat{\mu}'_{yt-1} = -\frac{1}{(1+\omega)^{t-1}} \frac{g}{V} \hat{\mu}'_{Dt} N_t; \quad (23.1)$$

thus

$$1 + \omega = \frac{\hat{\mu}'_{yt}}{\hat{\mu}'_{yt-1}} + \frac{g/V\ \hat{\mu}'_{Dt}\ N_t}{\hat{\mu}'_{yt-1}} \quad (23.2)$$

From (23.2) the ratio of undiscounted successive periods' marginal utilities of consumption plus an adjustment for disutility of increasing waste densities is equated with the social rate of time preference factor, $1 + \omega$.

This highly simplified model is very similar in structure and conclusions to models of a firm operating a single mine, except in this case instead of extracting resources from a finite capacity mine, we are "filling up" an assumed ambient natural environment with waste (Cummings and Burt 1969; Brown 1969). Also, there are some interesting analogies between this model and certain discrete time models in the theory of capital (Dorfman 1969). However, this model is much too simple in terms of at least three groupings of characteristics. First, there is no limit on the magnitudes of material flow or resource extraction per unit time except for penalties imposed by increasing waste densities. Extractive and renewable resources are assumed to be quite literally free. The second major limitation is with regard to the assumptions of a nonprogressive economy facing an inert natural environment where waste recycling, reduction in obsolescence rates, technological change, savings rates, investment in recycling processes, the environment's assimilative capability, and other factors are not

---

$$\sum_{t=1}^{\tau} \mu_t \left(y_t, \underline{K} + \frac{g}{V} \sum_{j=1}^{t-1} y_j N_j \right) N_t \qquad t = 1, \ldots, \tau. \quad (b)$$

The terminal condition $D_{\tau+1} \leq \overline{K}$ can be rewritten as $\overline{K} \geq \frac{g}{V} \sum_{t=1}^{\tau} y_t N_t + \underline{K}$. Forming a Lagrangian expression from (b) with the terminal condition as a constraint and differentiating with respect to y_t:

$$\frac{\partial L}{\partial y_t} = \mu'_{yt} N_t - N_t \frac{g}{V} \sum_{j=t+1}^{\tau} \mu'_{Dj} N_j - \lambda_\tau \frac{g}{V} N_t = 0 \qquad t = 1, \ldots, \tau; \quad (c)$$

where λ_τ is a Lagrangian multiplier associated with the terminal condition and has the same interpretation as λ_τ in equation (19.3). This first-order condition indicates that during each period, material flow per capita be increased to the point where marginal utility of consumption per capita is equated with the sum of: marginal disutility of increasing waste densities for current and future generations and a shadow price associated with the life-yielding capacity of the environment. By summing (19.2) from t to τ and substituting this result into (19.1), a first-order condition identical to (c) is obtained from the first-order necessary conditions given in the text. [I am indebted to R. Strotz, without implying responsibility, for correction of errors in this footnote contained in an earlier draft.]

allowed to alter continuously over time the magnitudes and disutilities of waste flows. Third, the model is extremely aggregative in that identical utility functions and strictly equal distribution of waste densities are presumed. In what follows, I shall attempt to remove some of these limitations. But before proceeding, several tentative conclusions can be inferred from the earlier model. First, "economic products" which contain raw materials and therefore create waste during their production and consumption will contribute to the overall problem of waste management at some point in time, unless these "goods" are not subject to obsolescence; for example, knowledge. Second, if there are meaningful finite limits to the natural environment, then an increasing GNP-material flow implies that increasing disutilities will emanate from environmental degradation and contamination; that is, provided the waste-generating technology (g in our model) is relatively constant (not substantially decreasing) over time and our assumptions with regard to the form of μ_{Dt} are acceptable. Third, if the first two premises are not without some element of validity, waste generating processes in both production and consumption sectors should be taxed at relatively high rates in the near future. Also, these taxes should reflect the current and future magnitudes of marginal social damages (or disutilities) of waste flows.

IV. THE RATE OF USE OF RESOURCES

Issues emerging from environmental management arise not only from the optimal rate of waste generation in a closed medium but also with regard to the rate of extractive (or renewable) resource exploitation. Earlier it was presumed that material resources were virtually free so that the only relevant issue regarding environmental management was the utilization of a scarce inert environment. But if extractive resources are finite in magnitude and can for all practical purposes be exhausted, then environmental management involves a "conjunctive use" type of allocation problem where one must consider simultaneously rates of extraction *and* rates of waste generation. Thus, the "pure" mining problem must be coupled with the "pure" pollution problem and such questions as, Which will we run out of first, air to breathe or fossil fuels to pollute the air we breathe? become relevant.

For expositional purposes, I shall assume an initial finite stock of an extractive resource which is equal to Q_t at the beginning of period t. Then

$$Q_{t+1} = Q_t - R_t \qquad t = 1, \ldots, \tau; \qquad (24)$$

where R_t denotes, as previously, the amount of resources extracted in period t. Also, upper and lower limits will be stipulated for Q:

$$Q_{r+1} \geq \underline{L} \geq 0 \tag{25.1}$$

$$Q_1 = \bar{L}; \tag{25.2}$$

with $\underline{L}$ and $\bar{L}$ constants equal to the terminal and initial stock of extractive resources, respectively.[8]

In order to consider the possibilities of exhausting extractive resources and substitutions between labor and resources in producing consumable goods, excluding services, I shall introduce several changes into the model given in sections II and III. Also, instead of assuming raw materials are totally transformed into waste during the current period, a one-period extraction-waste generation lag will be assumed. Thus,

$$R_t = W_{t+1} + [\text{a residual determined by (28.1) and (29.1)}] \tag{26}$$

defines the materials balance relationship.[9] It will also be assumed that the total population is employed in each period so that population equals the labor force. A homogeneous production function of degree one is assumed in which substitution exists between raw materials and labor:

$$y_t N_t = F(R_t, N_t) = f(r_t) \cdot N_t, \tag{27}$$

with r_t denoting extractive resources per capita. It is also assumed that this technological relationship fulfills the usual first and second order diminishing marginal-factor productivity conditions, namely $f' > 0$, $f'' < 0$. It is assumed that waste flows resulting from the production process are directly related to the quantity of extractive resources:

$$W_{it+1} = H(R_t) \tag{28.1}$$

or

$$W_{it+1} = h(r_t) \cdot N_t. \tag{28.2}$$

[8] In the case depicted here the change in stock of resources equals flow—a purely extractive process. Alternatively, if the resource is renewable—i.e., animal or plant populations—(24) would need to include a relationship for biological growth. It has become common practice to relate fish population growth rates to the initial mass of fish (Beverton and Holt 1957; Lotka 1956; Smith 1968; Smith 1969). In terms of our notation and discrete variables, and provided $E(Q_t)$ denotes the discrete time growth-biomass relationship, (24) would then be altered to:

$$Q_{t+1} - Q_t = E(Q_t) - R_t \qquad t = 1, \ldots, \tau.$$

For simplicity (24) will be applied, though it is to be noted that the model will generally accommodate biological growth relationships of the above type.

[9] As long as there is a "mass balance" in that raw materials extraction equals waste flows in each period or even over very short gestation-production periods, savings, recycling, or other long-term activities that markedly reduce current waste flows per unit of product must by definition be nearly zero. Thus, in order to accommodate such waste reducing possibilities, it is necessary to adjust the mass-balance relationship (d'Arge and Kneese 1969). However, the theoretical possibility of continuous recycling within a production cycle does exist, though I shall not treat this case except via a constraint on recycling in a variant of the model which is developed later.

25

Finally, waste flows originating in the consumption sector are presumed to be related to the amount of goods produced and consumed:

$$W_{ft+1} = G(F_t) \tag{29.1}$$

or

$$W_{ft+1} = g(y_t) \cdot N_t. \tag{29.2}$$

Relation (29.1) yields a one-to-one correspondence between waste flows and final goods produced if no saving or recycling occurs. However, in what follows such an equality will not be assumed. Given (27), (28.2), and (29.2), total waste flows can be defined in terms of r_t and y_t:

$$W_{t+1} = h(r_t) \cdot N_t + g(y_t) \cdot N_t \tag{30}$$

and thus from (17.1):

$$D_{t+1} - D_t = \frac{1}{V} [h(r_{t-1}) + g(y_{t-1})] N_{t-1}. \tag{31}$$

Social costs (or disutilities) emanating from the loss of psychic and aesthetic values attached to undisturbed environments are imposed by the extraction of resources; i.e., strip mining of bituminous coal, which causes disruption to the landscape; reductions in river flow; offshore oil derricks and oil spills; forest removal; and soil erosion. Therefore it seems appropriate within the context of the model studied to include within the welfare-utility relation a per capita loss function for disturbing the natural environment through extraction (or distortions in interspecies equilibrium). Let us add such a loss function of the following form:

$$\mu_Q(Q_t) \cdot N_t \tag{32}$$

with $\mu'_{Qt} > 0$, $\mu''_{Qt} < 0$. These conditions imply that the stock of natural resources offers some pristine enjoyment so that a reduction in their availability (or their disturbance) causes increasing per capita marginal disutility. Some nonconservationists may argue with the assumptions regarding the rates of change of this utility function, but I believe they are reasonably defensible. The per capita utility function that emerges is:

$$\mu_t(y_t, D_t, Q_t) = \mu_{yt}(y_t) - \mu_{Dt}(D_t) + \mu_{Qt}(Q_t). \tag{33}$$

With these assumptions, a Lagrangian function can be established:

$$L = \sum_{t=1}^{\tau} \mu_t(y_t, D_t, Q_t)N_t$$
$$+ \sum_{t=1}^{\tau} \lambda_t \left(D_t + \frac{1}{V} [h(r_{t-1}) + g(y_{t-1})]N_{t-1} - D_{t+1} \right)$$

26

$$+ \sum_{t=1}^{\tau} \rho_t(Q_t - r_t N_t - Q_{t+1}) \tag{34}$$

$$+ \sum_{t=1}^{\tau} \eta_t[f(r_t) - y_t]N_t$$
$$+ \psi_{\tau+1}(D_{\tau+1} - \bar{K}) + \lambda_o(\underline{K} - D_1)$$
$$+ \rho_{\tau+1}(Q_{\tau+1} - \underline{L}) + \rho_o(\bar{L} - Q_1)$$

with y_t, r_t, D_t, $Q_t > 0$. The first-order conditions for this model are:

$$\frac{\partial L}{\partial y_t} = \mu'_{y_t} N_t + \lambda_{t+1} g' \cdot \frac{1}{V} \cdot N_t - \eta_t N_t = 0 \qquad t = 1, \ldots, \tau \tag{35.1}$$

$$\frac{\partial L}{\partial r_t} = \lambda_{t+1} \cdot h' \cdot \frac{1}{V} N_t - \rho_t N_t + \eta_t f' \cdot N_t = 0 \quad t = 1, \ldots, \tau \tag{35.2}$$

$$\frac{\partial L}{\partial D_t} = -\mu'_{D_t} N_t + \lambda_t - \lambda_{t-1} = 0 \qquad t = 1, \ldots, \tau \tag{35.3}$$

$$\frac{\partial L}{\partial Q_t} = \mu'_{Q_t} N_t + \rho_t - \rho_{t-1} = 0 \qquad t = 1, \ldots, \tau \tag{35.4}$$

$$\frac{\partial L}{\partial D_{\tau+1}} = \psi_{\tau+1} - \lambda_\tau = 0 \tag{35.5}$$

$$\frac{\partial L}{\partial Q_{\tau+1}} = \rho_{\tau+1} - \rho_\tau = 0; \tag{35.6}$$

where ρ_t and η_t are Lagrangian multipliers that can be interpreted as the utility value of an additional unit of extractive resource and consumption per capita that become "available by magic" during period t (Dorfman 1969). Thus, η_t is a price for consumption goods during period t and ρ_t is a shadow price for extractive resources during period t. Given these interpretations, first-order conditions (35.1) indicate that in each period discounted per capita marginal utility is equated with discounted per capita marginal disutility associated with a small change in per capita consumption. The discounted per capita marginal disutility is measured by the sum of the marginal disutility of waste generated by the increment in product flow and the price of the product. The assumption of a one-period delay between extraction-production-consumption and waste generation results in a shadow price of the environment's unutilized density being for the next period (λ_{t+1}) rather than for the current period as was the case earlier.

The second set of first-order conditions (35.2) is of primary interest, however, since they relate how the rate of resource extraction should be optimally established. They indicate that in each period the discounted marginal value product of an additional unit of extractive resources per capita be equated with the sum of the discounted marginal disutility for waste generated by this unit resource flow and the shadow price (for environmental disruption) of extractive resources:

$$\eta_t f'_t = \lambda_{t+1} \frac{h'_t}{V} + \rho_t \qquad t = 1, \ldots, \tau. \qquad (36)$$

The first-order conditions (35.3) and (35.4) indicate that the shadow prices for waste density and resource extraction should be changing according to the magnitudes of disutilities arising from increasing waste densities and the despoilment of the environment through extraction of natural resources.

The first-order conditions above are for a hypothetical finite-lived economy where the allocation problem boils down to a joint determination of rates of resource exploitation and production of wastes. The two relationships $h(r_t)$ and $g(y_t)$ determine the efficiency of the economy in the production of wastes per unit of produced and consumed product. It is important to reinterpret these relationships in terms of other, more conventional, concepts of recycling, obsolescence, saving, and the production of durable goods.

Savings hypotheses in most neoclassical models of economic growth indicate that a certain proportion of production is not consumed currently, and thus in our terminology does not contribute to current waste flow. However, obsolescence or decay rates in these same models indicate the proportion of accumulated saving-investment that does currently enter as waste. Thus, the relationship $g(y_t)$ (relating waste flow from the consumption sector to the amount of goods produced) can be thought of as embodying both accumulation rates and depreciation rates for durable goods in the consumption sector.[10] Additionally, in the simplified model the $g(y_t)$ relationship implicitly contains recycling rates from the consumption sector back into the consumption sector. The processes of depreciation, consumption-saving, and recycling (within the consumption sector) are therefore all submerged in $g(y_t)$, and certainly some of the most impor-

---

[10] As a simple example of one interpretation for the function $g(y_t)$, if we assume a given stock of durable goods in the consumption sector equal to K_t, with accumulation and depreciation rates of s and k, respectively:

$$K_{t+1} - K_t = sF_t - \kappa K_t.$$

If for some reason the stock of durable consumption goods is kept in a constant relation with material flows, then $K_t = \beta F_t$, and waste flows from the consumption sector in period $t + 1$ in terms of our model would be a linear function of material flow in period t:

$$W_{f\,t+1} = (1 - s + \kappa\beta)F_t.$$

However, if β was not constant, waste flowing from the consumption sector would be determined not only by current material flow but also by the historical pattern of accumulation of durable goods.

tant policy questions with regard to environmental pollution require that these processes be separated. However, they all share a common (but generally equal) influence on waste flows since each directly affects pollution loads per unit of final product. At this stage not much more can be said than that a positive shift in savings rates or rates of recycle tends to reduce waste flows, while positive shifts in obsolescence rates will increase waste flows.

The $h(r_t)$ function links rates of raw materials extraction directly to the magnitude of wastes flow from the production sector. Thus, this relationship embodies such important determinants of pollution loads as rates of obsolescence and decay of machinery and equipment, and efficiency of raw materials conversion. Generally, every decision a firm makes that influences the technique and rate of production will also indirectly influence pollution emissions. In consequence, $h(r_t)$ is most certainly a gross oversimplification and, like gross investment in the national income accounts, conceals more than it reveals.

In the simplified paradigms examined thus far, the possibility of recycling from the consumption sector back into the production sector has not been examined. However, such a path for recycling appears to be one of the most important facets of managing a closed resource system. The current recycling of old automobiles for their metal content and introduction of returnable aluminum cans are only two examples of the many types of recycling between production and consumption sectors that are currently economically feasible or could be made so via subsidies.

One way of including such intersector recycling in my last model would be by defining a new decision variable, Z_t, representing the amount of recycled materials from consumption to production sectors during time interval t. Hypothetically, Z_t should also be included as a separate argument of the production function (27) since it might be expected a priori that recycled material would be less productive than "original" raw materials. Equation (27) should be amended to

$$F_t = f(r_t, z_t) \cdot N_t \qquad \text{(with } z_t = Z_t/N_t \text{ and } f'_{rt} > f'_{zt}) \qquad (37)$$

and the relationship (29.1) for waste flows from the final consumption sector would change to

$$W_{ft+1} = g(y_t, z_t) \cdot N_t. \qquad (38)$$

It should be expected that the magnitude of recycling between consumption and production sectors will also influence waste flows emanating from the production process such that (28.1) also needs to be amended to

$$W_{it+1} = h(r_t, z_t) \cdot N_t. \qquad (39)$$

No effective limit is established on the magnitude of recycling in each period, in that the variable Z_t could increase, allowing per capita material flow to increase while maintaining gross waste flows at less than initial materials extraction. In order to constrain Z_t in a definite manner, I shall presume the magnitude of total recycled products Z_t in any production period is directly related to raw materials extraction:

$$Z_t \leq B(R_t) = b(r_t)N_t; \tag{40}$$

with $B' > 0$, and $B'' < 0$ so that recycling possibilities increase to a maximum but at a decreasing rate with raw materials extraction.

Coupling these modifications for recycling between production and consumption sectors to the earlier Lagrangian expression (34), a new set of first-order conditions are derivable. Such a complete derivation will not be analyzed here since many of the marginal conditions remain the same, except that h'_t and g'_t become partial derivatives. If we define δ_t as a discounted Lagrangian multiplier for the added constraints for Z_t given by (40) and with $\delta_t > / < 0$, then

$$\frac{\partial L}{\partial z_t} = \lambda_{t+1} \frac{1}{V}(h'_z + g'_z)N_t + \eta_t f'_z N_t - \delta_t N_t = 0 \qquad t = 1, \ldots, \tau \tag{41}$$

and for r_t the conditions (35.2) change to

$$\frac{\partial L}{\partial r_t} = \lambda_{t+1} h'_r \frac{1}{V} N_t - \rho_t N_t + \eta_t f'_r N_t + \delta_t b'_r N_t = 0 \qquad t = 1, \ldots, \tau \tag{42}$$

where h'_j, g'_j, and f'_j denote partial derivatives with respect to the jth argument.

Clearly, from (41), recycling between production and consumption sectors should be valued in each period as the difference between the marginal value product of recycled material ($\eta_t f'_z$) and the increase, resulting from recycling, in marginal disutility associated with waste density $[\lambda_{t+1}(1/V)(h'_z + g'_z)]$. Further, equation (42) indicates that resource extraction has an additional value in recycling determined by (40) which must be added to its initial marginal value product as given in (36), that is, provided $\eta_t f'_z > \lambda_{t+1}(1/V)(h'_z + g'_z)$ at the optimum. [11]

[11] Actually, two cases arise if $Z_t \leq B(R_t)$ is specified as a strict equality, since δ_t then can be either positive or negative. If, at the optimum, the marginal value product of recycled materials exceeds the marginal value product of recycled materials-induced wastes, then the shadow price (δ_t) for recycling is positive. This positive shadow price must be added as a value for resources that are extracted and contribute to recycled materials via constraint equality (40). Alternatively, if the marginal value product of recycled materials is less than the marginal disutility of wastes generated, the shadow price (δ_t) is negative and must be subtracted from the valuation of extracted resources.

Throughout the discussion of first-order conditions defining the optimum in a closed resource system, I have omitted comparisons with what might result in a nonregulated economy. Yet it is obvious that if the closed-medium analogy contains some degree of validity, and disutilities are associated with increasing waste densities and disturbance of the natural environment, a hypothetical economy characterized by individual, unconstrained decisions will be inefficient in its utilization of the environment. Not only will the closed medium be used up too rapidly, but the economy's uncoordinated choices or piecemeal planning with regard to resource extraction and pollution rates will generally result in an inefficient path leading toward decimation.

V. SUMMARY AND CONCLUSIONS

A series of highly simplified paradigms were developed that related the economy to the natural environment in terms of resource extraction and waste emissions or accumulation. Conjunctive utilization of the environment (both as a source of natural resources and as a medium for waste discharge) was briefly analyzed. It was argued that the hypothetical economy could achieve an optimum path of consumption and period of survival only by imposing regulations on both extraction of natural resources and waste disposal that reflected the natural environment's presumed finite waste-holding capacity and the availability of extractive resources. Given the degree of interdependence between magnitudes of resource extraction and waste accumulation, it was argued that a rational policy toward utilizing the environment cannot be piecemeal or independent. Policies with regard to resource extraction indirectly affect the magnitude of waste flows and thus cannot be separated from policies attempting to regulate environmental pollution. If the closed resource system analogy is even approximately correct, then unfettered, unregulated production and consumption will ultimately result in earlier decimation of the population, or at least yield inefficient levels of waste densities and consumption.

Population was treated in each model as exogenously determined, and increasing at a constant rate. In terms of a closed resource system, it appears essential to curb population growth at some point or treat it as an endogenous variable and derive optimal population levels for each period (Dasgupta 1969). A viable population, even at subsistence standards of living, will usually cause some amount of waste accumulation. The level of population (along with standards of living) determines to a large extent magnitudes of waste flows. The central implication is therefore that a truly optimal extraction and waste accumulation program must be considered

31

concurrently with a population program. The models analyzed in this paper are then in essence "second-best" models in which population cannot be optimally adjusted according to the general availability (or lack of it) of the natural environment. However, if population is assumed to be endogenous in the model developed in section III, a Meade type of population rule is implied (Meade 1955); namely that population should be altered within periods so that in each period population is increased to the point at which the total utility of the individual added equals disutilities of individuals already there in terms both of forgone waste-holding capacity and of reductions of the material flow per capita necessary to provide for the individual.

From this brief description of interrelations between rates of waste flow and such acknowledged economic entities as savings rates, depreciation rates, and production of durables versus nondurable goods, it is clear that macroeconomic policies will intimately affect the magnitude of waste flows. A fiscal policy that emphasizes maintenance of high levels of aggregate demand quite innocently also accelerates rates of waste generation and accumulation. Monetary policies aimed at easing credit have a simultaneously positive and negative impact: they increase waste flows via a positive shift in consumption expenditure but encourage investment and thus retard the flows of goods immediately consumed. Selective instruments such as investment tax credits, depletion allowances, and capital gains provisions also have direct and indirect effects on the rate of consumption and the distribution of production between current consumption and savings and therefore influence the rate of environmental deterioration. It is interesting to ask whether the opponents of the oil depletion allowance raised the question of whether such an allowance actually increased the rate of waste flows, particularly emissions of carbon monoxide and oxides of nitrogen. This summary is not meant to be an analysis or even a statement on the effects of economic policies on generation of wastes. However, this most limited exposition, I believe, suggests that macroeconomic policy instruments have a definite and often unrecognized impact on the natural environment through their effects on rates of resource extraction *and* growth in consumption per capita.

Policies such as accelerated depreciation and even policies directed toward balance-of-payments equilibrium influence rates of waste generation. In recent decades, the United States has become a net importer of natural resources and net exporter of consumer durables. This balance indicates that we may very well have become a net importer of waste emissions (Vanek 1963). Most certainly, the current terms of trade *do not* reflect long-term social costs (or disutilities) associated with the resulting waste accumulation.

To summarize my major arguments, the processes of pollution and extraction are common characteristics of any economy, Robinson Crusoe and upward. They are not separable entities to be studied in isolation without regard to their physical and biological interdependencies unless the economy resides in an open resource system characterized by limitless natural resources, including air sheds and algae sinks. In fact, the rational utilization of the natural environment by man requires careful planning of rates of resource extraction and pollutant emissions, where one rate is highly dependent on the other. In a growing economy, recycling, savings rates, and rates of technical or physical obsolescence are intimately connected to resource use and waste flows, and thus, cumulative short-term government policies may have a long-term impact on the environment. In order to place some of the extremely abstract and possibly unreasonable arguments of this paper in perspective, I shall end with a quote attributed to Anaximander of Miletus, written about 590 B.C.:

> That from which all things are born is also the cause of their coming to an end, as is meet, for they pay reparations and atonement to each other for their mutual injustice in the order of time.

REFERENCES

Ayres, R. U., and A. V. Kneese. 1968. Environmental pollution. In U.S. Congress, Joint Economic Committee, *Federal Programs for the Development of Human Resources*, vol. 2. Washington, D.C.: Government Printing Office.
———. 1969. Production, consumption and externalities. *American Economic Review* 59:282–97.
Barnett, H. J., and C. Morse. 1963. *Scarcity and growth*. Baltimore: Johns Hopkins Press for Resources for the Future.
Beverton, R. J., and S. V. Holt. 1957. *On the dynamics of exploited fish population*, vol. 19. London: Ministry of Agriculture.
Boulding, K. 1966. The economics of the coming spaceship earth. In *Environmental quality in a growing economy*, ed. H. Jarrett, pp. 3–14. Baltimore: Johns Hopkins Press for Resources for the Future.
Brown, G. 1969. An optimal program for managing common property resources with congestion externalities. Unpublished manuscript, University of Washington, Department of Economics.
Coontz, S. 1966. *Productive labour and effective demand*. New York: A. M. Kelley.
Cummings, R. G., and O. R. Burt. 1969. The economics of production from natural resources: Note. *American Economic Review* 59:985–90.
Daly, H. 1968. Economics as a life science. *Journal of Political Economy* 76; no. 3:392–406.

d'Arge, R. C., and A. V. Kneese. 1969. General equilibrium and pervasive externalities: The case of environmental pollution. Unpublished manuscript.

Dasgupta, P. S. 1969. On the concept of optimum population. *Review of Economic Studies* 36:295–318.

Dorfman, R. 1969. An economic interpretation of optimal control theory. *American Economic Review* 59:817–31.

Leighton, P. 1964. The air resource. In *Proceedings of statewide conference on Man In California — 1980's*. Sacramento, California: State of California, January 27 and 28, 1964.

Lotka, A. J. 1956. *Elements of mathematical biology*. New York: Dover Publications.

Meade, J. E. 1955. *Trade and welfare*. London: Oxford University Press.

Rothenberg, J. 1970. The economics of congestion and pollution: An integrated view. *American Economic Review* 60:114–21.

Scitovsky, T. 1966. External diseconomies in the modern economy. *Western Economic Journal* 3:197–202.

Shell, K. 1967. *Essays on the theory of optimal economic growth*. Cambridge, Mass.: MIT Press.

Smith, V. L. 1968. The economics of production from natural resources. *American Economic Review* 58:409–31.

———. 1969. On models of commercial fishing. *Journal of Political Economy* 77:187–98.

Vanek, J. 1963. *The natural resource content of United States foreign trade, 1870–1955*. Cambridge, Mass.: MIT Press.

2. *A Materials-Process-Product Model*

Robert U. Ayres

INTRODUCTION AND BACKGROUND

Real, as opposed to rhetorical, progress toward improved environmental management in the future is likely to depend increasingly on the availability of detailed knowledge of the specific physical and chemical processes that occur in the production and use of goods. Whether the optimum environmental management strategy is to concentrate on regulation and enforcement—as at present—or to alter the price structure so as to eliminate or compensate for market failures, as many economists would advocate, it quickly becomes apparent that one cannot expect simply to put an absolute stop to all waste discharges that may have a deleterious effect on the environment. The awkward fact is that *all* materials that are converted to useful goods eventually outlive their usefulness and become waste products.[1] The same is true of energy. These are simple consequences of the basic physical laws of conservation, even though they seem to be somewhat at odds with the traditional language (at least) of economics, where one speaks of "final" consumption as though the physical substances involved actually disappeared. Obviously, they do not.

Since wastes, as such, cannot be eliminated by decree, the aim of environmental management is to minimize the disutilities resulting from economic activities as they now take place. To do so, one must know a good deal about available alternatives. Thus waste products could, in principle, be collected and reprocessed—or the wastes might be treated in some way to make them less dangerous or obnoxious. Or the production process

[1] Residuals in the terminology used elsewhere in this book.

35

might be changed so that less harmful by-products would result. Or, conceivably, the inadvertent consumer (of wastes) could be innoculated against or otherwise protected from their harmful effects. Each alternative involves certain economic costs, as well as possible benefits. A prerequisite to analyzing these alternatives is detailed knowledge of relevant economic and technological relationships.

One specific form of analysis that deserves special note in this context is forecasting. Almost the first step in designing a rational program of environmental management activities is to carry out a surveillance of the existing situation and project it forward in time. This provides a basis for assessing the future effects of alternative control programs (as well as their costs), and thus a means for setting priorities and allocating resources.

In many areas of government concern the future can be adequately portrayed in terms of measures of the intensity of economic activity such as output, employment, consumer credit, housing starts, car loadings, machine-tool orders, and the like. However, in the case of the environmental area this is not so. Forecasts of residuals cannot in general be made on the basis of economic activity alone. There is no inherent connection between them, since residuals are functions of the technology in use, not the end product.[2] It is an elementary point, though often overlooked, that alternative technologies are often available to produce a given product (or service), differing only slightly in cost but perhaps radically in other respects—including residuals output. An example that deserves to be taken more seriously than it has been to date is the closed-cycle external combustion engine as an alternative to the open-cycle internal combustion engine for automotive vehicles. Or one might point to the fossil-fuel burning power plant and its nuclear rival.

To rectify this deficiency, both for purposes of forecasting residuals and—it is hoped—to facilitate other kinds of analysis needed for environmental management purposes, a new sort of model is needed that combines economic and technological elements. Such a model is proposed in this paper.

GENERAL THEORY

In recent years it has increasingly been recognized that environmental problems cannot be discussed adequately in terms of existing economic measures or models. Whereas the physical "goods" produced by the

[2] As pointed out in the discussion, residuals are a function of the desired characteristics of the end product and of the nature of the raw materials used, as well as of the production technology. For a given product, raw material and production technology affect generation of residuals. [Editor's note.]

economy and exchanged in the marketplace are intimately bound up with well-defined economic measures of value (prices and costs), there are no equivalent measures with which the economist can readily analyze unpriced externalities of the production process. Lacking the mechanism of the market to relate value to physical quantity, the economist must revert to dealing with quantity itself. Thus models are needed that describe the movements of physical materials through the economy to supplement models describing the movements of dollars (Ayres and Kneese 1968). This emphasis on physical materials flow, rather than dollar flow, imposes a new set of requirements on the form of the model.

Most economic models hitherto have focused on the factors of production in a framework of analysis based on sectors distinguished by type of final product. The usual typology is the "Standard Industrial Classification" or SIC code. Since final products are the results of a rather complex combination of fabricating steps or chemical reactions, there is very little correlation between SIC categories and materials or processes involved in production. Hence, the stability of input-output relationships or so-called interindustry coefficients depends substantially on the degree of aggregation of the sectors—that is, on the inertia of large numbers. Relations between process and product are obscured virtually to the point of invisibility. Consequently, forecasts of economic growth or residuals production as a function of technological change, for instance, can only be done "in the large" by interindustry coefficient trend extrapolation—though good data are almost nonexistent—or "in the small" by making a detailed individual study of the actual configuration of an individual plant. There is no middle ground between the two levels of analysis, however. Projections from macro-data are generally useless on the micro-scale and vice versa.

This paper constitutes a preliminary exploration of the possibility that these deficiencies can be remedied by utilizing a different, though not necessarily more detailed, description of the economy. Both subdivision and aggregation are essential for analysis, but the SIC typology is not necessarily optimum for all analytical purposes. In particular, studies of the interrelationship between technological change and the economy would appear to be far more tractable in a context that takes advantage of the features of the terrain, so to speak, rather than cutting across country. Specifically, a model based on three fundamental classifications is proposed: (a) *materials*, based on physico-chemical composition and mode of utilization; (b) *processes*, based on the relations between the number and the type of material outputs; and (c) *final products*, which will be grouped in accordance with the SIC code already mentioned, primarily so that the results can be used in conjunction with conventional input-output models. The two (new) classification schemes will be described later.

The proposed model is a generalization of the well-known Walras-Cassel general equilibrium model, extended to include intermediate consumption *by process* and also including unpriced material inputs such as air and water, and unpriced outputs (residuals) such as combustion products and solids. This approach was previously utilized with a conventional input-output model where "sectors" were defined in the SIC typology, but physical intersectoral flows were considered (Ayres and Kneese 1969). Related approaches have been proposed by Cumberland and Hibbs (1970) and Leontief (1970). Energy and nonmaterial "services" are not treated explicitly by the present formulation except as heat-content or value-added during processing steps. However, energy could be treated explicitly as though it were a material substance, but this would involve some additional complexity.[3]

The following variables will be used:

resources (raw materials) 1 ... M

$$r^1 \quad \ldots\ldots\ldots\ldots \quad r^M$$

material inputs to process 1 ... N

$$X_1 \quad \ldots\ldots\ldots\ldots \quad X_N$$

final products 1 ... P

$$Y_1 \quad \ldots\ldots\ldots\ldots \quad Y_P.$$

All variables are measured in units of mass (pounds). The M basic raw materials are allocated to the P final products as follows:

$$r^1 = a_1^1 \, Y_1 + a_2^1 \, Y_2 + \ldots + a_P^1 \, Y_P$$
$$r^M = a_1^M \, Y_1 + a_2^M \, Y_2 + \ldots + a_N^M \, Y_P \tag{1a}$$

or

$$r^k = \sum_{l=1}^{P} a_l^k \, Y_l. \tag{1b}$$

The a_l^k coefficients define a matrix; a typical coefficient can be interpreted as the fraction of the lth final product which is composed of the kth basic resource. Since materials are neither created nor destroyed, the fractions must, by definition, add up to unity; viz.,

---

[3] This would provide the possibility of analysis of tradeoffs between material and energy residuals, and between them and other factor inputs to production. [Editor's note.]

$$\sum_{l=1}^{M} a_l^k = 1 \qquad (2)$$

for all l. This actually constitutes P separate constraints. The identification of the "final" product may be rather arbitrary, since recycling is clearly an important possibility. However, final products can also be viewed as raw materials and the mathematical treatment of the return flows does not introduce any particular difficulty.

Equation (1) can easily be solved to yield the distribution of the various resources among final products; viz.,

$$Y_l = \sum_{k=1}^{M} A_l^k r^k \qquad (3)$$

where

$$A_l^k = a_l^k \frac{Y_l}{r^k}. \qquad (4)$$

For a sufficiently aggregated level of analysis, the a_l^k or A_l^k coefficients might be determined to a reasonable degree of accuracy from standard sources of data. Thus A_l^k might be derived directly from statistics compiled by U.S. government agencies such as the Department of Agriculture, the Bureau of Mines, and the Bureau of the Census, while the a_l^k would have to be inferred by ad hoc analyses of various products (including residuals streams). It can be verified quickly by substitution that the sum of A_l^k over l is also equal to unity. Since the coefficients are not independent, both types of data may be used.

To introduce intermediate processing steps, we define the coefficients c_{ij}^k as the fraction of the kth material input to the jth process which flows from the ith process.[4] The quantity of material used in the jth process was previously denoted X_j, whence the product $c_{ij}^k X_j$ represents the quantity of material k flowing from process i to process j. Thus

$$c_{0j}^k X_j$$

represents the *unprocessed* material inputs to process j, and summing over all N processes we obtain

$$r^k = \sum_{j=1}^{N} c_{0j}^k X_j, \qquad (5)$$

[4] Either input or output coefficients could be defined; the choice is a matter of convenience and orientation. Output coefficients are derivable from input coefficients and vice versa.

since the kth resource must be entirely accounted for as unprocessed inputs to various processes. To allow for the possibility that some raw materials (e.g., air and water) are consumed without being otherwise processed, we define "final" consumption as the Nth process. The total quantity of material k consumed must then be divided up among the P final products and must be equal to the sum of the material inputs to the Nth process from all other processes:

$$\sum_{j=0}^{N-1} c_{jN}^{k} X_N = \sum_{l=1}^{P} a_l^k Y_l = r^k. \tag{6}$$

Again, expression (5) can be solved for the distribution of the various raw materials as inputs to various processes; viz.,

$$X_j = \sum_{k=1}^{M} C_j^k r^k \tag{7}$$

where

$$C_j^k = c_{0j}^k \frac{X_j}{r^k} \tag{8}$$

and

$$\sum_{k=1}^{M} c_{0j}^k = 1 \tag{9}$$

for all j. This relation comprises N separate constraints. Although basic materials may be combined and recombined—both physically and chemically—they are not created or destroyed by processing. Hence the material output of every process stage can be accounted for as an input to some other process or to "final" consumption.

Of course each final product Y_l involves material outputs from various processes, whence

$$Y_l = \sum_{j=0}^{N-1} \sum_{k=1}^{M} b_{jl}^k X_j = \sum_{j=1}^{N-1} \sum_{k=1}^{M} b_{jl}^k X_j + b_{0l}^k X_0. \tag{10}$$

The coefficient b_{jl}^k represents the fractional output of the jth process operating on the Kth material that contributes directly to the lth final product without further intermediate processing. The case $j = 0$ cannot be interpreted so neatly; however the product $b_{0l}^k X_0$ clearly represents the contribution to Y from unprocessed raw materials (e.g., air and water). Substituting (3) and (7) we obtain the interesting relationship

$$\sum_{j=1}^{N-1} \frac{b_{jl}^m}{b_{0l}^m} \left(\frac{c_{0j}^k - a_l^k}{c_{00}^k - a_l^m} \right) \frac{X_j}{X_0} = -1 \qquad (11)$$

which must be satisfied for all values of k, l, and m. Thus (11) actually comprises M^2P independent constraints.

In general, the r^k and Y_l would be given along with the a_l^k (or A_l^k). It might be necessary to solve for the b_{jl}^k or c_{mn}^k coefficients, of which there are MNP or MN^2, respectively.

It is clearly appropriate at this point to introduce the concept of value-added by processing. Conventionally one introduces a set of basic resource prices (prior to processing) per unit quantity

$$u^1 \ldots \ldots \ldots u^M \qquad \text{(or } u^k\text{)}$$

and a set of "final" product prices, per unit quantity, determined by the market:[5]

$$v_1 \ldots \ldots \ldots v_p \qquad \text{(or } v_l\text{)}.$$

Conceptually, we may suppose that the unit value of each material resource gains a characteristic increment (value added) as it passes through a given processing stage. This can be further broken down in terms of fixed (capital) and variable (labor and energy) costs associated with processing, plus profit to the processor. The value-added for the kth resource passing through the jth process, per unit quantity, can be denoted

$$w_j^k, \qquad \begin{array}{l} k = 1, \ldots M \\ j = 1, \ldots N - 1. \end{array}$$

Of course the Nth process (consumption) adds no value but, rather, "consumes" it. Value-added by the jth process ($j \neq N$) can be computed by summing over all materials processed.

$$\sum_{i=0}^{N-1} \sum_{k=1}^{M} C_{ij}^k w_j^k X_j.$$

Value-added to the kth raw material by *all* processes would be given by the expression

$$\sum_{i,j=0}^{N-1} C_{ij}^k w_j^k X_j.$$

Combining the above, one obtains an expression for the value of the final

---

[5] Again, the case of residuals requires special treatment.

product in terms of the value-added at each processing stage, plus the value of basic raw materials:

$$v_l Y_l = \sum_{k=1}^{M} \sum_{j=1}^{N-1} \left\{ b_{jl}^k \left[W_j^k X_j + \sum_{m=1}^{N-1} \sum_{n=j}^{N-1} C_{mn}^k W_n^k X_n \right] \right\} + \sum_{k=1}^{M} A_l^k u^k r^k. \quad (12)$$

| value of lth final product | fraction of output of jth process on kth material going to lth product | value-added by jth process | value-added by prior processing steps other than jth | basic material value |

This mathematical formalism may conceal more than it reveals, except to the dedicated theoretician. Through equation (11), it is an elaborate statement of the principle of conservation of mass (i.e., materials)—extended, if desired, to include conservation of energy—with all its detailed implications in terms of the relationships between inputs and outputs. Defining unit prices, or unit value-added, introduces the possibility of describing a dynamic system, with one (or more) equilibrium solutions. In a previous paper, the extended system, including physical flows to and from the environment, with associated "shadow prices," was shown to be mathematically equivalent to the familiar Walras-Cassel model (Ayres and Kneese 1969). Thus, arguments regarding the existence and uniqueness of solutions applicable to that model can presumably be carried over to the extended system, notwithstanding differences in nomenclature or taxonomy. Hence such questions, however dear to the mathematician, need not detain us further at this stage. It is more important to consider the pros and cons of the new approach in a real-world context.

TAXONOMIC CONSIDERATIONS

The basic criteria for a successful typology are: (a) that the correct classification of every entity to be classified (in this case, processes) be unambiguous (no overlap); (b) that all possible cases be covered (no gaps); (c) that the number of classes be small enough to manipulate, but large enough to permit adequate detail; and (d) that any entity should clearly have similarities with others in the same category and differences from those in other categories. The first and second requirements are equivalent to the mathematical concepts of orthogonality and completeness. If these conditions are met absolutely, any complex set of entities—whether materials, processes, or industries—can be broken down into a set of components each of which is characterized in terms of generally applicable variables, or descriptors. The breakdown may, or may not, be unique. Unfortunately, the third and fourth criteria are difficult to satisfy rigorously—wherein much controversy is generated.

In the case of the conventional I-O model the approach that has been widely accepted is known as the Standard Industrial Classification (SIC) system, used by the Bureau of the Census. Like the Dewey Decimal System for books, it can be (and has been) stretched arbitrarily to cover every known industry. Thus criteria (a) and (b) hold true almost by definition.

As regards the number of categories (i.e., the degree of disaggregation) and their commonalities and differences, there is more to be said. In economic terms, similarities *within* classes and differences *between* classes are expressed in terms of substitutability and competitiveness. That is to say, every product within a category should be substitutable for every other—hence compete for the same market—while no substitution or competition should be possible across class boundaries.

In practice, of course, this requirement leads to a high degree of disaggregation and conflicts with the requirement that the number of categories be relatively small for ease of manipulation. Within aggregated industry-groups, there is a considerable degree of nonsubstitutibility. On the other hand, there is certainly some substitution across sector boundaries; e.g., between aluminum and steel. The sector boundaries can be defined, in practice, by minimizing the cross-elasticities between each sector and all others; i.e., the response of output in any sector to changes in the prices of goods from other sectors (Chenery and Clark 1959).

In the case of materials and processes, it seems plausible that differences and similarities may be easier to justify, since they can be related in many cases to variables with a multiplicity of discrete values. (For this reason, the temptation to utilize indices with a continuous spectrum of values such as conductivity, hardness, melting point, deformability, etc., has been resisted.) This claim can best be substantiated by displaying specific candidate taxonomic schemes, which will be done later.

The optimum degree of aggregation or disaggregation for a material or process classification remains an open question, however. At the outset, one necessarily proceeds to some degree by hunch, modified by trial and error. The factors that put a limit on disaggregation are *data availability* and *data processing capability*. The latter restriction is less severe today than it was a decade or two ago and can, perhaps, be disregarded in comparison with the former. If data are to be obtained from standard sources, e.g., the Census of Manufactures, a fair degree of aggregation is a practical necessity. However, it is not clear that this level of aggregation can be reconciled with the criteria of similarity (i.e., homogeneity) within a sector. Some processes which are generically similar (such as fastening by means of a zipper or by means of a staple) may have no commonality in terms of costs, energy requirements, residuals, output, etc. On the other hand, it may be feasible to obtain usable data at a sufficiently disaggregated level by ad hoc engineering-economic studies of particular materials and processes within a specified industry. The latter alternative seems initially more promising, even though generalizing therefrom is far less automatic. However, an ability to generalize from a single industry to the whole U.S. economy seems inessential at present, although worth considering in the future, if exploratory applications of the model prove sufficiently fruitful.

The approach which will generally be recommended hereafter, then, is something of a compromise: to select an industry (defined, perhaps, by two-digit or three-digit SIC code) and apply the materials-process taxonomy and formulation *within* the confines of the industry. This may eliminate some of the objections that might be raised against using either the industrial classification or the materials-process classification scheme to the exclusion of the other. In any event, it makes the data acquisition problem more manageable, which is an important consideration.

Table 2.1 suggests a basic method of classification of materials by *physical form*—an extension and elaboration of the familiar "solid, liquid, gas" trichotomy. The table lists six simple forms (solid, granular, filamentary, mesh, liquid, and vapor) and sixteen "composite" forms (solid-solid, solid-granule, etc.), with examples of each. Most of these distinctions are obvious enough to need no explanation. However, to minimize confusion in interpretation, a Solid (with a capital S) is taken to be an indivisible, homogeneous, three-dimensional object which retains its shape under normal environmental stresses, such as the force of gravitation, for a reasonable length of time. Glass, soap, butter, or "hard" fats and plastics are included in this category. Inhomogeneous or conglomerate natural solid materials such as wood, stone, concrete, or meat are usually composites: thus wood consists of cellulose fibers cemented together by lignin, while animal tissue consists of filamentary strands (muscle and nerve cells) intermixed with other cells of a more globular structure, such as fat. Evidently the granule category covers a wide range of sizes, shapes, and sorts of granules differing from filaments primarily in shape; both would be solids under a microscope. The inclusion of mesh as a simple category (rather than a composite of the form F-F) is somewhat arbitrary, but it is convenient since materials in this form play such a major role in industry.

Table 2.2 introduces another dimension; viz., *electrochemical type*. The six categories listed are not distinguished as clearly as might be desired, since complex structural characteristics are involved. The selection of water as the sine qua non of solubility is based on the ubiquity of H_2O on

Table 2.1. Classification of Materials by Form

Simple Forms	*Example*
S: Solid	wood, stone, glass, metal castings
G: Granular or powder	sand, sawdust, metal powder, cells
F: Filamentary	hair, feathers, vegetable fiber, muscle, synthetic fiber, wire, etc.
M: Mesh (equivalent to F-F)	paper, woven textiles, wire, screens, etc.
L: Liquid or fluid	water, fats and oils, etc.
V: Vapor or gas	air

Selected Composite Forms	*Example*
S-S: Solid-solid (laminated structure)	plywood
S-G: Solid-granule	frozen soil, concrete
S-F: Solid-filament	fiberglass, fiberboard
S-M: Solid-mesh	epoxy-impregnated fabric
S-L: Liquid in Solid matrix	wet sponge
S-V: Vapor in Solid matrix	foam rubber, pumice, coke
G-G: Granule-granule	mixture of granulated or powdered materials
G-F: Granule-filament	plant or animal tissue
G-L: Granule-liquid (slurry, solution)[a]	mud, paint, syrup, brine
G-V: Granule-vapor	dust cloud
F-L: Filament-liquid (gel)	gelatin, silica-gel
F-V: Filament-vapor	cotton fluff
M-L: Mesh-liquid	wet cloth or paper
L-L: Liquid-liquid (emulsion)	cream, gravy
L-V: Liquid droplet in vapor (aerosol)	aerosol spray (water, paint, etc.)
V-L: Vapor in liquid (foam)	soap suds

(Other composites are conceivable and will be considered as appropriate in the model)

[a] By convention, a solution of polar or nonpolar solid material in a liquid is classed as a granule-liquid (G-L) composite (rather than a solid-liquid or filament-liquid, etc.).

the surface of the earth and in all aspects of human endeavor. Other polar solvents such as ammonia (NH_3) might be mentioned, but most compounds which dissolve in water will also dissolve in ammonia. The alternative focus on solubility in nonpolar hydrocarbons is simply based on the fact that hydrocarbons (such as benzene or carbon tetrachloride) are the most familiar nonpolar solvents, and that nonpolar compounds tend to dissolve in nonpolar solvents and *not* in polar solvents. There are organic compounds (and even hydrocarbons) in each group. The "insoluble" materials, on the other hand, seem to divide most conveniently into the organics and inorganics. The former group includes rubber, teflon, lignin, coal, cellulose, and many proteins. The latter comprises igneous rocks, gem stones, glass, many metallic oxides, silicates, carbonates, sulfides, and so on. It also includes such exotic materials as semiconductors. Insoluble organic solids are often used as thermal or electric insulators, fabrics,

45

Table 2.2. Electro-Chemical Classification, Basic Material Forms

Material type	S: Solid	G: Granular	F: Filamentary	M: Mesh	L: Liquid	V: Vapor
				Examples		
M_1 Metals only (conductors)	metals or alloys	metal powder or filings	metal whisks or wire	wirescreen	molten metal	n.a.
M_2 Polar electrolytes, soluble in H_2O	metal chlorides, nitrates, sulfates, hydroxides, some phosphates, some carbonates	powdered salts			fused salts H_2SO_4, HNO_3, H_2CO_3, NH_4OH,	HCL
M_3 Polar nonelectrolytes, soluble in H_2O	sugars, amino acids, soap	powdered: sugar soap amino acids	spun sugar		alcohols, H_2O, ethers, organic acids, phenols	SO_2, SO_3 NO, NO_2 NH_3, O_2
M_4 Nonpolar compounds, soluble in nonpolar HC (benzene, etc.)	resins, plastics, waxes, fats,	tetraethyl, lead, iodine	many synthetic polymers, e.g., rayon	rayon cloth	hydrocarbons, saturates, olefins, aromatics, bromine	chlorine
M_5 Insoluble, organic compounds (insulators)	rubber, teflon, lignin, coal, some proteins, cellulose	powdered coal, etc.	hair and wool, silk, muscle fiber, cotton, jute, wood pulp (cellulose)	wool, silk, cotton, linen, cloth, sponge	latex, fluorocarbons	freons, refrigerants
M_6 Insoluble, inorganic compounds (insulators)	metal oxides, silicates, phosphates, carbonates, igneous rocks, glass	powdered oxides, powdered glass, sand, clay, soil, gravel, sulfur	asbestos, glass fiber	asbestos or glass cloth	fused rock, molten glass, liquid nitrogen	helium, nitrogen, carbon dioxide, carbon monoxide, hydrogen, fluorine

n.a. = not applicable.

46

and heat transfer fluids, but seldom as structural materials. Inorganic solids tend to be harder and less flexible, more often used for structural purposes.

It is convenient at this point to combine the two material classification schemes into a single one. This is done in table 2.3, which identifies *possible* composite materials by electrochemical type. By convention, the material designated by column is assumed to be *implanted in* materials designated by row. The matrix is not necessarily symmetrical across the diagonal. Thus, granules can be implanted *in* a liquid medium (as a slurry) but not vice versa. And vapor bubbles can be implanted in a liquid (as a foam),

Table 2.3. Possible Composite Materials, by Electrochemical Type

	Solid						Granule						Filament				Mesh				Liquid						Vapor				
	M₁	M₂	M₃	M₄	M₅	M₆	M₁	M₂	M₃	M₄	M₅	M₆	M₁	M₄	M₅	M₆	M₁	M₄	M₅	M₆	M₁	M₂	M₃	M₄	M₅	M₆	M₂	M₃	M₄	M₅	M₆
S M₁																	×										×				×
M₂									×	×					×																
M₃									×	×																					
M₄	×				×	×	×			×	×	×	×	×	×	×	×	×	×	×	×	×			×	×	×		×	×	
M₅	×			×		×	×			×	×	×	×	×	×	×	×	×	×	×	×	×	×	×	×	×	×	×	×	×	
M₆	×			×	×		×				×	×	×			×	×	×		×	×	×	×	×	×	×	×	×	×	×	
G M₁								×	×	×	×	×	×	×	×	×					×	×	×	×	×		?	×	×	×	×
M₂							×		×	×	×	×	×	×	×	×					×	×	×	×	×				×	×	×
M₃							×	×		×	×	×	×	×	×	×					×	×	×	×	×				×	×	×
M₄							×	×	×		×	×	×	×	×	×					×	×			×	×	×	×		×	×
M₅							×	×	×	×		×	×	×	×	×					×	×	×	×	×	×	×	×	×	×	×
M₆							×	×	×	×	×		×	×	×	×					×	×	×	×	×	×	×	×	×	×	×
F M₁	×	×	×	×	×	×	×	×	×	×	×	×		×	×	×													×		
M₄	×	×	×	×	×	×	×	×	×	×	×	×	×		×	×															
M₅	×	×	×	×	×	×	×	×	×	×	×	×	×	×		×							×								
M₆	×	×	×	×	×	×	×	×	×	×	×	×	×	×	×																
Me M₁							×			×	×	×									×	×	×	×	×		×	×	×	×	
M₄							×			×	×	×					×		×	×	×	×			×	×	×	×		×	×
M₅							×			×	×	×					×	×		×	×	×	×	×	×	×	×	×	×	×	×
M₆							×			×	×	×					×	×	×		×	×	×	×	×	×	×	×	×	×	×
L M₁										×				×										×					×		
M₂							×			×	×	×	×	×	×	×					×			×	×		×	×	×	×	×
M₃							×			×	×	×	×	×	×	×					×	×		×	×		×	×	×	×	×
M₄							×	×	×		×	×	×		×	×					×	×	×		×		×	×	×	×	×
M₅							×	×	×	×	×	×	×	×	×	×					×	×	×	×			×	×	×	×	×
M₆							×	×	×	×	×	×	×	×	×	×											×	×	×	×	×
V M₂							?	?		×	×	×		×	×	×					×	×	×	×	×			×	×	×	×
M₃							×			×	×	×	×	×	×	×					×	×	×	×	×		×		×	×	×
M₄							×	×	×		×	×	×		×	×					×	×	×	×	×		×	×			
M₅							×	×	×	×	×	×	×	×	×	×					×	×	×	×	×		×	×	×		×
M₆							×	×	×	×	×	×	×	×	×	×					×	×	×	×	×		×	×	×	×	

47

while liquid droplets can be implanted in a vapor, but the two are not equivalent.

To distinguish between processes "in the large" (i.e., macroprocesses), such as "ore reduction" or "petroleum refining," and the process-elements into which they can be broken down on closer analysis, a set of micro-processes is defined, as shown in table 2.4.

Table 2.4. Elementary Microprocesses

P_1 Transportation (solids or fluids)
$P_{1.1}$ Vehicle, self-propelled (truck) (Solid or containerized fluid)
$P_{1.2}$ Vehicle, passive (pallet, cable car, pneumatic tube, etc.) "
$P_{1.3}$ Conveyor belt "
$P_{1.4}$ Gravity flow (channel or pipe) (Fluid)
$P_{1.5}$ Pressure flow (pump or pipe) "
$P_{1.6}$ Convective flow "
$P_{1.7}$ Capillary flow "

P_2 Change of energy state (solid or fluid)
$P_{2.1}$ Irradiation
$P_{2.2}$ Electrification or magnetization
$P_{2.3}$ Heating
    $_{2.3.1}$ No change of phase
    $_{2.3.2}$ Change of phase
$P_{2.4}$ Refrigeration
    $_{2.4.1}$ No change of phase
    $_{2.4.2}$ Change of phase

P_3 Change in physical form (mainly solids)
$P_{3.1}$ Pressure forming (or compression, for fluids)
$P_{3.2}$ Extension or expansion (or evacuation, for gases)
$P_{3.3}$ Torsion (twist)
$P_{3.4}$ Shear (bend)
$P_{3.5}$ Alignment of fibers or filaments (carding, comb)
$P_{3.6}$ Winding of fibers or filaments (cone, quill, spool)
$P_{3.7}$ Randomization of fibers or filaments (felting)

P_4 Physical integration (solids or mesh)
$P_{4.1}$ Fusion or sintering
$P_{4.2}$ Adhesion
$P_{4.3}$ Weaving of filaments (spinning, braiding, roving, etc.)
$P_{4.4}$ Mechanical joining (sewing, riveting, screwing, bolting, nailing, etc.)
$P_{4.5}$ Implantation in a surrounding medium

48

Table 2.4. (Continued)

P_5 Physical disintegration (solids or mesh) ⟶○– – – – –▸
   $P_{5.1}$ Shock
      $_{5.1.1}$ Mechanical impact (chopping, splitting, etc.)
      $_{5.1.2}$ Explosive impact (blasting)
      $_{5.1.3}$ Acoustic
   $P_{5.2}$ Tooth cutting (sawing, slicing, drilling, milling, etc.)
   $P_{5.3}$ Crushing
   $P_{5.4}$ Tearing or picking

P_6 Physical association
   $P_{6.1}$ Mechanical stirring or blending
   $P_{6.2}$ Mixing by acoustic agitation
   $P_{6.3}$ Entrainment and suspension by moving fluid stream
   $P_{6.4}$ Solution
   $P_{6.5}$ Absorption
   $P_{6.6}$ Adsorption
   $P_{6.7}$ Electrostatic deposition
   $P_{6.8}$ Diffusion

P_7 Physical dissociation or separation
   $P_{7.1}$ Mechanical dismantling
   $P_{7.2}$ Sifting and sorting
   $P_{7.3}$ Filtration
   $P_{7.4}$ Centrifugal separation
   $P_{7.5}$ Flocculation/precipitation
   $P_{7.6}$ Settling/draining
   $P_{7.7}$ Crystallization
   $P_{7.8}$ Evaporation, melting, or sublimation (see $P_{2.3.2}$ or $P_{3.2}$)
   $P_{7.9}$ Condensation or freezing (see $P_{2.4.3}$ or $P_{3.1}$)

P_8 Surface treatment or finishing (solids)
   $P_{8.1}$ Surface removal
      $P_{8.1.1}$ Abrasion (grinding, polishing, sanding, napping, etc.)
      $P_{8.1.2}$ Etching
      $P_{8.1.3}$ Coating removal (pickling, scaling, bleaching, stripping)
   $P_{8.2}$ Surface nonadditive treatment
      $P_{8.2.1}$ Work hardening
      $P_{8.2.2}$ Heat treatment
      $P_{8.2.3}$ Pressing
   $P_{8.3}$ Surface additive treatment
      $P_{8.3.1}$ Lubrication
      $P_{8.3.2}$ Wetting or fulling (detergent, surfactant)
      $P_{8.3.3}$ Coating (paint, dye, wax, shellac, oil polish, etc.)
      $P_{8.3.4}$ Metal plating
      $P_{8.3.5}$ Reactant coating (anodizing, passivating, nitriding, carbonizing, etc.)

Table 2.4. (Continued)

P_9 Chemical dissociation or decomposition
  $P_{9.1}$ Thermal activation (e.g., thermal cracking, dehydration, etc.)
  $P_{9.2}$ Electrolytic (e.g., anode reactions)
  $P_{9.3}$ Catalytic intermediary (e.g., catalytic cracking)
  $P_{9.4}$ Hydrolysis (e.g., ions in solution)
  $P_{9.5}$ Photolysis
  $P_{9.6}$ Biological digestion (e.g., proteins → amino acids)

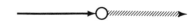

P_{10} Chemical association or synthesis
  $P_{10.1}$ Thermal activation (e.g., combustion)
  $P_{10.2}$ Electrolytic (e.g., cathode reactions)
  $P_{10.3}$ Catalytic intermediary (e.g., polymerization)
  $P_{10.4}$ Hydration
  $P_{10.5}$ Photochemical reaction (e.g., smog)
  $P_{10.6}$ Biological synthesis (e.g., amino acids → proteins)

P_{11} Isomerization

At the one-digit level of aggregation, two basic types of change occur. Each of these broad classes can be subdivided according to the number of inputs and outputs. Processes P_1 through P_8 (except $P_{8.1.3}$ and $P_{8.3.5}$) involve physical changes: in chemical engineering terminology, these are *unit operations;* the remainder involve chemical changes and are generally denoted *unit processes* in chemical engineering texts. A symbolic graphical representation is helpful. The agent that accomplishes the process—whether it be a machine, a tool, a form of energy, or a catalyst—is represented as a blank circle. Inputs enter from the left, outputs leave to the right. It will be noted that basic process types P_1 through P_6 and also P_{10} and P_{11} do *not* involve coproducts or byproducts, while P_7, P_8, and P_9 do so.

There are several definitions that require explanation. For instance, absorption ($P_{6.5}$) is classed as a type of physical *association* even though it is frequently used in conjunction with dewatering, which one might intuitively think of as a separation process. For consistency, we have similarly classed adsorption ($P_{6.6}$) and electrostatic deposition ($P_{6.7}$) even though both are often used in practice to separate impurities from a gas stream. Absorption and diffusion are frequently confused. In table 2.4 and hereafter, absorption is assumed to involve a porous or granular absorber, while diffusion is a spontaneous interdispersal of fluids. Note also, that biological processes are arbitrarily distinguished from others. These decisions are, in the last analysis, matters of convention in which internal consistency is the major concern.

In several cases processes which are normally considered together have been subdivided into component parts. Thus *distillation* is not defined separately, but is broken down into separate stages of evaporation and condensation. Similarly, complex chemical reactions such as ion-exchange can best be considered as sequences of dissociation (P_9) and reassociation (P_{10}). The fact that both may occur within a single physical system— e.g., an electric battery—does not alter the fact that they are conceptually distinct events and either may occur without the other.

Since all possible *macro*processes consist of sequences of all possible *micro*processes, acting on all possible materials, and all possible sequences can be built up from sets of ordered pairs of microprocesses, it is important to eliminate from the outset any ordered pairs of processes which are not compatible with particular materials. Thus the process of weaving is only applicable to filaments; it is not applicable to other material forms, regardless of electrochemical composition. Similarly, mechanical deformation applies only to solids, filaments, or meshes, while electrostatic deposition applies only to granules or vapors. This sort of analysis will eliminate the majority of the permutations that might otherwise have had to be considered.

Table 2.5 displays in matrix form those microprocesses which are compatible with simple materials. Table 2.6 displays those microprocesses which are compatible with *possible* composite materials (derived from table 2.3). A more detailed breakdown of the possible composites indicated in table 2.6 by electrochemical type would occupy too much space to show here.

The constraints (as it were) introduced by tables 2.3, 2.5, and 2.6 will be supplemented by broader restrictions on relationships among the microprocesses allowed in the particular industry being studied. Thus it is convenient to define four generalized process stages:

Stage 1 — Raw material preparation
(Mining, harvesting, and crude physical separation);
Stage 2 — Chemical treatment;
Stage 3 — Physical treatment and fabrication;
Stage 4 — Finishing.

Table 2.5. Microprocesses Applicable to Simple Material Forms

Material type	Phase	P_2 .1	P_2 .2	P_2 .3.1	P_2 .3.2	P_2 .4.1	P_2 .4.2	P_3 .1	P_3 .2	P_3 .3	P_3 .4	P_3 .5	P_3 .6	P_3 .7	P_4 .1	P_4 .2	P_4 .3	P_4 .4	P_4 .5	P_5 .1	P_5 .2	P_5 .3	P_5 .4	P_8 1.1	P_8 1.2	P_8 2.1	P_8 2.2	P_8 2.3	P_8 3.1	P_8 3.2	P_8 3.3	P_8 3.4	P_8 3.5	P_9 .1	P_9 .3	P_9 .5	P_9 .6	P_9 .9	P_{11} .1
M_1 Metal or alloy (conductors)	S	X	X	X	X	X		X	X	X					X	X	X	X	X	X	X		X			X	X		X	X	X	X	X						
	G	X	X	X	X	X			X	X					X	X		X	X								X		X	X	X	X	X						
	F	X	X	X	X	X			X						X	X		X	X		X					X	X		X	X	X	X	X						
	M	X	X	X	X	X									X	X			X		X					X	X			X	X	X	X						
	L			X	X	X																																	
M_2 Polar electrolytes, soluble in H_2O	S	X	X	X	X	X	X	X	X		X				X	X		X	?			X												X	X	?		X	
	G	X	X	X	X	X	X				X				X	X		X	?			X												X	X	?		X	
	L	X	X			X														X																			
	V	X	X			X																																	
M_3 Polar non-electrolytes, soluble in H_2O	S	X	X	X	X	X	X		X						X	X		X	?	X		X												X	X	?		X	X
	G	X	X	X	X	X	X				X				X	X		X	?			X												X	X	?		X	
	L	X	X			X																																	
	V	X	X			X																																	
M_4 Nonpolar compounds, soluble in nonpolar HC	S	X	X	X	X	X	X	X	X	X		X	X	X	X	X	X	X	X	X	X	X	X			?	X	X	X	X	X			X	X	X	X	X	X
	G	X	X	X	X	X		X	X	X					X	X		X	X		X	X					X	X	X	X	X			X	X	X	X	X	X
	F	X	X	X	X	X			X	X					X	X		X	X		X	X					X		X	X	X								
	M	X	X	X	X	X			X						X	X			X		X						X			X	X								
	L	X	X	X	X	X			X						X	X			X		X						X			X	X								
	V	X	X																																				
M_5 Insoluble organic compounds (insulators)	S	X	X	X	X	X		X	X	X		X	X	X	X	X	X	X	X	X	X	X	X			?	X	X	X	X	X			X	X	X		X	X
	G	X	X	X	X	X		X	X	X					X	X		X	X		X	X					X	X	X	X	X								
	F	X	X	X	X	X			X	X					X	X		X	X		X						X		X	X	X								
	M	X	X	X	X	X			X						X	X			X		X						X			X	X								
	L			X	X	X			X						X	X			X		X						X			X	X								
M_6 Insoluble inorganic compounds (insulators)	S	X	X	X	X	X	X	X	X	X		X	X	X	X	X	X	X	X	X	X	X	X			?	X	X	X	X	X			X	X	X		X	X
	G	X	X	X	X	X	X	X	X	X					X	X		X	X		X	X					X	X	X	X	X			X	X	X		X	
	F	X	X	X	X	X			X	X					X	X		X	X		X						X		X	X	X								
	M	X	X	X	X	X			X						X	X			X		X						X			X	X								
	L	X	X	X	X	X			X						X	X			X		X						X			X	X								
	V	?																																					

52

Table 2.6. Microprocesses Affecting Composite Materials

Composite material type	6.1	6.2	6.3	6.4	6.5	6.6	6.7	6.8	7.1	7.2	7.3	7.4	7.5	7.6	7.7	7.8	7.9	8·1.3	9.2	9.4	10.1	10.2	10.3	10.4	10.5	10.6
S-S									X							X		X			X					
G-S							X									X					X					
F-S																X					X					
M-S																X					X					
L-S																X					X					
V-S									X												X					
G-G														X		X	X				X					
G-F (F-G =)	X	X			X	X	X			X		X				X			X		X	X	X	X		
L-G (F-G =)	X	X			X	X	X			X		X				X			X		X	X	X	X		
V-G (F-G =)						X						X?				X					X					
F-F												X?				X					X					
G-M					X	X					X	X				X			X		X	X	X	X		
L-M					X	X					X	X				X			X		X	X	X	X		
V-M	X	X				X	X					X		X			X				X					
G-L[a]	X	X	X	X				X				X	X	X	X	X	X		X	X	X	X	X	X		X
F-L	X	X	X	X								X	X	X		X	X		X		X	X	X	X	X	
L-L	X	X		X								X		X		X	X		X		X	X	X	X?	X	
V-L		X		X				X						X			X		X		X	X	X	X	X	
G-V		X	X					X			X	X		X			X		X		X	X	X	X	X	
F-V		X	X								X	X		X					X		X	X	X	X	X	
L-V		X										X		X							X			X	X	
V-V								X						X							X			X	X	

a (Includes solutions.) By convention, a solution of polar or nonpolar solid material in a liquid is classed as a granule-liquid (G-L) composite (rather than a solid-liquid or filament-liquid, etc.).

Of course, as indicated by the generalized flow diagram, figure 2.1, either stage 2 or stage 3 (or both) may be skipped in some cases.

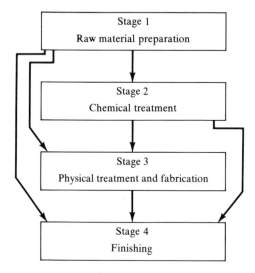

Figure 2.1. Generalized process flow diagram.

Each of these stages may be analyzed separately, to elucidate the various possible paths. We note that transportation processes (P_1) may (and do) occur at virtually any point in a sequence without affecting any other process step.[6] Thus we can omit such steps from further consideration. The basic processes that can occur in stage 1 are:

> P_2 Energy input
> P_5 Physical disintegration
> P_6 Physical association
> P_7 Physical dissociation.

Of course P_6 may involve the use of intermediate materials (other than the raw material in question) such as water, explosives, detergents, or chemicals. Prior processing, such as purification, deionization, or heating, is often necessary; however (with the exception of energy inputs) such treatment is characterized as chemical treatment or "finishing" for the chemical intermediate in question. Thus stage 1 can be analyzed in terms of the flow diagram shown in figure 2.2. The P_6 step can be skipped;

---

[6] It was pointed out in the discussion that mode of transport—i.e., wet, dry—can affect not only residuals generation in the transport process but also may affect residuals generation in prior or subsequent steps, fruit and vegetable canning being an example. [Editor's note.]

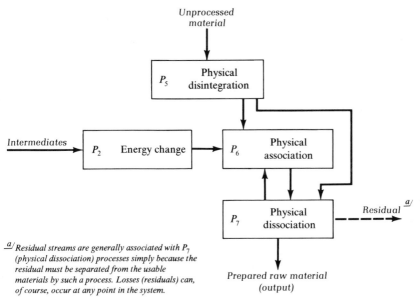

a/ *Residual streams are generally associated with P_7 (physical dissociation) processes simply because the residual must be separated from the usable materials by such a process. Losses (residuals) can, of course, occur at any point in the system.*

Figure 2.2. Stage 1 flow diagram: Raw material preparation.

alternatively the P_6–P_7 loop can be cycled several times with the same, or different, chemical intermediates. Examples of this sort of loop would be successive washings of wool or coal. Figures 2.3 to 2.5 show the basic flows in the other stages of processing. All of these relationships can be expressed in matrix form, as indicated in table 2.7.

In table 2.7 the symbol (1) in the i–j^{th} matrix element signifies that the sequence $P_i \rightarrow P_j$ is likely to occur in stage (1). This possible sequence is represented by an arrow between P_i and P_j on the flow chart for stage 1 (figure 2.2). Ideally, figures 2.2–2.5 should specify processes at the two-digit or three-digit level of disaggregation shown in table 2.4, and table 2.7 should be similarly expanded to accommodate the finer grain.

USE OF THE MODEL FOR FORECASTING

The key to the use of the Materials-Process-Product (MPP) model for economic or technological analysis is the availability of data to define meaningful process input (or output) coefficients. It is my basic hypothesis that input coefficients can be determined with reasonable and sufficient accuracy from an ad hoc engineering-economic analysis of an industry.

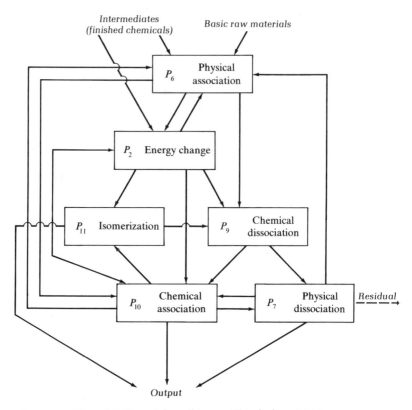

Figure 2.3. Stage 2 flow diagram: Chemical treatment.

The data primarily required are: (a) a materials flow diagram in which the principal processing steps are identified; (b) the average flows along the various paths; and (c) the fixed and variable costs (or value-added), energy requirements, and material losses for each link. To test the applicability of the model to an actual case, a materials flow diagram and the corresponding materials input-output matrix were prepared for beet sugar production. These are shown in figure 2.6 and table 2.8, respectively. Each entry in the table represents the outputs of the step of the production operation represented by the row as inputs into the step represented by the column. The last two columns indicate the product outputs and the residuals, respectively, from the indicated steps. Illustrative data on unit costs and measures of efficiency for the wool reprocessing industry are shown in table 2.9. It appears that significant data can be acquired from a combination of direct and indirect sources without detailed knowledge of proprietary processes or equipment, although the importance of obtain-

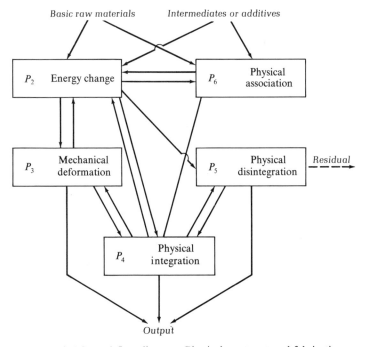

Figure 2.4. Stage 3 flow diagram: Physical treatment and fabrication.

ing some degree of cooperation from the industry involved must not be minimized.[7]

The first stage of analysis is based upon the assumption that the flow relationships are *characteristic* of the technology; i.e., that the technology uniquely determines the ratios between various inputs and outputs (as well as the fixed and variable costs of processing) even though the reverse is not true. If this deterministic relationship is valid, then it follows, first, that the probable flow relationships can be inferred from a study of the technology. Second, and more to the point, a forecast of the specific technology will probably result in a direct corollary forecast of the requisite material-flow relationships. Indeed, since technological forecasts are necessarily focused on functional capabilities, rather than on design details, the material-flow relationships themselves may be regarded as indices of technological change.

It should be emphasized that material-flow relationships may also be affected by factors other than changes in material processing technology.

---

[7] There was considerable disagreement in the discussion concerning the availability of data. [Editor's note.]

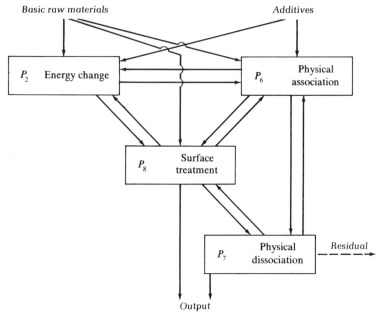

Figure 2.5. Stage 4 flow diagram: Finishing.

Changes in raw material characteristics would be one such factor. For instance, there is a distinct long-term decline in the average quality of ore mined. This is a consequence of the exploitation of the richest sources first, and is likely to continue more or less indefinitely. This clearly has important consequences for some industries. Changes in end-product requirements (i.e., demand) also have an obvious effect on materials-flow relationships. Thus demand for softer toilet tissue or higher quality newsprint would significantly change processes in the pulp and paper industry.

Of course much, if not most, technological change occurs incrementally, without major process or input substitutions. This kind of change would be reflected in perfectly straightforward trend extrapolations. For instance, one index of machine tool efficiency is material wastage. The increasing sophistication of computer-controlled machine tools would be reflected by gradual changes in the ratios of loss to output for lathes, milling machines, and similar "tooth-cutting" processes. Other improvements in material-forming technology would be reflected in decreased energy consumption per unit output, or decreased capital cost per unit output, etc. Another illustration might be the increased efficacy of detergents, reflected in decreased usage per unit output from a washing process. In fact, virtually

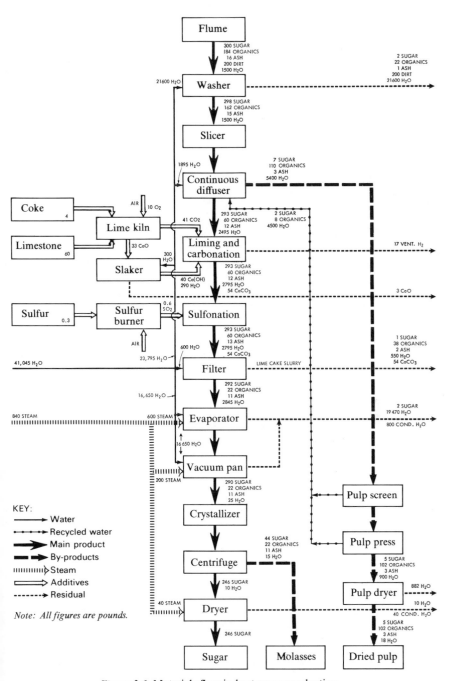

Figure 2.6. Materials flow in beet sugar production.

Table 2.7. Process Sequences in Relation to Process Stages

Input	Output										
	P_1	P_2	P_3	P_4	P_5	P_6	P_7	P_8	P_9	P_{10}	P_{11}
P_1		③④			①	② ③④		④			
P_2			③	③	① ③	③④		④	②	②	②
P_3	③	③	③								
P_4	③	③	③		③						
P_5	③			③		①	①				
P_6		② ③④		③			① ④	④	②	②	
P_7	①② ④						①② ④	④			②
P_8	④	④					④	④			
P_9	②						②				
P_{10}		②					②	②			②
P_{11}	②							②			

any index of technological capability can be related directly to a particular process or sequences of processes.

To forecast residuals, then, one would proceed as follows:

1. Identify major elements of demand.
2. Identify major sources of raw materials.
3. Identify major existing processes.
4. Project one or more (e.g., high, medium, low) future trends for each of the above. Process trends will be given in terms of relevant figures-of-merit such as energy requirements per unit output,[8] material loss per unit output, etc.

[8] If energy is a major factor, the model can be extended to include energy flow explicitly, as mentioned previously.

5. Look for possibilities of major changes in demand patterns, raw material supplies, policy, or technological breakthroughs that could lead to accelerated rates of substitution of one material or process for another.

A more interesting application of the model, for economists, would be to examine the impact of changes in the incentive structure, e.g., shifts in taxes, subsidies, depreciation schedules, import quotas, tariffs, and rules for computing rates. To explore these issues, some theorizing about the market behavior of materials-processing firms is needed.

It can probably be assumed that a profit-maximizing firm will attempt to develop a processing system that minimizes the sum of fixed and variable costs for its final products, in order to maximize the difference between its costs and the market price it can expect to receive for its products. If several alternative processing schemes are available, the one that minimizes "value added" should tend to drive out the others (in time). Of course, to the extent that capital replacement is involved, the time required for this to occur may be quite long. By the same token, the difference between the most efficient and least efficient processes, in some industries, may be considerable. (The most efficient existing process in an industry is, by the way, an effective lower limit to what the industry laggards will be doing at some future time.)

In an industry where more than one processing alternative can be identified, changes in the economic climate will have pronounced differential effects on the costs and profitability of the various options. For instance, an effluent charge resulting in a higher cost for disposing of certain residuals-streams may tend to favor a processing system resulting in less of those unwanted by-products. This is, qualitatively, the expected result of imposing effluent charges. The MPP model, however, opens up the prospect of quantitative analysis along these lines, using straightforward network analysis or critical path techniques. For instance, one could compute the process-path (among any number of alternatives) that minimizes value added with or without constraints on maximum allowable residuals output.[9] Thus, among other things, the model seems to have some potential as a tool for policy making.

The usefulness of the model evidently depends on the availability of adequate data on fixed and variable costs per unit input (or output) and other measures of efficiency for different basic processes as applied to various materials. Although a wide range of possible sources can be

[9] For specified final product and nature and quality of raw material inputs. Where mixes of residuals outputs are involved, it is not easy to establish relevant constraints in the absence of damage functions. [Editor's note.]

Table 2.8. Materials Input-Output Matrix for Beet Sugar Production

		1 Washer	2 Slicer	3 Continuous diffuser	4 Lime kiln	5 Slaker	6 Liming & carbonation	7 Sulfur burner	8 Sulfonation	9 Filter	10 Evaporator
Beets	S = Sugar	300									
	O = Organics	184									
	A = Ash & Dirt	216									
COKE = C					4						
CaO					19						
CO₂					41						
Sulfur								0.3			
Oxygen = O₂					10.7			0.3			
H₂O		1,500 21,600		63.95		300				16,650 600	16,650 600 steam
1 Washer → Slicer			298 = S 162 = O 15 = A 1,500 = H₂O								
2 Slicer				298 = S 162 = O 15 = A 1,500 = H₂O							
3 Continuous diffuser							293 = S 60 = O 12 = A 2,495 = H₂O				
4 Lime kiln						33 = CaO	41 = CO₂				
5 Slaker							40 = Ca(OH)₂ (= 21 = CaO + 19 = H₂O) 290 = H₂O				

6 Liming & carbonation	$293=S$, $60=O$, $12=A$, $54=CaCO_3$, $2{,}795=H_2O$							$292=S$, $22=O$, $11=A$, $2{,}845=H_2O$	
7 Sulfur burner	$0.6=SO_2$ $(0.3=O, 0.3=S)$								
8 Sulfonation	$293=S$, $60=O$, $13=A$, $54=CaCO_3$ $(=17=CaO+37=CO_2)$, $2{,}795=H_2O$								
9 Filter									
10 Evaporator									
11 Vacuum pan									
12 Crystallizer									
13 Centrifuge									
14 Dryer									
15 Pulp screen									
16 Pulp press							$2=S$, $8=O$, $4{,}500=H_2O$		
17 Pulp dryer									

63

Table 2.8. Materials Input-Output Matrix for Beet Sugar Production (continued)

	11 Vacuum pan	12 Crystalizer	13 Centrifuge	14 Dryer	15 Pulp screen	16 Pulp press	17 Pulp dryer	Product	Residual
Beets S = Sugar									
O = Organics									
A = Ash & Dirt									
COKE = C									
CaO									
CO_2									
Sulfur									
Oxygen = O_2									
H_2O	1,650 200 steam			40 steam					
1 Washer → Slicer									2 = S 22 = O 201 dirt 21,600 = H_2O
2 Slicer									
3 Continuous diffuser				7 = S, 110 = O 3 = A 5,400 = H_2O					
4 Lime kiln									
5 Slaker									3 = CaO

	Col 1	Col 2	Col 3	Col 4	Col 5	Col 6	Col 7	Col 8
6 Liming & carbonation	$17 = H_2$							
7 Sulfur burner								
8 Sulfonation								
9 Filter	$1 = S, 38 = 0$ $2 = A, 54 = CaCO_3$ $550 = H_2O$							
10 Evaporator	$2 = S$ $800 = H_2O$ (L) $19{,}270 = H_2O$ (V)							$292 = S, 22 = 0$ $11 = A$ $225 = H_2O$
11 Vacuum pan	$200 = H_2O$ (V)						$290 = S, 22 = 0$ $11 = A$ $25 = H_2O$	
12 Crystallizer						$290 = S, 22 = 0$ $11 = A$ $25 = H_2O$		
13 Centrifuge	Molasses $44 = S, 22 = 0$ $11 = A, 25 = H_2O$				$246 = S$ $10 = H_2O$			
14 Dryer	Sugar 246 $40 = H_2O$ (L) $10 = H_2O$ (V)							
15 Pulp screen			$5 = S, 102 = 0$ $3 = A$ $5{,}400 = H_2O$					
16 Pulp press		$5 = S, 102 = 0$ $3 = A$ $900 = H_2O$						
17 Pulp dryer	Dried Pulp $5 = S, 102 = 0$ $3 = A, 18 = H_2O$ $882 = H_2O$ (V)							

Table 2.9. Unit Costs and Measures of Efficiency

Process	Form of matter	Type of plant	Typical cost				Measures of efficiency		
			Fixed cost per unit capacity		Variable cost per unit capacity		Energy cost per unit output		Material loss in process
			Total cost	Cost of hot water	Total cost	Cost of hot water	BTU	KWH	
			($/lb. dww)	($/lb. dww)	($/lb. dww)	($/lb. dww)	($/lb. dww)	($/lb. dww)	(percentage)
Fulling	M,L	a	.004	.0010	.041	.0140		.0016	1
		c	.007	.0006	.041	.0083		.0016	1
Scouring	M,L	a	.002	.0010	.048		.0089	.0006	Neg.
		b		.0006			.0155		Neg.
		c	.005	.0022	.048		.0097	.0006	Neg.
		d		.0014					Neg.
Stripping	M,L	a	.003	.00040	.029	.0060	.0024	.0003	Neg.
		b		.00013		.0023	.0072		Neg.
		c	.008	.00080	.027	.0064	.0029	.0003	Neg.
		d		.00060		.0023			Neg.
Dyeing	M,L	a	.004	.00020	.107	.0030	.0018	.0003	Neg.
		b		.00010		.0017	.0030		Neg.
		c	.007	.00040	.107	.0027	.0020	.0003	Neg.
		d		.00030		.0017			Neg.

Note: M = mesh; L = liquid.
Flow-through processes in plants are based on lb. dry wool weight (dww)—where:

a. Plant is as it exists currently (equipment totally depreciated) with existing liquid-flow rate.

b. Plant as in a above, with liquid-flow rate half of present level.

c. Plant with equipment replaced at current prices, with existing liquid-flow rate.

d. Plant as c above, with liquid-flow rate half of present level.

Source: International Research and Technology Corp.

ROBERT U. AYRES

identified, the available data are spotty (or worse) both as to coverage and quality. Nevertheless, in view of the tremendous quantity of technical-economic literature, it should not be out of the question for even a small organization to accomplish a compilation of this sort. The first iteration might well be accomplished by pooling the knowledge of a small group of experienced engineering consultants. Valuable cross-checks could then be obtained by utilizing published data on capital/output ratios and labor productivity in various industries.

The fact that alternative macroprocesses actually in use within an industry may vary considerably in efficiency—whether measured in terms of unit cost, residuals output, or both—has already been noted in passing. It was pointed out that this may be of considerable value in forecasting the future direction of an industry. By the same token, the discrepancies between process efficiencies *across* industry lines (defined by standard industrial classification) is likely to be even greater. That is, an innovative, technologically advanced industry may be processing a given material for a given purpose in a backward industry. The way mechanical connections are made in the conventional building industry, for instance, bears almost no resemblance to the way functionally similar connections are made in the aerospace or electronics industries. Implementation of the MPP model across industry boundaries would turn up a wealth of specific instances of this sort. Such an analysis, if carried out systematically, would offer a very useful guide to opportunities for technological cross-fertilization and, perhaps, for high-payoff investments in research and development.

REFERENCES

Ayres, R. U., and A. V. Kneese. 1968. Environmental pollution. *Federal programs for the development of human resources*, vol. 2. Washington, D.C.: Government Printing Office.
———. 1969. Production, consumption and externalities. *American Economic Review* 59, no. 3:282–97.
Chenery, H. G., and P. G. Clark. 1959. *Interindustry economics*. New York: John Wiley and Sons.
Cumberland, J. H., and J. R. Hibbs. 1970. Alternative future environments: Some economic aspects. Paper read at the Institute for Management Sciences Symposium, March 9, 1970, at National Bureau of Standards, Washington, D.C.
Leontief, W. 1970. Environmental repercussions and the economic structure: An input-output approach. In "A challenge to social scientists," paper presented at the International Symposium on Environmental Disruption, International Social Science Council, Tokyo, Japan.

67

3. Observations on the Economics of Irreplaceable Assets

John V. Krutilla, Charles J. Cicchetti,
A. Myrick Freeman III, and Clifford S. Russell

I. INTRODUCTION

Production has commanded the attention of economists throughout the history of economic analysis. There has been a much smaller volume of literature on the economics of irreproducible assets, among which would be nonrenewable natural resources. Recently, however, a shift of emphasis, if not a major reorientation, may be detected toward a "new conservation" that formulates the natural resources issue in somewhat different terms, having first perceived technology (given tastes) as largely the determinant of the value of particular natural endowments. Taking some liberties, one might look upon natural resources as being "produced" by the advances in technology that permit previously uneconomic stocks of mass and sources of energy to be converted into economic "natural resources." In short, much of the literature on conservation addressing the distinction between "renewable" and "nonrenewable" resources may be of limited relevance in today's world.[1]

However, together with the advances in material well-being that technology has provided, somewhat different problems have been emerging for economists to consider. Some of these stem from the result of non-

We are indebted to our colleagues at Resources for the Future; to faculty and students of the 1969 Natural Resources Institute, Oregon State University; and to Darwin Nelsen, Donald Sander, and Arnold Quint of the Federal Power Commission for many helpful observations and suggestions during the preparation of this study. We also wish to acknowledge comments and suggestions on an earlier draft of this paper from Gardner Brown, Richard Judy, and V. Kerry Smith.

[1] The most vigorous statement of this position would be that of Barnett and Morse (1963).

uniform incidence of technological progress (Baumol 1967), or the asymmetry in the implications of technological advances for different uses of natural endowments (Krutilla 1967). In the former we have the case of different degrees of technological progressiveness among different sectors of the economy. In the latter we differentiate between natural endowments as factors of production, or intermediate goods, that are transformed through some production technology either into other goods in process or into final consumption goods, on the one hand, and natural endowments that directly give rise to stimuli eliciting satisfaction in an ultimate consumption of final-good sense, on the other. If a natural resource is used as a good in process, technology may provide a wide spectrum of substitutes for the particular input without significantly altering the final product either in appearance or performance. We can conceive of printed circuits substituting for copper wire in communication equipment requiring very dissimilar materials—hence providing substitution possibilities governed by the technologies in question—without affecting the quality of the transmission or reception. Here an elastic recipe of alternative ingredients in production may produce a "consumer-undifferentiable" final product appealing equally well to identical preferences for the final good.

If the natural endowment enters in some sense directly into the utility function of individuals, on the other hand, substitution becomes more difficult. At the final consumption stage, for given preferences, technology is likely to be less availing. Final product development through new technology may affect the cross-elasticity of demand for services of irreproducible assets, but if the utility enjoyed is in significant part derived from the "accident of fortune" attribute, there is reason to question the closeness of any contrived substitute. Lithography, for example, has brought the works of the masters into the homes of all who choose such reproductions; there is no evidence, however, that it has adversely affected the value of the originals as it would have had the reproductions in any sense been reasonably close substitutes. We would argue, then, that there is a greater range of substitution possibilities among produced goods designed to cater to given tastes than between producible and irreproducible goods.

One might suggest, then, that the ability to produce or replicate facilities producing final consumption goods to gratify given tastes will lie at the base of the distinction between producible and irreplaceable assets. Irreplaceability, of course, will be a function of the closeness of substitutes in final consumption. With this as a point of departure, at least three classes of "irreplaceable assets" can be distinguished. One would be "gifts of individual genius" such as the work of Leonardo da Vinci or Rembrandt. A second might be called "gifts of collective genius," represented by the cultural antiquities of Egypt, Greece, and Rome, among others.

Finally, we have the "gifts of nature," namely the accidents of geomorphology, biological evolution, and ecological succession.

The three classes of irreplaceable assets identified above may have different resource allocative implications. The real cost of preserving da Vinci's *Mona Lisa*, for example, is not really appreciable. On the other hand, the preservation of cultural antiquities may involve a different order of costs. That is, the preservation of the Roman Coliseum, or one of the other antiquities in a densely populated metropolitan area, may involve opportunity costs of substantial size by virtue of the fact that such antiquities may occupy sites that have high locational value for other economic activities. We may be excused for assuming that the cultural relics of such distinction meet their opportunity costs through the economic rents generated by tourists and other considerations. But ruins of lesser distinction—those of nearly insignificant character—under readily conceivable circumstances may have opportunity costs which exceed the potential value from preserving them as cultural assets.

Issues of similar character, of course, underlie conflicts over the allocation of gifts of nature. Perhaps the first, and certainly a classic one, in the United States was the case of Hetch Hetchy Valley, shortly after the turn of the century. Here a scenic resource in the Yosemite National Park, comparable in grandeur to Yosemite Valley, was dedicated to serve as a municipal water supply reservoir for the city of San Francisco. At current issue are the alternative incompatible purposes to which Hells Canyon may be devoted—as a national park or monument, being the deepest gorge on the continent, or for use as a hydroelectric site.

Where the preservation of irreplaceable assets have opportunity costs—namely the opportunity returns foreclosed from alternative uses of the resources reflected in, or required by, preservation—these must be given consideration. But, if the value of the output stream from different alternative incompatible uses is affected differently by technological change, the current evaluation of the assets yielding these services must reflect this. In section II this issue will be analyzed in the case of a gift of nature. Quantitative results of the analysis are presented in section III to serve as a basis for comparing the differences that may occur in evaluation of the alternative incompatible purposes in a practical case, when the differences in the incidence of technological advance are neglected.

While in the illustrative case in section III the results are sufficient to justify preserving the natural environment, the analysis might have revealed an opportunity cost exceeding the preservation value if estimated, as conventionally, without reference to the *option value* inherent in preserving an irreplaceable asset. If the opportunity returns from the two alternatives had been close, but had favored development at the expense

71

of preserving the natural environment, following Weisbrod (1964), we would have to consider whether or not the inclusion of option value would affect the decision at the margin. But as the existence of option value, independent of consumer surplus (already reflected in our computation of the preservation values) has itself been questioned (Long 1967), the problem will be addressed rigorously in section IV. Section V reviews the areas in which further research is suggested.

II. ASYMMETRIC IMPLICATIONS OF TECHNOLOGICAL ADVANCE FOR THE VALUE OF IRREPLACEABLE ASSETS IN CONTRAST WITH PRODUCED GOODS

In this section we use the attributes inherent in the current celebrated case of Hells Canyon (Federal Power Commission [FPC] hearings) to illustrate the methods used to introduce the effects of technological asymmetry, where relevant, in resource allocation decisions. The unique geomorphologic characteristics of Hells Canyon qualifiy its preservation under the Wild and Scenic Rivers Act (FPC hearings, exhibit R-624). At the same time, because of the narrowness of the gorge, steepness of its walls, and volume of flow in this reach of the Snake River, the canyon provides exceptionally fine sites for hydroelectric development. Thus we find a case where the preservation of a "gift of nature" is likely to have opportunity costs (and vice versa) so that a meaningful economic issue is posed. Moreover, we know that there have been advances in technology in the production of energy from alternative nonhydroelectric sources. We also are justified in regarding the canyon and its environment as not producible by man; hence if the natural environment is altered by development, a decision with an adverse irreversible consequence for an irreproducible asset will have been taken. The latter raises the question of option value, which will be discussed in section IV, as well as asymmetry in the implications of technological progress. In this section, however, we confine ourselves to the latter issue.

The Development Alternative

Consider now the proposed hydroelectric alternative to retaining the environment in its current condition. The technology of a given time is incorporated into the dam and powerhouse in such a facility at the time it is built, and will fix the costs of generation over the economic life of the facility. The benefits, on the other hand, being governed by the costs of the most economical alternative source[2] (electrical energy being so stand-arized a commodity) does not remain constant over the life of the hydro-electric facility. The cost of energy produced in thermal electric stations declined steadily, in real terms, over the past half century, and by about 4.5 per cent per year over the past two decades. This was partly due to the decrease in cost per kilowatt of capacity, and partly to the increased efficiency in the utilization of fuel. If the life of the alternative thermal source is shorter than that of the hydroelectric facility (and the real cost of the more technologically advanced replacement capacity is lower than at the time of the hydroelectric project construction), then the capacity benefits of the hydroelectric facility would be lower upon the hypothesized retirement and replacement of the thermal alternative with which the hydro is being compared.

Moreover, the effects of advances in technology of thermal generation have not been restricted to the capacity component of costs. Gains made in thermal efficiency also would have implications for the valuation of hydroelectric facilities. As the plant factor on technologically advanced new plants is higher than the system load factor, the difference in factors represents the percentage of capacity that can generate "economy energy" to displace energy produced by the most uneconomic plant in the system. A given plant, when new, enters the system at, say, 90 per cent plant factor; but as it ages, it is used a progressively smaller proportion of the time so that by the twentieth year it operates at, say, only 30 per cent plant factor.[3] Accordingly, the relevant energy cost would be given by the weighted average of the original and the advanced technology, with the costs related to the advanced technology figuring progressively more significantly as the relevant annual costs until the original thermal alternative is replaced (say, in the thirtieth year). At that time both the energy and capacity values

[2] The benefit from hydroelectric development can be represented as:

$$b_d = B_d - C_d - B_a + C_a;$$

where b_d = net benefit from development alternative,
B_d = gross benefit from development alternative,
C_d = cost of the hydroelectricity produced,
B_a = gross benefit from the alternative source of power,
C_a = cost of alternative power produced.

Since the alternative to the hydroelectric source, for comparative purposes, is designed to produce identical services, B_d equals B_a, hence cancels out. Accordingly, the net benefit, b_d is equal to $C_a - C_d$, or the resource savings, if any, from development of the hydroelectric resource. See Peter O. Steiner (1965).

[3] Federal Power Commission studies indicate that historically, for fossil fuel plants, the plant factor has fallen to 20 per cent by the twentieth year. For computational convenience we use an initial plant factor of 90 per cent and a 3 percentage point per year plant factor decay to give us a plant factor of 30 per cent in the twentieth year and retirement in the thirtieth year.

would be governed by the state of technology of the thirty-first, not the original, year. Thereafter, the capacity value would remain constant from the thirty-first to the fiftieth year, but the energy values would again begin to decline because the relevant costs used for evaluation purposes would again become a blend of the level of technology of the thirty-first year and the advances in technology from the thirty-first to the fiftieth years.

Formally this can be shown by the model below:[4]

Over the first 30-year period, taken as the useful life of a thermal facility, let PVC_t represent the present value of annual costs per kilowatt of the thermal alternative in year t:

$$PVC_1 = C_I + E(8760F)$$

$$PVC_2 = \left\{ C_I + [E8760(F - k)] + \frac{E}{(1 + r)}(8760k) \right\} \left(\frac{1}{(1 + i)} \right)$$

.
.
.

$$PVC_n$$

$$= \left\{ C_I + E[8760[F - (n - 1)k]] + \frac{E}{(1 + r)^{n-1}}[8760(n - 1)k] \right\} \left(\frac{1}{1 + i} \right)^{n-1}$$

for $1 < n < 30$;

where C_1 = capacity cost/KW/yr. during first 30-year period,

E = energy cost/KWh,

F = the plant factor (.90),

k = a constant representing the time decay of the plant factor (.03),

i = the discount rate,

r = the annual rate of technological progress.

---

[4] Two points should be noted in connection with the technological change model presented below. In the Hells Canyon case, we are talking about an almost exclusively hydroelectric system, with a thermal plant at this stage in the system's development as the realistic alternative to the hydro project. The model developed is appropriate to the case in which as yet no thermal plants exist in the system to which the new project is being added. Were we considering a mixed hydro-thermal, or a predominantly thermal system, the thermal alternative to the hydro project would be credited immediately, rather than gradually over time, with the benefits of displacing uneconomic energy generated in the system. Secondly, the details of the computational model used here are based on historical experience with technology that is not likely to be the same as the technology to be employed in the future. However, we do not know the details of the future technology sufficiently well to be able to specify a computational model based on it. The strategem employed here, then, is to use the results from the computational model based on past and current technology and argue, by analogy, that the effects for valuation purpose of the relevant future technology would be of the same or greater order of magnitude.

74

Writing out the nth term yields:

$$PVC_n = \frac{C_I}{(1+i)^{n-1}} + \frac{8760EF}{(1+i)^{n-1}} - \frac{8760Ek(n-1)}{(1+i)^{n-1}} + \frac{8760Ek(n-1)}{[(1+r)(1+i)]^{n-1}}.$$

These terms can be summed individually, using standard formulas for geometric progressions, and then factored to form:

$$PVC_{1,\ldots,30} = \sum_{n=1}^{30} PVC_n$$

$$= (C_I + 8760EF)\left[\frac{1-a^{30}}{1-a}\right] - \frac{8760Ek}{i}\left\{\frac{1-a^{29}}{1-a} - 29a^{29}\right\}$$

$$+ \frac{8760Ek}{(1+r)(1+i)-1}\left\{\frac{1-b^{29}}{1-b} - 29b^{29}\right\};$$

where $a = \left(\frac{1}{1+i}\right)$

$$b = \frac{1}{(1+r)(1+i)}.$$

Over years 31, ..., 50 the cost expressions are similar except that we are dealing with only a 20-year additional period and all terms thus get discounted by a factor of $(1/1+i)^{30}$. Hence, using similar formulas for the sum of geometric series, the present value of annual costs per kilowatt from this latter period is determined to be

$$PVC_{31,\ldots,50} = \sum_{n=31}^{50} PVC_n = \left(\frac{1}{1+i}\right)^{30}\left\{(C_{II} + 8760E'F)\left[\frac{1-a^{20}}{1-a}\right]\right.$$

$$- \frac{8760E'k}{i}\left[\frac{1-a^{19}}{1-a} - 19a^{19}\right] + \frac{8760E'k}{(1+r)(1+i)-1}\left[\frac{1-b^{19}}{1-b} - 19b^{19}\right]\right\};$$

where $C_{II} = \frac{C_I}{(1+r)^{30}}$

$$E' = \frac{E}{(1+r)^{30}}.$$

The overall present value is

$$PVC_{1,\ldots,50} = PVC_1 + \ldots + PVC_{30} + PVC_{31} + \ldots + PVC_{50}.$$

Traditional analyses are based essentially on the model given below.

$$K = \sum_{n=1}^{50} \frac{[C_I + E(8760F)]}{(1+i)^{n-1}}$$

or, which is equivalent,

$$= [C_I + E(8760F)]\left[\frac{1 - a^{50}}{1 - a}\right]$$

to be consistent with previous notation.

The adjustment factors in table 3.1 are obtained as follows:

$$K/PVC_{1,\ldots,50}$$

The Preservation Alternative

Consider next the preservation alternative. The value of any quantity of service consumed per unit time is measured by the area under the demand schedule. When the facility providing the service is a reusable, nondepreciating asset, such as a natural environment protected against destruction or degradation, the value of benefits is the area under the demand curve for each time period the natural area is used. If time is given the customary value of one year, the gross benefit of the natural area would be approximated by the sum of discounted annual benefits. The present value can then be compared with the capital investment (if any), the present value of annual operating costs (if any), and also the opportunity cost, or net present value of the most economical alternative use precluded by retention of the area for uses compatible with existing environmental conditions in the canyon.[5]

If the demand for the services of the area grows, congestion externalities eventually will arise. That is, a point will be reached beyond which the use

[5] To establish consistency in the treatment of the developmental and preservation benefits, we represent the benefit derivation model for the preservation alternative as below:

$$b_p = B_p - C_p - B_a' + C_a';$$

where b_p = net benefit from preservation alternative,
  B_p = gross benefit from preservation alternative,
  C_p = cost of providing services from the preservation alternative,
  B_a' = gross recreation benefit from alternative to preservation,
  C_a' = cost of providing recreational services alternative to the services provided by the canyon preserved in present condition.

Now, since the canyon in an undeveloped state is a gift of nature, the costs (other than opportunity costs accounted for in b_d, footnote 2) are zero. We have:

$$b_p = B_p - B_a' + C_a'.$$

However, since we look to produced assets' services as alternatives, and assuming free entry into the recreational services industry, we would expect that the leisure formerly consumed in Hells Canyon facilities would be distributed across the alternatives impinging at the margins. Now, since benefits at the margin under the circumstance would equal the costs at the margin, B_a' and C_a' would be equal. Accordingly, $b_p = B_p$, which corresponds to the results presented in table 3.4.

of the area by one more individual per unit time will result in a lessening of the utility obtained by others using the area. We have taken this point to be the capacity of Hells Canyon for the purpose of our analysis. If the marginal benefits of additional users exceed the marginal congestion costs they inflict on others, total benefits could be increased by relaxing the constraint. But we seek to define a quantity of constant quality services whose value represents a lower-bound estimate of the preservation benefit. Implicit in this position, of course, is the assumption that pricing will be employed in practice to ration use to the constraint level.

Growth in the demand for services of the area and a capacity constraint introduce some complications in the analysis. First, as income, population, and tastes change through time, the usual ceteris paribus assumptions must be relaxed. Accordingly, the shape and area under the demand curve may be expected to change with temporal shifts in the demand curve. Such shifts must be incorporated into the benefit estimating procedure and treated separately. Secondly, the capacity constraint presents another complication since it sets a limit on the range over which the quantity demanded can be summed without further adjustment.

The Analytical Model. So long as the additional use of the area by an individual diminishes neither the possibility nor quality of enjoyment of simultaneous use of that area by another, it is proper to think of a zero long-run marginal cost of producing one more user day of service in the canyon area. Therefore the supply schedule would be horizontal and coincident with the quantity axis. As demand shifts in this range of output, where there is excess supply at zero price, the market adjustment mechanism causes an increase in the quantity consumed.

Until the area in question reaches its capacity, this price-signal, quantity-response adjustment is applicable for explaining "stable" dynamic equilibrium. But as capacity is reached, and the quantity supplied becomes fixed, the market reaches equilibrium by having excess quantity demanded as the signaling device and variations in price as the adjustment mechanism. For this range—i.e., after an area reaches its recreational carrying capacity— the underlying supply curve is perfectly inelastic. As Keynes (1964, p. 300) pointed out:

> . . . in general, the demand for some services and commodities will reach a level beyond which their supply is . . . perfectly inelastic, whilst in other directions there is still a substantial surplus of resources without employment. Thus as output increases, [the economy grows] a series of "bottlenecks" will be successively reached, where the supply of particular commodities ceases to be elastic and their prices have to rise to whatever level is necessary to divert demand into other directions. . . .

For producible commodities (even recreation facilities such as Disney-land) this inelastic supply curve is a short-run phenomenon, but for nonproducible areas this short-run supply curve is also the long-run supply curve. Regardless of the range of output—i.e., before capacity ($t < k$ and $0 < Q_d < Q_k$) or beyond (when $k \geq t$ and $Q_d \geq Q_k$)—primary interest lies in the estimation of benefits under the implicit assumption of efficient rationing; that is, a zero user price is charged before capacity and a positive price is used as the rationing device after capacity[6] is reached and excess quantity demand occurs at the present prices.

The first important consideration is: "Why and how does the shift in demand curve vary through time?"

There are three classes of parameters—population (*Pop*), income (*I*), and taste (*T*) (a multivariate proxy term)—which may vary over time and cause the demand schedule to shift in price-quantity space. Two of these forces or factors are readily interpreted geometrically,[7] although conventional economic analysis is sometimes guilty of overlooking the subtle differences between Marshallian and Walrasian analyses; i.e., whether shifts in these parameters will effect pressure on the quantity demand at any given price, the price people are willing to pay for any given quantity, or both.

Taking population increase first, a plausible hypothesis is that new members will have preferences similar to those of existing members so that for any constant price, percentage growth in quantity demanded will be proportional to percentage growth in population. If preferences are strictly similar, so that we are simply adding identical demand curves horizontally, the percentage change in quantity demanded will equal the percentage change in population, or the elasticity of quantity demanded to population size will be unity at all price levels.

If population doubled, assuming a constant unit population-quantity elasticity, the quantity demanded at zero price (figure 3.1) would increase from 4 to 8, at price P' from 2 to 4, at P^* it would remain at zero. The effect then is the nonparallel shift from D_1 to D_2 as indicated in figure 3.1, which is the type of shift we usually hypothesize implicitly when we speak of variations in population. A parallel shift, on the other hand, would require the quantity demand to increase by the same absolute amount for all prices. This latter effect is a special case that requires all new people (as population grows) to have a perfectly price inelastic demand for this commodity. The horizontal shift from D_1 to D_2 indicated in figure 3.1,

---

[6] See J. Seneca (1970) for a discussion of the estimation of welfare or benefits when price is not permitted to act as the rationing device.

[7] See Shepherd (1933) and the comment by F. L. Thomsen for an early example of this controversy.

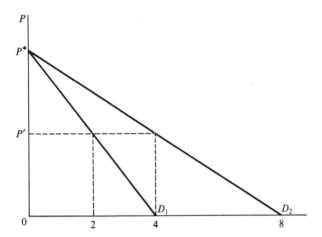

Figure 3.1. Equiproportional horizontal shifts in demand.

and the short-run assumption of constant tastes, are the most plausible assumptions we could make and are most likely to reflect the effect of population growth on the demand schedule in two-dimensional price-quantity space.

Another component of the shift in the demand schedule results from increased consumer incomes. It is not generally as clear in this particular case as with population growth, whether an increase in income should be considered as a shift in quantity demanded for a given price or a shift in demand price for a given quantity. However, where there is an inelastic supply of nonproducible goods (the case under consideration), the demand-price variation seems more general and preferable.

First, if a good is nonproducible and thus fixed in supply, as the stocks of other goods and services produced grow, the value (price) of this good in fixed supply would be expected to grow relative to the value (price) of a commodity whose stock is growing for each individual. As the price of the other goods (producible) falls relative to the good in fixed supply, the quantity demanded of these producible goods increases, resulting in diminishing marginal utility from these commodities relative to the fixed commodity. This is shown diagrammatically in figure 3.2.

As technological change occurs and the real incomes of individuals grow, society finds the marginal cost of Y (services of a nonproducible asset) grows relative to the marginal cost of X (producible goods). This is indicated by the change in the slope of the production possibility curves, the rate of product transformation, as indicated in figure 3.2 for each value of initial Y or nonproducible asset.

79

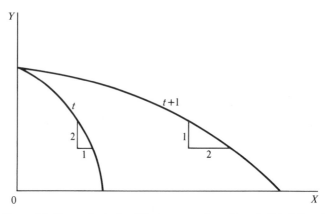

Figure 3.2. Change in trade-off between services of producible (X) and irreproducible (Y) assets as technology advances in former.

Therefore:

$$\frac{dY}{dX_t} = -2 = \frac{MC_x}{MC_y} \qquad \text{for time} = t;$$

$$\frac{dY}{dX_{t+1}} = -\tfrac{1}{2} = \frac{MC_x}{MC_y} \qquad \text{for time} = t+1;$$

$$\Delta MC_y \gg \Delta MC_x \text{ as } t \text{ goes from } t \text{ to } t+1.$$

Assuming now perfectly competitive markets, the ratios of marginal costs would be set equal to the ratios of the respective prices, and the resultant expression would be:

$$\frac{MC_x}{MC_y} = \frac{P_x}{P_y} = \frac{\text{price of producible goods}}{\text{price of goods in fixed supply}}.$$

Combining these last two results, it follows that the passage of time results in an increase in the price of y relative to the price of x; i.e., $\Delta P_y \gg \Delta P_x$ as t varies from t to $t+1$. Similarly, the value of the area under the relevant portion of the demand curve for services in fixed supply increases in response to increments in supply of producible goods and services.

A second, but not unrelated, reason for expecting pressure from growing income to affect the price people are willing to pay for a visit to Hells Canyon (P_y) can be based on the underlying demand conditions, but the nonproducible element of a wilderness experience, if the source becomes congested, is certainly implicitly at work in the analysis. If we define visits to Hells Canyon (Q_y) to be a relative luxury in the conventional Walrasian sense

$$\left(e_{Q_y I} = \frac{dQ_y}{dI} \cdot \frac{I}{Q_y} > 1, \text{ where } I = \text{income} \right)$$

then, in a two-good world, the conventional weighted income elasticity for all other goods must be less than unity:

$$\left(e_{Q_zI} = \frac{dQ_z}{dI} \cdot \frac{I}{Q_z} < 1 \right).$$

If we further assume that the cross elasticity between other goods (Q_z) and willingness to pay for Hells Canyon visits (P_y) is positive, then in this simplified two-good world we are assuming all other goods are substitutes for visits to Hells Canyon, and stated in total derivative elasticity form,

$$e_{Q_zP_y} = \frac{dQ_z}{dP_y} \cdot \frac{P_y}{Q_z} > 0.$$

If technological change increases the quantity of other goods available and lowers their price, then a cross-elasticity effect, as well as the conventional income effect, is at work. By using the chain rule and ignoring partial derivatives, we can construct a new elasticity that combines both of these effects with only one independent variable, income:[8]

$$e_{Q_zI} \cdot \frac{1}{e_{Q_zP_y}} = \frac{dQ_z}{Q_z} \cdot \frac{I}{dI} \cdot \frac{dP_y}{P_y} \cdot \frac{Q_z}{dQ_z}$$

$$= \frac{dP_y}{P_y} \cdot \frac{I}{dI} = e_{P_yI}.$$

In concluding this discussion, if the vertical component of shift in the demand schedule due to income variation is as suggested above, we might expect a constant percentage increase in willingness to pay per percentage increase in income for a given quantity. As income varies, the shift is of the nature shown in figure 3.3 (from D_1 to D_2).

A third component of shift in demand indicated above was taste. Tastes may be thought of as affecting the numerical values or signs and the

---

[8] A numerical example might better explain this new parameter. Assume

$$e_{Q_zI} = \frac{dQ_z}{Q_z} \cdot \frac{I}{dI} = \frac{1 - k_y \cdot e_{Q_yI}}{k_z} = 0.75;$$

where k_y = per cent of income spent on good Q_y (Hells Canyon)
and k_z = per cent of income spent on good Q_z (all other goods)
and let $e_{Q_zP_y} = 0.5$.
Then

$$e_{P_zI} = e_{Q_zI} \cdot \frac{1}{e_{Q_zP_y}} = \frac{3}{4} \cdot \frac{2}{1} = \frac{3}{2} = 1.5.$$

If the effect of technological change is to spend relatively less money on necessities and the marginal utility of these goods also falls, the pressure is to increase the elasticity of willingness to pay for Hells Canyon visits relative to income growth, e_{P_y}.

81

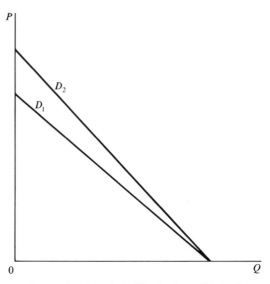

Figure 3.3. Equiproportional vertical shifts in demand price for every quantity.

explicit elasticities[9] of population to quantity (horizontal) and income to price (vertical) over time. For example, in the initial time period population might be growing at, say, 1.5 per cent per year but the quantity demanded at zero price might be growing at 10 per cent per year. However, the rate of change of tastes for the population at large favoring this kind of recreational activity might begin to decline as a "saturation level" is approached, so that eventually demand would reflect only additions to population and incomes rather than an increasing proportion of the population participating. Tastes may change over time and affect willingness to pay, for there is evidence that much recreation, particularly wilderness related, is a luxury good (Cicchetti, Seneca, and Davidson 1969). There is no compelling reason, however, to expect that this elasticity will be constant as income changes over time. Thus, variation in tastes may enter the analysis also through changes in the elasticity of prices to income through time.

The "Composite" Benefit Computational Model. Until now we have deliberately avoided being specific about the nature of the "preservation values." There are several services that a natural area like Hells Canyon

[9] I.e., $\dfrac{(\Delta \text{ Quantity})/(\text{Quantity})}{(\Delta \text{ Population})/(\text{Population})}$ and $\dfrac{(\Delta \text{ Price or value})/(\text{Price or value})}{(\Delta \text{ Income})/(\text{Income})}$.

82

can provide (Krutilla 1967; Fisher 1970). Through advances in economic analysis, the values of some of these have become measurable (e.g., the value of outdoor recreation resources), while the values of others are not yet open to economic measurement (e.g., the option value of preserving rare scientific research materials). For this reason we will not try to calculate the present value of services yielded from the canyon if preserved in its present condition, since we do not know how to measure it in toto. Instead, we ask what this value would need to be in order to equal or exceed the present value of the developmental alternative. And to get a better handle on the problem, we ask additionally what the base year's annual benefit would need to be to have a present value equal to or greater than the developmental alternative. The latter step is of considerable analytic assistance by virtue of the difference in the relation between the initial year's benefit and the total present value for the two alternative uses of the area. This is because of the asymmetry in the behavior of the value of the output streams from the two incompatible uses of the site. We show this in exaggerated form for illustrative purposes in the present value computational models below.

The development alternative:

$$PV_d = \sum_{t=1}^{T} \frac{b_0/(1+r)^t}{(1+i)^t} \, ;$$

where PV_d is the present value of developmental benefits,

b_0 is the initial, or base year's benefit,

T is the relevant terminal year,

i is the discount rate,

r is the simplified representation of the technological change model presented in section II under the head "The Development Alternative."

The preservation alternative:

$$PV_p = \sum_{t=1}^{T'} \frac{b_0'(1+\alpha)^t}{(1+i)^t} \, ;$$

where PV_p is the present value of the benefits from preserving the area in its natural condition,

b_0' is the initial, or base, year's benefit,

T' is the relevant terminal year,

i is the discount rate,

α is the rate of growth in annual benefits.

We assume that T, or the terminal year, is given by the year in which the discounted annual benefits fall to zero for practical purposes[10] or, for convenience in computation, fall to $0.01 per $1.00 of initial year's benefits.

Accordingly, although the annual benefit of the developmental alternative in the initial year may be quite large, and in fact the net present value as computed[11] is impressive, given the relation between α and i in the present value computational model for preservation benefits, the initial year's benefits of the latter may need to be only very modest. What we wish to do, then, is to compute the present value of one dollar's worth of initial year's "composite" preservation benefits for use in determining what the total initial year's preservation benefits would need to be in order to equal or exceed the present value of developmental benefits. This is done by dividing the present value of $1.00 of initial year's benefits growing at α into the present value of developmental benefits; i.e., to give us our required initial year's preservation benefits.

The problem of computing the present value of $1.00 of initial year's benefits growing at α occupies our attention next. The benefit per dollar of initial year's (composite) benefits of a nonproducible natural area is computed by considering the various possible shifts in demand through time given the "reverse L-shaped" supply schedule. We also assume that price is used as a rationing device. Thus:

b_0 = $1.00 of initial year's benefits;
P_0 = initial vertical axis intercepts (see figure 3.4);
Q_0 = initial horizontal axis intercept;
$D_0 D_0'$ = initial year's composite computational demand schedule;
r_v = rate of growth in vertical component of shift, related to the increase in per capita income, assuming a constant (income-price) elasticity

$$\frac{\Delta P_v}{P_v} \cdot \frac{I}{\Delta I}\bigg| Q = Q_0;$$

γ = the historical rate of growth in the quantity demanded for $P = 0$; i.e., horizontal component of demand shift at zero price. γ is constant up until capacity (year k);
k = the year the area reaches recreational carrying capacity;
d = the rate of decay of γ after year k which brings the rate of change in horizontal component of demand shift to rate of growth of population;

---

[10] For demonstration of the correctness of this criterion, see Fisher (1970).

[11] The "net" present value, of course, does not reflect the opportunity costs of converting an existing recreational area into a hydroelectric storage reservoir, which is a principal task of this exercise.

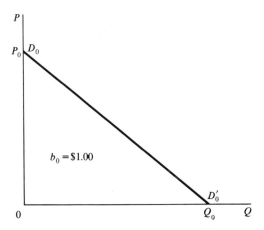

Figure 3.4. Hypothesized initial years' demand schedule for computations.

m = the year in which the rate of the horizontal component of demand shift equals the rate of growth of population;

i = rate of discount.

Equations

$$P_t = (1 + r_v)^t P_0$$
$$Q_t = (1 + \gamma)^t Q_0 \text{ for } t \leq k$$
$$Q_t = Q_{t-1}(1 + \gamma_t) \text{ for } t > k,$$

where $\gamma_t = \gamma(1 + d)^{t-k}$

and $d = \left[\dfrac{\gamma \text{ population}}{\gamma} \right]^{\frac{1}{m-k}} - 1.$

$$PV_b^0 = \sum_{t=1}^{\infty} \frac{b_t}{(1 + i)^t}$$

$$b_t = \text{½} P_t Q_t \text{ for } t \leq k;$$

i.e., the area under the composite computational demand schedule $D_t D_t$.

$$b_t = \text{½} P_t Q_t - \tfrac{1}{2} P_t^* Q_t^* \text{ for } t > k;$$

where $\dfrac{P_t^*}{Q_t^*} = \tan \theta_t = \dfrac{P_t}{Q_t}$

$\therefore \quad P_t^* = Q_t^* \cdot \dfrac{P_t}{Q_t}$

85

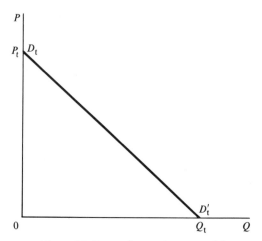

Figure 3.5. Demand curve in year $y \leq k$.

and $\quad Q_t^* = Q_t - Q_k$

and $\quad b_t = \frac{1}{2}P_tQ_t - \frac{1}{2}(Q_t - Q_k)^2 \dfrac{P_t}{Q_t}$ for $t > k$

$\therefore \quad PV_b^0 = b_t(t \leq k) + b_t(t > k)$, appropriately summed and discounted.

An important parameter of the system is the annual per cent increase in benefits. This is derived as follows:

$$b_t = \tfrac{1}{2}P_tQ_t \text{ for } t \leq k$$
$$= \tfrac{1}{2}[P_0(1 + r_y)^t][Q_0(1 + \gamma)^t]$$
$$= \tfrac{1}{2}P_0Q_0[(1 + r_y)(1 + \gamma)]^t$$

but $\quad 1 = \tfrac{1}{2}P_0Q_0$

$\therefore \qquad b_t = (1 + r_y\gamma + r_y + \gamma)^t$

$$\frac{db_t}{dt} = (1 + r_y\gamma + r_y + \gamma)^t \text{ Ln } (1 + r_y\gamma + r_y + \gamma)$$

annual per cent change in benefits $= \dfrac{\dfrac{db_t}{dt}}{b_t}$

$\therefore \quad \dfrac{\dfrac{db_t}{dt}}{b_t} = \dfrac{(1 + r_y\gamma + r_y + \gamma)^t \text{ Ln } (1 + r_y\gamma + r_y + \gamma)}{(1 + r_y\gamma + r_y + \gamma)^t}$

$$= \text{Ln} (1 + r_y\gamma + r_y + \gamma)$$
$$\text{for } t \leq k.$$

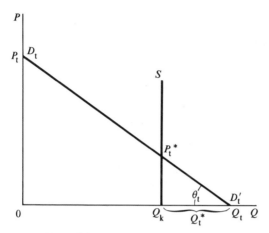

Figure 3.6. Demand curve in year $t > k$.

Finally, the slope of the initial composite computational demand schedule (the area under which is equal to unity) may be varied and the effect measured, since:

$$P = a + sQ,$$

$$\frac{P_0 \cdot Q_0}{2} = 1$$

and
$$P_0 = P \text{ when } Q = 0$$
$$Q_0 = Q \text{ when } P = 0$$

$\therefore$
$$P = P_0 + sQ$$

$$s = \frac{P_0}{Q_0}$$

$$sQ = P_0$$

and
$$P_0 Q_0 = 2$$
$$sQ_0^2 = 2$$

$\therefore$
$$Q_0 = \sqrt{2}/s \text{ and } P_0 = sQ_0.$$

This last result allows us to calculate benefits for various initial slopes as well as varying demand shifts and supply constraints, thus completing the general derivation for computing benefits through time for linear demand schedules.

By use of this model to calculate the present value of a dollar's worth of initial year's benefits, we can obtain, of course, the initial year's benefits required to justify retaining the canyon area in its present uses. The latter can be further decomposed by putting the initial year's benefits on an expected value per user basis. That is, if

87

U_0 = expected number of users in the initial year;

B_0 = the required initial year's benefits to justify preserving the canyon in its present condition;

B_0/U_0 = the expected average user value required to justify preserving the canyon area in its present type of uses.

Then this further decomposition permits us to observe the number of recreational (and/or other) users, estimate the average price or value per recreation day required, and compare this value or price with what is known about prices paid for similar types of recreational experiences.

In the following section we present the quantitative results obtained from application of this methodology to the current Hells Canyon issue.

III. QUANTITATIVE RESULTS OF METHODOLOGY APPLIED TO HELLS CANYON RESOURCE ALLOCATION PROBLEM

In this section the computational results of the models presented in section II will be displayed in a series of tables.

In the case of the technological change model, the quantitative results will depend both on investment per unit capacity of the alternative thermal source, itself partly depending on the interest rate, and on the cost per kilowatt hour of thermal energy. Finally, the rate of advance in technical efficiency itself enters into the calculation of the difference between the results obtained when technological advance is, and when it is not, introduced explicitly into the analysis. For our purposes, we have relied on construction cost data provided by FPC staff witness Joseph J. A. Jessell (FPC hearings, and exhibit R-54-B); we have used opportunity cost of capital of 9 per cent, but with estimates provided alternatively using 8 per cent and 10 per cent for purposes of sensitivity analyses; rates of technological progress of between 3 per cent and 5 per cent per year, to bracket what is believed to be the relevant range;[12] and energy costs, again supplied by FPC staff witnesses, of 0.98 mills per kilowatt hour in the early stage, ranging to 1.28 mills per kilowatt hour in the later period of analysis (I. Paul Chavez in FPC hearings, and exhibit R-107-B). The adjustment factors for introducing the influence of technological change into the analysis are given in table 3.1.

Accordingly, for any given interest rate (and hence capacity cost per kilowatt); rate of technological change; and energy costs in mills per kilowatt hour; the generation costs (sum of capacity and energy costs) would be adjusted as indicated (divided) by the values given in table 3.1 to obtain

[12] Data on technological change computed from Electrical World's biennial "Steam Station Cost Surveys," 1950–68.

Table 3.1. Overstatement of Hydroelectric Capacity and Energy Values
Resulting from Neglect of Influence of Technological Advances

Discount rate/year	Techno- logical advance rate/year	Conventionally estimated benefits as a percentage of actual benefits when adjusted for influence of technological advance, for various capacity and energy costs		
(i)	(r_t)	($/kw)	(Percentage at 0.98 mills per kwh)	(Percentage at 1.22 mills per kwh)	(Percentage at 1.28 mills per kwh)
0.08	0.03	27.43	107.4	107.9	108.0
	0.04		109.0	109.6	109.7
	0.05		110.2	110.9	111.1
0.09	0.03	30.08	105.9	106.4	106.5
	0.04		107.2	107.7	107.8
	0.05		108.2	108.8	108.9
0.10	0.03	32.89	104.8	105.1	105.2
	0.04		105.8	106.2	106.3
	0.05		106.5	107.1	107.2

Source: FPC hearings, exhibit R-670, table 1, p. 3.

the adjusted alternative cost — hence, the benefits of the proposed hydro-electric development.[13]

In connection with the composite benefit computational model, the present value of one dollar's worth of initial year's benefit is a function of both the rate of growth in annual benefits, α, and the discount rate, i. But, from examination of the model, it is apparent that annual benefits do not grow at a uniform rate over time depending on the values that are taken by γ, r_y, k, d, and m. Since k represents the "recreational carrying capacity" which is defined as the capacity of the area to accommodate recreation seekers without eroding the quality of the recreational experience, the k's and γ's are related. The particular values taken (i.e., γ of 10 per cent and k of 20 years), with alternative assumptions for purposes of sensitivity analyses, were chosen for reasons given elsewhere.[14] A discount rate of 9 per cent, with alternatives of 8 and 10 per cent, was the result of independent study (Eckstein and Harberger 1968; Seagraves 1970). The selection of the value of m of 50 years, with alternative assumptions of 40 and 60, was governed both by the rate of growth of general demand for wilderness or primitive area recreation and by the estimated "saturation level" for such recreational participation for the population as a whole. Finally, the range of values for r_y was taken from what we know about the conventional income elasticity of demand (as reinterpreted

---

[13] See Krutilla testimony in FPC hearings, transcript pp. R–5842–43 and exhibits R–669, R–669–A, and R–671, R–671–A, for detailed explanation of the derivation of benefits using a technological change model.

[14] Krutilla testimony in FPC hearings, transcript pp. R–5864–66 and R–5872.

in the light of fixed supply services, see p. 81) for this kind of recreation activity (Cicchetti, Seneca, and Davidson 1969) and growth in per capita income over the past two or three decades.

The results of our "preferred" values, with alternatives given for changes in assumptions, are shown in table 3.2. These present-value computations can next be divided into the net present value of the water resource development project (i.e., the hydroelectric power value, along with incidental flood control and related multipurpose development benefits), to yield the initial year's preservation benefit that (growing at α and discounted at i) would have a present value equal to the present value of development. The corresponding initial year's preservation benefits are shown in table 3.3.

What can we learn from this that we cannot learn from the traditional analysis of comparable situations requiring the allocation of "gifts of nature" between two incompatible alternatives?

Let us take for illustration, subject later to sensitivity analysis, the computed initial year's preservation benefit corresponding to i of 9 per cent, r_t of 0.04, γ of 10 per cent, k of 20 years, m of 50 years, and r_y of 0.05; namely, \$80,122. Is this a preservation benefit we might expect to be equaled or exceeded by the first year the hydroelectric project would otherwise go into operation? In many cases we would have only the sketchiest information and would have to make such a comparison on a judgmental basis. In the case of Hells Canyon, we obtained rather better

Table 3.2. Present Value of One Dollar's Worth of Initial Year's Preservation Benefits Growing at α

r_y	$\gamma = 7.5\%$ $k = 25$ years	$\gamma = 10\%$ $k = 20$ years	$\gamma = 12.5\%$ $k = 15$ years
$i = 8$ per cent, $m = 50$ years			
0.04	\$134.08	\$169.86	\$173.90
0.05	211.72	263.49	262.12
0.06	385.10	467.30	449.00
$i = 9$ per cent, $m = 50$ years			
0.04	93.67	120.07	125.89
0.05	136.12	172.35	176.25
0.06	214.76	267.10	264.49
$i = 10$ per cent, $m = 50$ years			
0.04	69.28	89.45	95.71
0.05	95.15	121.91	127.68
0.06	138.17	174.85	178.66

Where: i = discount rate;
   r_y = annual rate of growth of price per user day;
   γ = annual rate of growth of quantity demanded at given price;
   k = number of years after initial year in which carrying capacity constraint becomes effective;
   m = number of years after initial year in which γ falls to rate of growth of population.

90

Table 3.3. Initial Year's Preservation Benefits (Growing at α) Required in Order to Have Present Value Equal to That of Development

r_y	$\gamma = 7.5\%$ $k = 25$ years	$\gamma = 10\%$ $k = 20$ years	$\gamma = 12.5\%$ $k = 15$ years
$i = 8$ per cent, $m = 50$ years, $r_t = 0.04$, $PV_d = \$18,540,000$[a]			
0.04	\$138,276	\$109,149	\$106,613
0.05	87,568	70,363	70,731
0.06	48,143	39,674	41,292
$i = 9$ per cent, $m = 50$ years, $r_t = 0.04$, $PV_d = \$13,809,000$[a]			
0.04	147,422	115,008	109,691
0.05	101,447	80,122	78,336
0.06	64,300	51,700	52,210
$i = 10$ per cent, $m = 50$ years, $r_t = 0.04$, $PV_d = \$9,861,000$[a]			
0.04	142,335	110,240	103,030
0.05	103,626	80,888	77,232
0.06	71,369	56,397	55,194

Where: i = discount rate;
r_y = annual rate of growth in price per user day;
γ = annual rate of growth of quantity demanded at given price;
k = number of years following initial year upon which carrying capacity constraint becomes effective;
m = number of years after initial year upon which γ falls to rate of growth of population;
PV_d = present value of development;
r_t = annual rate of technological progress.
[a] *Source:* FPC hearings, exhibit R-671.

information and shall return to the matter later. But for now, we have the sum of $80,000 as the benchmark that we feel is necessary to justify, on economic grounds, allocation of the resource to uses compatible with retention of the area in its present condition. This sum of $80,000 compares with the sum of $2.9 million, which represents the "levelized" annual benefit from the hydroelectric development, when neither adjustments for technological progress have been made in hydroelectric power value computations, nor any site value (i.e., present value of opportunity returns foreclosed by altering the present use of the canyon) is imputed to costs. Typically then, the question would be raised as to whether or not the preservation value is equal to or greater than the $2.9 million annual benefits from development.

Let us now consider the readily quantifiable benefits from the existing uses of the canyon. These are based on studies conducted by the fish and game departments of the states of Oregon and Idaho, in collaboration with the U.S. Forest Service, and are displayed, along with our imputation of values per user day, in table 3.4.[15] From this table one could argue, for

[15] In table 3.4 we assume linear demand functions; hence the imputed average value per user day, multiplied by total number of user days, gives us a value equal to the total area under the demand curve.

Table 3.4. Illustrative Opportunity Costs of Altering Free-Flowing River and Related Canyon Environment by Development of High Mountain Sheep

Quantified losses	Recreation days 1969[a]	Visitor days 1969[b]	Visitor days 1976
Stream-based recreation:[c]			
Total of boat counter survey	18,755	28,132	51,000
Upstream of Salmon-Snake confluence	9,622	14,439	26,000
Nonboat access:			
Imnaha-Dug Bar	9,678	14,517	26,000
Pittsburgh Landing	9,643	14,464	26,000
Hells Canyon downstream:			
Boat anglers	2,472	1,000	1,800
Bank anglers	9,559	2,333	4,000
Total stream use above Salmon River	40,974 plus[d]	46,753 plus[d]	84,000 at $5.00/day = $420,000
Hunting, canyon area[e]			
Big game	7,050	7,050	7,000 at $25.00/day = $175,000
Upland birds	1,110	1,110	1,000 at $10.00/day = $ 10,000
Diminished valued of hunting experience[f]	18,000	18,000	29,000 at $10.00/day = $290,000
Total quantified losses		$895,000 ± 25%	

Unevaluated losses:
1. Unmitigated anadromous fish losses outside impact area.
2. Unmitigated resident fish losses:
   a) Stream fishing downstream from high mountain sheep.
3. Option value of rare geomorphological-biological-ecological phenomena.
4. Others.

a "Recreation days" corresponds to definition in President's Water Resources Council, *Policies, Standards and Procedures in the Formulation, Evaluation and Review of Plans for Use and Development of Water and Related Land Resources*, 87th Cong. 2d sess. S. Doc. 97, 29 May 1962, *Supp. 1, Senate Document No. 97*; namely, an individual engaging in recreation for any "reasonable portion of a day." In this particular study, time involved must be minimum of one hour.

b "Visitor day" corresponds to the President's Recreational Advisory Council (now, Environmental Quality Council) *Coordination Bulletin No. 6* definition of a visitor day as a twelve-hour day. Operationally, the total number of hours, divided by twelve, will give the appropriate "visitor day" estimate.

c *Source: An Evaluation of Recreational Use on the Snake River in the High Mountain Sheep Impact Area*, Survey by Oregon State Game Commission and Idaho State Fish and Game Department in cooperation with U.S. Forest Service, Report dated January 1970 and memorandum, W. B. Hall, Liaison Officer, Wallowa-Whitman National Forest, dated January 20, 1970.

d Scenic flights and trail use via Saddle Creek and Battle Creek Trails were not included in the survey. Thus, estimates given represent an underreporting of an unevaluated amount.

e *Source:* "Middle Snake River Study, Idaho, Oregon and Washington," Joint Report of the Bureau of Commercial Fisheries and Bureau of Sports Fisheries and Wildlife in *Department of the Interior Resource Study of the Middle Snake* (April 1968). Tables 10 and 11.

f The figure of 18,000 hunter days is based on witness William E. Pitney's estimate at FPC hearings of 15,000 big-game-hunter days on the Oregon side, and estimated 10,000 hunter days on the Idaho side (provided in letter from Monte Richards, Coordinator, Idaho Basin Investigations, Idaho Fish and Game Department, dated February 13, 1970), for a total of 25,000 hunter days (excluding small game, i.e., principally upland birds) in the Canyon area, less estimated losses of 7,000 hunter days. This provides the estimated 1969 total of 18,000 hunter days which growing at estimated 5 per cent per year for deer hunting and 9 per cent per year for elk hunting, would total 29,000 hunter days by 1976.

example, that the preservation benefits shown are roughly only a third as large as those that would be required in comparisons based on traditional quantitative analysis of similar cases. By introducing the differential incidence of technological progress on the mutually exclusive alternatives for Hells Canyon, we reach quite a different conclusion. The initial year's preservation benefit, subject to reevaluation on the basis of sensitivity tests, appears to be of an order of magnitude larger than that necessary for the present value to equal or exceed the present value of the development alternative. Thus we get results significantly different from those obtained by traditional analysis.

What about the sensitivity of these conclusions to the particular values given to the variables used in our two simulation models? Sensitivity tests can be performed with the data contained in tables 3.1 and 3.2, along with additional information available from computer runs. Some of these checks are displayed in table 3.5.

Given the estimated user days and imputed value per user day, it follows that the conclusions regarding the relative economic values of the two alternatives are not sensitive within a reasonable range, to the particular values chosen for the variables and parameters used in the computational models.

However, another set of tests is needed when exponential growth rates are being used. We might regard these as "plausibility analyses." They would test, for example, the plausibility of the ratio of the implicit price to the projected per capita income in the terminal year, to ensure credibility of the results. Similarly, they would test the plausibility of the ratio of the terminal year's preservation benefit, say, to the GNP in the terminal year. The year at which the growth rate in quantity of wilderness-type outdoor recreation services demanded falls to the rate of growth of the population must also be checked to ensure that the implicit population participation rate is reasonable. Such tests were performed in connection

Table 3.5. Sensitivity of Estimated Initial Year's Required Preservation Benefits Changes in Value of Variables and Parameters (at $i = 9$ per cent)

| Variable | Variation in variable | | Per cent change | Per cent change in preservation benefit |
	from	to		
r_y	0.04	0.05	25%	39% to 49%
r_t	0.04	0.05	25	25
k^a	20 yrs.	25 yrs.	25	30 to 40
γ	10%	12.5%	25	−4 to +7
m	40 yrs.	50 yrs.	25	3

[a] The 25 per cent change in years before capacity is reached translates into a 40 per cent change in carrying capacity at the growth rate of 10 per cent used here.

94

with the Hells Canyon case in order to avoid problems which otherwise would stem from use of unbounded estimates.

Finally, since the readily observed initial year's benefits appeared to be in excess of the minimum that would be required to have their present value exceeded by the present value of developmental benefits, the analysis was concluded at that point. On the other hand, since the analysis relies implicitly on the price-compensating measure of consumer surplus and does not include consideration of option value, the resulting estimate is a lower-bound estimate of the preservation value. In circumstances in which the present value of the output stream from the developmental alternative would exceed that of the preservation alternative, as calculated above, a question might still arise as to whether the comparative values are sufficient to justify the allocation to developmental purposes on economic grounds. This set of issues is explored in section IV.

IV. CONSUMER SURPLUS AND OPTION VALUE

When the alternatives that are being considered can be reduced to a comparison of "development" or "preservation" benefits, and further, when the preserved benefits are either common property or the nonexclusion condition obtains, several problems arise. One relevant issue is whether preservation benefits should be measured by how much users of the preserved area are willing to pay to preserve existing uses of the area, or the amount users must be paid to give up voluntarily the right to continue use of the area in question. The first alternative is the "price compensating" measure of consumer surplus; while the second is the "price equivalent" consumer surplus.

Uncertainty in demand in the future is a separate but related issue. Weisbrod (1964) pointed out that when several plausible conditions hold, an additional measure of benefits or value, which he called option value, should be considered. The first of these conditions is that there are individuals who are uncertain about future demand of the commodity or service in question, or are infrequent consumers; among these will be some who will never use the service. The second condition is that a decision about supplying the service in the future is about to be made and, should the service be curtailed in supply, reestablishing or expanding it would be very costly or even technically impossible. Finally, there must be no practicable way for the resource owner providing the service in question to collect the option value (premiums for assured availability in the future) because exclusion (i.e., ability to identify all who would benefit from assured availability and to exclude same for failure to pay the premiums) is not possible.

The discussion[16] which followed Weisbrod's concept of option value has centered around the relationship between option value and consumer surplus and the possibility of double counting if, as Weisbrod assumed, a discriminating monopolist controlled the service in question. The purpose of the following analysis is (a) to consider the two measures of consumer surplus and (b) to define option price and option value rigorously and to distinguish these concepts from the two measures of consumer surplus so that double counting will not arise.[17]

Price-Compensating and Price-Equivalent Measures of Consumer Surplus

Hicks (1941, 1943) in his classic work on demand theory provided economists with several measures of consumer surplus. Economics is based upon utility theory which for most practical purposes is nonquantifiable. In addition, economists agree that "value in use" will be greater than "value in exchange" for nonmarginal users. Accordingly, quantifiable cardinal approximations for ordinal utility differences between the two play a central role in public sector economic analysis.

Two measures that yield monetary values have been utilized here. One is measured by the amount of money that can be extracted from an individual so as to leave no surplus or difference between value in use and value in exchange. This amount is the monetary approximation of the price-compensating measure of consumer surplus.

Figure 3.7 shows this diagrammatically. An individual has an initial income of $\$Y_0$. If he bought none of good X he would be on indifference curve I_1. If X were supplied at the relative price indicated by the slopes of the budget lines B_1 and B_2, the individual could move to an indifference

[16] Millard Long (1967) has argued that option value and consumer surplus are identical and Cotton Lindsay (1969), has countered by stating that uncertainty in demand was overlooked by Long and is the main factor in the difference between option value and consumer surplus. Zeckhauser (1969) has referred to the fact that when a perfectly discriminating monopolist controls an industry, all users of the service are just as well off as if that service was not available. The difference between our subsequent treatment of uncertainty in demand and Zeckhauser's analysis is that we insist that the option value problem observed by Weisbrod is important only when the terms of the future option are specified by the option purchase.

[17] A value is also likely to be associated with certain nonusers benefiting from the terms of the option. Such individuals might receive utility and therefore be willing to pay for the preservation of existing facilities or services in "bequest" to future generations. However, in order to clarify the Long-Lindsay issue, we restrict the following discussion to those who are potential demanders of the service in question, whether "certain" or "uncertain" demanders.

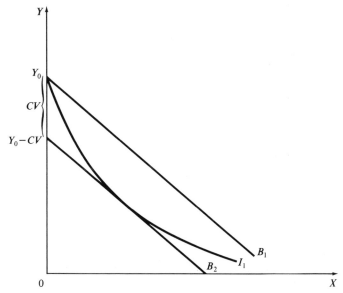

Figure 3.7. The price-compensating measure of consumer surplus.

curve higher than I_1. If now a charge were placed on the individual that would allow him to purchase at the given relative prices, yet would leave him on the same level of utility as he would be without the good, the amount would be CV, which is the price-compensating measure of consumer surplus.

The price-equivalent measure of consumer surplus is an alternative. It is the amount of numeraire (money income in dollars) that an individual who is presently consuming good X at a given set of prices must be paid to give up the right to continue consuming X. It is measured by determining the increment to present income that is necessary to permit him to stay on his highest attainable indifference curve while eliminating the consumption of X (see figure 3.8).

With prices given by the slope of B_1 and income given by Y_0, the individual would maximize his utility at E on indifference curve I_2. If the individual were to give up his right to consume X at the given set of prices, he would do so only if he were paid EV. This is the price equivalent measure of consumer's surplus.

Henderson (1941) and Patinkin (1963) have shown that the choice of measure depends on the particular case under consideration. Brown (1968) has pointed out that when new products are contemplated it is necessary to use the price-compensating measure of consumer surplus. On the other hand, if a good is being withdrawn, the price-equivalent measure of con-

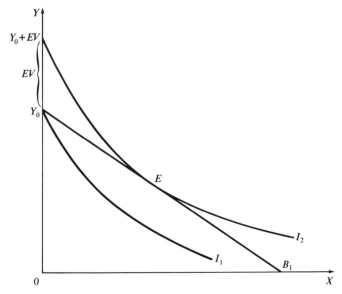

Figure 3.8. The price-equivalent measure of consumer surplus.

sumer surplus becomes appropriate.[18] Moreover, both Hicks and Henderson have established that the price-equivalent measure for normal goods is always equal to (for constant marginal utility of income) or greater than (for diminishing marginal utility of income) the price-compensating measure of consumer surplus.

Option Value Defined

When an asset providing services without close substitutes is under consideration, we have from the time of Dupuit recognized the need to take the present value of the area under the demand curve as its worth for allocation purposes; its measurement was considered above. When, in addition, there are individuals who are uncertain potential demanders of the

---

[18] This, of course, assumes the relevance of the "status quo" point. To do so may raise a question of appropriately vested rights in the status quo. For purposes of our analysis of the Hells Canyon case (section III) we note that the Supreme Court remanded for rehearing the FPC's previous action that would have had the effect of altering the conditions of use for what were largely public lands in that area. One of the grounds for so doing was that the court had found no evidence that the commission had considered, in the light of outstanding natural features of the area, whether the area should be developed. This would imply that the court felt that current use enjoyed some equity status that needed to be considered. The court's opinion thus is consistent with the Hicks-Kaldor compensation principle; namely, that gainers from the change in use must be able to compensate the losers out of their gains. Such a test, of course, would involve the price-equivalent measure of consumer surplus.

services of such an existing asset, under given conditions, Weisbrod has identified an additional value, i.e., option value, that should also be taken into account in a decision regarding the continuation or discontinuance of the services of the facility in question. The Weisbrod conditions, in addition to uncertainty of demand, involve a situation where the asset is not readily producible (or reproducible), and where its services are nonstorable, have no close substitutes, and have doubtful availability in the future. In addition, Weisbrod assumed the good or service was controlled by a perfectly discriminating monopolist. We clarify this assumption and analyze option value by considering the conditions under which a perfectly discriminating monopolist would choose a two-part pricing system to maximize his profits instead of charging a single discriminating price at the time of purchase. The two-part price mechanism at work in our analysis is that an option ticket is sold in the present to individuals who are uncertain about future demand for services such as visits to a hospital, use of a train from Ithaca to New York City, or visits to Hells Canyon, and the terms of future prices are fixed by this option ticket or purchase. We call the maximum price the individual would be willing to pay the option price, and assume for simplicity that the marginal rate of time preference is zero.

The nature of the option value can be understood by examining the behavior of an individual confronted with the above conditions. We do this by employing the Von Neumann-Morgenstern analysis of various plays in a nonzero sum, two-person game. The game is outlined schematically in figure 3.9. It has eight possible plays (outcomes) and three moves

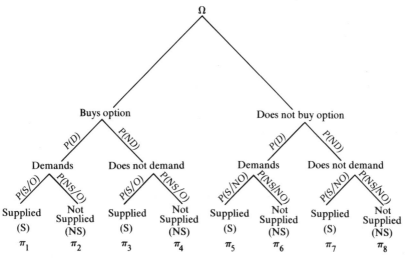

Figure 3.9. The option value game tree.

—one is personal (discretionary; he buys or does not buy the option) and two are chance moves (the service is supplied in future or is not supplied; is demanded or is not demanded).

It is important to make the distinction between the terms option price and option value. Option price is the amount an individual would pay to keep the right to consume the good for a fixed set of prices. We define option value (OV) as the difference between the maximum option price (OP) and expected value of consumer surplus ($\overline{CS}$):

$$OV \equiv OP - \overline{CS} \qquad (1)$$

We will show that option value exists and is positive for a risk-averse individual with uncertain demand, and that an option value can be associated with either the CV or EV measure of consumer surplus.

Several other terms are defined as follows:

$P(D) \equiv$ probability of demand,
$P(S/O) \equiv$ probability of supply given that the option is purchased;
$P(S/NO) \equiv$ probability of supply given that the option is not purchased.

To simplify the analysis, and to keep Weisbrod's basic conditions, it will be assumed that the service is originally supplied by a perfectly discriminating monopolist and, further, that the service is only supplied if the option price is paid, i.e.,

$$P(S/O) = 1. \qquad (2)$$

$$P(S/NO) = 0. \qquad (3)$$

Several cases can now be considered. In the first it is assumed that the individual is a certain demander, i.e., $P(D) = 1$; and that he is consuming at the existing relative price and income represented by income Y_0 and the budget curve B_1 in figure 3.10.

In figure 3.10 income is measured along the vertical axis and the quantity of X is measured along the horizontal axis. The level of utility is initially U_5. This is the level of utility associated with the π_5 outcome of the game tree, since π_5 is the case where an individual does not pay the option, demands good X, and good X is supplied at a given set of prices. If a perfectly discriminating monopolist charges the maximum possible option price for the right to continue consumption at the given prices, he could extract OP_1 from the individual. If OP_1 is collected from the individual at the given relative prices (slope of $B_1 = B_1'$), then U_1 which corresponds to π_1 in the game tree is the relevant indifference curve, remaining income is ($Y_0 - OP_1$), and the budget line is B_1'. If the option price is not paid, then the relevant budget line is B_2; i.e., good X is not supplied at any price and

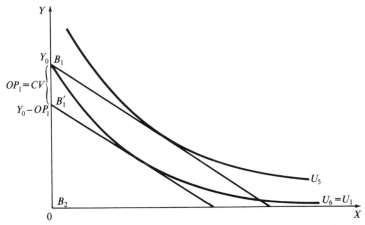

Figure 3.10. Option value and consumer surplus for a certain demander.

the relevant indifference curve is U_6 ($= U_1$). This corresponds to π_6 in the game tree. In this case the good is demanded but not supplied since the option price was not paid. The maximum option price, which is defined above by OP_1, is identical to the price-compensating measure of consumer surplus (CV) defined in the preceding section. Given that OP_1 is the price of the option, the individual is indifferent between buying the option and doing without. In other words, the expected utility of buying the option $(\bar{U}_0)$ equals the expected utility of not buying the option $(\bar{U}_{NO})$.[19]

Long (1967) correctly pointed out that option value is zero for individuals who are certain demanders and stated that option price and consumer surplus were identical. In defense of Weisbrod, Lindsay (1969) countered by stating that uncertainty in demand must be present for there to be option value. By relaxing only one assumption in case 1 we can

---

[19] To verify this:
$$\bar{U}_0 = P_1U_1 + P_2U_2 + P_3U_3 + P_4U_4;$$
where P_i is the joint probability corresponding to $\pi_i(i = 1, 8)$.

But $P_2 = P_3 = P_4 = 0$ in case 1,

∴ $\bar{U}_0 = P_1U_1 = P(D) \cdot P(S/O) \cdot U_1 = 1 \cdot U_1 = U_1,$

and $\bar{U}_{NO} = P_5U_5 + P_6U_6 + P_7U_7 + P_8U_8$

but $P_5 = P_7 = P_8 = 0$ in case 1

∴ $\bar{U}_{NO} = P_6U_6 = P(D) \cdot P(NS/NO) \cdot U_6 = 1 \cdot U_6 = U_6$

∴ $\bar{U}_0 = \bar{U}_{NO}.$

Option value is zero since
$$\overline{CV} = P(D) \cdot CV = 1 \cdot CV = OP_1 \tag{4}$$

and from (1)

∴ $OV = OP_1 - \overline{CV} = 0. \tag{5}$

examine these arguments for case 2 where $P(D) \neq 1$; further, we will assume $P(D) = \frac{1}{2}$ for illustrative purposes.

Our problem is to determine the maximum option price (OP_2^*) that the person would be willing to pay to guarantee the opportunity to consume X at the prevailing price ratios—in the face of his own uncertainty about demand. The maximum option price that could be extracted by the perfectly discriminating monopolist would be the one which would make $\bar{U}_O = \bar{U}_{NO}$. The actual price charged for the option determines (given the probabilities) $\bar{U}_0$. Therefore we will first determine $\bar{U}_{NO}$, then find the option price which will make $\bar{U}_0$ equal to it.

In figure 3.11 two new indifference curves, U_3 and U_8, represent the preference mapping of the individual in the event that in the future he does not demand the good. Since future demand is a probabilistic event, either the U_3–U_8 mapping or the U_5–U_6 mapping will appear in the future, but not both. In other words, either your house catches fire and you demand the services of a fire engine or your house does not catch fire and you do not demand the services of the fire engine. Still an uncertain demander must consider both sets of preferences as relevant to his decision on buying the option. To make the choice problem solvable, there must be some way of making the utilities of the two alternative mappings com-

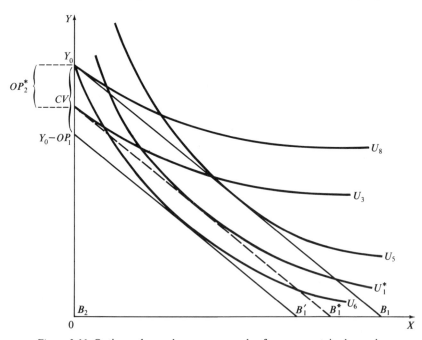

Figure 3.11. Option value and consumer surplus for an uncertain demander.

102

mensurable. We have proceeded as follows to derive a rule for comparing the utilities from the two alternative mappings. For any level of disposable income (e.g., Y_0), if the individual did not demand the good he would choose a consumption point on the Y axis and experience a certain level of utility (e.g., U_8); if he were to demand the good (assuming that it is available), he would choose a tangency point on the budget line associated with that point, and experience a given level of utility (e.g., U_5). We assume that the alternative outcomes have the same utility. Thus $U_8 = U_5$.

We can now define $\bar{U}_{NO}$ as follows:

$$\bar{U}_{NO} = P_5 U_5 + P_6 U_6 + P_7 U_7 + P_8 U_8 \tag{6}$$

where

$$P_5 = P_7 = 0, \text{ and } P_6 = P_8 = \tfrac{1}{2}$$

$$\bar{U}_{NO} = P(D) \cdot P(NS/NO) \cdot U_6 + P(ND) \cdot P(NS/NO) \cdot U_8 \tag{7}$$

$$= \frac{U_6}{2} + \frac{U_8}{2} \tag{8}$$

$$= \frac{U_6}{2} + \frac{U_5}{2}. \tag{9}$$

If the individual buys the option at some price less than OP_1 (the option price under certainty of demand), his budget line will be somewhere between B_1' and B_1 in figure 3.11. If the good is available, and he demands it, he can attain U_1^*. With this information we can define $\bar{U}_0$ as follows:

$$\bar{U}_0 = P_1 U_1^* + P_2 U_2 + P_3 U_3 + P_4 U_4 \tag{10}$$

where

$$P_2 = P_4 = 0, \text{ and } P_1 = P_3 = \tfrac{1}{2},$$

$$\therefore \quad \bar{U}_O = P(D) \cdot P(S/O) \cdot U_1^* + P(ND) \cdot P(S/O) \cdot U_3 \tag{11}$$

$$\bar{U}_0 = \tfrac{1}{2} U_1^* + \tfrac{1}{2} U_3. \tag{12}$$

Following our rule for making utilities commensurate,

$$U_1^* = U_3 \tag{13}$$

and

$$\bar{U}_0 = U_1^*. \tag{14}$$

The maximum option price, OP_2^*, is the one which makes

$$U_1^* = \bar{U}_{NO} = \tfrac{1}{2} (U_6 + U_5); \tag{15}$$

103

i.e., it is the one which places U_1^* half way between $U_6 (= U_1)$ and U_5. After finding OP_2^* we must find out whether it is greater than, equal to, or less than the expected value of consumer surplus where this is

$$\overline{CV} = P(D) \cdot CV \qquad (16)$$
$$= \tfrac{1}{2} OP_1.$$

If OP_2^* exceeds ½ OP_1, then option value is positive. To generalize:

$$OV \equiv OP_2^* - \overline{CV} = OP_2^* - P(D) \cdot OP_1 \qquad (17)$$

$$\therefore \qquad OV \gtrless O \quad \text{as} \quad OP_2^* \gtrless P(D) \cdot OP_1. \qquad (18)$$

In order to determine whether the maximum option price exceeds or is less than the expected compensating variation, we can translate figure 3.11 into the Friedman-Savage type diagram in figure 3.12, for an individual defined as a risk averter, i.e.,

$$\frac{dU}{dY} > 0; \ \frac{d^2U}{dY^2} < 0.$$

This curve maps utility and Y, given that X is zero. U_1^* is the midpoint on the utility axis between U_6 and U_5. The income level associated with U_1^* is $Y_0 - OP_2^*$; and the difference between this point and Y_0 is the maximum possible option price (OP_2^*). That OP_2^* is greater than the expected consumer surplus or ½ OP_1 can readily be seen by examining the Y axis of figure 3.12. The individual is indifferent between paying OP_2^* to assure realizing U_1^* with certainty and paying nothing and having an equal probability of realizing U_5 or U_6. Since the utility curve for Y is concave, this willingness to pay is more than half of OP_1, and the difference is true option value (OV_c). In this light, option value is a risk-aversion premium.

It can readily be shown that with constant marginal utility of Y as shown by a linear total utility function, OP_2^* and ½ OP_1 would be equal and option value would be zero. But this would imply that the income elasticity of demand for X was zero. Also a gambler with a utility function that is concave upward will have a negative option value.

By way of summary then, the above discussion indicates that because the various approximations of consumer surplus are monetary, when uncertainty enters the problem the level of income associated with the level of expected utility would be less than, equal to, or greater than the expected level of money income and consumer surplus depending on whether the individual is risk averse, risk neutral, or risk seeking. This occurs in the present discussion only for uncertain demanders, since certain demanders would only pay their full consumer surplus and the expected yield versus

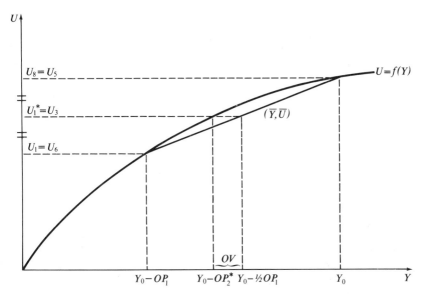

Figure 3.12. Option value in the case of a risk averter.

the expected utility comparison does not arise. We further simplified the discussion by assuming that individuals maximize expected utility rather than utility. The game tree used permits analysis of higher moments in the utility dimension and, given definitions of risk aversion similar to those used in this analysis, we can demonstrate that a positive or negative increment to option value might exist even for the certain demander. For example, if the variance about the level of expected utility of the no-option case exceeds the variance about the level of expected utility of the option case, then individuals who are averse to dispersion about the level of expected utility would pay a greater option price. To consider such situations would, however, lead us too far astray in the current discussion.[20]

The second extension of this model is into the realm of supply uncertainty. In the preceding analysis we kept the game honest, that is, consumers who did not pay the option were not allowed the possibility of a free ride; $P(S/NO) = O$. We also assumed that the producer of the good or service kept his word when the option was purchased; $P(S/O) = 1$. The framework of the preceding section can be used to show that even in the case of the certain demander there will still be positive option value for

---

[20] For a discussion of the problem and some of the pitfalls see the papers that appeared in an exchange in the early 1950s in *Econometrica* 20 (1952):661–79, by Wold, Savage, Manne, Charnes, Samuelson, and Malinvaud, in response to a paper by M. Allais, "Le Comportement de L'Homme Rationnel Devant Le Risque: Critique Des Postulats et Axiomes De L'Ecole Américaine," *Econometrica* 21 (1953):503–46.

risk averters when there is either kind of uncertainty in supply—either $P(S/O) < 1$ or $P(S/NO) > O$—as long as $P(S/NO) \geq P(S/O)$. In either case the maximum option price will fall, but it will still exceed the expected consumer surplus for risk averters and option value will therefore be positive, that is, unless $P(S/NO) \geq P(S/O)$.

Finally, in the same way that two alternative approximations for consumer surplus exist, as demonstrated above, there are two alternative measures of option value. The second is based upon the amount an individual must be compensated to give up his right to consume the good or service and is related to the price-equivalent measure of consumer surplus. The general conclusions are similar; i.e., that this measure of option value is positive for a risk averter. Some subtle differences should be pointed out, however, since this case is applicable when an existing service is being stopped and the potential users are being bribed to voluntarily give up their right to purchase or use this good or service at the present set of prices.

When there are uncertain users, $P(D) \neq 1$, the relevant plays become π_2, π_4, π_5, and π_7, since the assumption of honoring the option in this case means that the good will not be supplied if the option is paid to present users of the resource. $P(NS/O) = 1$, and the good is supplied if no option is secured by present users; i.e., $P(S/NO) = 1$. A second difference is that the utility associated with the preferred outcomes in the option branch of the game tree would exceed similar outcomes in the no-option branch. A final difference is that in the price-equivalent case there is no difference in utility between the two relevant no-option outcomes, but the U_4 outcome on the option side exceeds the U_2 outcome. In other words, if one is bribed to give up the right to use Hells Canyon and future conditions develop so that one does not demand this service (U_4), then one is better off than if future conditions result in one's demanding a visit to Hells Canyon (U_2), but it is not available.

Figure 3.13 shows the indifference curves for the various outcomes under the assumption that the probability of demand is $\frac{1}{2}$. The individual's initial income level is Y_0. If the individual does not receive the option payment, he either demands the good and realizes U_5 or does not demand the good and experiences U_7. U_5 equals U_7 by assumption. If he received an option payment of $\overline{EV}$ ($= \frac{1}{2} EV$), he is at U_2' if he demands the good, but at U_4' if he does not. We know that

$$\bar{U}_O = P_2 U_2' + P_4 U_4'.$$

Figure 3.14 shows at this monetary equivalent option price, $\overline{EV}$, the utility of the expected value of income with the $\overline{EV}$ option price, $\bar{U}_0'$, is less than the utility of the expected value of not accepting the option, $U_5 = \bar{U}_{NO}$.

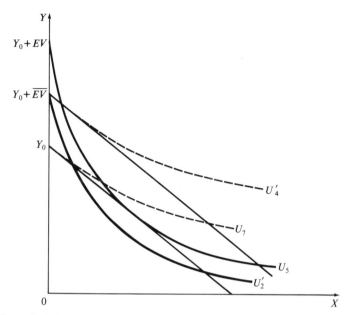

Figure 3.13. The price-equivalent consumer surplus for an uncertain demander.

The option payment must be increased to make $\bar{U}_O = \bar{U}_{NO}$. This would mean that both U_4' and U_2' would move along the utility function in the northeast direction to U_4^* and U_2^* respectively until the absolute value of the utility difference (when $P(D) = \frac{1}{2}$) between U_2^* and U_5 equaled the difference between U_5 and U_4^*. The amount that the option price must be increased over $\overline{EV}$ when U_4' moves to U_4^* is the option value in terms of the price-equivalent measure. Further, for a risk-averse individual $OV_E > OV_c$, just as the price-equivalent measure exceeds the price-compensating measure of consumer surplus if an individual has diminishing marginal utility of money.

For a gambler, the expected value of the price equivalent variation exceeds the minimum option price required and therefore option value is negative. Furthermore, the price-compensating measure of consumer surplus exceeds the price-equivalent measure for a gambler. Similarly, the absolute value of the option value compensating measure, OV_c, would exceed the absolute value of the option value equivalent measure, OV_E.

In conclusion, the analyst must first decide on the appropriate measure of consumer surplus and then determine whether there are uncertain demanders and if they are risk averse. If the answers are affirmative, the appropriate measure of utility would not be only the expected value of consumer surplus but that value plus some positive increment representing

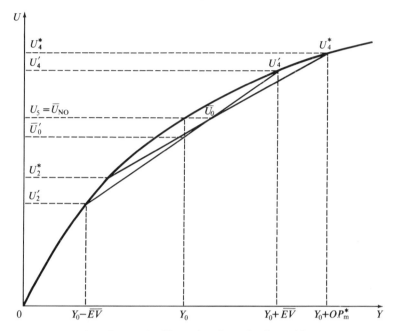

Figure 3.14. Expected utility and option value for a risk averter.

option value. For policy analysis it would be valuable to have some idea of the relative magnitude of option value.

From figure 3.12 it is possible to see what the effect of changing probability of demand has on the relationship between option value and expected consumer surplus. Figure 3.15 relates these quantities to the probability of demand. The linear function shows the relationship between expected value of consumer surplus by either measure and $P(D)$. Above it lies the maximum option price function. The vertical distance between them is the option value as a function of $P(D)$. At probabilities close to one, option value is both small and a small percentage of expected consumer surplus. But at middle and low probabilities, option value is large relative to expected consumer surplus. Thus, where there is a large number of low probability demanders, omission of the option value benefit could result in a significant understatement of benefits.

Accordingly, when irreplaceable assets are at issue in a world of uncertainty, there is need, as Weisbrod correctly perceived, to include a consideration of option value in addition to the consumer surplus in question. This is significant, however, only when the decision depends upon the option value; i.e., when the option value is critical to the resource allocation decision.

108

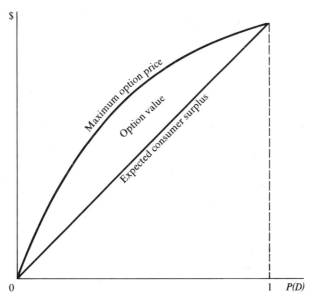

Figure 3.15. Option value and the probability of demand.

V. CONCLUSIONS AND OBSERVATIONS ON
ADDITIONAL RESEARCH

In section IV we established the theoretical relevance of option value to resource allocation decisions. To be of practical use, however, the Weisbrod insight must be made operational and research into the amount that people would be willing to pay for various services, given uncertainty in either supply or demand, should grow out of the theoretical discussion of option value. Several approaches might be considered. First, it seems possible that the difference between an individual's subjective and objective probability of using a given service could be measured in an attempt to determine whether a particular potential user is either overly optimistic or pessimistic. From this, work could be done toward a nonmonetary basis for classifying the respondent as either risk averse, neutral, or risk seeking. Second, the differences between an individual's estimation of the amount he would be willing to pay and the amount he would have to be compensated to surrender the right to use the service in question might be investigated. By having estimates of both of these measures of consumer surplus and the subjective measure of probability of use for different types of users and nonusers, a quantitative measure of option value might be developed.

A second area for future research would be to relax the assumption of a two-good world, implicit in our analysis, where all goods and services are competitive with visits to Hells Canyon. In practical terms this would have the effect of separating the composite vertical shift parameter r_y, whose effect on the benefit level is shown to be greatest in our sensitivity tests, into its differential components of conventional income and cross elasticities, and simultaneously extending the analysis to at least a three-good world. Here goods and services could be complementary to, as well as substitutes for, services of natural areas.

A third area of further research involves the notion of carrying capacity of assets the services of which can be extended to additional individuals but only at reduction in service quality. In our composite computational demand model we attempted to avoid the difficult problem associated with the combination of potential recreational activities that were involved. Because some of these are complementary and some are likely to be competitive, this will have some implications for the appropriate concept and measure of carrying capacity and the interaction among simultaneous participation in given recreational activities. Moreover, we found that the sensitivity of our conclusions to the assumption of carrying capacity constraint was not significant because of the comparatively large difference in the value of the output streams for the two incompatible uses. In other cases where the differences would be smaller, the conclusions might well depend on the specific assumptions regarding the capacity constraint. Accordingly, one of the areas meriting more intensive research involves the further elaboration of the concept of carrying capacity for each of several recreational activities and their computation or estimation, in order to permit better allocation decisions involving such incompatible uses of given resources.

The specific rate of technological advance in the source of supply of outputs alternative to their provision by the development alternative is significant for the present value of the latter. In the case under study, while the effect of introducing technological change into the evaluation of the hydroelectrical development affected the *gross benefits* by roughly only 5 to 10 per cent, the *net benefits*, and hence the present value, was reduced to roughly 50 per cent since the thermal alternative was a close competitor to the hydroelectric facility. The leverage from including modifications for technological advance must be recognized where two sources of supply of identical services are so nearly competitive. With changes taking place in the composition of the thermal alternatives to hydro, and the tendency for specialization in use of the different prime movers, this area might merit additional research.

Perhaps more significant, however, is the need to investigate more fully

110

the presumption of asymmetric implications of technological progress for the value of attributes of the natural environment when used as intermediate goods, compared with their retention as assets supplying final consumption services. Irreproducibility, it might be argued, is not synonymous with irreplaceability. If reasonably good substitutes can be found, by reliance on product development, the argument for the presumption of differential effects of technological progress is weakened; or if not weakened, the value that is selected for our r_y of section III, at least, would not remain unaffected. This problem doubtless merits additional attention, although a reconnaissance needs to be completed before a strategy of research can be suggested.

REFERENCES

Barnett, Harold J., and Chandler Morse. 1963. *Scarcity and growth: The economics of natural resource availability*. Baltimore: Johns Hopkins Press for Resources for the Future.

Baumol, W. J. 1967. Macroeconomics of unbalanced growth. *American Economic Review* 57:415–26.

Brown, G. 1968. Policy questions and measures of consumer's surplus. Unpublished paper, Department of Economics, University of Washington.

Cicchetti, C., J. Seneca, and P. Davidson. 1969. *The demand and supply of outdoor recreation*. Washington, D.C.: U.S. Department of the Interior.

Eckstein, O., and A. Harberger. 1968. *Economic analysis of public investment decisions: Interest rate policy and discounting analysis*. Hearings before the Subcommittee on Economy in Government of the Joint Economic Committee. 90 Cong. 2d sess. Washington, D.C.: Government Printing Office.

Federal Power Commission. In the matter of: Pacific Northwest Power Company and Washington Public Power Supply System, Projects nos. 2243/2273.

Fisher, Anthony. 1970. The optimum use of natural areas. Paper presented at the Western Economic Association meeting.

Henderson, A. 1941. Consumer surplus and compensating variation. *Review of Economic Studies* 8:117–21.

Hicks, J. R. 1941. The rehabilitation of consumer surplus. *Review of Economic Studies* 8:108–16.

―――. 1943. The four consumer's surpluses. *Review of Economic Studies* 11:31–41.

Keynes, John M. 1964. *The general theory of employment, interest and money*. New York: Harbinger, Inc., p. 300.

Krutilla, J. V. 1967. Conservation reconsidered. *American Economic Review* 57:777–86.

Lindsay, C. 1969. Option demand and consumer surplus. *Quarterly Journal of Economics* 83:344–46.

Long, M. 1967. Collective consumption services of individual consumption goods: Comment. *Quarterly Journal of Economics* 81:351–52.

Patinkin, D. 1963. Demand curves and consumer's surplus. In Carl F. Christ et al., *Measurement in economics*. Stanford, Calif.: Stanford University Press.

Seagraves, J. A. 1970. More on the social rate of discount. *Quarterly Journal of Economics* 84:430–50.

Seneca, J. 1970. The welfare effects of zero pricing of public goods. *Public Choice* 8:101–10.

Shepherd, Godfrey. 1933. Vertical and horizontal shifts in demand curves. *Journal of Farm Economics* 15:723–29, and comment by F. L. Thomsen, ibid. 566–70.

Steiner, Peter O. 1965. The role of alternative cost in project design and selection. *Quarterly Journal of Economics* 79:421–22.

Weisbrod, B. 1964. Collective consumption services of individual consumption goods. *Quarterly Journal of Economics* 78:471–77.

Zeckhauser, R. 1969. Uncertainty and the need for collective action. In U.S. Congress, Joint Economic Committee: *The analysis and evaluation of public expenditures: The PPB System*. 91 Cong., 1st sess.

PART II

DEVELOPING MANAGEMENT PROGRAMS

4. A Quantitative Framework for Residuals Management Decisions

Clifford S. Russell and *Walter O. Spofford, Jr.*

I. INTRODUCTION

It is almost impossible these days to be unaware of "environmental quality" as a major public issue in the United States and, indeed, throughout the industrialized world.[1] The explosion of interest, since President Nixon made known his intention to stress "quality" in the 1970 State-of-the-Union message, has been nothing short of phenomenal; it has even received the ultimate contemporary honor, cover stories in the national news weeklies. But what are the prospects that this currently heightened concern will result in solutions even to the most obvious problems such as the pollution of waterways near urban and industrial areas, and the refuse disposal crises striking some of our cities? One is tempted to conclude that these prospects are dim, so long as the prescription for action is ever larger doses of the same medicines we have tried over the last

The authors are indebted to Betty Duenckel and Iris Long of Resources for the Future for their effort in linking together IBM's linear programming code, MPS–360, with subroutines coded in FORTRAN. The authors also wish to thank Tze-Wen Chi of Harvard University for suggesting to them that MPS–360 could be used as the master program within which FORTRAN coded subroutines could be included.

[1] Japan is apparently suffering fairly severe environmental damage as part of the cost of her recent impressive growth rate. But private enterprise economies are not the only ones with problems; even the Soviet Union has its environmental quality disputes. In recent years, for example, a great controversy has surrounded the decision to build a paper mill on Lake Baikal, thus endangering that water body's unique ecological system. The mill is now operating but with much stricter effluent controls than were originally planned, and it is still the target of criticism.

decade and found wanting. Let us, however, go beyond this vague pessimism and suggest several basic reasons for the problems experienced in achieving what appears to be a widely shared social goal, significant improvement in environmental quality in the United States. Then, as a means of introducing this paper, we will indicate the relevance of our work to these problems.

The most fundamental difficulty we face in obtaining effective public (or even private) action on environmental quality is that there is not even general agreement on what we are talking about, let alone on what the goals are or should be. Some people have in mind the very broadest definitions of environmental quality and want government action in the arts, in urban design and location, and in population planning. Others are content to demand that the salmon should be reintroduced into a cleaned-up Connecticut River.

Even if we had general agreement on the scope of the issue, however, so long as we have differing incomes and tastes and so long as we earn most of our income from ownership or management of, or employment in, private-sector business firms, we can expect that there will be disagreement on practically every specific proposal for action designed to "improve" environmental quality. And thus a second reason for our failure to improve our situation is that we have not yet developed efficient institutions for balancing competing desires concerning aspects of environmental quality.[2] Indeed, one might characterize the general problem of environmental quality management as that of providing both institutions and price-quantity decisions for the allocation of common property resources for which the familiar private market mechanisms are inadequate.

A third reason for concern about our past methods is that they have almost always attacked environmental questions on a fragmented basis.[3] In particular, water pollution, air pollution, solid waste disposal, pesticide use, and transportation have each been studied in isolation. The making of such "cuts" in the larger system of man's environment implies either that there are no links between the relevant systems or that any links that do exist are adequately represented by market prices. And adequate

[2] To a large extent, only the courts are currently available to those who would attempt to influence a particular decision such as whether or not a dam should be built.
Some have objected to this rather dark characterization of the present situation, claiming that at all levels—local, state, and federal—existing legislative, administrative, and regulatory institutions are, in fact, becoming more and more efficient in this area. The disagreement may hinge on differing definitions of efficiency.

[3] Milton Heath, who has worked with federal and state authorities on environmental quality issues, disagrees with this statement. We are willing to admit that there may be a trend in the direction of unification, but we also feel that the past record of fragmentation speaks for itself.

116

representation by market prices in turn means that these prices represent marginal social costs and not simply marginal private costs.

To what extent is this study relevant to the solution of the problems we have just described?[4] To answer this question let us define the limits of our work, and in the course of doing so point out the contributions we hope it will make. We propose a quantitative framework for the analysis of regional problems of residuals management.[5] Or, put somewhat differently, we hope to provide a tool that will assist decision makers in balancing the competing uses of the physical environment involved in the disposal of the leftovers from man's production and consumption activities and the use of that same environment, again by man, for breathing, drinking, viewing, and recreating. Thus, from the point of view of the first problem raised above, it is what we leave out that is most significant. We are not concerned, for example, with the quality aspects of man's structures, or with the events and environment within them (except insofar as the costs of maintaining a particular internal environment are affected by residuals in the external environment). We make no claim, of course, that our choice of problems is "right," or that it is what we ought to mean in speaking of "environmental quality." We do, however, feel that residuals management represents a very important subset of the overall quality problem and one that can, without too much difficulty, be separated from other aspects, such as the preservation of unique scenic or geologic areas, the encouragement of cultural activities, and the promotion of visual quality in urban architecture.

The question of the limits of our study is also relevant to the third problem mentioned above, that of the piecemeal nature of current decisions. Our framework is designed to deal explicitly with at least the major

---

[4] There are, of course, several other reasons behind the slippage between concern and action. One is lack of funds; with local tax bases and borrowing capacity heavily strained and the states in very little better shape, only the Federal treasury seems to have the necessary flow of funds to finance sewage treatment works and new methods of dealing with solid wastes. Yet appropriations in these areas have been relatively small. Another reason is lack of specific information at every level; e.g., production process substitution possibilities and costs, pre-discharge treatment costs, environmental transmission mechanisms, and damages to those affected by the discharges.

[5] A residual is a quantity of material or energy left over when, in the course of a human production or consumption activity, inputs are converted into outputs. Examples are waste heat from thermal-electric generation and fruit or vegetable trimmings in canning. How do we know what is going to be left over? A widely useful, but not infallible, rule of thumb is simply to identify as products those material or energy outputs that have prices in normally existing markets (not prices established by an environmental management agency). Outputs that are not so priced are the residual outputs. Notice that this definition depends on the particular price set governing over the time span of reference. Since changes in relative prices obviously can and do occur, it is important in modeling to trace as many physical flows as seems practical in order to investigate sensitivity of the product-residual breakdown to these changes.

forms of residuals: air-borne, water-borne, and solid wastes.[6] As already pointed out, the separation of decisions about the management of these various residuals may lead to distortions because appropriate prices are not available for valuing the results of direct interactions not explicitly included in the separate models. Our model reflects the physical tradeoffs possible among forms of residuals in production and subsequent modifications—for example, treatment—and follows the various forms through the physical environment to the receptors where the damages are incurred.[7]

This study is not designed to make a direct contribution to the solution of the second problem noted above, that of the lack of institutions for balancing competing demands affecting environmental quality, and we do not offer any explicit designs for such institutions. The framework we present does, however, carry with it certain implications about the nature of the institutions that we would find desirable. First, we see such institutions as being organized on a regional level, where the region would be defined in terms of the physical scope of the residuals problem (the area within which the externalities resulting from residuals discharges are relatively important). Second, we visualize a regional management authority as having for its primary mission the reflection, in the actual conditions facing firms and consumers in the region, of these externalities. The authority would achieve this goal by imposing effluent charges or discharge constraints on the activities of the region, and it would arrive at the desired set of such charges or limits by choosing the set that did the best job of fulfilling some *objective*. The objective might be one of pure economic efficiency, or more probably one of efficiency tempered by some considerations of "equity" and political influence in the distribution of benefits, damages, and costs within the region.[8] Our model is visualized as the staff

[6] In principle, another major energy residual in addition to heat, namely noise, may also be handled within our model. At present there is not sufficient information for doing so, and beyond that there is the question of the separability of noise from other residuals. Separability depends on the extent of nonmarket interaction between noise and other residuals problems whether in production processes, in the physical environment, or in the creation of damages.

Another classification is into material and energy residuals, the former encompassing gaseous, liquid, and solid residuals. Neither classification is perfect. [Editor's note.]

[7] Receptors may, in a physical sense, include not only man, but also plants, animals, and inanimate objects. The damages suffered by the latter nonhuman receptors are, however, evaluated from the human point of view, even if that view includes a measure of mutual sympathy and a feeling for the intrinsic worth of the natural order.

[8] For one view of the appropriate manner of including political considerations in models designed to assist in decision making, see Robert Dorfman, "General Equilibrium with Public Goods," in *Public Economics*, ed. S. Margolis and H. Guiton (London: Macmillan, 1969). Edwin Haefele, in "Environmental Quality as a Problem of Social Choice," chap. 8 of this book, makes a case for legislative policy making bodies in fields such as environmental quality and shows how they can reflect individual preferences through vote trading.

tool by which information on the region's residuals generation, modification[9] and discharge possibilities; on its natural environment and the dilution, transportation and transformation, accumulation and storage of the discharged residuals therein; and on the activities suffering damages from the resulting concentrations of residuals, may be combined with the chosen objective function to find a "best" set of policy instruments (charges and limits) for imposition by the line section of the authority.

This model has evolved out of discussions and prior work at Resources for the Future concerning the appropriate characterization of the residuals management problem.[10] As shown in figure 4.1, we have found it useful to think of the problem in terms of flows of residuals from human production and consumption activities (reflecting decisions about production mixes, levels, and methods; treatment and recycle alternatives, etc.) through the transforming environment (in which dilution, transportation, decay, and other processes may take place), to the receptors including man and the plants, animals, and inanimate objects of economic, aesthetic, or other interest to him (possibly after the application of final protective measures such as air filtration or water chlorination). In the overall system, these flows of residuals and the resulting damages give rise to corresponding flows of information from the large and diffuse group of receptors to such generalized response organizations as conservation groups, city governments, and state legislatures. The information ultimately reaches whatever more specialized environmental quality management agencies exist and have jurisdiction, and these in turn take whatever actions seem both desirable and politically feasible. Such actions may include limiting discharges, requiring certain levels of treatment (or building treatment plants), imposing effluent charges, subsidizing recycling operations, modifying the assimilative capacity of the environment, or installing collective final protective measures. Whatever actions such agencies take will modify the ultimate damages and hence the content of the information being fed back into the response organization. Presumably at some point the management agency will decide that the costs of action to reduce further residuals concentrations reaching receptors will no longer be justified by the resulting

[9] The term modification encompasses the entire range of alternative ways of handling residuals after they have been generated—materials recovery, by-product production, and treatment. The first two have been identified herein in the production process options. See page 122. [Editor's note.]

[10] For an excellent recent example of such work, see Blair T. Bower et al., *Waste Management: Generation and Disposal of Solid, Liquid and Gaseous Wastes in the New York Region* (New York: Regional Plan Association, 1968). Related work of a theoretical, general equilibrium nature is represented by A. V. Kneese and R. C. d'Arge, "Pervasive External Costs and the Response of Society," in U.S. Congress, Joint Economic Committee, Subcommittee on Economy in Government, *The Analysis and Evaluation of Public Expenditures: The PPB System*, 91st Cong. 1st sess., 1969.

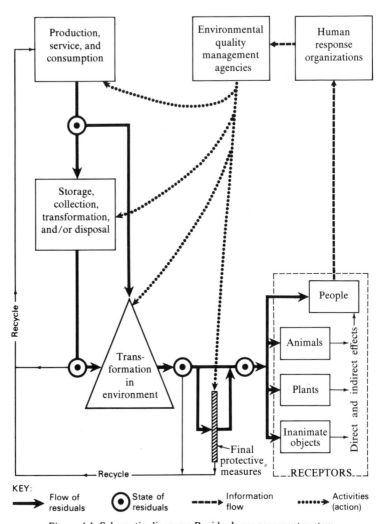

Figure 4.1. Schematic diagram: Residuals management system.

decreases in damages (all these adjusted for the equity and political influence factors referred to above). At such a point, we can say that "a solution" to the residuals management problem has been reached.

Our model, then, has been set up to achieve two goals. One is to reflect the view of the residuals management problem that we have described. The other is to make the problem amenable to explicit mathematical optimization. The outputs from our model may then be viewed as basic inputs to the political process, making use of available information in a relatively efficient way. To achieve these two basic goals, we have adopted

120

an overall model which is built from three blocks: (a) a model of production (and consumption) in which residuals discharges are determined along with processes and production levels; (b) a set of environmental models which transform, transport, dilute, and decay the discharged residuals, producing ambient concentrations at grid points in the regional environment; and (c) damage functions reflecting the impact of those ambient concentrations on receptors.[11]

None of these individual submodels is, in concept, original with us; nor, indeed, is the idea of combining input-output type models with more or less sophisticated environmental models,[12] although we have added certain features to some of these models that make them better suited to our purposes. But our most important contribution, we feel, is that we have devised a workable system for optimizing in which these several basic models *and* at least the three major forms of residuals are included in a single computational framework.

The key element of this, as of any optimization model, is, of course, the objective function. In defining this function, we choose to confine ourselves to the economic efficiency criterion, and in simplest terms our objective function becomes the algebraic sum of the gross benefits to society from its production/consumption activities, the traditional input costs associated with production, the costs of modification and transportation of the residuals generated, and the damages attributable to those residuals discharged to the environment.[13]

---

[11] This computational method and the problems involved in making it converge on "a solution" are discussed more completely later in this chapter.

[12] For an example of work along this line, see Walter Isard et al., "On the Linkage of Socio-Economic and Ecologic Systems," in *The Regional Science Association Papers* 21 (1968):79–100.

[13] There is nothing particularly unusual about this choice, but two of its features might usefully be amplified before we mention the other components of the model. First, we should, in principle, like to deal with gross benefits in the sense of gross willingness to pay for a particular level of consumption. This is because we wish to be able to discuss and judge among nonmarginal changes in patterns of production and consumption. The marginal valuation represented by a market price is only a useful guide for very small changes in output.

The second point worth additional comment is the makeup of the item we have called the traditional input costs of production. The basic rule here is that we should include the opportunity costs associated with various inputs such as labor, raw materials, etc. Thus, what is included in a particular application depends both on our time horizon and our assumptions about input mobility (the existence of other opportunities). For a relatively short horizon, capital and most labor may well be considered immobile and may thus be costed at zero in the objective function. In general, the longer the horizon the fewer the inputs which will be lacking in alternative opportunities.

It is interesting to note in passing that the use of willingness to pay, corrected for the associated internal and external costs, is conceptually close to the concept of the "net rent" attributable to the environment, a notion that others seem to have found attractive.

Maximization of this overall objective function is accomplished by computations involving the three component parts of our model. (See figure 4.2 for a schematic representation of these components and their links with each other.)

1. *A linear programming industry model* that relates inputs and outputs of the various production processes and consumption activities at specified locations within a region, including the unit amounts and types of residuals generated by the production of each product; the costs of transforming these residuals from one form to another (i.e., gaseous to liquid in the scrubbing of stack gases); the costs of transporting the residuals from one place to another; and the cost of any final discharge-related activity such as landfill operations.

The industry model permits choices among production processes, raw material input mixes, recycle of residuals, by-product production, and in-plant adjustments and improvement, all of which can reduce the total quantity of residuals generated. That is, the residuals generated are *not* assumed to be fixed either in form or in quantity. This model also allows for choices among transformation processes and hence among the possible forms of the residual to be disposed of in the natural environment and, to a limited extent, among the locations at which discharge is accomplished.

2. *Environmental diffusion models* which describe the fate of various residuals after their discharge into the environment. Essentially these models may be thought of as transformation functions operating on a vector of residuals discharges and yielding another vector of ambient concentrations at grid points throughout the environment. Between the discharge point and receptor locations, the residual may be diluted in the relatively large volume of air or water in the natural world, transformed from one form to another (as in the decay of oxygen-demanding organics), accumulated or stored and, of course, transported to another place.[14]

Analogous to the more familiar physical diffusion models could be models of ecological systems which reflect the transmission over time and space (as through a food chain) of the impact on natural systems of a particular residual discharge or set of ambient concentrations. Instead of residuals concentrations as the end-products of this type of model, we could obtain estimates of the populations of species of direct interest to man, such as sport fish or rare and endangered animals.

3. A set of *receptor-damage functions* relating the concentration of

---

[14] We also discuss very briefly methods for including explicitly as management alternatives direct intervention in the physical environment, as in the provision of low-flow augmentation or in-stream aeration. Inclusion of these alternatives involves certain additions to the basic linear programming model just introduced and, of course, changes in the environmental diffusion models themselves.

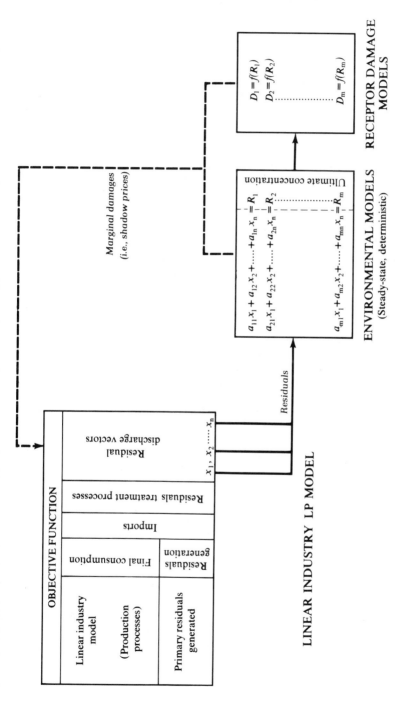

Figure 4.2. Schematic diagram of residuals-environmental quality planning model.

residuals in the environment to the resulting damages, whether these are sustained directly by humans, or indirectly through the medium of such receptors as plants or animals in which man has a commercial, scientific, or aesthetic interest. Thus, for example, ideally we should like to have functions relating human exposure to atmospheric residuals, such as sulfur and nitrogen oxides, to damages in terms of chronic or acute health effects. In addition, we should like to know what damages may accrue because of the action of these same gaseous compounds (perhaps in combination with atmospheric humidity) on houses and plants. So far, adequate damage functions have not been estimated for any phase of the residuals problem and consequently in our computations aimed at testing this framework we have been forced to use arbitrary functions.[15]

The linkage between the components of our model and the method of optimum-seeking may be explained heuristically as follows. Consider solving the linear programming model initially with no restrictions or prices on the discharge of residuals. Using this initial set of residual discharges as inputs to the diffusion models and the resulting ambient concentrations as the arguments of the damage functions, we may then calculate the marginal damages attributable to each discharge; that is, the change in total damages that would result if that discharge were changed by a small amount. These marginal damages are then applied as interim effluent charges on the discharge activities in the linear model and that model solved again for a new set of production, consumption, treatment, and discharge activities.

Another way of looking at this procedure is as a steepest ascent technique for solving a nonlinear programming problem.[16] The objective function is

[15] It is likely that for the foreseeable future damage functions will be unavailable for the effects of most residuals of concern to decision makers. Under these conditions one entirely respectable alternative is to calculate the costs of meeting several different sets of standards on ambient concentrations. The decision on which standard set to opt for involves then an implicit judgment, by the public or its elected or appointed representatives, on marginal benefits (reduction in damages), weighed against an explicit measure of costs. When we are dealing with a number of residuals and of locations at which concentrations are constrained, the problem of choosing a relatively small number of alternative quality standards becomes rather difficult.

This procedure may even seem the better one if we believe that individual preferences concerning public goods (such as clean air) are only revealed through the political process. In this view the expert estimation of damage functions involving such goods may only serve to prejudge the issue and to improperly constrain the appropriate political decision-making body. See Haefele, chap. 8 of this book.

[16] If the environmental diffusion models may be written as linear functions (constant transfer coefficients) and if the damage functions are linear or piecewise linear with increasing marginal damages, our system may be written as a single large linear programming problem. We employ the division and iterative computing technique described in order to maintain flexibility for dealing with such complications as simulation models of the environment or interaction between residuals in the environment or in the creation of damages.

linearized locally, using marginal damages as "fixed" residuals discharge prices, and because the constraint set is also linear, the resulting problem may be solved by using standard linear programming methods. This linearized subproblem is solved subject to suitable bounds on the allowable distance that a decision variable may move in a single iteration. The objective function is then linearized again around the new temporary solution point and so on until a local optimum is reached.

The following assumptions are basic to the first-phase models described more fully below. Most of them are made with the obvious and practical aim of simplifying the version of the world to be modeled.

First, we assume a static economic world so that time does not enter as a decision variable in our production model. Second, we assume that the physical world is deterministic and steady state; that is, the attributes of the dispersion and diffusion models are known with certainty and do not vary with time. Third, we assume that interactions among residuals in the environment do not occur,[17] and that decay rates, where applicable, are independent of the quantities of the residual present (as well as of the presence of other residuals). Fourth, we assume that damages are functions of single residuals only; that, for example, damages attributable to SO_2 concentrations in the atmosphere are independent of the concentration of particulates (although such interactions could be handled quite easily by our nonlinear, iterative technique).

Before proceeding with a more detailed discussion of our models and associated techniques, it might be helpful to mention a set of problems which, if they have not done so already, will undoubtedly trouble the reader at some point along the way. These difficulties arise, in general, because of the pervasive character of the externalities with which a residuals-management agency, and hence a model like ours, must deal. Almost all of man's activities within any region are affected to some extent by externalities involving the residuals of his production or consumption activities. This implies that a completely satisfactory decision model requires, in principle, a general equilibrium analysis of the economic situation including all external costs and benefits.[18] But construction and application of general equilibrium models for actual situations will almost certainly be prohibitively expensive because of data gathering problems and the expense and difficulty of manipulating the very large resulting models. Consequently, management models, such as the one proposed in this paper, will be based on only a partial equilibrium description of the regional economy.

---

[17] We do not, for example, attempt to include the reactions between hydrocarbons and nitrogen oxides associated with the production of photochemical smog.

[18] See, for example, Kneese and d'Arge, "Pervasive External Costs."

The fundamental problem is, of course, that our partial equilibrium model's description of the region must inevitably be incomplete and inadequate for any save relatively small changes in consumption, production, or employment levels. Any demand functions we use, for example, will typically have been estimated on the basis of relatively small variations in prices and quantities. If the indicated solution for the region involves significantly lower consumption levels (for whatever combination of reasons) it will be highly suspect on the grounds that these functions do not adequately represent the rising value of marginal willingness to pay as consumption decreases. Similarly, if regional unemployment would increase significantly under the management solution, we must be careful in evaluating our estimates of factor mobility (implicit in the factor prices we have used) since these are probably based on experience with a relatively small range of unemployment.

II. EXPOSITION OF METHODOLOGY

Although it is intuitively appealing and quite proper (within the economic framework we have established here) to use marginal damages as "shadow prices" or effluent taxes in each iteration on the residuals discharged to the environment, it might be helpful for the reader if we digressed a little in order to develop the basis for this iterative procedure in a more rigorous manner. After that, we will continue with a discussion of the industry linear programming model, ambient concentrations of residuals, damage functions, and finally, marginal damages.

2.1. *Model Development: Some Basic Considerations*

For a particular region, our aim is to choose the levels of production, of consumption, of treatment activities, and of resulting damages that maximize a given economic objective. In order to achieve this goal, we must (a) specify an appropriate objective function; (b) specify a constraint set for relating, and in some cases limiting, the values that the various decision variables can assume; and (c) choose an appropriate computational technique for finding an optimal solution.

Objective Function. We have chosen as a criterion, at least initially, the maximization of regional economic efficiency. In its most general form, the objective function may be thought of as having six parts: (a) gross consumption benefits, i.e., total willingness to pay, B; (b) opportunity costs of traditional production inputs (including recirculation, etc.), C_p; (c) residual

126

treatment costs, C_{RT}; (d) costs of modifying the environment to reduce receptor damages, e.g., in-stream reaeration and low-flow augmentation, C_{ME}; (e) costs of final protective measures, e.g., water treatment facilities, C_{FP}; and (f) subsequent damages to man caused by ambient concentrations of residuals in the environment, D. Stated more formally,

$$
\begin{aligned}
F = B(q_i, i = 1, \ldots, k_1) - C_p(q_i, i = 1, \ldots, k_1) \\
- C_{RT}(w_i, i = 1, \ldots, k_2) - C_{ME}(s_i, i = 1, \ldots, k_3) \\
- C_{FP}(R_i, i = 1, \ldots, k_4; y_i, i = 1, \ldots, k_4) \\
- D(y_i, i = 1, \ldots, k_5), \quad (2.1\text{-}1)
\end{aligned}
$$

where

F = value of the objective function;
q_i = activity levels of k_1 production processes;
w_i = activity levels of k_2 residuals treatment processes;
s_i = activity levels of k_3 processes for modifying the environment;
R_i = ambient concentrations of residuals at k_4 receptor locations;
y_i = ultimate ambient concentrations of residuals resulting in damages to receptors at k_5 locations.

Ordinarily, this function is nonlinear. Very often, however, it is possible to transform a nonlinear function into a piecewise linear form. If the constraint set is also linear, the problem may then be solved as a standard linear programming problem.

The Constraint Set. Material (and energy) flows from raw material inputs to the production processes, through the production processes to final products and residuals, through the environment to final protective devices and ultimately to receptors are characterized in our model by a series of mathematical expressions. These relationships comprise what is known as the *constraint set* in that they relate—in this case because of the laws of conservation of mass and energy, and of resource scarcity—the activity levels of the various decision variables. Some of these relationships are truly linear; others, although not strictly linear, traditionally have been expressed in linear form (e.g., production relationships);[19] while still others assume a linear form only under certain conditions (i.e., expressions for relating ambient concentrations of residuals and their rates of discharge under steady state conditions where residuals do not interact in the natural environment). It is this last set of relationships that we want to examine in more detail.

[19] So that linear programming methods may be employed for solving the industry problem, this particular set of relationships is usually expressed in linear form.

If we denote as X a vector of residual discharges to the environment from production and consumption activities of the region; as S an output vector from activities employed to modify the environment, e.g., additional stream flow and dissolved oxygen; and as R a vector of ambient concentrations of residuals at the various receptor locations, the relationship among them may be expressed functionally as:

$$R = f(X, S). \qquad (2.1\text{–}2)$$

This is a general expression for all environmental disperson formulations. If this relationship is available to us at all, it will be in one of three forms: (a) a linear expression, (b) a nonlinear analytical expression, or (c) a simulation model.

When residuals interact in the natural environment (e.g., oxides of nitrogen, hydrocarbons, and sunlight in the production of photochemical smog; or heat and its effect on the rate of change in the biochemical oxygen demand, BOD, of organic material in a river), equation (2.1–2) will be nonlinear. Also, when low-flow augmentation is considered explicitly as a decision variable, equation (2.1–2) will assume a nonlinear form.[20] In short, only when we make the assumptions presented in the introduction— i.e., deterministic steady state conditions, no interactions among residuals in the natural environment, and no explicit treatment of modifications to the environment (specifically, low-flow augmentation)—will equation (2.1–2) result in a linear expression.[21]

Some Considerations for Choosing an Appropriate Optimization Scheme. The forms of both the objective function and the constraint set dictate the appropriate computational tool or tools that need be employed for obtaining a solution. We must now search for a computational methodology for specifying an optimal management plan within the framework of our model. Because we intend to deal with large numbers of variables and constraints, we will confine our exploration to computer-oriented optimizing techniques.

As has been demonstrated thus far in this section, the general regional environmental quality management model without alteration does not lend itself readily to solution by linear programming methods as both the objective function and the constraint set are apt to be nonlinear. Furthermore, some of the relationships that represent the behavior of residuals in the natural environment may be established only through simulation

---

[20] In-stream aeration will add additional *linear* constraints to the problem.

[21] There are, however, other ways of dealing with low-flow augmentation. One way would be to solve the remainder of the model for a reasonably small number of levels of low-flow augmentation and choose that scheme which maximizes net benefits.

and are not available in analytical form at all. However, by redefining the original problem, we might be able to (a) eliminate the nonlinear (and simulation model) constraints and/or (b) transform the objective function into a linear or piecewise linear form, but probably not without some sacrifice in flexibility and loss in scope. The question here is what form we should strive for in our model. On the one hand we would like to maintain as many of the significant features as possible; on the other hand, we want to be able to solve the problem. From an operational standpoint, it is more convenient to deal with linear constraint sets than with the nonlinear variety.[22] Hence, we have decided—at least initially—to limit our model to constraints of a linear analytical form. We will, however, attempt to deal with a nonlinear objective function.

What can be done in our management problem to eliminate the nonlinear (and/or simulation model) constraints? As suggested above, if we assume deterministic, steady state conditions in the environment with residuals that do not interact, and eliminate certain modifications to the environment from explicit treatment as decision variables, the constraint set, equation (2.1–2), will, in fact, be entirely linear and thus none of the constraints would have to be eliminated. Ambient concentrations of residuals, R, could be included explicitly within the model along with final protective measures and ultimate concentrations of residuals. If the damage functions can be linearized and if these functions have the proper shape for linear programming treatment, this particular form of the problem could be solved as a large linear programming problem.

If, on the other hand, we wished to treat explicitly interactions among residuals in the environment or modifications to the environment (such as low-flow augmentation), or perhaps even more important if we do not have analytical expressions—either linear or nonlinear—for relating inputs to and outputs from the environment (for example, simulation models of ecosystems may be all that are available to us), these relationships would have to be eliminated as constraints (but not from the problem, as will be seen later on) in order to maintain an entirely linear constraint set.[23] One way of achieving this and still reflecting costs of final protective measures and receptor damages in regional environmental quality management decisions is to eliminate explicit treatment of the related decision

[22] Considerable progress has, however, been made in the last decade in the development of general, nonlinear algorithms that can handle nonlinear constraints of both the equality and inequality type. See, for example, F. A. Fiacco and G. P. McCormick, *Nonlinear Programming: Sequential Unconstrained Minimization Techniques* (New York: John Wiley and Sons, 1968).
[23] Because most standard optimization schemes require that constraints be in analytical form, it would be necessary to eliminate the simulation model "link" as part of our traditional constraint set anyway.

variables (i.e., R and Y) and, instead, reflect the respective marginal costs and damages through prices on the residuals discharged to the environment.[24] We can best get around this in our model by constructing a new set of "damage" functions which represents, for each residual and a spectrum of concentration levels, the minimum of damages to receptors plus costs of final protective measures.[25] Consequently, from this point on, the term damage function implies the minimum of receptor damages plus costs of final protective measures for all ambient concentration levels, R.

With this relatively minor alteration of our original problem, we have apparently eliminated the necessity for nonlinear (and simulation type) relationships in the constraint set of the optimization model. And this is important to us when we go to expand our model *beyond* the first-phase assumptions listed previously in the introduction (section I). We have, however, added to the nonlinearity of the objective function.[26] This will be seen more clearly below where we derive the new objective function. This revised form is a compromise between a complete and explicit treatment of the entire management problem in a single model on the one hand, and what we think is an operational methodology on the other.

Before we leave this section, the original objective function, equation (2.1–1), should be rewritten to reflect these changes. The revised form of the objective function follows.

$$
\begin{aligned}
F = \; & B(q_i, i = 1, \ldots, k_1) - C_p(q_i, i = 1, \ldots, k_1) \\
& - C_{RT}(w_i, i = 1, \ldots, k_2) - C_{ME}(s_i, i = 1, \ldots, k_3) \\
& - DC(x_i, i = 1, \ldots, k_6; s_i, i = 1, \ldots, k_3)^{27} \quad (2.1\text{–}3)
\end{aligned}
$$

where x_i = activity levels of k_6 residual discharge activities.

A Nonlinear Programming Technique. In this section, we describe a programming technique for optimizing a nonlinear objective function subject to a set of linear equality and inequality constraints. From an operational

[24] Equality constraints may always be used to eliminate variables in an optimization problem. Here, we are proposing to use the equality relationships, equation (2.1–2), to eliminate explicit treatment of ambient concentrations, $R_i^{(k)}$, as variables.

[25] If the final protective measures are linked to receptors directly and if their activity levels are not related to activity levels of other processes in the model, this minimization procedure may be performed independently of the LP interindustry model. For a more complete discussion of this point, see section 2.4.

Combining the costs of final protective measures together with receptor damages to form a joint "damage" function is not a requirement of our approach. Each could be treated separately. Whenever possible, however, it is convenient to combine them.

[26] No longer, for example, will it be possible to use the piecewise linear approach for the objective function, as prices, in some cases, will be functions of other than the associated variables.

[27] The notation DC represents the minimum of receptor damages plus costs of final protective measures; i.e., $DC = [D + C_{FP}]_{\min}$.

standpoint it has much appeal to us in that a standard linear programming algorithm may be used for determining successively better positions along the response surface.[28]

The scheme we describe is based on the gradient method of nonlinear programming. The technique consists of linearizing the response surface in the vicinity of a feasible point, $X^{(k)}$.[29] To do this, we construct a tangent plane at this point by employing the first two terms of a Taylor's series expansion (up to first partial derivatives). This linear approximation to the nonlinear response surface will, in general, be most accurate in the vicinity of the point X^k and less accurate as one moves farther away from this point. Because of this, a set of "artificial" bounds, i.e., constraints, is imposed on the system to restrict the selection of the next position along the response surface to that portion of the surface most closely approximated by the newly created linear surface. The selection of the appropriate set of artificial bounds is analogous to choosing a step size in other gradient methods of nonlinear programming.

Because the newly created subproblem is in a linear form, we are able to make use of standard linear programming techniques for finding a new optimal point, $X^{(k+1)}$. This point locates the maximum value of the linearized objective function within the artificially confined area of the response surface. Because, in general, the linearized surface will not match the original nonlinear surface, the original nonlinear objective function must be evaluated at this point to determine whether or not this new point, $X^{(k+1)}$, is, in fact, a better position than the previously determined one, $X^{(k)}$. That is, the following condition must be satisfied:

$$F[X^{(k+1)}] > F[X^{(k)}]. \qquad (2.1\text{--}4)$$

If this condition is satisfied, a new tangent plane is constructed at the point $X^{(k+1)}$ and a new set of artificial bounds is placed around this point. As before, a linear programming code is employed to find a new position, $X^{(k+2)}$, which maximizes the linearized objective function, and so on until a local optimum is reached.[30]

---

[28] The response surface is the surface described by the objective function, $F(X)$, and delimited by the constraint sets, $AX \leq B$ and $X \geq 0$.

[29] $X^{(k)}$ is a feasible point if it satisfies the constraint sets $AX \leq B$ and $X \geq 0$.

[30] This procedure, like all gradient methods, finds only the local optimum. If the response surface contains more than one optimum, the problem becomes one of finding the *global* optimum. One way of approaching this is to start the procedure at different points within the feasible region, R, defined by the constraint sets $AX \leq B$ and $X \geq 0$, where the starting points may be chosen at random. For techniques on random starts within a feasible region defined by the constraints $AX \leq B$ and $X \geq 0$, see P. P. Rogers, *Random Methods for Non-Convex Programming* (Ph.D. diss., Harvard University, June 1966).

131

For any of the gradient procedures, two computations are necessary at each step: (a) the direction of travel, e.g., the local gradient (a vector quantity),[31] and (b) the length of the step (a scalar quantity). The rationale used in developing expressions for these are unrelated; although, operationally, the *direction* must be known in order to compute an "optimal" step length.[32]

For the method described here, a linear programming algorithm is used (a) to determine, implicitly, the best direction of travel among a series of vectors formed by all feasible vertices of the constraint set (original constraint set as well as the artificial bounds) and the position vector, $X^{(k)}$,[33] and (b) to determine, again implicitly, the maximum distance, δ_1, of travel in a given direction such that none of the constraints will be violated. Evaluation of the distance δ_2 to the nearest maximum in the direction of travel must be made in a separate computation as is the case for all gradient methods. The essential features of this procedure follow.

Consider the following optimization problem:

$$\max\{F = f(X)\} \tag{2.1--5}$$

$$h_i(X) = 0 \qquad i = 1, \ldots, m < n \tag{2.1--6}$$

$$g_i(X) \geq 0 \qquad i = m + 1, \ldots, p \tag{2.1--7}$$

$$x_i \geq 0 \qquad i = 1, \ldots, n \tag{2.1--8}$$

where $f(X)$ is a nonlinear objective function; $h_i(X) = 0$, $i = 1, \ldots, m$, is a set of linear equality constraints; $g_i(X) \geq 0$, $i = m + 1, \ldots, p$, is a set of linear inequality constraints; and x_i, $i = 1, \ldots n$, is a vector of decision variables.

The response surface described by the objective function, $F(X)$, may be approximated in the neighborhood of a feasible point $X^{(k)}$ by expanding

---

[31] The gradient, ∇F, is a vector of first order partial derivatives of the function $F(x_1, x_2, \ldots, x_n)$ computed at a point, $X^{(k)}$; i.e., $\nabla F \equiv \hat{e}_1 \dfrac{\partial F}{\partial x_1} + \hat{e}_2 \dfrac{\partial F}{\partial x_2} + \ldots + \hat{e}_n \dfrac{\partial F}{\partial x_n}$, where $\hat{e}_1, \hat{e}_2, \ldots, \hat{e}_n$ are unit vectors in the 1, 2, $\ldots$, n^{th} orthogonal directions respectively. The gradient points locally in the direction of the maximum increase (or decrease) of the response surface; i.e., $\Delta F_{\max}$.

[32] Every direction has associated with it an "optimal" step length. The optimal step is defined here as the distance to the nearest local optimum (if one exists) formed by the intersection of the response surface and the plane of the direction vector, S. The direction of travel used in most gradient methods is the one that yields the maximum increase (decrease) in the value of the objective function within the feasible region, R.

[33] When the artificial bounds are set according to the gradient, the selected direction of travel will be the gradient for all unconstrained interior points and the most feasible direction of travel for all constrained points. The *most feasible direction* is the vector that makes the smallest angle θ with the gradient and which for a small step in that direction will violate none of the constraints, $AX \leq B$ and $X \geq 0$.

132

the Taylor's series at that point. When terms of second order and above are neglected, the following linear relationship results:

$$F[X^{(k+1)}] = F[X^{(k)}] + \nabla F[X^{(k)}] \cdot [X^{(k+1)} - X^{(k)}]. \qquad (2.1\text{-}9)$$

Rearranging terms in equation (2.1–9) yields:

$$F[X^{(k+1)}] = \nabla F[X^{(k)}] \cdot X^{(k+1)} - \nabla F[X^{(k)}] \cdot X^{(k)} + F[X^{(k)}], \qquad (2.1\text{-}10)$$

where in the $(k + 1)^{\text{th}}$ step, $F[X^{(k)}]$, $\nabla F[X^{(k)}]$, and $X^{(k)}$ may be considered constants.

The problem now becomes one of maximizing the quantity,

$$F[X^{(k+1)}] = \nabla F[X^{(k)}] \cdot X^{(k+1)} + \gamma \qquad (2.1\text{-}11)$$

where γ is a constant, subject to (a) a set of linear equality constraints, equation (2.1–6); (b) a set of linear inequality constraints, equation (2.1–7); and (c) a set of bounds or "artificial constraints" on the allowable range of the decision variables, X, at the next step; i.e.,

$$x_j \leq \beta_j \qquad j = 1, \ldots, n - m^{34} \qquad (2.1\text{-}12)$$

$$x_j \geq \alpha_j \qquad j = 1, \ldots, n - m, \qquad (2.1\text{-}13)$$

where α and β are the lower and upper bounds respectively. Clearly, this modified problem may be solved as a linear programming subproblem (if there is a solution).

Artificial constraints are used in this particular gradient method as a way of specifying or constraining the distance, δ_2; i.e., the "optimal" distance (however defined) in the most feasible direction of travel. In general, there should be one upper and one lower bound on the decision variables for each degree of freedom of the problem; i.e., $n - m$. Any more artificial constraints than these would be redundant, as the n decision variables are not truly independent, but are related by the m equality constraints. The right-hand sides, α_j and β_j, of the artificial constraints will, in general, change for each iteration of the L.P. subproblem. They are recomputed for the $(k + 1)^{\text{th}}$ step from (a) the location of the kth step in the feasible region, $X^{(k)}$, and (b) the length of the step δ_2 (however selected). Specifically, the upper and lower bounds for the $(k + 1)^{\text{th}}$ iteration may be expressed as

[34] The quantity $(n - m)$ is equal to the degrees of freedom of the problem. In general, one pair of upper and lower bounds is required in the scheme for each degree of freedom. The number of artificial bounds may be further reduced by noting that for variables associated with constant first derivatives, the optimal solution will not be interior for these variables but on the boundary of the feasible region, R. However, this additional reduction of artificial bounds will, in general, preclude the use of the gradient as the direction of travel during the ascent procedure.

$$\alpha_j = x_j^{(k)} - |\delta_{2j}^{(k+1)}| \qquad (2.1\text{-}14)$$

$$\beta_j = x_j^{(k)} + |\delta_{2j}^{(k+1)}| \qquad (2.1\text{-}15)$$

where $|\delta_{2j}|$ is the absolute value of the component of the step length in the jth direction.

For most gradient procedures, the selection of the step length, δ_2, is based on the direction of travel. The main drawback of this approach is that the only direction of travel readily available to us is the gradient. The most feasible direction of travel, if other than the gradient, is not evaluated explicitly. In situations where solutions are apt to be on the boundary of the feasible region, R, defined by the constraint sets $AX \leq B$, and $X \geq 0$, or in situations where equality constraints are present, the most feasible direction will not, in fact, be the gradient. Because we do not determine explicitly the most feasible direction of travel at each step, we have only two choices available to us: (a) establish direction by setting our artificial bounds according to the gradient[35] or (b) step in an arbitrary direction of increase in the value of the objective function, for example, by preselecting a vector of constant step sizes which are reduced in magnitude by some predetermined fraction when in any one step (iteration) in the ascent scheme a reduction in the value of the objective function results.

If we decide to set our bounds according to the direction of the gradient, the step size, δ_2, may be computed from the following expression:

$$\delta_2^{(k+1)} = \lambda \nabla F[X^{(k)}] \qquad (2.1\text{-}16)$$

where λ is a scalar multiple of the gradient, the magnitude of which may be specified by any one of a variety of techniques presented in the literature.[36] The jth component of the step size may be expressed as

$$\delta_{2j}^{(k+1)} = \lambda \nabla F_j[X^{(k)}] \quad \text{for} \quad \delta_{2j}^{(k+1)} \geq \delta \min^{37} \qquad (2.1\text{-}17)$$

If we do not know a priori the most feasible direction of travel at a point, $X^{(k)}$, and if we do not use the gradient vector which is readily available to us, how do we choose a direction of travel and its associated step length? For these cases, other, perhaps less rational, approaches might be

---

[35] For interior points with no equality constraints, this computation enables us to step in the direction of the gradient or otherwise in the most feasible direction.

[36] See, for example, T. Saaty and J. Bram, *Nonlinear Mathematics* (New York: McGraw-Hill Book Company, 1964), pp. 72, 75, 76, 126.

[37] $\delta_{\min}$ is employed here to facilitate "climbing" to a constrained maximum. If $\delta_{\min}$ were allowed to equal zero (unless, of course, λ also equals zero) it is conceivable that under certain conditions the process would stop short of the constrained maximum, thereby registering an optimal solution having a smaller value of the objective function than the actual constrained maximum.

taken. For example, one might select an initial step size set based on the range of all possible values for each decision variable within the feasible region, R, defined by the constraint sets $AX \leq B$ and $X \geq 0$. Associated with this approach would be the added feature of incorporating scale directly.[38] Given the range[39] for each variable, $R_j, j = 1, \ldots, (n - m)$, the initial step size, $\delta_{2j}^{(1)}$, might be computed from the following expression:

$$\delta_{2j}^{(1)} = \frac{R_j}{D} \qquad j = 1, \ldots, (n - m); \qquad (2.1-18)$$

where D equals an arbitrary number greater than one and less than, say, ten. When, in any iteration, a reduction in the value of the nonlinear objective function results, the initial step size could be shortened; for example,

$$\delta_{2j}^{(2)} = \frac{\delta_{2j}^{(1)}}{D} \qquad j = 1, \ldots, (n - m), \qquad (2.1-19)$$

and the process continued from the point of the maximum value (thus far) in the objective function.

This process may be thought of as dividing the feasible region, R, into units of equal size and stepping from vertex to vertex until no better point can be found. At that point, the feasible region is subdivided again into even smaller units and the process is continued until no better point can be found, and so on.

It should be apparent by now that central to the efficiency of this method is the selection of an appropriate set of artificial bounds at each step in the ascent procedure. The main problem with the step size procedure suggested above is that all elements of the step size vector are reduced in the same proportion at the same time. A better procedure might be to reduce elements of this vector selectively, possibly using information about the dual values from the linear programming subproblem. In any case, this is an area where additional work might be warranted.

A Linearized Objective Function. How does our environmental quality management problem fit into this scheme? When we attempt to fit our revised objective function, equation (2.1–3) into the linearized form, equation (2.1–11), the following function obtains:

---

[38] Scale might also be incorporated by dividing the value of each variable by the range of feasible values; i.e.,

$$\bar{x}_j = \frac{x_j}{R_j} \qquad j = 1, \ldots, n.$$

[39] Values for the range could, in most cases, be obtained from knowledge of the various processes and activities involved.

$$F = \left(\frac{\partial B}{\partial q}\right) \cdot Q - \left(\frac{\partial C_p}{\partial q}\right) \cdot Q - \left(\frac{\partial C_{RT}}{\partial W}\right) \cdot W$$

$$- \left(\frac{\partial C_{ME}}{\partial S} + \frac{\partial DC}{\partial S}\right) \cdot S - \left(\frac{\partial DC}{\partial X}\right) \cdot X + \gamma \qquad (2.1\text{--}20)$$

where $\partial B/\partial q$ is a vector of prices on final products, $\partial C_p/\partial q$ is a vector of marginal opportunity costs of traditional production inputs, $\partial C_{RT}/\partial W$ is a vector of marginal costs for residuals treatment, $\partial C_{ME}/\partial S$ is a vector of marginal costs for modifying the environment, $\partial DC/\partial S$ is a vector of marginal benefits associated with modifying the environment, $\partial DC/\partial X$ is a vector of marginal damages associated with the discharge of residuals in the environment, and Q, W, S, and X are activity levels of final products, residuals treatment, environmental modifications, and residuals discharged to the environment respectively.

In our problem, through assumptions or transformations of the original variables or both, prices on final products, traditional production cost coefficients, and all the residuals treatment cost coefficients are considered constants. And for quite restrictive conditions pertaining to the environment, residuals in the environment, and damage functions (together with transformations of appropriate variables), we could, in fact, consider marginal damages as constants. If we then eliminate explicit consideration of modifications to the environment as decision variables, all the cost coefficients in equation (2.1–20) would be constants and thus we could solve this wholly as a large L.P. problem.

However, in order to maintain a completely linear system, we would have had to have made many assumptions and restrictions regarding the nature of the environment. We feel that some of these restrictions would severely limit the future usefulness of this model. Consequently, we have decided to retain some of the more interesting features of this model;[40] and thus the need for the more general nonlinear framework. The objective function that we will be using in most of our work—at least in the beginning—may be written in the following form:

$$F = p \cdot Q - c_p \cdot I - c_{RT} \cdot W - \left(\frac{\partial DC}{\partial X}\right) \cdot X + \gamma. \qquad (2.1\text{--}21)$$

where I = activity levels of traditional production inputs. When modifications to the environment are treated explicitly in our model, equation (2.1–21) expands to:

[40] For example, damages as functions of more than one residual, interactions of residuals in the environment, modifications to the environment, and environmental simulation studies cannot be included in the purely linear programming framework. Approximations can, in some cases, be made and then checked and/or adjusted but that puts the problem in the realm of nonlinear programming.

$$F = p \cdot Q - c_p \cdot I - c_{RT} \cdot W - \left(\frac{\partial C_{ME}}{\partial S} + \frac{\partial DC}{\partial S}\right) \cdot S$$

$$- \left(\frac{\partial DC}{\partial X}\right) \cdot X + \gamma. \qquad (2.1\text{--}22)$$

Given a linear constraint set for relating the decision variables, equations (2.1–21) and (2.1–22) may be solved, in steps, as a linear programming problem.

It should be apparent to the reader that these objective functions provide the rationale for dividing the model up, as we did, into three parts: (a) a linear industry model, (b) environmental models, and (c) damage functions. The latter two models are used jointly, but quite separately from the former; the link being the marginal damages and benefits, $\partial DC/\partial X$ and $\partial DC/\partial S$ respectively. For each iteration of the overall management model, the marginal damages, $\partial DC/\partial X$, are computed separately using the environmental and damage models and are returned as *shadow prices* on residuals discharged to the environment in the following iteration in the L.P. industry model. If modifications to the environment were treated explicitly, a similar computation would be made for evaluating marginal costs and benefits, $\partial C_{ME}/\partial S$ and $\partial DC/\partial S$, respectively. These values would also be returned to the L.P. model at each iteration. This iterative procedure is continued until a local optimum is found.[41] It should be apparent from the foregoing discussion that what we are actually doing in this iterative procedure is constructing a local tangent plane at a point to approximate the shape of the response surface in the vicinity of that point and moving to consecutively better positions along this surface.

An important advantage of dividing the problem up as we did is that from both administrative and personnel standpoints, the problem separates very nicely along the lines of the various disciplines involved; i.e., an industry economic model, water and air diffusion models (and later, we hope, models of ecosystems), and damage functions. Each portion of the model may be developed separately, tested separately, and need be joined together only for actual production runs. That is, the L.P. industry model may be operated alone for any price set desired on the discharge of residuals to the environment. Also, environmental models may be run separately for various levels of inputs of residuals from production and consumption activities in the region. This is certainly a desirable feature when initially developing the models and later when evaluating the reasonableness of various management alternatives.

[41] See footnote 30.

2.2. The Linear Programming Model of Production and Residual Transformation

The basic economic building block in our environmental quality management model is a part describing and permitting choice among available alternatives for the production of goods and the transformation of the resulting residuals.[42] In this section our goals for this part of the larger model are discussed and the actual framework adopted is described. We also indicate the modifications made to permit application of the iterative solution technique outlined above.

One fundamental aim in this part of our model, as we have pointed out, is the inclusion of significant nonmarket interconnections between forms of residuals. Thus, for example, a firm's decision to treat its organic discharges to a watercourse implies the generation of a sludge which must also be disposed of in some way. The decision to transport the sludge to a landfill site means that the original water-borne residuals problem has been at least partially transformed into a solid waste problem. Similarly, incineration of the sludge and disposal of the ash implies both new airborne residuals and a solid waste residual.

A second objective is the reflection of nontreatment alternatives in residuals management. Most important, our model is designed to include alternative production processes reflecting different input choices (e.g., coal of two different sulfur contents) and different amounts of recirculation of various residuals-bearing streams (e.g., once-through cooling or cooling tower recirculation). This, we hope, is another improvement on the conventional approach in the environmental quality literature, which has dealt very nearly exclusively with treatment alternatives (and occasionally with such collective alternatives as low-flow augmentation).[43] The consideration of process-change[44] alternatives frequently will allow given quality stand-

---

[42] We plan, in later expansions of this basic model, to include certain consumption activities directly. This may be most efficiently done by expanding the present production submodel, which matter is discussed further later in this section.

[43] See, however, the work of Robert E. Kohn for St. Louis; for example, "A Linear Programming Model for Air Pollution Control: A Pilot Study of the St. Louis Airshed," (paper presented at the 62nd Annual Meeting of the Air Pollution Control Association, New York, June 22–26, 1969). Kohn has gathered a considerable amount of data on "control" measures which, in our terminology, include both process changes and treatment. The range of alternatives is classified and discussed in A. V. Kneese and B. T. Bower, *Managing Water Quality: Economics, Technology, Institutions* (Baltimore: Johns Hopkins Press for Resources for the Future, 1968). For example, see table 1, p. 42. No application is made to a particular region.

[44] Includes raw material change, materials recovery, and by-product production. [Editor's note.]

ards to be attained more cheaply. The neglect of such alternatives will almost always result in the exaggeration of the expense of achieving a desired quality goal and hence may have undesirable political side effects.

Finally, we show how the demand functions necessary to our objective function, which is based on willingness to pay, may be included in the linear model. This is a straightforward application of piecewise-linear gross benefit functions (step demand functions). There is, however, a problem of the availability of the necessary information from which to construct the linearized versions of market demand functions. Since a number of wide-scale demand estimation studies have already been reported in the economics literature, and since necessary data are continually being generated at an enormous rate in this record-keeping economy, one can be fairly sanguine about the availability of *some* data in this area for virtually any product. It may, on the other hand, be necessary to settle for relations estimated for different sets of underlying conditions or, potentially more significant, from studies concentrating on demonstrating an econometric technique rather than providing useful results.

When, however, we think about explicitly including in the model the residuals from consumption activities, additional and more difficult problems arise because of the necessity of deciding on the appropriate degree of disaggregation over goods and consumers. A detailed discussion of these difficulties is beyond the scope of this paper, but we may suggest here the essence of the matter. In principle, we might wish to work with a completely disaggregated description of a region's demand patterns, for then the differences in costs associated with different types and quantities of consumption residuals generated at different locations in the region could be fully reflected in the solution. (The cost differences would include primarily those of collection, if the residual is collected by a system of pipes or trucks; if direct discharge by households were practiced, the differences in the patterns of external damages would clearly be of principal interest.) As a practical matter, of course, we could not begin to deal with a problem of that size and complexity, so we will have to aggregate to reduce the number of goods and the number of consumption locations. Consequently, we confine ourselves here to the discussion of techniques for inserting consumption residuals into the model at a given level of aggregation.

Description of the Linear Production Model Structure. We first describe the general form of the linear production (L.P.) model and then consider the specific version chosen for our initial didactic model. Let us begin by writing the familiar general form for a maximizing linear programming problem:

$$\max c'x$$
$$\text{subject to } Ax \leq b \qquad (2.2\text{--}1)$$
$$x \geq 0,$$

where c is a vector of "prices"; b, a vector of constraint levels; x, a vector of activity levels; and A, a matrix defining the relationships among the activity levels which form the constraints. Figure 4.3 summarizes our version of this model schematically; its features are described in greater detail below.[45]

Beginning with the A matrix, we note that it may be thought of as being divided into two basic sets of constraints (or rows): those on production of and demand for goods and on input availability; and those on the handling of residuals generated in production. Vertically, we may divide it into four major groups of activity vectors (columns): (a) production; (b) demand (and importation); (c) by-product extraction, raw material recovery, treatment, and transport of residuals; and (d) discharge of residuals. The x vector (activity levels) is divided into groups of activities corresponding to the vertical division of A. The b vector will contain zeroes wherever the constraints are in the form of continuity conditions; and nonzero entries for upper limits (for example, input availability) and lower limits (for example, minimum production requirements). The continuity conditions will be equalities; the limits, inequalities. The coefficients of the objective function are divided into groups of prices and costs corresponding to the x vector. An important point to note here is that we may attach effluent charges to each of the discharge activities, reflecting the marginal external damages attributable to that discharge. (See sections 2.1, 2.3, and 2.5 for discussion of the linkage making such a marginal damage attribution possible.)

The sign conventions chosen for the A matrix are that the production of a good and the *input* of a residual to a treatment process are both plus entries, while all standard inputs to production and all residuals generated in production (or in later transformation) are minus entries. In addition, the entries in the demand vectors are negative and those in the import activities positive. Given these conventions, the constraints may be characterized as follows:

Production/demand:
+ production + imports − demand must be equal to zero;[46]

[45] For a more complete discussion of this linear production model, see C. S. Russell, "Models for the Investigation of Industrial Response to Residuals Management Actions," *Swedish Journal of Economics* (April 1971).

[46] As we have pointed out, we actually use stepwise linear demand functions; this complicates the situation somewhat since a constraint is required to bound each segment.

Figure 4.3. Schematic of models of industrial production, residuals generation, treatment, and discharge.

Columns / Rows	Production alternatives $X_1...X_H$	Sale and import of products $Y_1...Y_N, M$	By-product extraction $B_1...B_J$	Raw material recovery $W_1...W_K$	Treatment and transport of residuals $T_1...T_L...V_1...V_M$	Discharges of residuals $D_1...D_G$	Right-hand side
Production and sale	$+\bar{e}_{X_1}...+\bar{e}_{X_H}$	$-\bar{e}_{V_1}...-\bar{e}_{V_N}$	$+\bar{b}_1...+\bar{b}_J$				≥ 0
Input availability	$-\bar{p}_{X_1}...-\bar{p}_{X_H}$			$+\bar{w}_1...+\bar{w}_K$			$\geq -\bar{P}$
Primary residuals[a]	$-\bar{r}_{X_1}...-\bar{r}_{X_H}$		$+\bar{e}_{B_1}...+\bar{e}_{B_J}$	$+\bar{e}_{W_1}...+\bar{e}_{W_K}$	$+\bar{e}_{T_1}...$ $+\bar{e}_{V_1}...$	$+\bar{e}_{D_1}...$	$= 0$
Secondary residuals[a]			$-\bar{r}_{B_1}...-\bar{r}_{B_J}$	$-\bar{r}_{W_1}...-\bar{r}_{W_K}$	$-\bar{r}_{T_1}...+\bar{e}_{T_L}...+\bar{e}_{V_M}...$ $-r_{V_1}$ $-r_{V_M}$ $-r_{T_L}$ Etc.	$+\bar{e}_{D_g}...+\bar{e}_{D_G}$	$= 0$ . . . $= 0$
Objective function	Costs of production	Prices of output	Costs of extraction	Costs of recovery	Costs of treatment and transport	Possible effluent charges	

Note: The $\bar{e}$ are column vectors of zeroes and ones. A particular vector $\bar{e}$ has the number of row elements corresponding to the constraint set in which it appears. The occurrence of ones is determined by the function of the column in which the vector appears. Thus, in e_{X_1}, a one appears in the row corresponding to the output of process X_1.

[a] For further discussion of the structure of these constraints, see the text.

Factor and raw material inputs:
- input implied by production must be greater than or equal to the negative of the availability;[47]

Residuals generation and handling:
- generation in production + amount taken into treatment processes + amount transported elsewhere + amount discharged must equal zero.

Secondary residuals—those generated in treatment and transport processes—will require additional constraints of this same general form, as we see below. This particular orientation of signs proved helpful in setting up the linear model initially, partly because it treats production as a positive entry and an input as a negative entry, the most widely familiar scheme. We emphasize that residuals generation is treated analogously to *inputs* to the production process.[48]

Since we have not yet introduced time explicitly into the model, the important characteristics of the residuals are type and location (e.g., BOD generated at plant *A*). Treatment processes act to change the chemical, physical, or biological form of the residuals while location of the residual is presumed to remain unchanged. Location is, however, changed and residual form held constant by transport activities, such as pipelines for water-borne wastes and trucks for fly ash precipitate. Ultimately, after any sequence of treatment and transport activities, the entire mass of material residuals and the original energy residual generated in production (plus any material or energy inputs to the treatment and transport processes) remain to be discharged into the natural environment.[49]

In general, then, the L.P. model is a fairly straightforward application of familiar interindustry analysis. Three features, however, deserve special comment. Two of these are built into the model: the techniques for dealing with residuals between initial generation and final discharge to the environment; and the artificial bounds placed on residuals discharge activities to

[47] In practice, one might wish to multiply through these rows by -1 to obtain $(+)$ input use $\leq (+)$ availability, with all b vector entries nonnegative.

[48] It is useful to think of residuals generation as an input, even though the material and energy flows are *out of* the process, because this points up the possibility of substituting other inputs for such generation. For example, in a thermal electric power plant, capital in the form of more efficient plant may be substituted not only for fresh heat input, but for waste heat production.

[49] It is, perhaps, worth reminding the reader that we are not concerned in this model with maintaining a *complete* energy and materials balance from raw material input to ultimate residual. While such a balance would be useful in forcing us to realize that at no stage in the production or transformation process does "extra" material or energy just conveniently appear or disappear, our choice to keep only partial account of our energy and material inputs is based on our own balancing of the marginal costs and benefits involved in completing these accounts.

142

facilitate the iterative solution method used on the overall model. The other feature could be built into the model but is not included in our present didactic version: the generation, treatment, and discharge of residuals related to final consumption.[50]

The treatment, transport, and discharge of residuals after their generation in production is based, first of all, on the row requirements that the total quantity of each residual generated at each location must be accounted for by some combination of these processes.[51] These row requirements (or continuity conditions) are of the form:

$$-r_{ix_h} \cdot X_h + T_l + V_m + D_g = 0 \qquad (2.2\text{--}2)$$
$$\text{(for all } i \text{ and for } h = 1, 2 \ldots, H)$$

(r_{ix_h} is the generation per unit of process operation.)[52] T_l is the amount of residual i shunted to treatment process l; V_m is the amount of residual i transported by transport process m; and D_g is the amount discharged by discharge activity g. In terms of the matrix and activity vector, we may write the same condition as:

$$
\text{Row } i \quad
\begin{bmatrix}
& & \cdots & & \\
\cdots -r_{ix_h} \cdots & \cdots +1 \cdots +1 \cdots +1 \\
& & \cdots &
\end{bmatrix}
\cdot
\begin{bmatrix}
\vdots \\ X_h \\ \vdots \\ T_l \\ \vdots \\ V_m \\ \vdots \\ D_g
\end{bmatrix}
=
\begin{bmatrix}
\vdots \\ 0 \\ \vdots
\end{bmatrix}
$$

$$(2.2\text{--}3)$$

[50] When we include management alternatives involving modification of the environment, the activity levels for these processes will be determined in the L.P. model using shadow prices discussed in section 2.5.

[51] By-product extraction and raw material recovery are conceptually similar to the processes we describe.

[52] It is important to recall that residuals are differentiated both by type of material or energy *and* by location. Thus, the generation of *BOD* at two different plants creates two *different* residuals.

There may, of course, be more than one process in each category which could apply to the residual i. (If one process applies to more than one residual, problems will be raised by the necessity for working with fixed proportions in generation and transformation.)

Conceptually, the discharge activities require no entries in any other rows (except in relation to the artificial bounds discussed below). The objective function entry for each discharge will, at every iterative stage after the first, be the marginal damages it causes, computed as described in section 2.5. However, the other two process types, transformation and transportation, result in changes in the form or location of residuals, and these changes must be accounted for in the model. This is done by introducing the necessary process outputs (as *negative* entries) in the process columns. Thus, the treatment process vector might appear as:

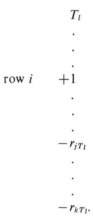

The entries, $-r_{jT_l}$, and $-r_{kT_l}$, indicate the quantities of residuals j and k respectively (again identified by type *and* location) generated when treatment process l is used to transform (treat) one unit of residual i. (We shall say for brevity that process l is "picking up" one unit of residual i.) If, then, in a particular solution process l is carried on at level T_l, the amount of the secondary residual, j, generated will be $T_l \cdot (r_{jT_l})$. In order to assure that all secondary residuals (all products of the transformation processes) are accounted for either by further treatment or transport, or by discharge to the environment, we put the same kind of continuity constraint on row j as that described for row i. With suitable substitution of the word "transport" for "treatment," these remarks apply without change to the set of processes that change only location and not type of residual.

The objective function entries for both kinds of processes represent the cost of "picking up" one unit of the particular residual that the process is designed to handle. Thus, for electrostatic precipitation of fly ash out of

144

stack gases, unit operation represents a ton of fly ash entering the precipitator. The secondary residuals generated are α percent of that ton in the
form of precipitate and $1 - \alpha$ percent in the form of particulates still in
the stack gas that continues through the precipitator. The objective function entry for the precipitator reflects the cost of building a precipitator
designed to remove α percent of the fly ash passing through it, expressed
per unit of entering fly ash.[53]

One additional capability of this system of including residuals generation and handling is worth noting. Certain transformation processes
typically occur in sequence, such as the primary-to-secondary-to-tertiary
treatment sequence for water-borne biodegradable residuals. Using the
above methods, it is a simple matter to reflect in the structure of the A
matrix a requirement that one process be used before another. This is
done by requiring that input to the second process come only from the
secondary residual "output" of the first process.

A second feature of the model we describe briefly is the set of bounds
added to control step size (the allowable movement between consecutive
solutions) in the iterative solution technique for the overall model. These
are upper and lower bounds on the levels of the discharge activities. In the
iteration procedure, the bounds are varied according to certain rules (discussed in section 2.1), the purpose being to confine the next solution to a
relatively small area of the feasible space at any one time. In general, the
area of confinement shrinks as the overall problem approaches a solution.
The general form of these constraints is:

$$D_{ij} \leq b_2 \qquad (2.2\text{--}4)$$
$$D_{ij} \geq b_1 \qquad \text{where } b_1 \geq 0,$$

where D_{ij} is the discharge of residual type i at location j.

If a single discharge activity exists for the particular residual and location, all that is required for the new constraints are the entries $+1$ in the
upper-limit and lower-limit constraint rows. Thus, for D_{ij} we have:

	Process j	D_{ij}	RHS	
Row i	$-r_{ij}$	$+1$	$= 0$	
Upper-limit row		$+1$	$\leq b_2$	(2.2--5)
Lower-limit row		$+1$	$\geq b_1.$	

[53] There is, of course, a problem here in trying to reflect both capital and operating
and maintenance costs of these processes. That is, scale effects will often make cost, in
principle, a function of level of activity, and with the function generally the wrong
"shape" for piecewise linear treatment. (When there are economies of scale, the segments would tend to "fill up" in the wrong order if special computational devices
were not employed.)

Where more than one activity represents the discharge of a single residual at a single point, the upper and lower limit rows contain $+1$'s for each of the separate activities, thus effectively summing the separate discharges. For example, assume that i, s, u, and v are all the same type of residual (as BOD from successive stages of a biological treatment plant). The discharges of these residuals are reasonably assumed to be occurring at the same *point*, the plant outfall. Hence, our limits may efficiently and correctly be placed on the total discharge. We would then have the following, extending the previous schematic of the relevant portion of the A matrix (the common residual type is called Z for notational clarity):

Row	D_i	D_s	D_u	D_v	Right-hand side	
i	$+1$				$= 0$	
s		$+1$			$= 0$	
u			$+1$		$= 0$	
v				$+1$	$= 0$	(2.2–6)
upper limit on Z	$+1$	$+1$	$+1$	$+1$	$\leq b_2$	
lower limit on Z	$+1$	$+1$	$+1$	$+1$	$\geq b_1$	

Finally, we consider another feature that up to now has not been introduced into our operating model: residuals generation in consumption activities; that is, by households.[54] Basically, two methods are open to us to accomplish this inclusion. In one, residuals generation is attached to the demand (or importation) activities in a manner analogous to that discussed above for production. This method has the conceptual advantage of linking generation of residuals by households directly to levels of consumption (hence, roughly, to material standards of living). Any attempt to apply it in practice, however, raises a number of difficult problems centering around the appropriate degree of aggregation over consumption goods and over households. Thus, for example, if we were considering domestic water-borne residuals, we would want to relate them to food consumption. But would we want to attempt to calculate the separate contribution to these residuals of consumption of each of ten groups, or 100 individual foodstuffs, or would we settle for a composite food-demand contribution factor? Similarly, how would we aggregate individual household demands (and hence residuals loads)? Over blocks, neighborhoods, or over entire cities?

[54] For simplicity, we confine our discussion to consumption activities. There is no difficulty in treating current government services in the same manner. However, investment activities raise a host of new problems that we prefer to avoid in this static model.

Clearly our answers to the above questions would reflect, among other things, the set of management alternatives assumed to be available. Thus, if prohibition of consumption of a particular good were feasible, or if differential charges on liquid wastes could be levied by neighborhood, we would wish to design the model so that these alternatives were compared fairly against others. Moving in this direction, of course, one very quickly comes up against the more fundamental question of the extent to which society is willing to interfere with consumer sovereignty to allow forced internalization of the costs implied by consumption residuals.

Assuming answers to these difficult questions, the technique of attaching domestic residuals generation to demand activities does allow interesting approaches to certain residuals management problems. Thus, for example, for those cases in which ⸻ production decisions govern the type and quantity ⸻ essary to include the appropriate production ⸻ production section of the model. Thus, for ex⸻ packaged in (at least) two alternative forms: ⸻ and (consumption) activities would then corr⸻ products. The residuals produced by the two c⸻ be identical except for the packaging material⸻ *consumption technology* may, in fact, offer cho⸻ ectors to be generated. For example, the residu⸻ sumption of transportation services from an a⸻ will vary depending on the attention given by the consumer to upkeep of muffler, fuel tank, piston rings, and any additional antipollution devices installed. This could also be reflected in alternative demand vectors producing different residuals and, presumably, characterized by different benefit entries in the objective function.

An alternative method of bringing in consumption residuals lacks both the conceptual appeal and the great practical difficulties attached to the demand-vector approach. In this second method, we simply assume generation coefficients per capita or per household, for example, for different subdivisions of the region under study and for the different residuals of interest. (Again, we must decide on the desired aggregation level.) Then the model is required to choose treatment, transport, and discharge activities such that the continuity conditions are satisfied and such that the sum of costs and external damage is minimized (where external damages attributable to discharges of domestic residuals will, of course, reflect the simultaneous existence of production residual discharges). In terms of the L.P. model, this method produces an essentially independent subproblem connected to the production side of the regional economy only through the damage functions relating to ambient concentrations, and hence to discharges through effluent charges, since marginal damages will depend

147

on the levels of production *and* consumption.[55] This assumption of constant domestic residuals generation is consistent with our partial equilibrium approach and will be more or less valid depending on the extent to which residuals management actions leave regional incomes unchanged; the greater any change in regional income implied by a management action, the more dangerous an assumption of fixed per capita generation.

2.3. *Ambient Concentrations of Residuals*

Environmental models—air and water dispersion, and models of ecosystems when available—may be used to describe the transport, transformation, and storage, throughout both space and time, of both energy and materials that have been disposed of in the environment as residuals from the production and consumption activities of man. For our purposes, we use these models to specify the steady state ambient concentrations of residuals at various points in space throughout the environment, given (a) a set of residuals discharge levels, and (b) a set of values for the environmental parameters; e.g., stream flow and velocity, water temperature, wind speed and direction, and atmospheric mixing depth.

Central to our methodology is our desire to relate marginal damages to types and sources of residuals. Consequently, for a particular residual, we need to be able to relate the quantity discharged from a production or consumption activity in the region to its contribution to the total ambient concentration at a given receptor location. In the most general case, we refer to this relationship as a *transfer function*. Under very special assumptions (deterministic, steady state models with noninteracting residuals), this transfer function degenerates to a constant and, thus, for our purposes here, will be referred to as a transfer coefficient.[56]

The numerical value of a transfer coefficient represents the change in ambient concentration of a given residual at a specified receptor location for a unit change in the rate of discharge of that residual from a single source in the region. The actual values of these coefficients are specified though the use of environmental dispersion models—atmospheric and stream—given a set of values for the appropriate environmental parameters: hydrological, meteorological, physical, biological, chemical, and

[55] The final discharges of consumption residuals will, of course, be subject to effluent charges reflecting marginal damages in the demand-vector approach as well.

The mutual dependence postulated here depends on the assumption the marginal damages are not constant over the range of ambient residuals concentrations.

[56] However, as will be seen later, these coefficients may in fact be functions of other decision variables that we may wish to consider explicitly; specifically, (a) modifications to the environment, e.g., low-flow augmentation, and (b) the presence of other residuals; e.g., heat and its effect on the BOD–DO relationship in a river.

148

so on. A good example for demonstrating how one would actually evaluate these coefficients is the relationship between the dissolved oxygen (DO) and biochemical oxygen demand (BOD) in streams.

In 1925 Streeter and Phelps[57] presented one of the earliest models developed specifically for the purpose of predicting water quality—DO-BOD relationship in streams. Their original formulation included a mechanism for carbonaceous oxidation—i.e., first stage BOD—only. They did not include effects of nitrogeneous oxidation (second stage BOD) on dissolved oxygen; production of oxygen through photosynthetic activity, as with algae; reduction of oxygen through plant respiration; and the effects of runoff, scour, sedimentation, and so on. Others[58] have subsequently added some of these refinements in their particular formulations of the dissolved oxygen relationship in streams. However, for illustrating the method of developing transfer coefficients, we lose no generality by using the classical Streeter-Phelps oxygen "sag" equation.

The dissolved oxygen level, DO, in a stream may be expressed as the difference between the DO saturation value and the dissolved oxygen deficit, DOD. That is,

$$DO = DO_{sat} - DOD. \qquad (2.3-1)$$

The dissolved oxygen saturation level, DO_{sat}, is a function of both temperature and "impurities"; e.g., the concentration of chlorides. The relationship between the dissolved oxygen deficit, DOD, at a point along the river and the BOD discharged at some upstream point may be expressed as[59]

$$DOD = \frac{K_1 L}{K_2 - K_1} [e^{-K_1 t} - e^{-K_2 t}] \qquad (2.3-2)$$

where

DOD = the dissolved oxygen deficit (DOD) at time, t, mg/L;

K_1 = BOD rate constant, days^{-1};

K_2 = the rate of reoxygenation of the body of water, days^{-1};

L = ultimate first-stage BOD concentration (i.e., carbonaceous demand) at point of discharge, mg/L;

t = time of travel from point of discharge, days.

[57] H. W. Streeter and E. B. Phelps, *A Study of the Pollution and Natural Purification of the Ohio River*, Public Health Bulletin No. 146 (Washington, D.C.: U.S. Public Health Service, 1925).

[58] See, for example, T. R. Camp, *Water and Its Impurities* (New York: Reinhold Publishing Co., 1963); and W. E. Dobbins, "BOD and Oxygen Relationships in Streams," *Journal of the Sanitary Engineering Division, Proceedings, ASCE* 90, no. SA3 (June 1964): 53–79. For an excellent summary of the DO relationship in streams, see also Donald J. O'Connor, "The Temporal and Spatial Distribution of Dissolved Oxygen in Streams," *Water Resources Research* 3, no. 1 (1967): 65–79.

[59] This expression does not include a term for the initial dissolved oxygen deficit. Here it is assumed to be equal to zero.

For a single source, the ultimate first-stage BOD, L, may be expressed as a function of the BOD discharge, XBOD (pounds per day), and the river flow, Q (pounds per day).

$$L = \left[\frac{XBOD}{Q}\right] \times 10^6 \qquad mg/L \qquad (2.3\text{–}3)$$

Substituting this expression into equation (2.3–2) and rearranging terms yields

$$DOD = a \cdot XBOD, \qquad (2.3\text{–}4)$$

where

$$a = \left[\frac{K_1}{K_2 - K_1}\right] \cdot \left[\frac{10^6}{Q}\right] \cdot [e^{-K_1 t} - e^{-K_2 t}]. \qquad (2.3\text{–}5)$$

The transfer coefficient for the dissolved oxygen deficit is expressed as a in equations (2.3–4) and (2.3–5). It is a function of the following parameters: K_1, K_2, Q, and t. Given the velocity of the river (together with values for the parameters K_1, K_2, and Q), this transfer coefficient may be evaluated for any discharge-receptor couple through the time parameter, t (where $t = $ distance/velocity).

Having this background regarding the development of appropriate expression for the transfer coefficients, we will now proceed with a general discussion of the evaluation of total ambient concentrations.

Under the simplifying assumptions we have made regarding the rates of discharge of residuals in the region, the hydrologic and meteorologic parameters, and the behavior of residuals in the environment, the ambient concentration of the kth residual at any point in the region as a result of the discharge from *one* source in the region may be expressed as:

$$R^{(k)} = a^{(k)} X^{(k)}, \qquad (2.3\text{–}6)$$

where

$R^{(k)}$ = ambient concentration of the kth residual;
$a^{(k)}$ = transfer coefficient for the kth residual;
$X^{(k)}$ = rate of discharge of the kth residual.

Given the distance between source and receptor, values for environmental parameters, and so on, the transfer coefficient, a, may be evaluated by using the appropriate environmental dispersion model. For a number of sources discharging the same residual, the ambient concentration of this residual at a given receptor location along the stream may be determined by summing up the contributions from all sources. Expressed mathematically,[60]

$$R = a_1 x_1 + a_2 x_2 + \ldots + a_n x_n, \qquad (2.3\text{–}7)$$

[60] This expression is for the kth residual even though we have neglected the superscripts here.

where the subscript represents the source. Here, each transfer coefficient, a_i, $i = 1, \ldots, n$ must be evaluated separately using the appropriate values of the parameters in the dispersion models. As one might expect, the spatial relationship of source and receptor plays a very important role in both the absolute and relative values of the transfer coefficients, a_i, $i = 1, \ldots, n$.

In the most general case, we will want to relate many receptor locations with all (or nearly all) sources in the region. This relationship may be expressed conveniently in matrix notation as

$$R = A \cdot X, \tag{2.3-8}$$

where R is a vector consisting of elements, R_i, $i = 1, \ldots, m$; A is a matrix of transfer coefficients containing the elements, a_{ij}, $i = 1, \ldots, m$, $j = 1, \ldots, n$, relating the ambient concentration at receptor location i to a unit discharge of a residual from source j; and X is a vector of residual discharge levels with elements, x_j, $j = 1, \ldots, n$.

For computational purposes, we consider a finite number of receptor locations. The river, for example, is subdivided into reaches with a single concentration representing average conditions in a given reach. We do the same for gaseous atmospheric residuals in that the region of interest is subdivided into grid squares. Residual sources may either be aggregated over a unit area—reach or grid square—or considered as individual sources depending upon the situation.

Given our first-phase assumptions, the transfer coefficients relating sources and receptors may be considered as constants. If, however, we wish to treat explicitly either low-flow augmentation or interactions among residuals in the environment, these coefficients become functions of other decision variables. This may be shown by referring to the expression for the DOD transfer coefficient, equation (2.3–5). This particular transfer coefficient is a function of river flow, Q, through its effect on dilution, river velocity (therefore travel time, t), and the parameter K_2; as well as of temperature through its effect on the parameters K_1, K_2, and L. Under these conditions, this coefficient is not truly constant (in our analysis) but a function of one or more of the other decision variables; specifically, effects of low-flow augmentation and heat discharges on the BOD-DO relationship in streams.

2.4. *Damage Functions*

In an ideal version of our management model there would be a set of functions relating damages per unit time to the ambient concentrations of residuals in the environment.[61] However, before showing formally how these relations would fit into our framework, it is worth stressing that we are, in fact, operating in a world in which very little is known about any actual damage functions. Indeed, it seems fair to characterize this section of the management problem as an enormous set of research needs.

We do have some knowledge of both water-based recreation benefits and water supply treatment costs in relation to raw water quality.[62] But virtually nothing has been done for air, water, or land "quality" in the area of aesthetics. And, more broadly, the damages associated with air pollution are still not fully understood in a qualitative sense, at least with respect to human health, let alone measured quantitatively.[63] Studies on air-pollution damage have generally relied on aggregated indices of presumed damages such as those thought to be provided by property value differentials.[64]

Of course, each of the activities for which damage functions might be estimated presents its own difficulties, both practical and conceptual, and a discussion of all of these problems is not within the scope of this paper. We might, however, suggest very briefly that all the activities share certain common problems related to the stance taken and assumptions made in establishing a management framework for a region. In particular, once we have delineated a region, our choice of objective function scope is still

[61] If ecological models are available and are used to predict species' populations, damage functions based on these populations as arguments would also be part of the complete model.

[62] A basic reference in the recreation area is M. Clawson and J. Knetsch, *Economics of Outdoor Recreation* (Baltimore: Johns Hopkins Press for Resources for the Future, 1966). See also P. Davidson, F. G. Adams, J. Seneca, "The Social Value of Water Recreational Facilities Resulting from an Improvement in Water Quality: The Delaware Estuary," in *Water Research*, ed. A. V. Kneese and S. C. Smith (Baltimore: Johns Hopkins Press for Resources for the Future, 1966); and J. B. Stevens, "Recreation Benefits from Water Pollution Control," *Water Resources Research*, 2, no. 2 (1966): 167–82. On water supply damages, see R. Frankel, "Water Quality Management: Engineering-Economic Factors in Municipal Waste Disposal," *Water Resources Research* 1, no. 2 (1965): 173–86; L. Koenig, "The Cost of Water Treatment," *Journal of the American Water Works Association* 59, no. 3 (March 1967): 290–336; R. Parlante, "A Guide to Treatment Costs," *Industrial Water Engineering* 5 (April 1963): 32–35; and W. L. Patterson and R. F. Banker, "Effects of Highly Mineralized Water on Household Plumbing and Appliances," *Journal of the American Water Works Association* 60, no. 9 (September 1968): 1060–69.

[63] See, for example, the interesting statistical results and biochemical hypotheses proposed by R. J. Hickey, "Ecological Statistical Studies Concerning Environmental Pollution and Chronic Disease," presented at a symposium of the Institute of Electrical and Electronic Engineers in April 1970. Also R. J. Hickey and E. H. Harner, "Ecology, Ethology and Genetic Polymorphism (University of Pennsylvania, Institute for Environmental Studies, 1969).

[64] For example, see R. G. Ridker, *Economic Costs of Air Pollution* (New York: Praeger, 1967).

open and has important implications for our damage measurements. For example, management objectives based on a national, state, or more local point of view are all possibilities. This choice provides the basis for deciding who and what to count, for example, in valuing the damages to water-based recreation resulting from the presence of certain residuals concentrations in the chosen section of river. Thus, from a national point of view we would count directly the personal welfare losses we attribute to both residents and nonresidents of the region, while for regional accounting we would include for nonresidents only the lost benefits *to the regional population* from reduced tourism. A related question arises in connection with our assumption about factor mobility (factor opportunity cost), since certain costs of high residuals concentrations will appear as expenditures for substitute services or facilities. The real social cost of these substitutes will depend on our assumption about the extent of factor unemployment. For example, if swimming pools are provided in place of natural swimming areas, the social cost of this action depends on whether or not the labor and capital involved in constructing pools would otherwise be unemployed.[65]

But in order to understand the model and its potential application with whatever damage functions are available, it will be worthwhile to discuss more fully the nature of the damage functions associated with a particular receptor location.

Consider, for example, a particular receptor location i. At any stage in the iterative solution process, identified with that location will be a vector of ambient residuals concentrations, $\{R_i^{(k)}\}$. Also identified with that location will be a set of human activities some of which will be affected by one or more of the K elements of $\{R_i^{(k)}\}$. For example, if location i were a suburban housing development, some of the important activities identified with it could be characterized as household cleaning, housing maintenance, landscaping and gardening, and more broadly, human existence, all of which are affected by atmospheric pollution. One can imagine measuring each of these effects, in terms of dollars, as the increased cost of carrying on an activity at a desired level for increasing concentrations of each residual. Thus, in our example, the damages associated with housing maintenance and SO_2 concentration would be the increased cost of paint, labor, etc. necessary to keep houses at i at some more or less well-defined state of repair and appearance when atmospheric moisture and sulfur dioxide were creating a kind of perpetual acid bath. Similarly, particulate

[65] For a fuller discussion of these points, though in a slightly different context, see C. S. Russell, D. G. Arey, and R. W. Kates, *Drought and Water Supply: The Implications of the Massachusetts Experience for Municipal Planning* (Baltimore: Johns Hopkins Press for Resources for the Future, 1970).

fallout increases the costs of housecleaning, and concentrations of such gases as nitrogen dioxide and hydrogen fluoride cause damage to trees and plants.

Some of the activities going on at our hypothetical suburban location are difficult to subsume under any name except a vague and all-inclusive one such as "life processes." That is, the individual people at this location are necessarily eating, drinking, breathing, smelling, seeing, and hearing. Residuals concentrations can impinge directly on these fundamental activities, as when a local stream is so grossly polluted as to be anaerobic or full of ugly floating solids, or when a nearby highway or airport creates noise pollution. The damages associated with these direct effects are probably among the most difficult to quantify since there is virtually no point at which receptors bring their own judgments about the severity of conditions up against the measuring rod of money. Indeed, one of the few possibilities for exploring these damages does seem to be through multivariate statistical analysis of masses of data on housing values under the assumption that, ceterus paribus, consumers will pay more for a home or apartment in an aesthetically pleasing setting.

Somewhat less direct, but perhaps even more important, are the health effects associated with breathing the air or drinking the `·ater at the receptor location.[66] These effects may be acute, as in the notorious inversion episodes in which concentrations of atmospheric residuals build up to very high levels over relatively short times; or they may be chronic, due to prolonged exposure to low concentrations (particularly, it seems, of SO_2 and NO_2) causing, it is hypothesized, an accumulation of genetic changes leading essentially to more rapid aging.[67] In either case, the measurement difficulties are great, first in establishing the physical relation between concentration of a residual and increased mortality or morbidity, and second, in estimating the social cost of these health effects.[68]

But let us assume for the moment that we have a set of relations between damages and residuals concentrations for, say, stream DO, suspended solids, and chlorides; atmospheric SO_2, NO_2, and particulates; and for land pollution caused by accumulations of solid wastes. We shall denote the concentration of the kth residual at location i as $R_i^{(k)}$. The next step for our purposes would be to sum up, for each residual, the damages attributable to that residual for all concentrations over some range 0 to $\bar{R}_i^{(k)}$. (That is, we would add vertically the individual activity damage functions associated with a particular residual.) This would give us a set of composite

---

[66] See Hickey and Harner, "Ecology, Ethology and Genetic Polymorphism"; and Hickey, "Ecological Statistical Studies."

[67] Ibid.

[68] Also important is the period of exposure to any particular concentration.

damage functions, one for each residual, for the individual location. Let us write such a composite relation as:

$$DM_i^{(k)} = f(R^{(k)}),\qquad (2.4\text{-}1)$$

where the notation is the same as that explained above. If such composite functions are available for each of the M locations in the region, the total regional damages attributable to the kth residual are:

$$D_T^{(k)} = \sum_{i=1}^{M} DM_i^{(k)}.\qquad (2.4\text{-}2)$$

The total regional damages from all K residuals are given by:

$$D_T = \sum_{k=1}^{K} D_T^{(k)}.\qquad (2.4\text{-}3)$$

Before we consider the manipulation of these damage functions, in combination with our environmental models, in order to obtain marginal damages attributable to specific discharges, we should add one other note about the nature of the functions themselves. For many activities, as residuals concentrations increase, actions may be taken to protect the receptors, to screen out the effects of these rising concentrations. Such actions have been referred to previously as "final protective measures"; examples are intake treatment of municipal water supply, air conditioning of homes and offices (to remove dirt and pollen, as well as to cool), and the erection of barriers between homes and unsightly landfill areas. We assume that our damage functions include, in fact, the sum of the costs of the final protective measures taken and the damages suffered in spite of those measures. To be more specific, we assume that each of our individual damage functions is the loci of minima of the sum of costs of appropriate final protective measures plus remaining damages.[69] Such a function may be thought of as being constructed as follows. First, consider a function relating costs of final protective measures plus remaining damages to the ultimate residual concentration *actually experienced* by the consumer. In general, the damages will be an increasing function of this concentration, while for any particular ambient concentration the costs of final protective measures will decrease with increased ultimate concentrations at the final

[69] Subject to the qualification raised in footnote 71, this minimization procedure can be assumed to be performed independently of the complete management model if we can assume that the final protective measures are linked to the receptors directly and not by the intermediate physical world as modeled in our diffusion models. In other words, we must be able to assume that the minimization does not involve any of the constraints of the larger model.

receptor.[70] For another, higher ambient concentration, the final protective measures' cost curve shifts up to the right while the final damage function is, of course, unchanged. Then, for each ambient concentration, there will be some minimum level of protection costs plus remaining damages (due to the associated "delivered" residuals concentrations). As the ambient residual concentration increases (quality decreases) this minimum of damage plus cost will increase. The resulting function, relating final damages plus final protective measure costs to ambient concentrations, is the function presented as equation (2.4–1).[71]

With these definitions and caveats in mind, we will return to the formal methods involved in manipulating damage functions and dispersion models in order to obtain marginal damages attributable to particular discharges.

2.5. Marginal Costs and Damages

One of the requirements of our approach to regional environmental quality management is that certain marginal costs and damages be recomputed at each iteration and returned to the L.P. model as prices on associated activities. For our first phase model, marginal damages associated with the discharge of residuals in the environment are used as "shadow prices" on the discharge of these residuals. In a future model, we hope to include two management alternatives for modifying the environment: (a) in-stream aeration, and (b) low-flow augmentation. For these alternatives, marginal costs and benefits of modifying the environment will also be computed at each iteration and their respective algebraic sums used as prices on the outputs of the aerators and low-flow augmentation scheme.

Marginal Damages. When explicit analytical expressions are available for relating (a) ambient concentrations to the discharge of residuals, and (b) damages to ambient concentrations, expressions for the marginal damages are derived by taking the appropriate partial derivatives of the total damage function. If enough simplifying assumptions are made, the desired analytical functions can usually be provided. However, there are

---

[70] The damage function facing the final consumer may not be a strictly increasing function of ambient concentration, but may fall over some range as the ambient concentration is increased. This is true, for example, for total dissolved solids in water supply where minimum damages correspond to a level of about 75–100 ppm.

[71] There are problems with this damage plus cost of final protective measures approach, since in general the activities considered as receptors in this section of the model may also be present as producers or consumers in the L.P. model. The actions of such activities with respect to, say, higher water-treatment costs may be to substitute other inputs for water withdrawals. But our model does not now include this kind of feedback in response to changing ambient concentrations.

some cases in which continuous analytical expressions are just not available. For some of these situations, simulation models for relating inputs to, and outputs from, the environment may be all we have to work with.

In the latter case, the necessary marginal damages may be evaluated numerically. For example, for the kth residual discharged, the environmental-damage models would be solved twice; the first time for the discharge vector $[x_1^{(k)}, x_2^{(k)}, \ldots, x_n^{(k)}]$, and the second time for a discharge vector with a small change in the quantity of one of the residuals discharged; i.e., $[x_1^{(k)}, x_2^{(k)} + \Delta x_2^{(k)}, \ldots, x_n^{(k)}]$. The difference between the total damages for two vectors above, $D_T[x_1^{(k)}, x_2^{(k)}, \ldots, x_n^{(k)}] - D_T[x_1^{(k)}, x_2^{(k)} + \Delta x_2^{(k)}, \ldots, x_n^{(k)}]$, divided by the difference in the quantity discharged, $\Delta x_2^{(k)}$ provides us with a measure of the marginal damages for the $x_2^{(k)}$ discharge source. As one might imagine, this approach involves very many computations and, consequently, almost certainly would prove quite costly. However, the discussion is included here to indicate to the reader that there are other ways of making the necessary computations of marginal damages when the more involved environmental simulation models are employed.

The remainder of this section will be confined to the formulation of marginal damages for the case where analytical functions are available.

An expression for the ambient concentrations of residuals at the various receptor locations was presented in section 2.3 as

$$R_i = \sum_{j=1}^{n} a_{ij} x_j \qquad i = 1, \ldots, m$$

or, in matrix notation

$$R = A \cdot X. \tag{2.3-8}$$

Total regional damages attributable to ambient concentrations of the kth residual were expressed in section 2.4 as

$$D_T^{(k)} = \sum_{i=1}^{m} DM_i^{(k)}, \tag{2.4-2}$$

where the term $DM_i^{(k)}$ represents the total damages at receptor location i associated with the ambient concentration of the kth residual. This relationship was expressed in section 2.4 as

$$DM^{(k)} = f(R_i^{(k)}). \tag{2.4-1}$$

For the remainder of this discussion on marginal damages, we will be dealing with only one residual. Hence, we omit the superscript (k) and equation (2.4-1) becomes

$$DM_i = f(R_i) \qquad i = 1, \ldots, m. \tag{2.5-1}$$

The marginal damages that we are concerned with in our model may be expressed as the partial derivatives of total damages, D_T, with respect to *each* of the residuals discharged; i.e.,

$$\frac{\partial D_T}{\partial x_1}, \frac{\partial D_T}{\partial x_2}, \dots, \frac{\partial D_T}{\partial x_j}, \dots, \frac{\partial D_T}{\partial x_n}.$$

Utilizing the expressions of equations (2.4–2), (2.3–8), and (2.5–1), and the definition of marginal damages expressed above, the following expressions obtain:

$$\frac{\partial D_T}{\partial x_j} = \sum_{i=1}^{m} \frac{dDM_i}{dR_i} \cdot \frac{\partial R_i}{\partial x_j} \qquad j = 1, \dots, n. \qquad (2.5\text{–}2)$$

From equation (2.3–8) we note that

$$\frac{\partial R_i}{\partial x_j} = a_{ij}, \qquad (2.5\text{–}3)$$

so that equation (2.5–2) may be rewritten as

$$\frac{\partial D_T}{\partial x_j} = \sum_{i=1}^{m} a_{ij} \cdot \frac{dDM_i}{dR_i} \qquad j = 1, \dots, n. \qquad (2.5\text{–}4)$$

This formulation for *marginal damages* may be written in the more general matrix notation as

$$\left(\frac{\partial D_T}{\partial X}\right) = A^T \cdot \left(\frac{dDM}{dR}\right). \qquad (2.5\text{–}5)$$

Equation (2.5–5) yields the vector of marginal damages that is returned, each iteration, to the industry model as shadow prices on the discharge of residuals to the environment.

Before we leave this section, it might be interesting to take a closer look at the formulation of marginal damages expressed as equations (2.5–4) and (2.5–5). Note that this expression is made up of two components: (a) transfer coefficients, a_{ij}; and (b) first derivatives—i.e., slopes—of the damage functions, dDM_i/dR_i. The values of the shadow prices that we use in the industry model, thus, vary according to the magnitudes of these two components. What factors, then, are involved in establishing the proper shadow prices? Clearly, for the simplified assumptions on which we base our model, marginal damages are functions of both the physical relationship between emitter and receptor, expressed through the transfer coefficients, a_{ij}, and the discharges of all the other emitters in the region, expressed through the slope of the damage function, dDM_i/dR_i, evaluated at the ambient concentration, $R_i = f(x_1, x_2, \dots, x_n)$. Thus, we see clearly from the above that: (a) in general, for the same quantities of residuals discharged per emitter, the marginal damages can be expected to increase in the future as the number of emitters and/or receptors increase in the region; and (b) for the same quantities of residuals discharged per emitter, the marginal damages may be changed through various location policies, such as zoning, affecting either or both dischargers and receptors.

Marginal Costs and Benefits of Modifying the Environment. A further requirement of our approach, when we include modifications to the environment explicitly as decision variables in our analysis, is the evaluation of their marginal costs and benefits. Here, we discuss briefly two such alternatives: (a) artificial reaeration of the river, and (b) a low-flow augmentation scheme consisting of one dam and reservoir.

In-stream Aeration.[72] Artificial aeration with air or oxygen is an alternative to reducing discharge for the purpose of maintaining the dissolved oxygen level of a body of water. The marginal costs of providing in-stream aeration varies directly with the river flow and the marginal cost of increasing the power output of the aerator, but inversely with the efficiency of the aerator and the "driving force"; i.e., the difference between the DO saturation level and the DO concentration at the aerator. But if we provide in-stream aeration, what are the marginal downstream costs and benefits associated with increasing the DO level of the stream? Increasing the DO level of the river results both in changes in DO-related damages to all downstream receptors and in increased marginal costs of providing downstream aeration units because the driving force is decreased.

In summary then, the marginal costs and benefits associated with the output of an aerator at location i may be expressed as the algebraic sum of: (a) marginal costs of providing that aerator; (b) marginal costs associated with the operation of all other downstream aerators; and (c) marginal benefits to all downstream receptors. This is the quantity that is returned to the linear model as a price on the output (measured in terms of the increased DO level at the aerator) of the aerator at location i.

---

[72] For a detailed analysis of the costs and technical aspects of in-stream aeration, see William Whipple, Jr., et al., *Instream Aeration of Polluted Rivers* (Water Resources Research Institute at Rutgers University, 1969). For a study of the economic trade-offs between artificial aeration and wastewater treatment facilities, see Leonard Ortolano, "Artificial Aeration and the Capacity Expansion of Wastewater Treatment Facilities," (Ph.D. diss., Harvard University, June 1969). For additional discussions of in-stream aeration see also E. J. Cleary, "The Re-aeration of Rivers," *Industrial Water Engineering* 3, no. 6 (June 1966): 16–21; and B. T. Bower, "The Economics of Water Quality Management" (Paper delivered at the International Scientific Symposium on Computers and Water Resources Management, Montpellier, France, May 27–29, 1970), pp. 27–31.

Low-Flow Augmentation.[73] Low-flow augmentation may be employed to improve the quality of a river during certain critical low-flow periods. In terms of water quality, the advantage of low-flow augmentation is that it provides dilution for all residuals in the river, not just for the organic material.

The costs[74] of providing low-flow augmentation include the costs of (a) acquiring the necessary land; (b) clearing the land; (c) construction of the dam; (d) construction of appurtenant structures, such as access roads; and (e) operation and maintenance. Costs of a dam and reservoir scheme, C_{LF}, increase with the volume of water, V, stored in the impoundment; i.e.,

$$C_{LF} = f(V). \tag{2.5-6}$$

The volume of the reservoir, V, required to meet a desired level of low flow, Q (with a given degree of confidence), may be expressed as

$$V = f(Q). \tag{2.5-7}$$

If both these functions—i.e., equations (2.5–6) and (2.5–7)—are known, the following expression may be used to evaluate the marginal costs of low-flow augmentation:

$$\frac{dC_{LF}}{dQ} = \frac{dC_{LF}}{dV} \cdot \frac{dV}{dQ} \tag{2.5-8}$$

But what kinds of downstream costs and benefits accrue to low-flow augmentation? From our previous discussion of transfer coefficients of a BOD–DO system, we know that increasing the flow reduces the dissolved oxygen deficit, and thus increases the DO level of the stream. We also know from the previous discussion of artificial aeration that an increased flow, Q, increases the marginal costs of raising the DO level of the water at the aerator.

In summary, the marginal costs and damages associated with a low-flow augmentation scheme may be expressed as the algebraic sum of: (a) marginal costs of the dam and reservoir; (b) marginal costs to all downstream aerators; and (c) marginal benefits to all downstream receptors. This quantity is returned to the linear model as a price on the activity level of the low-flow augmentation scheme.

[73] For a study of the economic trade-offs between low-flow augmentation and wastewater treatment facilities, see D. P. Loucks and H. D. Jacoby, "Flow Regulation for Water Quality Management," in "Models for Managing Regional Water Quality," ed. R. Dorfman, H. Jacoby, and H. A. Thomas, Jr. (Harvard University Press, forthcoming).

[74] We assume here that this is a single-purpose structure and, consequently, use for low-flow augmentation must bear the entire costs of construction, operation, and maintenance. Water for low-flow augmentation can also be obtained from ground water, an alternative currently under consideration by the Miami Conservancy District. See B. T. Bower, "The Economics of Water Quality Management."

III. DIDACTIC VERSION OF MANAGEMENT MODEL

In order to test our proposed quantitative procedure for specifying an optimal management plan, we assume the hypothetical region shown in figure 4.4. This region consists of a single river and two urban areas: city A, an industrial area; and city B, primarily a residential area. For demonstration purposes, we have chosen economic activities that interest us—i.e., those that involve some trade-offs among quantities and forms of residuals and for which data on production processes and residuals generated are readily available. Thus, initially, we include within our analysis two economic activities: (a) a beet sugar processing plant capable of processing 2,700 tons of beets per day;[75] and (b) a 400 MW thermal power generating facility.[76]

The basic assumption is that the plants themselves are in place and hence fixed in basic design, but that certain modifications and additions are possible. Thus, for example, the thermal efficiency of the power plant is fixed, as is its capacity (400 MW), but electrostatic precipitators or wet scrubbers may be installed for stack-gas treatment, and water cooling towers may be added to recirculate the condenser cooling water. The options indicated here are, then, those of an intermediate run (i.e., intermediate planning horizon). However, in an actual planning context, both shorter and longer runs would also be relevant. That is, we shall in general be faced with decisions about grass-roots design of production facilities as well as about operation of existing plants over a time span within which no modifications are feasible.

Within our intermediate time-span assumptions, we consider as manageagement options various alternative combinations of raw materials, production processes, and treatment activities for both the thermal power generating facility and the beet sugar processing plant.

Thermal Power Generating Facility

The thermal power plant production alternatives are based on combinations of the following elements: inputs of raw or prepared coal;[77] once-through or recirculated cooling water; no treatment or limestone injection plus wet scrubbing of the flue gas to remove sulfur dioxide; and various degrees of fly ash removal by electrostatic precipitation.

[75] See G. O. G. Löf and A. V. Kneese, *The Economics of Water Utilization in the Beet Sugar Industry* (Washington, D.C.: Resources for the Future, 1968).
[76] See P. H. Cootner and G. O. G. Löf, *Water Demand for Steam Electric Generation: An Economic Projection Model* (Washington, D.C.: Resources for the Future, 1966).
[77] Prepared coal has been subject to processes that lower its ash and sulfur content and raise the available BTU/ton.

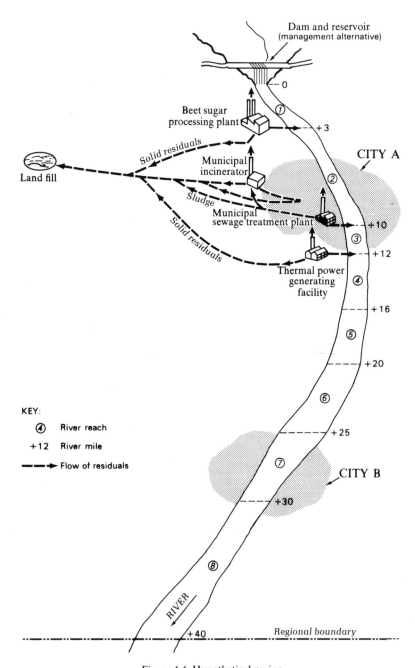

Figure 4.4. Hypothetical region.

The primary residuals from this process accounted for in our model are heat, sulfur dioxide, fly ash, and bottom ash. Waste heat emissions to the watercourse may be eliminated by the installation of a cooling tower. Sulfur dioxide discharges to the atmosphere may be reduced by opting for prepared coal or by employing limestone injection and wet scrubbing.[78] (This latter addition to the production process generates a wet slurry which may either be discharged to the stream, adding a load of suspended solids, or released to settling ponds, thereby reducing the ultimate suspended solids load to the stream, but producing a solid waste which must be trucked to a landfill site.) The fly ash (particulates) in the stack gas may be partially removed by electrostatic precipitation. The degree of removal may be 90, 95, or 98 per cent, and the precipitated ash is considered, along with the furnace or bottom ash, as a solid residual from the plant. This solid residual may be removed from the plant by either of two transportation alternatives, one of which represents a longer haul (presumably to a more remote landfill site) than the other.[79]

Beet Sugar Processing Plant

For the beet sugar plant, the alternative processes are differentiated by the extent of water recirculation and type of coal burned. There are four water-use alternatives: "typical use" as described by Löf and Kneese;[80] the addition of cooling water recirculation to the typical plant; the further addition of a small pond and the recirculation of some process water; and, finally, the substitution of a larger pond and a very high degree of recirculation. The recirculation of process water cuts down both on water withdrawals and on the discharge of BOD and suspended solids. Each of these alternative processes may be carried out by using either raw or prepared coal as the heat source. The primary residuals generated in production of sugar are heat, organic material measured by its biochemical oxygen demand (BOD), suspended solids, sulfur oxides, fly ash, and furnace ash. The water-borne residuals may either be dumped into the adjacent stream or treated in a standard wastewater treatment plant to the primary, secondary, or tertiary level. Treatment reduces the amount of BOD and suspended solids discharged to the river, but produces an organic sludge which must either be trucked away to a landfill or dewatered and in-

[78] Conceptually both could be used.

[79] Ceteris paribus the program will always choose the shorter and cheaper trip. But if aesthetic (or other) damages from landfill activities are greater at the close-in site, the shadow prices on the discharges will reflect this and will force the adoption of the longer haul.

[80] Löf and Kneese, *Economics of Water Utilization.*

cinerated.[81] The incineration, in turn, produces fly ash and bottom ash. The fly ash is assumed to be 95 per cent precipitated, so the ultimate residuals are a rather large amount of ash for trucking to some landfill site and a small amount of fly ash escaping up the incinerator stack.

The stack gases of the main plant boilers may be allowed to escape untreated, or electrostatic precipitators of 90, 95, or 98 per cent efficiency (in terms of fly ash removal) may be installed.

Residuals Discharged to the Environment

To make the simple model more interesting, while not expanding the set of decision variables, we have also provided a mechanism for handling the following "background" residuals: (a) organic and inorganic materials initially in the river; i.e., at river mile $0 + 0$, expressed by its BOD and suspended solids concentrations; (b) organic material (BOD) and suspended solids from a municipal wastewater treatment facility; (c) particulates and sulfur dioxide from stationary sources within city A, e.g., residential heating; (d) particulates from the incineration of sludge at the municipal wastewater treatment facility; (e) particulates and sulfur dioxide from the municipal incinerator; (f) suspended solids from wet scrubbing of effluent gases at the municipal incinerator; and (g) solids to landfill directly from city A, the municipal incinerator, and the wastewater treatment facility. Computer runs can be made using various levels of these background residuals for the purpose of sensitivity analysis. Although treated as parameters in the present model, in the future we hope to include some of these background residuals as decision variables.

The discharges of residuals from both the beet sugar processing plant and the thermal power generating facility, together with the background residuals discussed above are summarized in table 4.1.

The Region

Most of our attention will be focused on city A. City B is used only in our estimates of damages (or ambient standards as the case may be) to that city caused by changes in water quality. We assume that receptor damages caused by changes in water quality are suffered along the entire length of the river within the region and, thus, appropriate reaches of the river are defined in terms of receptor-use patterns. In the case of damages

---

[81] There is a choice of dewatering processes based on the conditioning chemical used. In one alternative, fly ash from the plant's electrostatic precipitators is used; in another, fly ash from the thermal plant is trucked in; and in a third, the standard polyelectrolyte additives are used.

Table 4.1. Forms of Residuals Discharged to the Environment

Activity production/treatment	Residual (or measurement of)		
	Discharged to the atmosphere	Discharged to the river	Discharged to the land
Decision variables:			
Beet sugar processing plant	particulates (fly ash)	BOD	bottom ash (furnace ash)
		suspended solids	
	sulfur dioxide		precipitate
	water vapor[a]	heat	sludge
			incinerator ash
Thermal power generating facility	particulates (fly ash)	suspended solids	bottom ash (furnace ash)
		heat	
	sulfur dioxide		precipitate
	water vapor[a]		settled solids
Background residuals:			
Municipal wastewater treatment facility	particulates	BOD suspended solids	sludge incinerator ash
Municipal incinerator	particulates sulfur dioxide	suspended solids	incinerator ash
City A	particulates sulfur dioxide		solid wastes
Background residuals (from outside the region)	particulates sulfur dioxide	BOD suspended solids	

[a] Water vapor is mainly from the cooling towers.

associated with air-borne residuals, we assume that all losses of economic significance occur within and around city A. In a more comprehensive analysis of this region, damages to city B would also be considered.

As discussed above, various residuals are generated in production and consumption activities. Also, material residuals may be converted from one form to another in production, consumption, and treatment processes, e.g., solids to liquids, gases to liquids, liquids to solids, etc. Regardless of form, however, all residuals are ultimately disposed of somewhere within our hypothetical region, either through recycling or direct discharge to the environment.[82] As indicated in table 4.1 residuals are finally discharged to: (a) the atmosphere; (b) the river; and/or (c) the land. We assume that solid residuals disposed of on the land remain there; that is, the links between land storage and ground or surface water are weak and thus may

[82] We could allow residuals "export," e.g., sludge dumping at sea, but this raises a number of difficult conceptual questions as well as creating political problems.

be neglected. Furthermore, we assume that solid residuals once on land do not enter the atmosphere either through dump fires or air-borne transport (winds), and that the landfill area—once the residuals are deposited there—represents a closed ecosystem. Consequently, we do not use environmental dispersion models to describe the transport or transformation of residuals in landfill areas.

We do, however, use atmospheric and stream dispersion models to describe the transport, transformation, and storage of residuals in these environments. Hence, we provide a brief description of the assumed characteristics both of the river and of the atmosphere of this hypothetical region.

The River

The river is used for water supply—industrial as well as municipal—water-based recreation, and industrial cooling water. River flows vary widely depending upon the time of year but low flows can be anticipated from late summer through early fall. The seven-day consecutive low flow expected on the average once in ten years is 500 cfs. This is the flow that we will be using (at least initially) to establish a residuals-environmental quality plan for the region; i.e., this will be used as the "design flow."[83]

In order to compute the dissolved oxygen (DO) concentration along the river for various BOD loadings and stream characteristics, it is convenient to subdivide the river into reaches. One possibility would be to divide the river up into sections which represent reaches between the various residuals outfalls. Other possibilities would be to divide the river into reaches depending upon the various receptor/use patterns along the river or to divide the river into sections for maintaining various minimum water-quality standards. For our purposes, a combination of these approaches is used.[84] For simplicity, we assume the physical characteristics of the river remain constant throughout the length of river within the region. We also assume that no significant tributaries enter the main

---

[83] As discussed previously in sections 2.1 and 2.5, there are at least two ways of improving the assimilative capability of the river; (a) low-flow augmentation, and (b) in-stream reaeration. We hope to include both these as management options in a future model. In addition, we do not mean to imply that the "design flow" approach to planning is the only or best approach. As indicated previously, we plan to include the effects of time variations in the assimilative capacity of the natural environment in future models.

[84] In an actual situation, one would also delineate reaches where stream flow and biochemical oxidation parameters remain relatively constant within each reach. In order to expedite the presentation, however, we have assumed that the various parameters remain constant throughout the entire length of the river within the region of interest.

stream within this section of the river. Hence, we assume that the carbonaceous, i.e., first stage, BOD rate constant, K_1, and the reoxygenation rate, K_2 (except for their dependency on temperature) are constants throughout the river within the region. Specifically, we have defined reaches: (a) between points of residuals discharges; (b) at sites of various receptor/use activities; and (c) at other intervals close enough that predetermined water quality gradients will not be exceeded.

The Atmosphere

The region shown in figure 4.4 is located in a valley between two mountain ranges oriented in a north–south direction. The geographical location of this region, together with its associated meteorological conditions, are such that the assimilative capacity of the atmosphere, although usually quite good, may at times be severely limited. That is, air pollution episodes have been experienced in the past.[85] Hence, for this particular region, we would be interested in examining two quite different meteorological conditions:[86] (a) episode situations where ventilation of the atmosphere is virtually nonexistent (ambient concentrations of residuals are not in a steady state); and (b) the more frequently observed meteorological condition where the prevailing winds are parallel to the mountain ranges and are from the south in the summer and from the north in the winter. In the latter case, the steady state ambient concentrations are a function of the ventilation factor.[87] (A numerical value for this factor is reported daily by the Weather Bureau as an early warning of potential air pollution conditions.) Use of the ventilation factor as a design criterion for the assimilative capacity of the atmosphere is analogous to the design river flow mentioned previously.[88]

So that residuals discharged to the atmosphere might be related to residual concentrations at various receptor/use points, the area in and around city A has been sectioned into two-mile grid squares as shown in

[85] Stagnating anticyclones that have lingered over the same area for four days or more have been associated with major air pollution episodes. See Julius Korshover, "Climatology of Stagnating Anticyclones East of the Rocky Mountains, 1936-1965," Environmental Health Series, Public Health Service Publication, no. 999-AP-34 (Cincinnati: Dept. of Health, Education, and Welfare, 1967).

[86] The present model includes a mechanism for describing ambient concentrations associated with both these conditions.

[87] The ventilation factor is the product of the mixing depth D and the average wind speed V. All other things being equal, the greater its numerical value, the smaller the ambient concentrations of residuals. See H. A. Panofsky, "Air Pollution Meteorology," *American Scientist* 57, no. 2 (1969), p. 283.

[88] Again, we do not mean to imply that the "design flow" approach to planning is the only or best alternative. In future models, we plan to explore the effects of time variations in the assimilative capacity of the atmosphere.

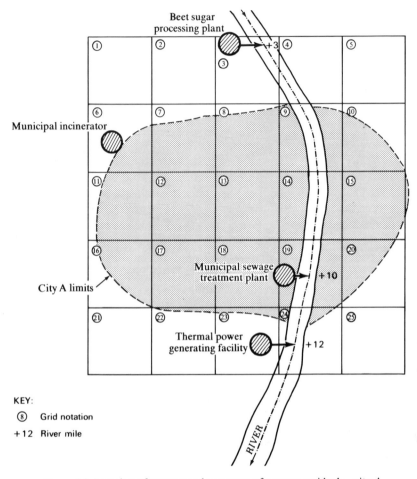

Figure 4.5. Location of sources and receptors of gaseous residuals—city A.

figure 4.5. Production/consumption activities that discharge large quantities of residuals to the environment are treated as point sources. All other activities located within a particular grid square are grouped and we assume the aggregated residual is discharged at the center point of the area. Similarly, receptors are assumed to be grouped at the center of each grid square and transfer coefficients[89]—between source and receptor—are computed accordingly.

[89] Transfer coefficients are used in our model to relate ambient concentrations of a specified residual to unit discharges of that residual from various sources in the region. For a more detailed exposition, see section 2.3.

CLIFFORD S. RUSSELL AND WALTER O. SPOFFORD

The Computer Program

The linear program that we are using for our computations is IBM's
hird generation L.P. code, MPS-360.[90] This is a master program in itself
ind cannot be used as an L.P. subroutine. However, it is able to interact
with other routines—e.g., FORTRAN coded routines—and so it is useful
or our purposes.

In order to construct the necessary tangent plane at each point, accord-
ng to equation (2.1–11), the gradient, ∇F, must be evaluated. Computer
ubroutines coded in FORTRAN are employed to make this computation.
Residual discharges from the industry linear model are used as inputs
o the environmental/damage models and the associated marginal damages
ire evaluated. These, in turn, are used as cost coefficient (i.e., price) inputs
o the linear model on the next iteration. This process is repeated until
one of the terminating conditions described below is met.[91]

The step size selector that we are now using is the latter of the two
schemes described in section 2.1, i.e., equations (2.1–18) and (2.1–19). We
chose this procedure over the former because most of the elements of the
gradient vector are constants. Consequently, we need artificial bounds for
only a relatively few variables (actually only for those activities discharging
residuals to the environment). The feasible range of each residual discharge variable is established by two methods and the larger of the two
values is automatically chosen. The first set of range values is estimated
from a knowledge of the processes and activities involved. The second set
of ranges is evaluated by first solving the industry linear model with
zero prices on residual discharge activities (this gives us a feasible upper
bound)[92] and then solving the model with prices on residual discharge
activities equal to marginal damages associated with the first solution
(this gives us a feasible lower bound). The absolute differences in the values
of the variables for these two program runs are used as the second set of
ranges.

The initial step size set is computed using equation (2.1–18). Various
values of D ($D = 2, 5,$ and 10) have been experimented with in an attempt
to improve the overall efficiency of this method. Although efficiency of
convergence depends upon a number of variables—such as initial starting
point, scale, shape of the response surface, and the relative values of the
step size vector—it would appear that the smaller values of D (i.e., $D = 2$

[90] IBM's linear programming code was chosen because IBM's 360 system was readily
available for our use.
[91] The efficiency of this method has been improved significantly by using the final basis
of the kth iteration as the initial basis of the $(k + 1)^{th}$ iteration. On a typical run, the
iterations *within* MPS–360 were reduced from fifty-two to four.
[92] Feasible, in that it satisfies all the linear constraints, $AX \leq B$.

and 5) establish a more efficient convergence than the larger value of D (i.e., $D = 10$). As suggested above, the step size scheme is an extremely important aspect of this method but, unfortunately, the weak link. Consequently, additional work will be needed along these lines in order to improve efficiency.

At present, we start the ascent process from a point (vector) that describes the residual discharge activity levels resulting from prices on discharge activities equal to the marginal damages that result from solving the same problem with zero prices on these activities. However, random feasible starts could easily be introduced, and are intended in the future.

The program is coded to end computations when any one of the following conditions is met:

1. The value of the objective function increases by no more than a specified amount;
2. The number of iterations equals the specified maximum number;
3. The number of different step size sets equals the specified maximum number.

If the program terminates because of condition 1, a test must then be made to determine whether or not this terminal point is actually at a local optimum.

The Results of a Test Run

In order to test the actual mechanics of this optimizing scheme, it has been necessary to generate appropriate data for production processes, treatment processes, transfer processes for residuals in the environment, and damage functions. Information about the beet sugar processing plant and the thermal power generating facility, as cited above, was taken from Löf and Kneese[93] and Cootner and Löf[94] respectively. The transfer coefficients for gaseous residuals have been assumed,[95] along with those for describing the concentration of suspended solids in the river. Transfer coefficients for both BOD–DO and temperature relationships in the river were computed by using appropriate dispersion models but by assuming values for the relevant parameters.

The shapes and magnitudes of the damage functions were also assumed. Although we realize that some damage functions are composed of both convex and concave portions, we have assumed (initially) simple convex

---

[93] Löf and Kneese, *Economics of Water Utilization.*
[94] Cootner and Löf, *Water Demand.*
[95] Transfer coefficients for this particular run were not based on episodic conditions.

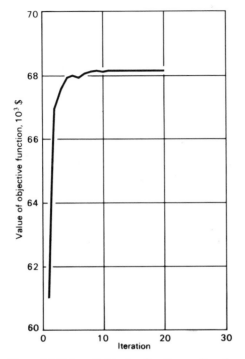

Figure 4.6. Value of objective function vs. iteration.

forms to insure a unique optimum.[96] These functions have been chosen specifically, however, to give reasonable solutions to our didactic residuals management problem.

Utilizing these data and information, the computer program (the master linear program and all the related subroutines) was run until a point close to the "optimum" was found.[97] In the example presented here, this point was found on the twentieth iteration. A plot of the value of the objective function vs. the number of iterations is presented as figure 4.6. It should be pointed out, however, that although the value of the objective function changed very little after the fifth or sixth iteration, the various discharge activity levels changed significantly. That is, a significant readjustment process was going on. This indicates that we are dealing with a flat response surface that is caused by the combined shapes of the benefit, cost, and damage functions. Because some of these shapes were assumed and do not

[96] This is not, however, a requirement of this method, as random starts could be used to explore a multipeaked surface.

[97] How close this point is to the actual optimum depends upon the criteria used to terminate the program. (See previous section, "The Computer Program.")

necessarily represent conditions of the real world, no conclusions should be drawn from this regarding expected shapes of actual response surfaces.

Table 4.2 depicts the residual discharge activity levels (both to the river and to the atmosphere) at the "optimal" solution; i.e., on the twentieth

Table 4.2. Discharge Activity Levels at "Optimal" Solution

Residual Vectors—Water (Iteration = 20)			
Reach number	BOD (10^3 lbs/day)	Suspended solids (10^3 lbs/day)	BTU (10^9 BTU/day)
1	0.0	0.0	0.0
2	25.7	319.0	1.09
3	43.0[a]	0.0	0.0
4	0.0	843.0	36.2
5	0.0	0.0	0.0
6	0.0	0.0	0.0
7	0.0	0.0	0.0
8	0.0	0.0	0.0

Residual Vectors—Air (Iteration = 20)		
Grid number	Particulates (tons/day)	Sulfur dioxide (tons/day)
1	0.0	0.0
2	0.0	0.0
3	6.34	6.86
4	0.0	0.0
5	0.0	0.0
6	0.0	0.0
7	0.0	0.0
8	0.0	0.0
9	0.0	0.0
10	0.0	0.0
11	0.0	0.0
12	0.0	0.0
13	0.0	0.0
14	0.0	0.0
15	0.0	0.0
16	0.0	0.0
17	0.0	0.0
18	0.0	0.0
19	0.0	0.0
20	0.0	0.0
21	0.0	0.0
22	0.0	0.0
23	18.7	13.9
24	0.0	0.0
25	0.0	0.0

[a] Assumed "background" residual from the municipal sewage treatment facility. This is the only background residual that was employed in this particular computer run.

CLIFFORD S. RUSSELL AND WALTER O. SPOFFORD

iteration. Given these discharge levels, table 4.3 represents the associated ambient steady state concentrations of these residuals in the various reaches of the river and grid squares of city *A*. Table 4.4 indicates for each residual, and at the optimal discharge levels (i.e., discharge levels on the twentieth

Table 4.3. Ambient Concentrations at "Optimal" Discharge Levels

Ambient Concentrations in River (Iteration = 20)

Reach number	DO saturation level (*mg/L*)	DO deficit (*mg/L*)	DO level (*mg/L*)	Suspended solids (*mg/L*)	Temperature (°F)
1	9.17	0.0	9.17	0	68.0
2	9.14	0.72	8.42	118	68.5
3	9.14	1.77	7.37	118	68.5
4	8.08	3.07	5.00	431	80.5
5	8.26	4.37	3.89	431	78.0
6	8.43	5.35	3.08	431	76.0
7	8.59	5.99	2.60	431	74.5
8	8.76	6.33	2.43	431	72.5

Ambient Concentrations of Air Pollutants

Grid number	Deposited particulates (*tons/sq.mi./day*)	Suspended particulates (*micrograms/ cubic meter*)	Sulfur dioxide (*parts per million*)
1	0.04	3.2	0.4
2	0.14	12.2	0.8
3	0.36	19.4	1.1
4	0.14	12.2	0.8
5	0.04	3.2	0.4
6	0.02	2.4	0.5
7	0.09	10.5	0.7
8	0.14	14.6	0.9
9	0.09	10.5	0.7
10	0.02	2.4	0.5
11	0.0	3.2	0.50
12	0.07	9.6	0.8
13	0.14	12.8	0.9
14	0.07	9.6	0.8
15	0.0	3.2	0.50
16	0.05	7.2	0.6
17	0.27	24.8	1.1
18	0.43	36.7	1.5
19	0.27	24.8	1.1
20	0.05	7.2	0.6
21	0.11	9.6	0.6
22	0.43	35.9	1.4
23	1.06	57.5	2.1
24	0.43	35.9	1.39
25	0.11	9.6	0.6

Note: Initial river temperature = 68.0°F.

173

Table 4.4. Marginal Damages at "Optimal" Discharge Levels
for All Reach and Grid Locations

Total Marginal Damages—BOD, Suspended Solids, Heat, Particulates, Sulfur Dioxide
(Iteration = 20)

Reach/grid number	BOD ($/lbs/day$)	Suspended solids ($/lbs/day$)	Heat ($/10^6 BTU/day$)	Particulates ($/tons/day$)	Sulfur dioxide ($/tons/day$)
1	0.076	0.00002	0.022	0.12	10.3
2	→0.075	→0.00002	→0.025	0.28	14.6
3	0.067	0.00002	0.035	→0.42	→16.5
4	→0.063	→0.00002	→0.039	0.28	14.6
5	0.053	0.00002	0.031	0.12	10.3
6	0.041	0.00001	0.024	0.12	13.9
7	0.025	0.00001	0.018	0.31	19.3
8	0.011	0.00000	0.009	0.42	21.5
9				0.31	19.3
10				0.12	13.9
11				0.16	16.2
12				0.41	22.5
13				0.56	25.0
14				0.41	22.5
15				0.16	16.2
16				0.30	16.7
17				0.73	23.7
18				0.98	26.7
19				0.73	23.7
20				0.30	16.7
21				0.35	14.1
22				0.83	20.5
23				→1.22	→23.4
24				0.82	20.5
25				0.35	14.1

Note: Arrows indicate the marginal damages for the beet sugar processing plant (river reach 2, grid square 3) and the thermal power generating facility (river reach 4, grid square 23).

iteration), the actual marginal damages attributable to an additional unit release for all reach and grid locations delineated in our hypothetical region. This table represents the marginal damages that are returned to the industry L.P. model as prices on the discharge of these residuals.

In table 4.5 we summarize the results (i.e., activity levels and values of the objective function) for three different price sets on residuals discharged to the environment. The first column under "Iteration" represents the resulting discharge levels for zero prices on discharge activities. The second column represents the discharge levels for prices on the discharge activities equal to the marginal damages resulting from the discharge levels of the first column. The third column depicts the discharge levels we obtain on iteration 20; i.e., the "optimal" set of discharge levels. As one might ex-

Table 4.5. Comparison of Results with Different Prices
on Residual Discharge Activities

Discharge activity	Residual	Units	Iteration		
			1[a]	2[b]	20[c]
Beet sugar	BOD	10^3 lbs/day	33.4	18.6	25.7
processing plant	Suspended solids	10^3 lbs/day	414	230	319
	Heat	10^9 BTU/day	2.38	0.0	1.09
	Particulates	tons/day	22.0	5.35	6.34
	SO_2	tons/day	6.86	6.86	6.86
	Solids[d]	tons/day	6.40	72.3	49.7
Thermal power generating facility	Suspended solids	10^3 lbs/day	0.0	904	843
	Heat	10^9 BTU/day	51.4	0.0	36.2
	Particulates	tons/day	277	0.19	18.7
	SO_2	tons/day	86.4	8.64	13.9
	Solids[e]	tons/day	80.6	109	108
Net private benefits, 1000$			72.8	67.4	69.7
Damages (externalities) 1000$			11.8	0.4	1.5
Objective function (net social welfare) 1000$			61.0	67.0	68.2

Note: Prices on solids were assumed to be constant, but not zero, in this analysis.
[a] Zero prices on residual discharge activities.
[b] Maximum prices on residual discharge activities.
[c] "Optimal" prices on residual discharge activities.
[d] Total solids from the beet sugar processing plant include a mixture of bottom ash, precipitated fly ash, organic sludge, and incinerator ash.
[e] Total solids from the thermal power generating facility include bottom ash, precipitated fly ash, and precipitated slurry solids.

pect, the net private gains (benefits less costs) are maximized for the situation represented by the first column. However, the externalities (i.e., damages) are also maximized for this strategy. Also, as one might expect, the damages are minimized for the strategy represented by the second column; but so are the net private gains. For the management plan represented by the third column, our so-called "optimal strategy," the social welfare of the region[98] (i.e., with all externalities internalized) is greater than that for either of the other two cases, even though this strategy represents neither the maximum net private gains nor the minimum external damages.

For selected residuals, we have depicted in figures 4.7 and 4.8 ambient concentrations vs. reach (or grid) for the various pricing strategies presented in table 4.5. Figure 4.7 indicates the variations of temperature and dissolved oxygen in the river for the different management schemes;

[98] Defined in section I.

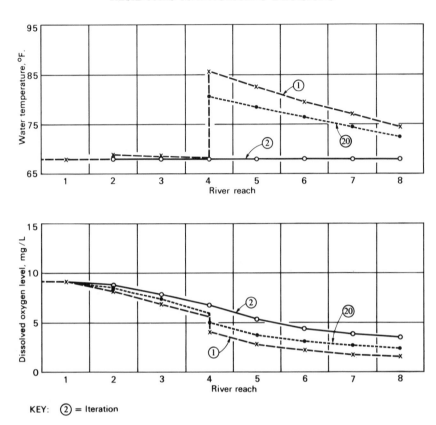

Figure 4.7. Comparison of results—temperature and dissolved oxygen profile in river.

figure 4.8 shows the distribution of sulfur dioxide concentrations in city *A* both for a sulfur dioxide effluent charge of zero and for the optimal price set (as previously defined) established by this iterative technique.

This brief account of the didactic model has been presented in order to provide the reader with a feeling for the operational aspects of this quantitative approach.

IV. SUMMARY AND CONCLUSIONS

In this paper we have described in general terms a quantitative framework designed to assist regional authorities in making decisions about residuals management policies. The framework deals explicitly with airborne, water-borne, and solid residuals and includes, in a linear program-

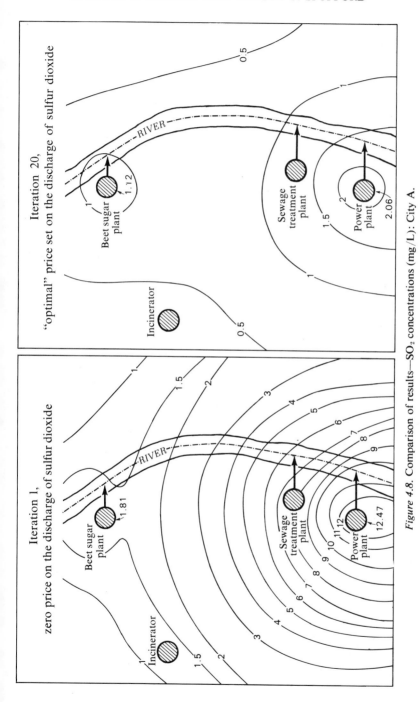

Figure 4.8. Comparison of results—SO₂ concentrations (mg/L): City A.

ming model of regional production, information about internal production process changes, recirculation alternatives, and end-of-pipe treatment processes, and their implications for the form and amount of residual discharges. (Residuals from consumption of products may also, in principle, be included.) These discharges are traced through the physical environment by a set of dispersion/diffusion models reflecting the atmospheric and watercourse characteristics of the region.[99] The damages caused by the resulting ambient residuals concentrations, and particularly the marginal damages attributable to individual discharges, are then calcuated, either analytically or numerically, depending on the type of environmental models used. These marginal damages are the link between the several submodels and the key to the optimizing method used to solve for the residuals management policy which maximizes a measure of regional welfare. (This measure includes the benefits from material production/consumption, the costs of residuals treatment at source, the costs of direct modification of the environment, and the remaining damages from ambient residuals concentrations.)

Even in the general form presented here, this model is useful both in identifying the kinds of information necessary for effective regional decision making and in structuring the problem of residuals management to suggest the areas in which several relevant disciplines may make important contributions. For example, in applying this model, the following broad research tasks would be faced:

1. The identification of at least the most significant residuals-generating industries of the region, and the study of their process changes, recirculation and treatment alternatives relevant to residuals discharges.[100] The aim would be to develop linear activity vectors describing the alternatives and to link these in an interindustry model. This would involve economists and engineers of several types, depending on the specific industries to be studied.

2. The building of necessary dispersion and diffusion models for the region. This might require hydrologists, meteorologists, and sanitary engineers.

3. The development of ecological models to parallel the physical transformation models. This would be a job for life scientists such as zoologists, botanists, and limnologists.

---

[99] As previously noted, ecological models could similarly be incorporated.

[100] For partial examples of the kind of studies necessary, see Cootner and Löf, *Water Demand*, and Kneese and Löf, *The Economics of Water Utilization*. A similar procedure would be required for other residuals generating activities, such as households and transportation.

4. To the extent possible, the estimation of damage functions for the region's receptor locations. This could involve any number of disciplines from medical science to fisheries biology, psychology, and economics.

As we have noted, at the moment areas 3 and 4 are the least well explored and developed.

Our own aims for this framework go beyond the general version presented here. As a first step, we have constructed a didactic version for a hypothetical region, in order to test our techniques, especially the optimizing technique. This version includes two industries, thermal electric generation and beet sugar processing, for which considerable information on residuals problems was already available at Resources for the Future. (The residuals we deal with are water-borne heat, BOD, and suspended solids; air-borne particulates and SO_2; and solids—furnace ash, precipitated fly ash, and sewage-treatment-plant sludge.) We use simple dispersion/diffusion models based on the assumed characteristics of the region's river and local meteorology. The damage functions for each residual and receptor location are arbitrarily constructed to introduce some play into the model. Ultimately we plan to use this model to explore solution sensitivity to the parameters of the physical models and the damage functions. This should assist us in evaluating the relative importance of the research gaps already noted. In addition we plan to use this model as a base for exploring the inclusion of consumption residuals, and the introduction of time through two-season, deterministic physical models and corresponding economic models allowing for such options as programmed discharges.

The next major step in our research will be an effort to apply this framework to an actual region to see whether it really will prove useful and practical under complicated real-world conditions. This work will involve us in all the problem areas cited above and our most important decisions will be on how far it is possible to simplify the representation of the chosen region without destroying the validity of the intended demonstration of practicality.

5. *Agricultural Pesticides: Productivity and Externalities*

Max R. Langham, Joseph C. Headley, and *W. Frank Edwards*

This paper is divided into four parts. In part I two simplified conceptual models are used to put the pesticide problem in context and to illuminate gaps in our knowledge. In parts II and III two empirical studies on the use of pesticides in agriculture are described. Part IV lists implications and conclusions of the research.

In the first of the empirical studies an attempt is made to estimate marginal productivities of selected agricultural chemicals and marginal rates of substitution between insecticides and land. The emphasis is on understanding and describing the economic behavior of agricultural producers who, if left to pursue their individual interests, would consider only the production alternatives open to them and the markets they face for inputs and final products, and thus ignore certain social costs that their decisions might impose upon other groups in society.

In the second empirical study we attempt to incorporate externalities into a benefit-cost analysis of the use of agricultural pesticides. The externalities of interest are those benefits and costs created by the use of agricultural pesticides that accrue to persons not acting in the role of producer and/or consumer of the product. In this study we attempt to evaluate, from a social welfare perspective, alternative policies for the use of pesticides.

In both studies, our focus is on pest control by chemicals. This method of control is widely used and is under the explicit direction of agricultural producers. Ecologists and others who have recognized the potential environmental danger of using large amounts of chemicals for pest control

This paper is based on research made possible by grants from Resources for the Future, Inc.

181

have stressed the importance of developing effective alternatives to chemicals. Alternative biological and integrated control methods have been described and discussed by the President's Science Advisory Council (1965). Society needs greater knowledge about all forms of pest control if it is to produce its food and fiber requirements with minimum disruption to the environment.

Both empirical studies also assume given qualities of agricultural products. For example, Florida vegetable producers sell largely on the fresh market and the objective of their pesticide spray program[1] is to produce a marketable crop. And what is marketable depends upon state regulations, which are in turn based on U.S. Department of Agriculture grades and standards and, at least in theory, on consumer preferences for "quality." Fewer pesticides could be used if consumers were willing to accept somewhat lower "quality" standards. Furthermore, quality standards often depend as much or more on a product's appearance than on its nutritive value. In searching for "optimum pest control" policies, it is important for society to remember that quality standards are variables.

PART I.   MAN-ENVIRONMENT INTERACTIONS

The natural environment is characterized by a stock of life-giving resources and a productive plant which turns out a flow of these resources. The existing stocks have resulted from an accumulation of flow resources through millenniums during which man did not exist or was too few in number and too lacking in knowledge to be of consequence to the environment.

All living organisms do of course have some power of control over their immediate environment, but man's unique ability to generate and store knowledge permitted him to obtain unusual power to influence the system that generated him. This capability has made man an important factor in the system.

Figure 5.1 presents a simple schematic diagram of the man-environment system. Man's ability to utilize resources to increase his physical well-being is shown as an input to his level of living. Since man cannot destroy nature's resources but can only change their form, there is a flow of waste materials (residuals) from man's level of living processes. These materials can be recycled for further use by man's technology, they can be discarded into the environment as effluents or waste materials, or in some cases they

---

[1] An individual agricultural producer's spray program for a particular crop is the sum total of his chemical spraying activities to control insects, diseases, et al., during a given season.

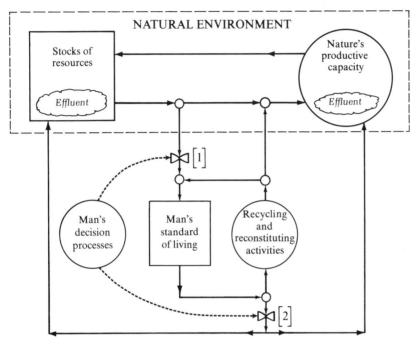

Figure 5.1. Flow diagram with feedback loops showing man's interaction with his environment.

can be reconstituted to their original form before being returned to the environment. The hourglass symbols can be visualized as valves and man has, so to speak, his corporate hand on them through his decision-making processes.

When man was fewer in number and lacked the knowledge to capture energy, his corporate hand had little power to open the valves. However, his geometrically increasing population and level of technology have strengthened this hand until it has become relatively easy for man to open the valves in order to exploit resources to improve his level of living.

However, in his willingness to open the valves, man has too often ignored the fact that environmental resources are produced and held in finite quantities. Consequently there are growing indications that man's activities are depleting and contaminating the stocks of resources and impairing the environmental productive processes. These indications are leading to a growing awareness of an optimum or desired equilibrium rate of flow through these valves. Man should not blindly devote his energies to continually opening these valves, but should seek the optimum "valve settings" so as to avoid irreparable damage to the environment.

The level of technology and the population determine the rate (valve 1) at which resources are borrowed from the natural system. An increase in the effective level of technology will generally result in an increase in the present value of a given amount of environmental services. If nature's biological rate of renewal is greater than the rate at which technology requires environmental services, then the amount borrowed will be repayable. However, if the rate at which the environment renews itself is less than the rate at which its services are borrowed, one or both of the following actions would be required—increased technology to recycle or reconstitute resources to offset the loss of natural environmental services (i.e., to shut off valve 2) and/or a decrease in the level of living in the future (making smaller withdrawals from the system).

It has been argued that the use of chemical pesticides in agriculture to enhance agricultural productivity has been at the expense of the future ability of the environment to control pests naturally. It is argued further that additional increases in technology can only postpone man's eventual day of reckoning when the environmental debt must be repaid.

Let us consider the hypothesis that natural environmental pest control resources are being depleted and look at some of the other issues in the pesticide controversy within the framework of the following simultaneous equation model:

$$\text{Production function: } F_t = f(F_{t-1}, X_{1,t}, \bar{L}_t, K_t) \tag{1}$$

$$\text{Environmental beneficence function: } E_t = h(E_{t-1}, P_t, X_{1,t}, X_{2,t}, K_t) \tag{2}$$

$$\text{Learning function: } K_t = q(K_{t-1}, X_{1,t}). \tag{3}$$

F_t, E_t, and K_t are endogenous variables. Disturbance terms have been omitted from the above equations. The model utilizes the following terminology and assumptions:

1. Man's standard of living at time t, F_t, is a function of man's standard of living in the previous period, F_{t-1}; man's effort, $X_{1,t}$; the beneficence of his environment, E_t; and his level of knowledge, K_t.

2. The beneficence of the environment to man and hence to F_t is defined conceptually as E_t. It is a function of the condition of the environment in the previous period, E_{t-1}; population, P_t; man's effort, $X_{1,t}$; his use of pesticides, $X_{2,t}$; and his level of knowledge, K_t.

3. Man's level of knowledge or state of the arts, K_t, is a function of knowledge in the previous period, K_{t-1}, and effort, $X_{1,t}$.

4. Man has control over X_1, X_2, and P.

5. The reduced form equations are twice differentiable.

184

The following relations illustrate the major gaps in our knowledge and hence the areas of major controversy.

$$\frac{\partial E_{t+s}}{\partial X_{2,t}} \overset{?}{\underset{<}{>}} 0 \tag{4}$$

How will the use of pesticides in period t affect the beneficence of the environment in future periods? If, for example, persistent pesticides do irreparable and continuing damage to certain life forms, the future beneficence might decrease, and the "less than" relation would hold in (4).

$$\frac{\partial^2 F_{t+s}}{\partial X_{1,t+s}\, \partial X_{2,t}} \overset{?}{\underset{<}{>}} 0 \tag{5}$$

$$\frac{\partial^2 F_{t+s}}{\partial E_{t+s}\, \partial X_{2,t}} \overset{?}{\underset{<}{>}} 0 \tag{6}$$

The evidence of increasing use of pesticides in recent years would lead one to suspect that the "greater than" inequality would hold in (5) and/or (6), for s values within the planning horizons of rational farmers. In equation (5) this would mean that the use of pesticides enhances the marginal productivity of man's effort in producing F. In equation (6) it would mean that the use of pesticides improves the marginal productivity of the environment, which one would normally expect to have a positive effect upon F. If neither of these relations hold, we would not expect farmers to increase their use of X_2. It should be noted, however, that the "greater than" relation might hold for small values of s in farmers' planning horizon and the "less than" relation for larger s values. This would be the case if pesticides had a temporary beneficial effect but a long-run detrimental effect.

$$\frac{\partial^2 E_{t+s}}{\partial X_{2,t+s}\, \partial X_{2,t}} \overset{?}{\underset{<}{>}} 0 \tag{7}$$

How will the use of pesticides in period t affect the environment's response to pesticides in future periods? If, for example, we must continuously apply greater quantities of pesticides to maintain environmental beneficence, the "less than" relation in (7) would hold.

Man's challenge (or Utopian dream?) is to make F, E, and K monotonically increasing functions of time. But many argue that the influence of an increasing P is such that F and E must move in opposite directions regardless of the level of K. They hold that it is impossible for man to have a rising standard of living and an amicable environment in the long run, unless the population is stabilized. To add to man's worries, some ecologists have hypothesized that if E falls below a certain level, the environment cannot restore itself and man will be doomed.

Unfortunately, because of the short-run static nature of our models and our limited knowledge about the long-run effects of persistent pesticides, our empirical measures have done more to explain man's willingness to use pesticides than to elucidate some of the critical issues suggested by conditions (4) through (7). Most empirical work has been in the nature of an accounting of present annual benefits in a static framework, and the question is posed, "Are these enough benefits to offset whatever costs are occurring?" We have seldom attempted to assess future benefits or costs from today's pesticide usage. Part of our difficulty may be caused by treating society as a static entity in our measures of costs and benefits. Society is a dynamic population of people, not a static entity, and we probably err considerably when we so willingly make intertemporal comparisons of utility as though this utility were accruing to the same being. Such an intertemporal comparison of utility between the living and those yet unborn is presumptuous to say the least, and if the long-run costs turn out to be greater than the long-run benefits, it amounts to "taxation without representation" for future generations.

There is no theoretical basis for making interpersonal comparisons of utility in situations involving income redistribution. But if the persons involved are living today and are able to react to policy decisions which concern their income distribution, a government has feedback to help guide policy. If on the other hand, a government today makes, as it must, decisions that affect the utility of future citizens, then it is on more dangerous grounds. The tendency will be to exploit resources today to raise the utility of persons living today. There is a particular danger of this exploitation when many of the people living today are seriously deprived, or worse, are on the verge of starvation.

As long as technology continues to "bail man out" and to let him enjoy an increasing standard of living, the next generation will never begrudge previous generations for some exploitation of resources for a better life. The danger is that man will propagate to the point where the requirements of technology become so great that he is faced with a declining standard of living (and possibly chaos).

Our social and environmental problems today begin to make us realize that perhaps man cannot rely on exploitative technology for an increasing level of living ad infinitum. If so, then perhaps one can, from a long-run social welfare point of view, argue for admitting only those technologies which are in general environmentally neutral[2]—a criterion that implies that we can, with suitable tests, determine what is environmentally neutral.

PART II. PRODUCTIVITY OF PESTICIDES[3]

Few studies have been made on the productivity of agricultural pesticides across firms and regions. In contrast, numerous estimates have been made of the production gained from individual experiments with chemical pest control in agriculture, many of which were reported at the Ribicoff hearings in 1963 (U.S. Senate 1965). Most of the prevailing opinion concerning pesticide productivity in agriculture represents an intuitive aggregation of the results of similar experiments, reinforced by a market for agricultural pesticides that has grown both in dollar volume and physical magnitude since the close of World War II.

Now that chemical pest control has come to be recognized as a potential source of a number of undesirable effects outside the agricultural producing firm, knowledge of the productivity of pesticides is essential to an informed change in the amounts of pesticides used, the kinds of materials used, and the ways these materials are dispersed.

Marginal Productivities of Pesticides

Headley (1968) estimated the marginal contribution of pesticide expenditures by combining data obtained from Farmer Cooperative Service estimates of expenditures for pesticides by state in 1963 with data from published farm income and expenses for that year. While these estimates have statistical and economic limitations, the results showed that one dollar of expenditure at the margin was associated with a four-dollar increase in the value of farm sales based on variations among state totals in 1963.

[2] By this we mean a technological development that will not be detrimental to endangered species of plants or animals that add to the beneficence of the environment, does not create an uncompensated nuisance to man, and leaves the environment essentially unchanged after the productive life of the development and/or consumptive activities it creates.

[3] Pesticides is a general term that includes chemicals used for the control of several broad categories of pests. Pesticides used to control insects are more specifically referred to as insecticides. Likewise, fungicides are used for controlling plant diseases, herbicides for undesirable weeds, miticides for mites, nematocides for nematodes, and rodenticides for controlling rodents. Though pesticides is a general term it is sometimes used in this and other writings to refer to insecticides or some other category or categories of pesticides. In such cases, the reader will normally have no trouble distinguishing the meaning of the word.

This estimate suggests that, while there may be pest, chemical, and crop situations where marginal expenditures were not this productive, the average effect of an increase or decrease in the mix of pesticides used by farmers would result in a four-unit change in output for a one-unit change in input (both in value terms). Headley's study did not provide insights into differences between types of farming or geographical areas nor into differences between chemicals in various uses.

Another study was undertaken by Headley to estimate the marginal contributions of pesticides in different uses in agriculture and in various regions of the country where the pesticide inputs were measured in ounces of technical material applied rather than expenditure values. Marginal contributions for herbicides, insecticides, and fertilizer for ten production regions and the nation are given in table 5.1 as computed from statistically estimated input–output functions.

These results have several interesting aspects. First, the marginal contribution of insecticide materials was positive in all regions with the exception of the North Plains, and the variable was dropped from the equation in that region. Second, the estimated contributions in all regions were in excess of what would constitute a weighted average cost per ounce of

Table 5.1. Estimated Marginal Contributions of Selected Farm Chemicals, by Region, 1964

| Region | Chemical category | | | |
	Herbicides in dollars per ounce	Insecticides in dollars per ounce	Fertilizer in dollars per ton	R^2 of estimating equation
Northeast		1.31[a]	157.39[a]	0.84
Appalachian	0.60	0.31	310.22[a]	0.76
Southeast		0.005	157.24[a]	0.94
Delta	0.22	0.30[a]	217.17	0.95
Corn Belt	2.38[a]	0.76	198.87[a]	0.75
Lake	−1.02	11.09[a]	388.35[a]	0.66
North Plains	0.13		302.71[a]	0.70
South Plains	1.05[a]	0.06[a]	158.66[a]	0.96
Mountain		13.85[a]	633.55[a]	0.88
Pacific		1.74[a]	669.71[a]	0.97
United States	−0.21	1.52[a]	270.31[a]	0.76

Note: All contributions computed at the geometric means for 1964.

[a] Estimates derived from partial regression coefficients that were significantly different from zero at $\alpha = 0.05$.

Sources: Pesticide use data were taken directly from data tapes of the U.S. Department of Agriculture Pesticide Use Survey conducted in 1964. Data on other farm inputs and crop sales were taken from U.S. Bureau of the Census, *Census of Agriculture, 1964, Statistics for the State and Counties*, Vol. 1 (Washington, D.C.: Government Printing Office, 1967). Individual state reports were used for those states included in the Pesticide Use Survey.

technical insecticide material, with the exceptions of the Southeast and the South Plains. Third, the production regions that are primarily cotton areas —such as the Appalachian, Southwest, Delta, and South Plains—showed lower estimates for insecticides. Fourth, the estimated marginal contribution of herbicides was largest in the Corn Belt where they are widely used, and the average estimated contribution in the national function showed herbicides with a negative contribution. Fifth, the estimated marginal contribution of fertilizer was uniformly large relative to the cost of a ton of normal analysis fertilizer and all estimates were positive.

It is reasonable to ask what these estimates might mean to those concerned with agriculture and policies directed at pest control in agriculture. If the estimates are valid, i.e., measure what they purport to measure, one interpretation is that the use of additional insecticides in the Southeast and the South Plains cannot be expected to generate much, if any, additional output. The same is true to some extent for the Delta and Appalachian regions. Similarly, the estimates suggest that a reduction in use of a given amount of technical material in these areas would result in a relatively small reduction in output compared to other regions. Why might this be so?

If the regions where productivity is estimated as low are essentially using all of the insecticides that they can and still get a positive effect, this could be the cause of the low estimate. The partial correlation coefficient relating insecticides and crop sales was low in these regions. The reason is not known. While it supports the hypothesis that high-use levels of inputs result in lowered marginal productivity, the result may be due to input complementarity. That is, some other input in the function may be measuring the effect of insecticides. Hired labor and fertilizer are two possibilities in this regard. In any case, the results do indicate that insecticide applications cannot be used to explain differences in output within the Southeast, South Plains, and perhaps the Appalachian regions.

For the remaining production regions, the results suggest considerable ability to explain differences, based on insecticide applications, in crop sales by county. The pattern seems to be that the more heterogeneous the agriculture, that is, crop production versus livestock or dairy, the more pronounced is the partial regression coefficient between insecticide use and crop sales. Therefore, these results are perhaps as much indicators of variation in output resulting from type of farming as they are indicators of variation resulting from insecticide use per se. This doubt is weakened somewhat, however, by the large statistically significant coefficients for commercial fertilizer that should also reflect variation caused by type of farming.

In spite of the limitations of the measurement device, the results for insecticides support the hypothesis that the marginal productivity of insecticides is least where the use is the most intensive. This conclusion certainly is consistent with our expectations based on economic theory.

The measurement of the marginal contribution of herbicides on a regional basis was not as consistent or as impressive as the results for insecticides. Table 5.1 shows that only in the Corn Belt and in the South Plains were the contributions based on statistically significant regression coefficients.

As a region, the Corn Belt uses more herbicide materials than any of the other regions, and the South Plains, while not the smallest regional user, was not the second largest.[4] It seems that these results run contrary to the economic theory hypothesis that was supported for insecticides. One explanation for the Corn Belt result could be that there were differences in the quantities of herbicides used among the counties in the sample and, since the preponderance of herbicide material used in the Corn Belt is applied to corn and soybeans, the two principal cash crops, the differences in output not explained by other inputs were attributed to herbicides. While the Corn Belt is the largest user of herbicides there was not, in 1964, the uniformity in use of herbicides on corn and soybeans from farm to farm that there was in the use of insecticides on cotton, for instance. Farmers who grow corn and soybeans in rotation with grain or pasture do not have the weed problems found under more intensive cultivation such as continuous corn programs. It is, therefore, argued that herbicide applications differentiated cash grain counties from more diversified ones in the Corn Belt in 1964 and, further, if the measure is valid, that the difference exists because of herbicides. Consistent with the expansion of the herbicide market since 1964, more recent surveys in Illinois show that herbicides are used on 70 to 80 per cent of the corn and soybeans in that state (Berry 1970).

Herbicide use in the South Plains region is largely devoted to grains, hay, and pasture including rangeland (Eichers et al. 1968). What the herbicide coefficient for this region measures is not clear. The dependent variable in the regression equation, crop sales, suggests that it is not measuring animal output from improved ranges and must, therefore, be an indication of variations in output due to higher production of grains such as barley, rice, and mixed grains. There is also the possibility that herbicide applications, to some extent, measured differences in intensity of farming among counties in the region.

For the nation as a whole, the herbicide variable did not perform as expected and its regression coefficient was negative and nonsignificant.

---

[4] See Theodore Eichers et al. (1968) for the regional use statistics tabulated for 1964.

This indicates that herbicides are not associated with the residual variance in crop output after other factors have been taken into account, either because its effect is measured by some other input such as fertilizer or because the national level of herbicide use is sufficient to deal with most of the important weed and brush problems. Given the rapid expansion of the herbicide market in the last five or six years, this may be worth considering.

Marginal Rates of Substitution Among Agricultural Inputs

As the U.S. Congress, state legislatures, and the USDA are faced with considerable pressure to act on the pesticide question as a part of the concern for the environment, it becomes necessary to consider various alternative forms of action. Some steps have been taken; e.g., cancelling registrations of certain compounds, doing more research on biological control, instituting integrated control, and using "clean" chemicals.

Production theory suggests still another possibility—the use of input substitution as an instrument of policy. Agricultural policy that restricts land use encourages the adoption of techniques such as chemical pest control as a means of enhancing the productivity of limited land combined with machinery, fertilizer, and new varieties of crops. So the policy has been one of substitution: substitution of technology for the natural resource, land. As this policy has altered the time pattern of land use, it has shifted the use of the natural ability of the biological system to control pests toward the present and has also put pressure on the disposal capacity of the system.

According to production theory, the marginal rate of substitution of one input for another is given by a ratio of their marginal products. In addition, an elasticity of substitution can be computed that measures the percentage change in one input, given a 1 per cent change in another input, while maintaining the same level of output.[5]

Before implementing an agricultural policy that encourages, for example, replacing pesticides with land, estimates of the relative changes in the levels of the inputs are needed to determine the inpact on input use and to assess the effects on agricultural output. The input–output functions estimated for the regions can provide a starting point for this idea.

In table 5.2 the marginal rates of substitution of cropland for insecticides and the elasticities of substitution of cropland for insecticides, both by region, are presented, based on the statistical input-output functions. The elasticity of substitution is the percentage decrease in ounces of tech-

[5] This is not the same definition of the elasticity of substitution as that found in Allen (1938), where the elasticity of substitution is defined as the percentage change in the input ratio for a one per cent change in the marginal rate of substitution.

nical insecticide material applied made possible by a 1 per cent increase in cropland with all other inputs held constant. The Northeast was not included in the production regions because of the absence of a coefficient for cropland; the North Plains were excluded because of the absence of a coefficient for insecticides in that region.

Large elasticities of substitution of cropland for insecticides were found in the Southeast and South Plains regions. In these regions the marginal contributions of insecticides were lowest (see table 5.1). In the other regions the elasticities ranged from −2.70 in the Appalachian region to −14.9 in the Delta.

By applying these estimates to the regions, or to the nation as a whole, an estimate can be made of the reduction of insecticides possible as land is returned to production. This provides a basis for evaluating the effect of using more land on insecticide use.

In 1967, the USDA estimated that 40.8 million acres of cropland were diverted from production under various government land retirement programs (U.S. Department of Agriculture, 1968). These programs included the Conservation Reserve, the feed grain programs for corn and grain sorghum, the cotton program, the cropland conversion program, and the cropland adjustment program. Most of this land is suitable for regular cultivation with no additional investment. If all of this land were returned to production the cropland base currently in use would increase by about 12 per cent.

The use of an estimate of the elasticity of substitution of cropland for insecticides of −6 to −7 for the United States leads to the conclusion that a 12 per cent increase in cropland harvested would reduce insecticide use by 70 to 80 per cent and maintain output.

Table 5.2. Marginal Rates of Substitution and Elasticity of Substitution of Cropland for Insecticides, by Region, 1964

Region	Marginal rate of substitution[a]	Elasticity of substitution[b]
Appalachian	−33.19	−2.70
Corn Belt	−10.03	−4.35
Delta	−256.47	−14.89
Lake	−0.80	−8.16
Pacific	−24.06	−6.49
Mountain	−0.97	−7.77
Southeast	−3,257.00	−326.67
South Plains	−547.17	−170.04
United States[c]	−13.24	−6.49

[a] Ounces of insecticide reduced per one acre increase in cropland.
[b] Percentage decrease in insecticides per one per cent increase in cropland.
[c] Excluding Alaska and Hawaii.

Such a substitution would have some repercussions. First, compared to present situations, return of this diverted cropland would mean that farmers would lose the government payments received currently under the program. Second, farm costs would be reduced by the amount of the value of the reduction in the use of insecticides plus application costs. Many costs on farms would remain unchanged, based on the assumption of the existence of a certain amount of underemployment of farm labor and excess machinery capacity.

Given this rather "rough and dirty" means of estimating the effect of such an action, the reasonableness of the result deserves discussion. The result requires the assumption that the land returned is of a quality equal to that in use. This we are sure is not the general rule. So, because this assumption is violated, the decrease in insecticide use would not be as dramatic as indicated. The result also requires that other inputs are sufficient to operate the added land at a level such that output lost by reducing insecticides could be made up from the added land. It is reasonably certain that the functions used for estimation are subject to some specification bias and that increasing cropland implies adding other correlated inputs, particularly seed, petroleum, and fertilizer. Therefore, farm costs would be increased to the extent that these additional inputs were required. Of course, the level of fertilizer use per acre would perhaps decline, since without insecticides insect damage would increase and the same level of fertility would no longer be profitable unless the prices for farm products were to increase. How much additional labor and machinery would be required has not been estimated. Finally, the effects of changes in the product mix of agriculture that would certainly occur under such a policy are ignored by the mathematical result. If farmers were to revert to use of rotations to control insects, weeds, and fungus in cash crop areas, relatively more forage and small grains might be produced. Finally, slightly more soil erosion may result from returning land to production that may be more susceptible to erosion than the land currently used for crops.

PART III. EXTERNALITIES AND THE USE OF PESTICIDE[6]

The research discussed in this section involved a slightly different aspect of the pesticide issue. While the comparison of marginal productivity with marginal cost is appropriate for the individual in deciding how much pesticide to use, it may *not* result in the "best" quantity from a social welfare perspective. This is because the marginal costs and/or marginal

[6] Some of the material in this section has been reported elsewhere (Edwards, Langham, and Headley, 1970).

benefits experienced by the individual may not coincide with those experienced by society as a whole. For example, a farmer's marginal cost of pesticides may include items such as the price he must pay for them, the cost of labor and machinery he uses to apply them, and so on. But his marginal cost does *not* include items like damage to wildlife, air and water quality, or human health. He only feels these indirectly as a member of society. To the extent that these consequences exist, they are partially borne by other members of society. This empirical study looks at these externalities and attempts to incorporate them into some measure of social welfare.

The Model

The model used for this analysis employed a measure of welfare consisting of consumers' plus producers' surplus, modified for observable externalities neglected in the surplus calculation. For each of the specified policies for use of pesticides, the model maximized this measure of welfare over production of the eight major crops in Dade County, Florida.[7] The model can be stated in general terms as follows.[8]

For a set of subjectively chosen pesticide usage policies, $r, r = 1, \ldots, s$, rank the associated estimates of welfare, W_r, where

$$W_r = \underset{\substack{y_j \\ z_i}}{\text{maximum:}} \quad \sum_{j=1}^{n} \left\{ \int_0^{y_j} [f_j(y_j) - g_j^r(y_j)] dy_j \right\}$$

$$- \sum_{i=1}^{m} [h_i(z_i)] \qquad \begin{aligned} j &= 1, \ldots, n \\ i &= 1, \ldots, m \\ r &= 1, \ldots, s \end{aligned}$$

[7] These crops are tomatoes, potatoes, beans, corn, squash, avocados, limes, mangos.

[8] In an earlier specification of the model, "flexibility constraints" were applied to the acreage of each crop in an effort to recognize the many factors—economic, technological, institutional, and sociological—that discourage large deviations from past cropping patterns. For the jth crop, the maximum and minimum flexibility constraints were specified as:

$$b_j \text{ (max)} = \frac{\sum_{t=2}^{m_1} \dfrac{y_j(t)}{y_j(t-1)}}{m_1} \qquad \text{for } y_j(t) > y_j(t-1)$$

$$b_j \text{ (min)} = \frac{\sum_{t=2}^{m_2} \dfrac{y_j(t)}{y_j(t-1)}}{m_2} \qquad \text{for } y_j(t) \leq y_j(t-1)$$

where m_1 and m_2 are the number of periods respectively. In the model runs these constraints were ineffective on the solution; therefore, we have omitted them from this specification of the model. For a discussion of the concept of a "flexibility constraint," see Henderson (1959).

194

where the maximization for a given policy r is subject to

1. $\sum_{j=1}^{n} a_{ij}^r y_j - z_i = 0$

2. $c_{ki}(z_i) \leq C_{ki}^*$ $\qquad\qquad k = 1, \ldots, p$

3. $y_j, z_i \geq 0$

where

$f_j(y_j)$ = demand function for the jth crop;
y_j = acres of the jth crop;
$g_j^r(y_j)$ = supply function for the jth crop under the rth policy alternative;
$h_i(z_i)$ = an "externality function," a functional relationship between observed external effects expressed in dollars, and the quantity of the ith pesticide used;
z_i = quantity of the ith pesticide used, measured in pounds of 100 per cent active material;
a_{ij}^r = the quantity of the ith pesticide used per acre of the jth crop under the rth policy;
$c_{ki}(z_i)$ = the quantity of the ith pesticide residue produced in the kth environmental element as a function of the ith pesticide; and
C_{ki}^* = an arbitrary upper limit on the ith pesticide residue in the kth environmental element—a parameter to be determined "politically."

Since the orientation of this section is toward externalities in pesticide use, we will confine our comments to the two portions of the model involving externalities neglected in the surplus calculation. These externalities are accommodated by the model in one of two ways. Those which can be objectively valued in monetary terms are recognized through the externality function, $h_i(z_i)$. Those which cannot be adequately valued in monetary terms are conceptually recognized through "environmental constraints." The "externality function" will be discussed first, followed by a description of the measurement of externalities in Dade County; finally the concept of an environmental constraint will be introduced.

The Externality Function

For the externality function, an attempt was made to bypass the physical cause and effect relationships that exist between pesticides and externalities. The effort was aimed at relating a dollar measure of the social costs of externalities to the amount of a pesticide being used. The objective was to obtain structural estimates of the function:

$$\text{Ext} = H[z_1, z_2] = \sum_{i=1}^{2} [h_i(z_i)] \qquad (8)$$

where Ext is a dollar measure of externalities and z_1 and z_2 are pounds of 100 percent concentrated chlorinated hydrocarbons and organic phosphates, respectively, used in Dade County.

Since time series or cross-sectional data were not available on external dollar damages or pesticide use, it was possible to observe only one point on the function. The explanations for the point estimates of pesticide usage and externalities are developed later. The purpose of this section is to explain how the point estimates were integrated into the model.

The diagnosis of pesticide poisoning of humans was found to be relatively imprecise. If pesticide poisoning had been diagnosed, it was usually attributed to an organic phosphate—most often parathion. The total cost estimate of about $4,600 for the 1966–67 crop year in Dade County included those cases about which there was doubt and, in this sense, was biased upward for the organic phosphates.

There was very little substantive information on externalities attributable to the chlorinated hydrocarbons. If damage were caused by this group of pesticides, it was of a chronic, long-term nature which could not be adequately observed and valued at the time of the study. In an effort to overcome this shortcoming partially, sensitivity analysis was used on the externality function to observe the effect of higher levels of damage on public welfare.

Our data could be illustrated as shown in figure 5.2. The point estimate of externalities arising from the organic phosphates in 1966–67 was $4,600, and the corresponding organic phosphate use on the eight crops was 136,000 lbs.[9] These two pieces of information were quite difficult to obtain and are subject to some rather serious limitations that are discussed later. Perhaps they serve more to indicate the difficulty of obtaining "hard" data (particularly the $4,600 estimate) than they do to provide "good" estimates. Even if one accepts this point estimate, there remains the question of the shape of the function that passes through this point. There was no way to observe empirically additional points on the function as a basis for estimating the functional form. Hence, it was necessary to assume a func-

---

[9] This estimate of organic phosphate use represents an estimate of the total amount applied. This amount includes some indeterminate amount of wastage that did not reach the target plants. The wastage is a function of such things as size and density of plants, method of application, and weather conditions.

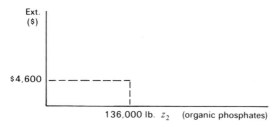

Figure 5.2. Point estimate of externalities arising from the agricultural use of organic phosphates.

tional form and to rely on sensitivity analysis for some indication of the solution's response to changes in this assumption.

We began by assuming a linear relation passing through the origin between externalities and organic phosphates and between externalities and chlorinated hydrocarbons. Thus the externality function could be depicted as:

$$Ext = \phi z_1 + \theta z_2 \qquad (9)$$

The observed level of acute externalities was \$4,600, so the value of θ necessary to pass the linear function through the origin and the observed point was .0338. The model was solved a number of times, allowing the coefficients of z_1 and z_2 to take on values between 0.0 and 5.0. These solutions, which we refer to as "Solution Set 1," will be discussed later.

The prevailing consensus was that, rather than being a linear function, the z_2 portion of the externality function was shaped as in figure 5.3. This figure implies that for organic phosphates, externalities increase at a decreasing rate.[10] In order to test the influence of this hypothesis on the model solution, the following externality function was used:

$$Ext = \phi z_1 + z_2^\lambda, \qquad (10)$$

where

ϕ varied from 0.0 to 5.0 in increments of 1.0,
$$\lambda = .708.$$

The parameter, λ, was established by forcing the function to pass through the origin and through the observed point on the function. These solutions, referred to as "Solution Set 2," will also be discussed later.

---

[10] The shape of the externality function relating to chlorinated hydrocarbons may increase at an increasing rate. However, for organic phosphates most externalities were associated with accidents which seem to increase, though at a decreasing rate with added usage.

197

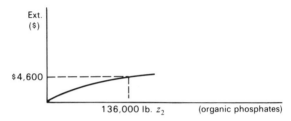

Figure 5.3. Hypothesized relationship for externalities arising from the agricultural use of organic phosphates.

Measuring Externalities

For purposes of empirical measurement an externality was defined as any "cost" created by the agricultural use of pesticides but not borne, or only partially borne, by the producers. This definition does not preclude the possibility of handling an external benefit as a negative cost. It is empirically operational, and is not inconsistent with that presented by Buchanan and Stubblebine (1962).

Although the estimation of externalities in Dade County was primarily based on information from two main sources, five sources were analyzed in an effort to be as comprehensive as possible.

The grower interview. A section of the questionnaire administered to growers in the area was devoted to questions about human sickness, damages to wildlife and domestic animals, and damage from drift among the growers.

The responses of the growers indicated that poisoning incidents were not increasing and probably were decreasing in spite of growing organic phosphate usage. Growers stated that education of spray men to the dangers of pesticides and safe ways of handling them has been a key factor in checking the rise of such incidents. It should be stressed that "safe ways of handling them" did not always coincide with "recommended ways." Only one grower stated that he required his men to wear protective clothing such as boots, gloves, and masks while spraying. The rest of the growers indicated that they made such equipment available but could not get their spray men to wear them. This equipment is very uncomfortable in the hot climate of south Florida, and most of the spray men would simply prefer to "take their chances" with the pesticides. Individual tolerance to pesticides among spray men seemed to vary a great deal. Some spray men were able to handle pesticides with no ill effects, while others tended to be very sensitive to them. In general, sensitive spray men did not remain

198

spray men very long. This natural selection process is also a possible explanation for the fact that pesticide sickness does not appear to be on the increase. It was also reported that some spray men refuse to apply the highly toxic organic phosphates such as parathion. This was not, however, observed to be very widespread.

Grower responses to questions about damage to domestic animals and wildlife were somewhat vague as to time of occurrence and extent of damage. In most cases this was probably due to lack of recollection. Many of the growers acknowledged fish-kills in the canals. Water was frequently taken out of the canals for irrigation and for mixing with pesticides. Some of this water eventually seeped back into the surface and ground waters, carrying with it some pesticide residues. It was also likely that some residues in the surface waters flowed down from the farming regions just north of Dade County. Growers also acknowledged that spray rigs were frequently washed out in the canals, increasing the pesticide residues. Most of the fish found in the canals and drainage ditches are what conservationists call "rough fish" (not considered suitable for human consumption), but the migratory laborers, nevertheless, eat them, and they are a part of the ecological system of the area.

Some wildlife could, of course, be classified as "pests" and were purposely poisoned by the growers. This was frequently the case with rats, blackbirds, crows, and raccoons. One grower stated that the robin was a pest to strawberry growers. Seagulls are very plentiful in the area, and several growers stated that they were sometimes killed by the pesticides. Three growers stated each had had one dog killed from drinking polluted water standing in the fields.

It is customary in Dade County to use honeybees to facilitate pollination on some of the blooming crops. Squash is the dominant example. Hives of honeybees are rented from beekeepers by the growers and placed around the field. One beekeeper, a past president of the Beekeepers' Association, was contacted about pesticide damage to the bees. He stated that such damage was very common, and that most beekeepers assumed they would lose a few bees when they were rented out. Bees, however, reproduce very quickly; therefore the economic loss was slight. He also said that most of the growers were using more caution, and that damage during the past two or three years was much less than it had been previously. Generally there was no cash settlement above rental cost when damage occurred.

Damage among growers from pesticide drift was also investigated. When such damage occurred, the growers usually settled the problem informally among themselves with the damaging party making compensation in one form or another. Sometimes the party causing the damage was unknown and the damaged party simply had to absorb the cost. In either case, the costs were limited to the producers as a group and were not construed as being external to the industry supply function. The trends toward fewer crops and larger crop fields have caused the drift problem to decline in recent years.

It is conceivable that external benefits may have been caused by pesticide drift. One grower located in the center of a number of growers who spray regularly may not have had to spray as much as he would otherwise because of the drift from the other growers and the protective pesticide barrier around his field. This is speculation, however, and we were unable to gather any data to substantiate such a hypothesis.

As a group, the growers were well insured. Not only did almost all of them carry workmen's compensation on their employees, but they also carried general liability to protect them in case they damaged the property of others. They did not, however, have insurance for cases where others damaged their property.

Insurance claims. A Florida state law requires all workmen's compensation claims to be filed with the Florida Industrial Commission. Industrial Commission data for Dade County for the years 1966 and 1967 were obtained and summarized.

All of the workmen's compensation claims reported to the Industrial Commission are classified into two groups—disabling and nondisabling, defined as follows:

Disabling injury: a work injury resulting in death, permanent impairment, or loss of time beyond the day or shift of occurrence.

Nondisabling injury: an injury arising out of and in the course of employment in which there is no loss of time beyond the day or shift of occurrence (Florida Industrial Commission, 1966 ed.).

Very little data are maintained on the nondisabling category. The number of injuries in this category is much greater than in the disabling category, but the cost per injury is much less.

The Industrial Commission categorizes its disabling injuries in a number of ways. The one which seemed most important for this research was "Disabling work injuries by agency." The "Agency of injury" identifies the object, substance, exposure, or bodily motion that directly produced or inflicted the injury. There are 53 agency categories, one of which is called "Poisons and infectious agents."

For the state as a whole the category "Poisons and infectious agents" is declining in importance (Edwards 1969, pp. 78–80). Percentages of number of injuries, days lost, and costs have all declined since 1962. The Dade

County cost figures for 1966 and 1967 are consistent with this finding. In 1966 the total cost for the agency was about $175,000 while in 1967 it was about $115,000.

Veterinarians. In order to get additional information on the effects of pesticides on domestic animals, arrangements were made to sample the records of three veterinarians in the area. Two were located approximately on the dividing line between the rural and urban areas, while the third was located in Homestead, the heart of the rural area. Samples as nearly random as possible were taken from each.[11] The frequency of pesticide calls was noted along with the diagnosis, the species, and the treatment. After sampling, a brief conversation was held with each veterinarian to see if the sample bore out his a priori notions. The veterinarians all stated, before seeing the sample results, that they would expect the frequency of pesticide cases to be a small fraction of 1 per cent. This agreed with sample results. They further said that they felt the incidence of pesticide calls was not increasing.

In sampling the veterinarian records, an effort was made to include all calls that might have been connected with pesticides even though some were questionable. Even so, the frequency of pesticide calls was extremely low and was far overshadowed by:

1. cases in which animals were hit by autos;
2. cases in which an animal swallowed a fishhook;
3. cases of tick paralysis;
4. cases of dog fights or cat fights.

Biologists. Biologists at the Everglades National Park and the research director for the National Audubon Society, located on Tavernier Key, were contacted in an effort to gather more information on pesticide damage to wildlife. Of all the areas touched upon by the research project, this

[11] The first veterinarian numbered his cases sequentially and had about 10,000 of them. Each case contained an average of 4.5 calls. Using a table of random numbers to determine the starting point, 909 cases were examined for a total of 4,090 calls. There was no relation between a case's sequence number and the dates of the calls contained therein.

The second veterinarian maintained his cases alphabetically, by last name of owner, and did not know how many he had. Ten small file drawers were involved so the first and last 150 calls in each drawer were arbitrarily examined. This veterinarian also kept a separate file for deceased cases, and all of these were examined.

The third veterinarian maintained his files alphabetically, by last name of owner, and they did not lend themselves well to sampling. For this veterinarian, all of the "D's" were examined—a total of 275 cases with four calls per case.

area—pesticide effects upon wildlife—was probably the most difficult to assess and the most difficult to speak about definitively.[12]

The mechanisms by which pesticides are transmitted, modified, and accumulated in the environment are not well understood, so it is impossible to determine the direct exposure of a given species in a locale even if one knows the quantity of pesticides being applied to agricultural crops in that area and in ecologically related areas. And even if the direct exposure level for a given species is known, there are at least two other areas of ignorance that prevent measurement of the effects on that species. First, we do not understand how sublethal exposure affects a given species; and second, we do not know how the effect on one species will affect other species through the ecological system. Research on the former is now moving along rapidly, but statistical evidence to date has been inconclusive and, in some cases, contradictory (Keith 1966; Lehner 1967; Locke, Chura, and Stewart 1966; USDA 1967; Woodwell 1967). Research on the latter is in its infancy, and results useful for policy formulation will probably not be available for several years.

Two conclusions that we hope are unbiased about the position of biologists were reached from discussions with them. First, biologists are far more afraid of chlorinated hydrocarbons as a group than of organic phosphates and would favor policies designed to encourage the substitution of organic phosphates for chlorinated hydrocarbons. This stems from a feeling that long-term, sublethal exposure to the chlorinated hydrocarbons is detrimental, primarily to the reproductive process. Since organic phosphates decompose quickly in the environment, their effects tend to be acute and are not likely to have hereditary ramifications. Second, while there is as yet no conclusive proof of the long-range detriment of low-exposure levels, the circumstantial evidence is increasing rapidly[13] (Kimball 1968).

In summary, the opposing positions seem to reduce to:

Biologist: "Until the chlorinated hydrocarbons are proved harmless, they should not be used."

Farmer: "Until the chlorinated hydrocarbons are proved harmful, they may be used."

Community Studies on Pesticides. Another source of information on externalities in Dade County was the Community Studies on Pesticides, a

[12] The reader who is interested in the effects of pesticides on wildlife is advised to read an evaluation by the National Academy of Sciences. See also The Study of Critical Environmental Problems (1970), pp. 126–36.

[13] There are ecologists who would disagree with this statement; i.e., who maintain that sufficient evidence has been accumulated to state definitely that long-range detrimental effects do occur. [Editor's note.]

program of the U.S. Public Health Service and the Florida Department of Public Health, under the direction of John E. Davies, M.D. At the time of this study the Community Studies program consisted of a nationwide series of epidemiological and ecological studies on levels of pesticides in the human population and environment of selected study areas. Contractual arrangements were made with state boards of health and medical schools or universities whereby the Public Health Service could arrange for and support investigations of the effects of pesticides upon human health. The typical program had two major facets—monitoring and epidemiology. The monitoring program attempted to determine the levels of pesticide residues, primarily chlorinated hydrocarbons, in human tissues and in the environment. The epidemiological facet sought to detect in occupationally exposed workers clinical illness or subtle biochemical changes that could be caused by pesticides.

The Dade County program was relatively new, having been set up in 1964, and did not have a great deal of output useful for our research, especially in the area of chronic or long-term damage. With time, their accumulated knowledge should constitute a valuable source of information on the "human health" aspect of the pesticide issue.

Concluding Remarks on Externalities in Dade County. The problem with many writings on the pesticide issue is that they quickly degenerate into an enumerative description of incidents in which pesticides represent either the culprit or the hero, depending on the side of the issue espoused by the writer. Conclusions cannot easily be drawn from such a process. For analytical purposes one would like to aggregate the incidents with some common measure, and incorporate them into a benefit-cost analysis.

The activities described above constituted the search for externalities in Dade County—the enumeration process. The job of reducing and aggregating the incidents to a common measure required some strong and somewhat arbitrary assumptions. Omissions and double counting of externalities also aggravated accurate measurement. Table 5.3 is a summary of the externality calculation used in the model.

This estimate is subject to three limitations. First, in the search for externalities, there was no guarantee that all externalities had been recognized and that none was double counted. It was felt that the more logical sources of information were exhausted, but this did not mean that all externalities were uncovered nor did it give a basis for measuring the confidence one could place in the enumeration.

A second limitation was that, by the nature of things, the list was probably biased toward external costs relative to external benefits. External costs were simply easier to observe since they tend to create controversy.

203

Table 5.3. Summary of the Externalities Incorporated in the
Empirical Model, Dade County, 1967

Nature of externality	Extent of damage	
Damage to humans[a]		
Compensation	$1,094[b]	
Medical	662	
Hospital	653	
Artificial members	27	
First aid	125	
Total 1		$2,561
Total 2[c]		3,227
Total 3[d]		3,470
Damage to domestic animals[e]	$1,120	
Total		$4,590

[a] Data from the Florida Industrial Commission serve as the basis for these figures. The agents, "Parathion" and "Insecticides not elsewhere classified," were added together.

[b] The original figure for this estimate was $547. According to Florida law, the maximum payable compensation is $46 per week. But the average weekly salary of Florida workers is $86.18. Therefore the original figure was doubled to try to reflect more accurately the true dollar loss.

[c] Total 2 represents a 26 per cent increase over total 1 because disabling damages, which must be estimated at the time of occurrence, have historically been underestimated. For a more complete explanation of this increase in cost, see the report, "Facts About Workmen's Compensation" (February, 1968), published by the Florida Industrial Commission, Research and Statistics Department, Caldwell Building, Tallahassee, Florida 32304.

[d] Total 3 represents an increase over total 2 to reflect the fact that the dollar cost of disabling claims in agriculture have historically comprised 93 per cent of the dollar cost of total claims.

[e] From data gathered from the veterinarians. Assumptions are that (a) all poisoning calls are included, whether or not they are designated "pesticide," "toad," or "lizard"; (b) a dead animal was assumed to be worth $50; and (c) an average veterinarian call was assumed to cost $10.

One grower stated, for example, that he hoped the adjacent grower's spray did drift over to his field (they were growing the same crop), but there was no way to quantify this phenomenon. The killing of certain pests, such as rats, might have had a beneficial effect on human health by holding down disease but, again, quantification was impossible. The "state of the arts," particularly in the area of ecological relationships, simply does not permit such quantification.

The third limitation stems from the fact that all observed externalities were acute as opposed to chronic. This point was made implicitly in the section entitled "Biologists." Biologists suspect that the persistent pesticides are harmful to reproduction, but the evidence for such a hypothesis is very fragmentary, and the data did not exist to permit us to recognize it in the model.

In summary, it can be stated that, despite very substantial research efforts to quantify externalities, very little "hard" data were uncovered.

Environmental Constraints

The environmental constraints in the model,

$$c_{ki}(z_1) \leq C_{ki}^* \qquad \begin{array}{l} k = 1, \ldots, p \\ i = 1, \ldots, m \end{array}$$

say that the residue of pesticide i in the kth environmental element shall not be allowed to exceed C_{ki}^*, a politically determined value. This constraint is extremely important from a conceptual point of view, for this is the route by which value judgments and externalities not amenable to monetary expression gain admission to the model and restrain the solution. But the data needed to activate the environmental constraint do not exist as of this writing, so the constraint could not be included in the model runs. The type of data needed for this constraint should be of great interest to ecologists and conservationists, for they frequently argue that wildlife, clear water, and beautiful sunsets are incommensurable, and that . . . "in a positivistic society, commensurables are automatically 'valued' above incommensurables" (Clement 1968, p. 17). Admittedly, the environmental constraints do not make commensurables out of incommensurables, but they might give an indication of what the incommensurables are costing in terms of market values.

Some recent studies, particularly those of the Patuxent Wildlife Research Center, approach the model's concept of an environmental constraint. For example, Stickel and Stickel (1968, p. 13) state, "Residues in brains of birds of several species killed under different conditions were of a similar magnitude. . . . The concentration of 30 ppm of DDT plus DDD appears to be a useful approximation for the beginning of zone of hazard, although some birds will die with lower amounts." We as a society might then make the value judgment, through our legislators and policy makers, that we would like to maintain the species' brain level of residue at or below 30 ppm. This figure would become the "politically determined value" in the environmental constraint.

Let us now consider the information that is needed for the remainder of the environmental constraint. Essentially what we need is the relation between brain residue levels and exposure levels for the given species, but we might have to use "quantity of pesticides applied" as a proxy variable for exposure level simply because it is the closest concept to "exposure levels" that we can actually measure. This will certainly introduce additional variability into the relationship since the quantity of pesticide applied is not perfectly correlated with exposure level. But if we hope to influence or regulate pesticide usage, then we must ultimately come back to those variables over which we have some control, commonly called "policy variables." If we could estimate the relation between pesticide residue in the brain of some species and the level of pesticide usage in the region, then we would have a function that can be directly admitted to the economic model.

We do not wish to try to play the role of ecologist, but it might be enlightening at this point to speculate on a few factors that seem to complicate the estimation of the relation between pesticide application and resulting brain residue level.

First, there are important intermediate stages of cause and effect. After the pesticide is applied, it disperses into the biosphere. The degree and form of dispersion depend upon climatic and geographic characteristics, the method of application, and the formulation of the pesticide. Next, the species under consideration is exposed to the pesticide either directly or indirectly through the food chain. Finally, the pesticide enters the body and is influenced by a number of physiological factors before it manifests itself as residue in the brain.

Second, these relationships are most likely time-related in the sense that a pesticide application today influences brain residues tomorrow. This problem is illustrated mathematically by relation (4) in part I.

Third, the relationships would be dynamic. In other words they might shift with changes in the physiology of the species, practices of pesticide use, and so forth.

Fourth, the relationships would probably vary from one broad geographic region to another.

Speculation such as this is very discouraging. Many individuals on both sides of the pesticide issue have thrown up their hands in despair and pushed blindly for policy that appeals to their basic emotional proclivities. However, it is our opinion that if such a process produces an optimal allocation of the public's resources, taking account of both "commensurables" and "incommensurables," it is purely by accident.

Since we do not yet have data and methodology to permit us to estimate the above relationships, let us consider a slightly different approach using two types of data that might make it possible to specify crude environmental constraints.

First, we need regular statistical series showing the quantities of pesticide residues in certain ecologically important elements of the environment, such as air, water, soil, and critical species of animals. This area of monitoring is currently progressing at the greatest speed and accumulating a sizeable body of data. One of the main sources for the documentation of such monitoring studies is the *Pesticides Monitoring Journal.*

Second, regular statistical series are needed that show the quantities of pesticides being injected into the environment by the various groups that use pesticides.[14] It might then be possible to relate statistically the pattern of usage with the pattern of monitored observations and hence formulate a relation that can be admitted to the model as an environmental constraint.

It should be pointed out that the manner in which an environmental constraint can be stated is very flexible. If, for example, we subscribe to the theory that chlorinated hydrocarbons inhibit calcium formation, we might think in terms of relating use of pesticides to the residue content of eggs in order to establish the constraint. The shadow price for such a constraint provides a basis for placing a monetary value on society's environmental value judgment.

In conclusion, the message of this section is cautiously optimistic. The natural sciences appear to be producing output which can be used in the foreseeable future by imaginative social scientists for policy decision models.[15]

Analytical Results, Implications, and Recommendations

The solution to the model for a specified policy consisted of: (a) the maximum value of the objective function, which was a measure of the net social benefits of the crops studied; (b) the crop acreages consistent with the above objective function and policy; and (c) the pounds of z_1 and z_2 consistent with the objective function and policy.

To date, two sets of solutions have been generated. These were referred to previously as Solution Set 1 and Solution Set 2, and are defined in terms of the form of the externality function.[16]

[14] Efforts to measure such quantities have been very limited. In 1964, Congress authorized an expanded program of research on the use of pesticides in agriculture (USDA 1967). One phase of the expanded program was to conduct a periodic farm survey to obtain information on the use of pesticides in different areas and on different crops and classes of livestock. While this program will no doubt generate very useful data in the future, its relevance for our research was limited for two reasons. First, there is approximately a two-year time lag before survey results are published; and second, no farms were sampled in Dade County and only a few in Florida as a whole.

[15] Donald Chant argues that the search for measurable, including monetary, externalities and for explicit environmental constraints is completely unrealistic, given the vast number of species for which allowable concentrations in brain or eggs would have to be determined. He argues for a policy posture that would preclude use of any material having the following characteristics: high persistence, high mobility, carcinogenic qualities, mutagenic qualities, and hormone interference in higher organisms. [Editor's note.]

[16] See page 197.

Solution Set 1

The externality function for this solution set was

$$C = \phi z_1 + \theta z_2,$$

where
$$\phi = 0, 1, \ldots, 20;$$
$$\theta = 0, .0338, 1, 2, 3, 4, 5.$$

The model was solved for policy 1, current pesticide usage practices, and for policy 2, a 50 per cent reduction in the per acre usage of chlorinated hydrocarbons. Under policy 2, three substitution rates were used between chlorinated hydrocarbons and organic phosphates, and a model solution was generated for each. It was found that within the range from 0.3 to 0.5 pounds of organic phosphates per pound of chlorinated hydrocarbons, the solution acreage was very stable, varying less than 0.01 per cent. This leads to the conclusion that the aggregate substitution rate between chlorinated hydrocarbons and organic phosphates is not a critical variable for the crops studied in Dade County and may not be worthy of much additional research expenditure. To avoid unnecessary complexity, all results presented in this section are for the middle value, or 0.4 pounds of organic phosphates for each 1.0 pound of chlorinated hydrocarbons.

With policy 1 and disregarding externalities entirely, the solution acreages for current pesticide use were:

Tomatoes	19,000 acres
Potatoes	7,700 acres
Beans	5,800 acres
Corn	1,650 acres
Squash	3,080 acres
Groves	10,340 acres

When the estimated acute externalities from organic phosphates were recognized ($\theta = .0338$), the solution acreages remained the same. When θ had acquired a value of 5.0, or about sixteen times the estimated level, the solution acreages were:

Tomatoes	18,800 acres
Potatoes	7,400 acres
Beans	5,800 acres
Corn	1,600 acres
Squash	3,080 acres
Groves	10,340 acres

At this point the use of chlorinated hydrocarbons had only fallen by 1.8 per cent and that of organic phosphates by 2.3 per cent.

Parametric programming on the externality coefficient for chlorinated hydrocarbons, ϕ, caused more extensive changes. At estimated levels of acute externalities (from organic phosphates), ($\theta = .0338$), and when ϕ was increased, the solution acreages for tomatoes and corn declined progressively while that for potatoes and beans hardly changed. When ϕ had acquired a value of 20, tomato acreage declined to 18,000 acres and corn to 400 acres. At this level of ϕ, the usage of chlorinated hydrocarbons had fallen by 26.2 per cent and organic phosphates by 10 per cent.

With policy 2—a 50 per cent reduction in use of hydrocarbons—two results stand out. First, as in policy 1, the solution acreages tended to be "stable" as the coefficients of z_1 and z_2 were varied. In general, very large changes in external "damage" levels caused very small changes in solution acreages.

Second, the value of the objective function fell only 1 per cent under policy 2 at observed externality levels.

Solution Set 2

The externality function for this solution set was

$$C = \phi z_1 + z_2^\lambda,$$

where

$$\phi = 0, 1, \ldots, 5,$$
$$\lambda = .708.$$

The model was again solved for policies 1 and 2. The differential in social welfare between policies 1 and 2 narrows with this hypothesis about the externality function. This result gives the opponents of persistent pesticides a stronger case for advocating the substitution of organic phosphates for chlorinated hydrocarbons.

IMPLICATIONS AND CONCLUSIONS

What general conclusions, then, can be drawn from our research results to date? It appears that a 50 per cent reduction in the use of chlorinated hydrocarbons could be effected with about a 1 per cent decline in the net social benefits of the crops studied. As yet we cannot say what would happen to welfare under policies of eliminating more than approximately 50 per cent of the chlorinated hydrocarbons. We are currently studying the effects of greater reduction in usage of chlorinated hydrocarbons. In Dade County it is entirely possible that agricultural production would be virtually wiped out, given current consumer attitudes toward produce quality. We would then import these vegetables and fruits from other countries where pests are less prevalent or pesticide regulations less stringent. Also we must remember that the effects of a policy change would not be distributed evenly across all farmers or across other members of society. Some would be hurt or helped more than others. The change in the welfare function of our model is an "average" of all these effects.

Furthermore, technology is changing in a way favorable to the substitution of less persistent for more persistent pesticides. Companies are concentrating their research efforts on developing new pesticides that are less persistent, and we can realistically expect that through time, cheaper and more effective nonpersistent pesticides will be developed.[17] This trend suggests a multi-stage versus a single-stage approach to reducing the usage of chlorinated hydrocarbons. In the multi-stage approach we may evaluate, for example, a 50 per cent reduction policy. If it improves or is not "too detrimental" to welfare, we pursue it. When it is accomplished, we again evaluate a 50 per cent reduction policy and again pursue it if it is not "too detrimental" to welfare. This process continues as long as welfare is improved or until the governing body decides that the price of further reduction is too high. At each stage of the process a new state of the arts prevails which the analyst may recognize in his model. The multi-stage approach would leave more flexibility for adjustment, more freedom for the farmers, and would permit the accumulation of valuable knowledge as the process continues. It would also contain less predictive error simply because the near future is easier to forecast. At the same time, it would not require an extensive length of time to achieve large reductions in the usage of persistent pesticides under a well-organized program.

However, decision making in the area of chemical pest control is fraught with an enormous amount of uncertainty. Policy makers in the Congress and in USDA are in an unenviable position of being under considerable pressure from a largely urban population to take positive steps to assure that irreversible damage to the environment is prevented. At the same time the pressure of hunger around the world and the welfare of the farmers and consumers at home make it extremely important that nothing be done to impair seriously the output of food and fiber.

The results of pesticide productivity studies indicate that chemical pesticides are currently making a definite positive contribution to agricultural output across the country. Given current pesticide-product price ratios, the level of adoption of the technology is high and expanding. However, as has been pointed out, this expansion has been encouraged by a price and income policy for agriculture that has restricted land inputs

[17] Increasing research is also underway on biological controls, combined chemical-biological controls, development of pest resistant strains. [Editor's note.]

and increased the relative price of cropland. If the price of pesticides does not reflect the full costs of their use because of spillover effects on the environment, both in contemporary and intertemporal senses, then the combination of pesticides and land that is used may not be the least cost combination from a social point of view.

Given such a disequilibrium situation, the direction of adjustment is easily discerned—reduce the level of chemical pest control relative to land used in the agricultural production system. It is not so easy to discern where to do so and by how much.

It seems that agricultural science is in a better position to assess the impact of a change in our system of pest control than it is to determine the full costs of pesticides. However, even in the former, orientation of research programs has provided few answers to questions relating to the time patterns of pest populations under various kinds of cultural practices, the impact of these populations on agricultural output, and the resulting adjustments in resource use. All of the effects and adjustments have impacts on the supply function for agriculture, agricultural income, and food and fiber prices. Patterns of regional specialization and even rural population can be influenced by the methods of pest control adopted.

We may be at a turning point in agricultural policy. For years the conventional position has been to restrict output by restricting acreage and to move surplus labor out of agriculture. This position is based on elementary demand theory and the rather tenuous argument, without benefit of rigorous demonstration, that the interest of society was being served. We may now be seeing, if not too clearly, the social costs of this policy.

REFERENCES

Allen, R. G. D. 1938. *Mathematical analysis for economists*. London: Macmillan and Co., Ltd., pp. 340–43.

Berry, John H. 1970. Effect of restricting the use of pesticides on corn-soybean farms. Paper presented at the Symposium on Economic Research on Pesticides for Policy Decision Making, U.S. Department of Agriculture, April 27–29, 1970, Washington, D.C.

Buchanan, James M., and William Craig Stubblebine. 1962. Externality. *Economica* 29:371–84.

Clement, Roland C. 1968. The pesticide problem. *Natural Resources Journal* 8, no. 1:11–22.

Edwards, W. F. 1969. Economic externalities in the agricultural use of pesticides and the evaluation of alternative policies. Ph.D. diss., University of Florida.

Edwards, W. F., M. R. Langham, and J. C. Headley. 1970. Pesticide residues and environmental economics. *Natural Resources Journal* 10, no. 4:719–41.

Eichers, Theodore, *et al.* 1968. *Quantities of pesticides used by farmers, 1964.* Agricultural Economic Report No. 131. U.S. Department of Agriculture, Economic Research Service.

Florida Industrial Commission. 1962–63, 1966, and 1967. *Analysis of work injuries covered by workmen's compensation.*

Headley, J. C. 1968. Estimating the productivity of agricultural pesticides. *American Journal of Agricultural Economics* 50, no. 1:13–23.

Henderson, James M. 1959. The utilization of agricultural land, a theoretical and empirical inquiry. *Review of Economics and Statistics* 41, no. 3:242–59.

Keith, J. A. 1966. Reproduction in a population of herring gulls (larus argentatus) contaminated by DDT. *Journal of Applied Ecology* 3 (Supplement):57–70.

Kimball, Thomas L. 1968. Changing trends in insect control. *N.A.C. News* 27, no. 1:8–9. (Remarks before the 35th Annual Meeting of the National Agricultural Chemicals Association, September 23, 1968, White Sulphur Springs, West Virginia.)

Lehner, Philip M., Thomas O. Boswell, and Frank Copeland. 1967. An evaluation of the effects of the aedes aegypti eradication program on wildlife in South Florida. *Pesticide Monitoring Journal* 1, no. 2:29–34.

Locke, Louis N., Nicholas J. Chura, and Paul A. Stewart. 1966. Spermatogenesis in bald eagles experimentally fed a diet containing DDT. *The Condor* 68, no. 5:297–502.

National Academy of Sciences—National Research Council. 1962. *Pest control and wildlife relationships: Part I. Evaluation of pesticide wildlife problems.* National Academy of Sciences—National Research Council Publication 920-A.

President's Science Advisory Committee. 1965. *Restoring the quality of our environment.* Report of the Environmental Pollution Panel. Appendix Y11.

Stickel, Lucille F., and William H. Stickel. 1968. Distribution of DDT residues in tissues of birds in relation to mortality, body condition, and time. (Paper presented at the Sixth Inter-American Conference on Toxicology and Occupational Medicine, August 26–29, 1968, Miami, Florida.)

The Study of Critical Environment Problems. 1970. *Man's impact on the global environment.* Cambridge, Mass.: MIT Press.

U.S. Department of Agriculture. 1968. *Agricultural statistics 1968.* Washington, D.C.: Government Printing Office.

U.S. Department of Agriculture, Economic Research Service. 1967. *Farmers' expenditures for pesticides in 1964.* Agricultural Economic Report No. 106. Washington, D.C.: Government Printing Office.

U.S. Department of the Interior, Fish and Wildlife Service. 1967. *Wildlife research problems programs progress, 1966.* Washington, D.C.: Government Printing Office.

U.S. Senate. 1965. Subcommittee on Reorganization and International Organizations of the Committee on Government Operations. *Interagency coordination in environmental hazards* (Pesticides). 88th Cong. 2d sess., March 1, 1965, Appendix I to Part I.

Woodwell, George M. 1967. Toxic substances and ecological cycles. *Scientific American* 216, no. 3:24–31.

6. Air Pollution Damage: Some Difficulties in Estimating the Value of Abatement

Lester B. Lave

I. INTRODUCTION

Constructing a benefit analysis for pollution abatement consists of finding out what consumers would pay (as a schedule) if there were no problems with knowledge, psychological realization, income distribution, decision making for others, myopia (and other problems with decisions over time), and public goods. That is, we want to know what consumers would pay for abatement if the economic world were optimal except for air pollution (and that only marginally incorrect).[1]

There are a number of approaches to deriving this schedule. One assumes that consumers know the benefit of pollution abatement (explicitly or implicitly); the problem then becomes how to tease out the answer from the consumer. If the consumer knows explicitly, we must ask him in a way that will elicit complete information and dissuade lying. If the consumer knows implicitly—i.e., his knowledge is reflected in his actions even though he may not be consciously aware of the problem—we must analyze his actions that are directly related to pollution. Another approach denies that the consumer has systematic knowledge of the benefits of pollution abatement. In this case, one must estimate the physical benefit and then find a way to translate this physical benefit into dollar terms.

Certainly the former approach is simpler and closer to a classical eco-

---

[1] A number of recent discussions concerns each of these problems. For example, if there are deviations from Pareto Optimality other than air pollution, the general theory of the second best is relevant (see Baumol and Bradford 1970; Davis and Whinston 1967; and Lerner 1970). The proper rate of discount is discussed in Arrow and Kurz (1970) and in Baumol (1968). The other points are considered in the review article on benefit-cost analysis by Prest and Turvey (1965).

213

nomic approach. It focuses our attention on the things that economists have the most experience with, namely estimating utility functions, demand functions, and splitting the pollution component of a price from other factors. However, I believe that this approach is not likely to lead to fruitful results.

Consumers are dreadfully ignorant of the benefit of abatement. Surveys tend to find that people are not willing to pay much for abatement.[2] This occurs in spite of the many obvious biases toward overstating the amount one would pay, as discussed in section III.

If consumers act as if they know the value of pollution abatement, then the market will reflect their actions in prices; for instance, residential land in unpolluted areas will carry a premium. I will explore this issue at length in section IV, but cannot resist throwing a stone in anticipation. Aside from the doubt that consumers really do reflect their knowledge of pollution in land rents, it is extremely difficult to split off the pollution component of the rent differential. A really serious difficulty here concerns the assumption that land rents must be in equilibrium at any time and must reflect consumer knowledge of pollution patterns over time and space. I find that these assumptions are not even reasonable approximations, as argued in section IV.

You cannot bet on a horse race unless there are contrary opinions. More careful work, principally in the form of more careful data collection, could resolve many difficulties and improve the answers from the implicit approach. In advocating the explicit approach to finding the value of pollution abatement, I am all too conscious of the additional difficulties I have introduced. It is a good deal simpler to estimate the component of what consumers now pay that is due to air pollution than to engage in the flight of fancy involved in determining what they would pay for a new (or "comparable") product. Economists are much better at the sort of hair splitting involved in separating demand into components than at estimating the demand for new product and services. However, if one doubts that consumers have knowledge and that market prices reflect implicit knowledge (gained by experience, even though the consumer may not realize the true costs), one has no alternative to adopting the explicit evaluation.

This approach means that I have two tasks: to quantify the physical damage function and then translate the physical damage into value terms. In some cases, the former task is quite easy. The effect of air pollution on visibility is directly measured. However, translating physical damage into

---

[2] For example, Ridker (1967, p. 82) found that people living in areas of high pollution were willing to pay less than $10 per year for a "complete" solution to the pollution problem.

value terms is never easy or straightforward. How much are consumers willing to pay for a clearer atmosphere? If one is sufficiently clever, various kinds of surrogates can be used to estimate this figure. For example, one might look at the premium paid for residential lots with good visibility. Generally, the task is very difficult. Other translations seem easy at first glance, only to prove to be terribly entangled. For example, we know that air pollution speeds the deterioration of many objects—clothes and auto tires.[3] However, if clothes are generally thrown away before they are worn out, and if tires are worn out by driving before pollution damage becomes a factor, the value added (or lost) because of pollution will be negligible.

The range of uncertainty, both in estimating the physical damage function and in translating it into value terms, is great. One can only hope to estimate rather conservative figures, lower and upper bounds for the dollar losses. This means that the value of pollution abatement will always cover a large range, although it is hoped that this will be small enough for major decisions about abatement not to depend on where the estimate falls within the range.

II. ESTIMATING THE PHYSICAL DAMAGE FUNCTION

The Physiological Mechanism

The damage function of interest is the effect of air pollution on human health. The precise question is how air pollution affects illness and death rates, including partial disability, absence from work, absence from school, and expenditures on health. How many days of life, good health, or work would be gained by a specified reduction in pollution? In attempting to answer these questions, a prime consideration is the lack of a theoretical model specifying the way air pollution affects health.[4] Although acute pollution episodes lead to increased mortality and aggravate chronic diseases, the predominant effect is more subtle and relates to increasing the incidence of chronic diseases. While the principal effect is probably associated with chronic respiratory diseases, the human body is sufficiently

---

[3] A good discussion of the effect of air pollution on inert materials is contained in Yocom (1962). This evidence is reviewed by Kneese (1967) who characterizes it as quite rough.

[4] A number of discussions have concerned the way that air pollution has been found to affect health (Ipsen, Ingenito, and Deane 1969; Ferris 1968; and Goldsmith 1965). However, these discussions tend to reason from available data without seeking to specify a physiological mechanism or build a general model that could generate predictions beyond what was observed.

complex so that other chronic diseases, such as heart disease, are aggravated. Medicine provides little insight as to which chronic disease might be aggravated, what time period is involved, or what would be reasonable effects. Thus, the investigation is necessarily a crude exploration for significant effects with little a priori knowledge to guide it.

Mortality or Morbidity?

Under these conditions, investigating morbidity is more likely to be fruitful than examining mortality. Death is the end of a complicated sequence that starts with an initial disease and may evolve in many ways; often the "immediate cause of death" will have little to do with the initial disease. The general deterioration in health can lead to death from a large number of unrelated causes. The optimal investigation would be one on morbidity rates for various respiratory and similar directly related diseases.

Unfortunately, data on morbidity rates, absence rates, and health expenditures are not available on any extensive basis. Whatever the merits of these data, I am forced to rely on mortality data.

The Value Added of Air Pollution

A number of problems are associated with analyzing mortality rates. Putting off death is worth little unless reasonably good health is restored. Keeping a patient alive, but in a coma, for a few extra days is worth nothing. In analyzing mortality rates, one must remember that everyone dies eventually. Lowering the bronchitis death rate among octogenarians probably does not add much value to pollution abatement. These people would have a short life expectancy even if they were completely healthy; little additional time would be added by abating pollution. Age-specific death rates are much better data than crude mortality rates; some results for age specific death rates are discussed under "Age Specific Mortality and Life Expectancy."

The Urban Factor

It has long been recognized that there is an urban factor in mortality. People living in large cities have higher total death rates and disease specific rates, which seem to be related directly to pollution. However, one must stop short of this obvious association. City dwellers tend to lead more strained, less healthy lives. They smoke more, tend to be more overweight, get less exercise, and generally lead a less healthy life. Air pollution must be separated from the other causes explaining this urban factor.[5]

Other environmental factors might be correlated with air pollution and consequently bias the estimated effect; e.g., radiation. Since fallout generally takes the form of radioactive particles that mingle with ordinary air pollution, one must be careful not to confuse these two effects. Other environmental factors have to do with occupational exposure and diet. Even nonenvironmental factors are known to be significant, e.g., genetic factors.[6]

The problem is similar to the earlier controversy over smoking.[7] It is virtually impossible to account for all possible factors that might be the "real" causes of ill health. In the absence of a theory specifying the nature of the relation, it is impossible to rule out various causes as insignificant or unrelated. This means that a great deal of evidence is necessary before one can conclude that there is an effect or what the magnitude of it is.

The problem is that skeptics can propose many factors as "the real cause" of the illness (rather than pollution). As a consequence, (a) all of one's time can be spent gathering data, (b) it will be found that there are no data of the sort that could test some hypotheses, (c) eventually other factors will be found that, no matter how implausible, explain illness variations about as well as the pollution data. Without a physiological mechanism, there is no limit to the number of possible causes. Eventually, as with smoking, the evidence of many studies and more carefully collected data should overwhelm the critics. At the end of section II under "Is There Really an Association?," I discuss some current objections to the association between air pollution and ill health.

Pollution and Smoking: Interactions?

In attempting to separate the effects of air pollution from other factors, significant interactions appear. For example, the death rate for smokers in a polluted atmosphere is much higher than that for smokers in a rural environment.[8] Where there are interactions, the question arises of how to parcel out the effect.

For example, Buell, Dunn, and Breslow (1967) contrast lung cancer mortality rates in the San Francisco–San Diego urban areas with rates in less urban counties. A nonsmoker experiences an increased risk equal to

[5] See, for example, the discussion of urban-rural comparisons of mortality rates in MacMahon, Pugh, and Ipsen (1960), pp. 149–53.
[6] For discussions of radiation, see Sternglass (1969) and Lave, Leindhardt, and Kaye (1970). Other factors are discussed by Ferris (1968).
[7] For example, see the review by Brownlee (1965).
[8] The evidence on a positive interaction effect between smoking and air pollution in raising the lung cancer mortality rate is reviewed by Buell and Dunn (1967).

33 per 100,000 man years by living in the urban area. For males smoking more than one pack a day, the increased risk of living in an urban area is 88 per 100,000 man years. (The nonsmoker would experience lung cancer mortality at rates of 11 and 44 per 100,000 man years in rural and urban settings while the man smoking more than a pack a day would experience rates of 138 and 226 per 100,000 man years.)

As a nation, we seem to be better at solving public than private problems. After half a dozen years of intensive campaigns, cigarette consumption is still rising. I suggest that the most realistic forecast involves allocating the interaction to air pollution and assuming that smoking will continue to rise.

Errors of Observation

In estimating the damage function, a major problem is caused by errors of observation in the data. Disease-specific mortality rates are especially susceptible to these errors. The cause of death may be determined by autopsy, by careful examination of medical history, or by more informal means. Unfortunately, only a small percentage of deaths are investigated by an autopsy. This means that misclassification can be of major importance in estimating mortality rates of certain diseases.

When the errors of observation occur only in the dependent variable and are random errors, least squares regression estimates are unbiased. The effect of the measurement errors is to enlarge the error term and lower the explanatory power of the regression. The parameter estimates will be unbiased.

A more important problem with measurement errors in the dependent variable is the possibility that misclassification may be nonrandom. It is likely that in urban areas autopsies are done more often and that more care is taken in determining the cause of death. This implies possible biases in the estimated coefficients. Perhaps the only way of handling the bias is to consider data covering only urban areas; e.g., compare Standard Metropolitan Statistical Areas (SMSAs) or census tracts within an SMSA.

Other errors of observation concern the independent variables. Socioeconomic variables are reported by the census decennially. This means that other years must be approximated. A special problem arises in connection with population. We know that population changes depend on socioeconomic variables, including employment. Thus, if population is incorrectly observed, the coefficients of the socioeconomic variables are likely to be biased because of a simultaneous equation problem. Even the air pollution variable may be biased insofar as it is a surrogate for employment (or industrial production) in a region.

218

The measurement of air pollution is subject to significant problems. First, no long time series are available. This means that current mortality rates are being correlated with current air pollution indices. However, air pollution some years in the past was a factor in causing the disease. Only insofar as current levels of pollution are representative of past levels will the estimates be even remotely correct. Furthermore, since pollution has worsened over time, the coefficients will be biased downward.

To see this, suppose that we are estimating a cross-section regression of mortality rates against current pollution indices for a number of cities. If the cities have the same rank (vis-à-vis pollution) over a long time period, the pollution coefficients will indicate the association. However, because pollution has become worse over time there will be a marked bias. Suppose the pollution index averaged 50 at about the time that the illness was first caused, whereas it currently averages 100. Then the estimated coefficient will be half the correct magnitude.

Another problem with pollution indices is that of determining how accurately a single index describes a region. Pollution varies markedly over time and place. A hilltop can be quite clean at the same time that the valley below is extremely polluted; one valley might be quite clean while a neighboring one is extremely polluted. There is no good way to condense a complex set of pollution indices, by region and by time, into a single or a few numbers. My despair at this problem is lessened only by remembering the previous point: pollution indices are being used as surrogates for the pollution levels of past years. I must always remind myself that the measured pollution indices are only remote surrogates for what is desired.

Nonlinear Relationships Between Pollution and Health

Virtually all of the work relating pollution to health has assumed a linear relation. At best, this assumption should be interpreted as an approximation over a limited range to a much more complicated function. Other forms, such as log linear, quadratic, and piecewise linear, are reported in table 6.1, together with the simple linear model.

The first column reports a regression where all variables are entered in a linear relation. The four pollution variables and four socioeconomic variables explain 80 per cent of the variation in the total mortality rate across the 117 SMSAs ($R^2 = 0.800$). The coefficient of min P indicates that an increase in the minimum biweekly level of measured particulates of one microgram per cubic meter (1 $\mu g/m^3$) would increase the total mortality rate by 0.049 per 10,000. While the value of t does not indicate that this coefficient is significantly greater than zero (a value of 1.65 would be required using a one-tailed test), the value is greater than 1.0. The co-

219

efficient of max P indicates that an increase in the maximum biweekly measurement of particulates of one microgram per cubic meter would increase the total mortality rate by 0.006 per 10,000. If the minimum and maximum sulfur readings were increased separately by 1 $\mu g/m^2$, the death rate would rise by 0.69 and 0.03 per 10,000 respectively. Similarly, the

Table 6.1. Alternative Specifications for Total Mortality Rate, 117 SMSAs

	Linear specification	All variables in logarithms	Piecewise linear specification	Quadratic specification
R^2	0.800	0.805	0.845	0.861
Constant	20.868	0.491	15.262	−5.615
Min P	0.049	0.033		0.162
	(1.22)	(1.68)		(1.14)
Min P^2				−0.001
				(−0.75)
Min $P \leq 29$			0.104	
			(0.59)	
$30 \leq P \leq 52$			0.054	
			(0.52)	
$53 \leq P \leq 75$			0.070	
			(0.89)	
$75 < P$			0.031	
			(0.50)	
Max P	0.006	−0.018		−0.032
	(0.98)	(−0.82)		(−1.51)
Max P^2 ($\times$ 1000)				0.0001
				(1.93)
Max $P \leq 296$			0.035	
			(0.57)	
$297 \leq P \leq 517$			0.032	
			(0.79)	
$518 \leq P \leq 738$			0.013	
			(0.40)	
$739 \leq P$			0.042	
			(1.44)	
Min S	0.069	0.026		0.190
	(2.87)	(2.57)		(3.37)
Min S^2				−0.0001
				(−2.60)
Min $S \leq 48$			0.045	
			(0.65)	
$49 \leq S \leq 95$			0.074	
			(1.84)	
$96 \leq S \leq 142$			0.088	
			(2.05)	
$143 \leq S$			0.027	
			(0.84)	
Max S	0.003	0.042		0.052
	(0.35)	(2.09)		(2.62)
Max S^2 ($\times$ 1000)				−0.0001
				(−2.66)

total mortality rate (per 10,000) would increase with increases in population density of one person per square mile, in nonwhite population of one percentage point, of older people by one percentage point, and of poor families of one percentage point separately by 0.001, 0.35, 6.68, and 0.09 respectively, other factors held constant.

Table 6.1. Continued

	Linear specification	All variables in logarithms	Piecewise linear specification	Quadratic specification
Max $S < 282$			0.075 (1.38)	
$283 \leq S \leq 501$			0.054 (1.59)	
$502 < S < 20$			0.034 (1.15)	
$721 \leq S$			0.013 (0.54)	
p/m^2	0.0001 (1.73)	0.021 (2.22)	0.002 (2.70)	0.001 (2.49)
N-w	0.035 (3.71)	0.004 (0.44)	0.035 (3.41)	−0.005 (−0.25)
$(N\text{-}w)^2$				0.001 (1.93)
> 65	0.668 (17.06)	0.523 (13.86)	0.648 (15.87)	0.838 (4.95)
$(> 65)^2$				−0.001 (−1.24)
Poor	0.009 (0.66)	0.114 (4.48)	0.011 (0.75)	0.173 (2.49)
$(Poor)^2 (\times 10)$				−0.0004 (−2.22)

Note: The figures in parentheses are the t statistics (the ratio of the regression coefficient to its standard error).

R^2: The coefficient of determination or per cent of variation explained by the regression.

Total mortality rate per 10,000 ($\mu = 91.3$, $\sigma = 15.3$).

Min P: Minimum particulates; i.e., biweekly minimum reading of suspended particulates ($\mu g/m^3$)($\mu = 45.5$, $\sigma = 18.6$).

Max P: Maximum particulates; i.e., biweekly maximum reading ($\mu g/m^3$)($\mu = 268.4$, $\sigma = 132.1$).

P: Arithmetic mean of readings ($\mu g/m^3$)($\mu = 118.1$, $\sigma = 40.9$).

Min S: Minimum sulfates; i.e., biweekly minimum reading of sulfates ($\mu g/m^3 \times 10$) ($\mu = 47.2$, $\sigma = 31.3$).

Max S: Maximum sulfates; i.e., biweekly maximum reading of sulfates ($\mu g/m^3 \times 10$) ($\mu = 228.4$, $\sigma = 124.4$).

S: Arithmetic mean of readings ($\mu g/m^3 \times 10$)($\mu = 99.6$, $\sigma = 52.9$).

p/m^2: Persons per square mile ($\mu = 756.2$, $\sigma = 1,370.5$).

N-w: Per cent nonwhites in population ($\times 10$) ($\mu = 125.1$, $\sigma = 104.0$).

> 65: Per cent population over 65 ($\times 10$) ($\mu = 84.0$, $\sigma = 21.2$).

Poor: Per cent families with income $< \$3,000$ ($\times 10$) ($\mu = 180.9$, $\sigma = 65.5$).

The second column reports a regression where all variables are transformed into logarithms. The implications of this log linear regression and the previous linear one are quite similar. For example, a 10 per cent increase in the minimum biweekly measurement for particulates would lead to an increase in mortality rate of 0.25 per cent according to the linear specification or 0.33 per cent according to the log linear specification. Equivalent comparisons for the other pollution variables are 0.18 and −0.18 for the maximum biweekly particulate reading, 0.34 and 0.26 for the minimum biweekly sulfate reading, and 0.09 and 0.42 for the maximum biweekly sulfate reading. If all four air pollution measures were to rise by 10 per cent together, the mortality rate would rise by 0.86 per cent according to the linear specification and 0.83 per cent according to the log linear specification.

The implication of the log linear specification is that a 10 per cent increase in population density would lead to a 0.21 per cent increase in the mortality rate, other factors held constant. Holding other factors constant, increases of 10 per cent in the nonwhite population, old population, and poor population would increase the death rate by 0.04 per cent, 5.23 per cent, and 1.14 per cent, respectively.

The third column reports a piecewise linear form where each of the pollution variables is split into four variables; each new variable represents a quartile of the original. This has the effect of approximating the relation between total mortality and air pollution by a series of line segments. Thus, the systematic decrease in the coefficients of min particulates carries the interpretation that the effect of this variable on total mortality decreases as the pollution level rises. For very unpolluted areas, a rise of 1 mg/m^3 would increase the mortality rate by 0.104 per 10,000; for polluted areas, this same rise would increase the mortality rate by only 0.031 per 10,000.

This result is corroborated by the quadratic regression reported in the fourth column. Here the pollution variables and some of the socioeconomic variables are entered as second degree polynomials. The effect for min particulates on the mortality rate is positive, but it decreases as the level of min particulates decreases. Note that the quadratic function reaches a maximum at a level of 90 and then turns down. Thus, at a level of 90, the total of min particulates no longer raises the death rate; at higher levels, it would lower the death rate. However, a level of 90 is .much greater than any observed reading. Thus, the quadratic form is really an approximation to the true form and one must be careful not to extrapolate the results outside the range of observed data.

The piecewise linear regression indicates that a linear specification is about as good as any for max particulates. The four coefficients hover around the same value. This result is not consistent with the log linear or quadratic specifications. The former indicates that mortality falls as max particulates increase. The latter indicates that max particulates reach a minimum at a level of 160, which is approximately the lowest observed value. Thus, the quadratic form indicates that the effect of max particulates rises with the level. This result offers support for the commonly held view that a small increase in pollution at really high levels is much worse than the same increase at low or moderate levels.

The piecewise linear regression indicates a falling effect with pollution for min sulfates, similar to that shown for min particulates. The quadratic form corroborates this effect. The same effect is shown for max sulfates, in both the piecewise linear and quadratic forms. Thus, three of the four pollution variables display decreasing effects as the pollution level increases. Only max particulates display the generally assumed relation of increasing effect with pollution level.

Quadratic forms for the socioeconomic variables are reported but will not be discussed.

In comparing the four alternative forms, one should note that all fit the data about equally well. The linear specification explains about 80 per cent of the variation in the total mortality rate while the quadratic specification explains 86 per cent of the variation. After accounting for the extra parameters estimated in the quadratic specification, the adjusted coefficients of determination are quite close.

The alternative specifications have approximately the same elasticities at the mean, although they have quite different elasticities at the extremes of the observed data. In contrast to the linear regression, the other three tend to agree that the marginal benefit of abatement is greatest in getting rid of the last bit of pollution (both particulates and sulfates). The only exception occurs with respect to max particulates in the quadratic specification. There seems to be a strong implication that health is best in those areas that are quite unpolluted at some time during the year.

There is little basis for choosing one specification over another. As long as they are being compared at the mean of the observed data, the implications are quite comparable. The linear specification is both simple and plausible. There seems to be no reason to substitute alternative forms for it and so it will be used for the rest of the estimation.

The failure of the maximum readings to show importance suggests that people are adjusting to pollution. Either sensitive people emigrate from polluted areas or they restrict their activity during particularly acute episodes. In any case, the policy implications are novel. They indicate that we should worry little about the maximum maximorum, but instead concentrate on reducing the minimum minimorum.

Which Measure of Pollution?

Having accepted a linear specification of the damage function, the next question is which pollutant is the real culprit and which measure of that pollutant the most relevant? Air pollution can take the form of suspended particulates, sulfur compounds, nitrogen compounds, photochemical smog, or various other chemicals. There is little data on pollutants other than the first two and so the results are confined to them. These pollutants can be measured in terms of the largest biweekly measurement throughout the year (max), the smallest biweekly measurement (min), and the arithmetic average of the biweekly measurements (mean). Attention has been centered on acute episodes and thus on maximum concentrations. However, chronic illnesses might be more closely related to one of the other two measures of pollution. For example, the body's defense mechanisms may be able to neutralize acute episodes, but are useless against prolonged exposure.

Eugene Seskin and I have collected data on max, mean, and min concentrations for both suspended particulates and sulfur compounds for 117 SMSAs. These have been entered in a series of regressions shown in table 6.2. The first row of the table is a regression explaining the total mortality rate in 117 SMSAs by the levels of air pollution and four socioeconomic variables. When the six pollution variables and four socioeconomic variables are entered together, they are so highly interrelated that only one pollution variable (min sulfate) makes a significant contribution to the explanatory power of the regression (given that the other five pollution variables are present). Two of the six pollution variables (max particulates and mean sulfates) actually have negative coefficients (although their standard errors are extremely large), indicating that the mortality rate should fall as either rises, other factors held constant. When there is as high a relation between the explanatory variables as there is among these ten variables, the estimates of the standard errors of the coefficients are biased upward, although the regression coefficients continue to be unbiased estimates. Essentially, the six pollution variables are measuring the same thing and so no single one is very important.

To determine which variables are most closely related to mortality, insignificant variables are dropped, as shown in the fifth row. Note that the coefficients of the surviving pollution variables (mean particulates and min sulfates) are virtually identical in the two regressions. Thus, these variables are so strong that their coefficients are affected little by the presence of other variables. Of the two, the sulfate variable seems to be stronger, both in terms of its significance level and its marginal effect. Three of the socioeconomic variables (population per square mile, per-

224

Table 6.2. Mortality Regressions Involving Air Pollution, 117 SMSAs

	Constant	Particulates			Sulfates			p/m²	Socioeconomic variables			R²
		min	max	mean	min	max	mean		N-w	≥65	Poor	
Total	18.973	0.005 (0.07)	-0.001 (-0.11)	0.036 (0.84)	0.067 (2.51)	0.005 (0.43)	-0.001 (-0.02)	0.001 (1.65)	0.037 (3.67)	0.676 (16.51)	0.011 (0.78)	0.828
<1 year	192.735	0.207 (0.87)	0.016 (0.42)	0.045 (0.28)	0.062 (0.61)	-0.070 (-1.65)	0.111 (0.89)	0.001 (0.40)	0.176 (4.59)	-0.073 (-0.46)	0.154 (2.92)	0.557
<28 days	141.388	0.037 (0.19)	0.008 (0.26)	0.101 (0.75)	0.090 (1.04)	-0.060 (-1.66)	0.070 (0.67)	0.001 (0.47)	0.106 (3.28)	0.119 (0.90)	0.048 (1.07)	0.306
Fetal	84.214	0.121 (0.48)	-0.008 (-0.20)	0.008 (0.04)	0.097 (0.89)	0.030 (0.66)	0.022 (0.17)	0.003 (1.42)	0.175 (4.30)	0.069 (0.42)	0.116 (2.06)	0.435
Total	19.607			0.041 (2.53)	0.071 (3.18)			0.001 (1.67)	0.041 (5.81)	0.687 (18.94)		0.827
<1 year	185.802	0.365 (2.82)							0.186 (6.52)		0.157 (3.38)	0.537
<28 days	149.428			0.083 (1.62)	0.120 (1.82)				0.098 (4.04)		0.056 (1.45)	0.271
Fetal	93.852	0.008 (1.37)					0.141 (2.67)		0.161 (5.33)		0.125 (2.49)	0.426
≤14 years	9.825							0.003 (1.61)	0.003 (2.11)	-0.044 (-7.42)	0.007 (3.38)	0.602
15–64 years	11.397			0.025 (2.82)				0.001 (3.19)	0.034 (6.73)	0.109 (5.31)	0.013 (1.31)	0.538
≥65 years	52.412			0.156 (4.58)					-0.066 (-6.47)			0.394

Note: The figures in parentheses are the *t* statistics (the ratio of the regression coefficient to its standard error).

R^2: The coefficient of determination or per cent of variation explained by the regression.

Total: Total mortality rate per 10,000 ($\mu = 91.3$, $\sigma = 15.3$).

<1 year: Death of infants under one year per 10,000 live births ($\mu = 254.3$, $\sigma = 36.4$).

<28 days: Death of infants under 28 days per 10,000 live births ($\mu = 187.3$, $\sigma = 24.5$).

Fetal: Stillborns per 10,000 live births ($\mu = 153.2$, $\sigma = 34.3$).

≤14 years: Deaths of children, 14 and younger, per 10,000 total population ($\mu = 8.2$, $\sigma = 1.8$).

15–64 years: Deaths of adults aged 15 to 64 per 10,000 total population ($\mu = 31.6$, $\sigma = 5.2$).

≥65 years: Deaths of adults 65 and older per 10,000 total population ($\mu = 51.5$, $\sigma = 14.4$).

Particulates: min—biweekly minimum reading of suspended particulates ($\mu g/m^3$) ($\mu = 45.5$, $\sigma = 18.6$).

max—biweekly maximum reading ($\mu g/m^3$) ($\mu = 268.4$, $\sigma = 132.1$).

mean—arithmetic mean of readings ($\mu g/m^3$) ($\mu = 118.1$, $\sigma = 40.9$).

Sulfates: min—biweekly minimum reading of sulfates ($\mu g/m^3 \times 10$) ($\mu = 47.2$, $\sigma = 31.3$).

max—biweekly maximum reading ($\mu g/m^3 \times 10$) ($\mu = 228.4$, $\sigma = 124.4$).

mean—arithmetic mean of readings ($\mu g/m^3 \times 10$) ($\mu = 99.6$, $\sigma = 52.9$).

p/m²: Persons per square mile ($\mu = 756.2$, $\sigma = 1,370.5$).

N-w: Per cent nonwhites in population ($\times 10$) ($\mu = 125.1$, $\sigma = 104.0$).

≥65: Per cent population 65 or older ($\times 10$) ($\mu = 84.0$, $\sigma = 21.2$).

Poor: Per cent families with income < $3,000 ($\times 10$) ($\mu = 180.9$, $\sigma = 65.5$).

Sources: The mortality rates, reported in *Vital Statistics*, are for 117 SMSAs in 1960; air pollution data are reported by the National Air Sampling Network; socioeconomic variables are reported by the 1960 Census. For a more complete description of these data, see Lave and Seskin (1970a).

centage of nonwhites in the population, and the percentage of old people in the population) continue to be significant variables. The implications of these variables are quite similar to those of the first regression in table 6.1.

Regressions explaining three categories of infant death rates are also shown in the table. For infants dying during their first year, the important pollution variable is min particulates. An increase of 1 $\mu g/m^3$ would result in an increase of 0.365 deaths per 10,000 live births. Only two of the socioeconomic variables contribute to the explanatory power of the regression (percentage of non-whites and percentage of poor). A one percentage point increase in each of the two categories would increase the death rate per 10,000 live births by 1.86 and 1.57 respectively. Just over half of the variation in the death rate across SMSAs is explained by the one pollution and two socioeconomic variables. Note that little explanatory power is lost in dropping insignificant variables since R^2 falls only from 0.557 to 0.537.

For infants dying during their first 28 days, the important pollution variables are mean particulates and min sulfates. An increase in the mean particulate level of 1 $\mu g/m^3$ would lead to an increased death rate of 0.083 per 10,000 live births. The same increase in min sulfates would lead to an increased death rate of 1.20 per 10,000 live births. The same two socioeconomic variables continue to be significant. Note that a much smaller percentage of the variation in the under 28-day death rate is explained by the regression. Apparently there are a number of major factors influencing the death rate that are not included.

The third infant death rate is for stillborns. Mean sulfates is the significant pollution variable; an increase of 1 $\mu g/m^3$ would lead to an increase in the fetal death rate of 1.41 per 10,000 live births. In addition to non-whites and poor families, population density is a significant socioeconomic variable. Almost half of the variation in the stillborn rate is explained by the regression.

The last three rows of the table show three age specific death rates, which will be described in the section on "Age Specific Mortality." For now, it should be noted that these three regressions tend to be generally consistent with the previous ones.

In another paper,[9] these variables are compared for a number of disease categories and then corroborated with data for another year. The second year's data shows that the relation is extremely stable across the two years. Depending on the particular disease, sulfates or particulates may be more important. Generally the important measures are the minimum, rather than the maximum, level of the pollutant.

---

[9] See Lave and Seskin (1970*b*).

LESTER B. LAVE

Episodic Relationships

One of the more difficult tasks, both conceptually and technically, is to isolate the component of a rise in the daily mortality rate that is associated with air pollution.[10] The difficulties are so great that most published studies are suspect. Correlating daily mortality rates with daily air pollution indices gives results that have little to do with the effect of air pollution on mortality. Many of the problems are common to all time series analysis, and many are peculiar to air pollution. For example, most hospitals have days in which elective surgery is concentrated and days when there is no elective surgery. This means that there is a built-in cycle of mortality increases which is independent of the level of air pollution. The same sort of effect stems from weekly and seasonal periods of activity. Shortly after a snow fall, the mortality rate rises from activities such as shoveling snow or from accidents. During certain seasons, people are more active and so the chance of an accident or heart attack rises.

The basic time series problem is that there is a high amount of autocorrelation in a daily series of mortality rates. The death rate is high today for many of the same reasons it was high yesterday. Before much sense can be made of the data, cyclical trends must be removed. Ideally, the cycles would be independent of the level of pollution. Unfortunately, however, almost all reasons for higher or lower mortality rates are connected with changes in air pollution. For example, the snowstorm that leads to heart attacks and accidents also washes the air of pollution. The meteorological reasons for heightened activity in the summer also tend to be reasons for higher pollution levels. The problem is that there are direct links between meteorology and pollution and between economic activity (such as three-day weekends) and pollution. These links make it difficult to distinguish between increased mortality resulting from air pollution and from other causes.

Another problem in examining increased mortality is that those who die are likely to be acutely ill. Either they have a chronic condition that is aggravated by the increased pollution or some acute condition is worsened. For the former category, there would seem to be little social gain from abating pollution. If the current episode does not result in death, later episodes are likely to do so. It is very difficult to know how many people fall into this category. So far as I know, no one has looked at age specific death rates, as is done in the next section. This means that one can not be sure whether the lives saved are worth much or little to society, whether

[10] For discussions of the problem see Hechter and Goldsmith (1961); Ipsen, Ingenito, and Deane (1969); and Rumford (1961). Many of the published studies relating daily mortality or morbidity and daily air pollution readings are listed in Lave and Seskin (1970a).

227

they are saved for a few days or for many years. It might be fruitful to focus on daily infant mortality, instead of looking at total death rates.

A more interesting investigation concerns the relation between morbidity and acute pollution. It would be useful to relate daily levels of air pollution with daily illness rates, absence from work, and expenditures on health. The cyclic problems discussed above still pertain. For example, pollution tends to be high on Friday and the absence rate is also high for unrelated reasons.

There are two ways of handling this cyclic difficulty. One involves getting an exogenous estimate of cycle and averaging over time. Seasonal and other cyclic trends in absences from work are probably quite similar across cities. If so, one might obtain an estimate of the cycle by finding a cycle common to a number of cities or by finding the cycle in an unpolluted city. The other possibility is that of aggregating data for a week or other period to get rid of the work part of the cycle. I am far from sanguine in suggesting aggregation. It is difficult to find a period that excludes the worst part of the cycle without going all the way to annual data. The longer the period, the more of the cycle is removed. But the longer the period, the fewer degrees of freedom are available and the longer the time series must be (with attendant changes in medical practice and other factors).

One final suggestion here would be the use of age specific death rates for mortality studies and the use of morbidity or work absence data along with mortality data.

Age Specific Mortality and Life Expectancy

Table 6.2 shows not only the total death rate, but age specific death rates. There are three categories of infant death rates (less than one year, less than 28 days, and stillborns), and death rates for children (under 15 years), adults (15 to 65); and the aged (over 65). By looking at the various mortality rates, one can get a better idea of who would be saved by pollution abatement.

Pollution is a significant explanatory variable for the three classes of infant death rates. For the less-than-one-year category, the minimum level of particulates is crucial; a 10 per cent decrease in min particulates would result in a 0.7 per cent reduction in this death rate. Ten per cent reductions in the mean particulate and min sulfate levels would result in a 0.8 per cent reduction in the less-than-28-day mortality rate. A 10 per cent reduction in the mean sulfate level would result in a 0.9 per cent reduction in the stillborn rate.

228

These effects could be translated into life expectancy terms by assuming that the infants who were saved by abating pollution would be healthy and have the normal life expectancy of other infants born at the same time. Assuming a 50 per cent reduction in the minimum level of particulates, the infant (less than one year) death rate would fall by 3.5 per cent. This fall in the death rate would add just under three years to the life expectancy of these infants.

The age specific regressions in the last three rows of table 6.2 are similar to the regressions reported above them. Just over 60 per cent of the variation in the pediatric death rate (persons under 15 years) across the 117 SMSAs is explained by the regressions. The significant pollution variable is min particulates; a 10 per cent reduction in min particulates would lead to a 0.4 per cent reduction in pediatric deaths. The important socio-economic variables are the proportions of the population that are nonwhite, older than 65, and poor.

For adults (aged 15 to 64), over 53 per cent of the variation across the SMSAs is explained. Both mean particulates and min sulfates are the important pollution variables and a 10 per cent increase in each would lead to a 1.3 per cent increase in the adult death rate. All four socioeconomic variables are significant.

For older people (65 or older), just under 40 per cent of the variation is explained. Min sulfates is the important pollution variation and a 10 per cent increase would lead to a 1.3 per cent increase in the death rate for these people. The only significant socioeconomic variable is the proportion of nonwhites in the population. Apparently there is a selection process so that nonwhites who can manage to survive to age 65 have higher life expectancy than whites of the same age.

These age specific results can be translated into life expectancy terms, assuming that someone saved has the life expectancy of the average person of his group. A 50 per cent reduction in air pollution (specifically in min particulates, mean particulates, and min sulfates) would add four or five years to the life expectancy of a newborn. Most of the increase in life expectancy would come during the first year of life, but there would be effects throughout the population.

These increases in life expectancy might be put into perspective by examining the effects of other social policies to improve health. For example, a 10 per cent reduction in the number of poor families would reduce the infant (under 1 year) death rate by 1.1 per cent. While this would have many social benefits beyond mortality reduction, in terms of mortality reduction this would be only slightly more effective than a 10 per cent reduction in air pollution, which would lower the infant death rate by 0.7 per cent.

I find it impressive that a 50 per cent reduction in air pollution would have nearly the same effect on life expectancy as giving up smoking. I can think of many smokers who would rather have moved to less polluted places and kept their smoking than gone through all the pain of giving up cigarettes in New York or Chicago.

Is There Really An Association?

Lave and Seskin (1970b) cite a large number of studies that relate ill health to air pollution. Regression studies for U.S. SMSAs are reported in tables 6.1 and 6.2 and analyzed in more detail in another manuscript (Lave and Seskin 1970b). However, as noted earlier, no single study manages to control for all factors that might be the real cause of the ill health. Has enough evidence been accumulated that we can conclude that there is an association? Would an unbiased observer be forced to conclude that the association has been established beyond a reasonable doubt?

I would argue that the association is beyond reasonable doubt. In order to claim that the association is spurious, a critic would have to argue that a third factor in each study was somehow correlated with air pollution and lent pollution a spurious significance. Two possible factors depend on the fact that air pollution tends to be concentrated in urban areas and tends to be worst in the areas where people of low socioeconomic status live.

Thus, one argument is that the effect is really an urban one. City dwellers probably smoke more than those living in rural areas, probably are more overweight, less exercised, more tense, and generally less healthy. This line of reasoning might lead one to doubt the association were it not for the fact that the relationship is at least as strong when comparing urban areas with each other as when comparing urban to rural areas.[11]

A second argument is that people of low social status tend to smoke more, have more exposure to occupational pollution, and tend to be less healthy. Thus, air pollution is merely acting as a surrogate for low socioeconomic status in the regressions. However, this objection falls before the fact that several measures of socioeconomic status are entered in the SMSA regressions. Their presence actually seems to enhance the significance of the pollution variables.

Trace elements in the water, radiation, genetic factors, and general life styles might also be argued to be the real cause. However, one must cite evidence that these factors are correlated with measured air pollution. Presumably, the proponent of a measure must be able to argue that his factor is a more plausible explanation of ill health than air pollution.

[11] See the literature summary in Lave and Seskin (1970a).

230

My conclusion is that the individual elasticities cannot be argued to be "true" but that the general magnitude cannot be doubted. I think that there is far too much evidence to be able to doubt the association. The abatement elasticities are insensitive to radical changes in the specification of the function, including the addition of meteorological variables, and are stable over a subsequent year of data (Lave and Seskin 1970*a*). The remaining uncertainty seems concentrated around the exact magnitudes of the elasticities, particularly for values quite far from the mean.

III. TRANSLATING THE EFFECT INTO DOLLAR TERMS

How much should society pay (as a schedule) to abate the physical effects described in the previous section? I would argue that the relevant question is what the consumer is willing to pay, when he has complete knowledge. If we could somehow inform the consumer of all the consequences of his decision and then perceive his demand for abatement, this would be the relevant schedule. Health in these terms is like any other good or service that he might purchase.

One might distinguish between what consumers are willing to pay and what they should be willing to pay. The answer to the first query is the one that might be given to the question: How much are you willing to pay to reduce the incidence of these diseases by 1 per cent (to you and your family)? The second might differ by considering consumer myopia, by considering society's interest in other members of his family, particularly his children, and by considering some issues that the individual might be unwilling or unable to consider properly.

Estimating the Demand Schedule for Abatement

The first problem in estimating the demand schedule for abatement is that air pollution is a local "public bad," with all of the consequent properties. This means that consumers are always motivated to misrepresent their preferences (Ridker 1967, p. 82). If the question is merely, "What would you pay?," the consumer should name an arbitrarily high figure, since the sum will not actually be collected. If the sum is to be collected, he should name an arbitrarily low figure, since this is the conventional problem of public goods. A responsible consumer might answer that he would be willing to pay little because it is not his problem, because he can have no appreciable effect, and because abating pollution for him will benefit everyone. However these biases may work out, consumers are never likely to give reasonable answers to the question and so another approach must be found.

231

A second problem is that the consumer is making decisions for the other members of his family. Particularly when these are children, society has an interest in the decision beyond that of the decision maker. Note that this observation is quite independent of the possibility that health might be a merit good. Society has an investment interest in the health of children, just as it does in their education.

Two final possibilities are that the consumer might be too myopic for his own interests, i.e., at a later time he might note that he regrets his previous decisions and would make different ones if he had a chance. And he either may not realize the consequences of certain illness (what disutility he would get from having them) or may be unwilling to think about the consequences of health matters in purely economic terms. At present many people prefer their physicians or others to make all decisions regarding health matters, rather than themselves having to think about marginal allocations between money and health.

All of these qualifications are made with the assumption that few consumers know the health consequences of air pollution, and that only a slightly larger number would know the consequences if they could be told in terms of increased incidence of various diseases.

Form of the Implied Benefit Model

Assume for a moment that a marginal improvement in health has a constant price attached to it over a small range. Since the effects of pollution on health are marginal, it seems quite reasonable that a constant value of health be used. Then one can translate the physical damage function immediately into a dollar benefit function by multiplying by the dollar price. This means that a linear damage function will give rise to a linear benefit function and a log linear damage function will be translated into a log linear benefit function.

The more general point here is that translating the physical damage function into a benefit function involves only a single step. The only additional piece of information required is the value of a unit increment. Even where the physical damage is sufficiently large that a schedule should be used instead of a constant price, the translation merely involves multiplying the demand schedule by the physical damage function.

Evaluating Low Probability Events

However, deriving the appropriate price for marginal health improvements is a difficult task. As Schelling (1968) has noted, people are not used to thinking of purchasing a marginal improvement in health and have little experience in valuing it. Furthermore, the form of the commodity is even more difficult. Abating pollution results in a lowering of the probability of dying or becoming ill from a particular disease. What the consumer is asked to value is a small reduction in the probability that he will die or become ill. Any time a consumer must put a price on a reduction in the probability of death this year from 1/1000 to 1/1050, he is going to have a difficult time.

I could suggest two possible solutions. The first is to translate the health improvement into life expectancy terms, as was done in section II under "Which Measure of Pollution?" How much would you be willing to pay for an additional three years of life expectancy? How much would you be willing to pay to add five years to the life expectancy of your children? The second possible solution is to search for comparable choices, as described in the next section.

Finding Programs with "Comparable" Health Improvements

Diligent search uncovers a number of cases where society values marginal health improvements. Individuals do so when they decide which optional safety features to put into an automobile; society does so in designing a highway, e.g., the width of the shoulder, the sharpness of turns, and lighting.[12] Individuals make the judgment when they decide whether to brush their teeth and see their physician and dentist for preventative maintenance. Society makes the judgment in public health programs such as those on the purity of water; the health aspects of garbage disposal; and mass innoculation programs for polio, smallpox, and German measles.

Unfortunately, these programs value marginal health improvements at a vast range of values. A child with leukemia is treated as if an extra few days of life are worth thousands of dollars. Poor children can grow up with rickets and many other indications of malnutrition because society is unwilling to spend a few hundred dollars over their lives for better food. Thus, one infers a wide range of values. Perhaps one might follow Klarman (1965) in looking at "comparable" programs to find values; this would tend to lessen the range, although it will continue to be very large.

One direct way of finding out how consumers value cleaner air is to examine expenditures on devices, such as filters and precipitators, that reduce pollution in homes, offices, and automobiles. I have the impression that these expenditures are becoming quite substantial, including the power

---

[12] Safety is treated as a service that the consumer may buy in Lave (1968). In that discussion of transportation safety, and of the role of government for aspects of safety which are public goods, much of the same approach is taken as in discussing increased health in the present manuscript.

bill for operating these devices. One might also attempt to estimate the component of air conditioning expenditure which is due to polluted air. Any air conditioner provides a low level of filtration to clean the air and make it less unpleasant. Many people allege that they installed automobile air conditioners to cut the pollution reaching them.

A Second Best World

Another way of stating this problem is to ask how funds should be spent (and reallocated) so as to achieve the greatest improvements in health. Even if we limit consideration to public health funds, a radical reallocation would take place. I suspect that funds for medical care would be drastically reduced and the funds would be reallocated toward better housing and food. I would conjecture that expenditures on air pollution abatement would increase in urban areas. As shown in section I under "The Physiological Mechanism," marginal reductions in air pollution have marked health effects.

This misallocation of funds makes it extremely difficult to prescribe how much should be spent on pollution abatement. Is the correct amount to be judged by the "best" public health program or the "worst" program? Are our consciences clear in advocating increased expenditures on pollution abatement when we know that the money might be spent better on housing and nutrition for the poor? (See Lave and Lave, forthcoming.)

IV. EFFECTS NOT CONNECTED WITH HEALTH

The health effects described in the previous two sections are quite narrow in scope. The primary investigations have been of mortality, with only slight attention to morbidity and absence rates. Mortality is pretty final, but there are some important effects that are unlikely to be represented, even indirectly, by the mortality rates. For example, there is evidence that asthmatics suffer more frequent attacks when the pollution level is high (Zeidberg, Prindle, and Landau 1971; Schoettlin and Landau 1961; Lewis, Gilkeson, and McCamdin 1962). The mortality effect is quite limited both because these people are unlikely to die from their asthma and because they are likely to respond to the polluted air by leaving the area or installing home air-filtration devices. Thus, there are health effects that are likely to be much more important than those indicated in the previous two sections.

From here, the effects get much more nebulous, but are still just as real. Pollution obscures visibility and there is some evidence that it decreases work ability marginally (National Academy of Sciences 1969). Certainly anyone in Los Angeles or my native Pittsburgh can testify to the high level of physical discomfort during one of the really unpleasant days. There are myriad effects that can be grouped under the headings of a "lower quality of life" when the air is polluted.

If it is difficult to value health effects, it is even more difficult to value reductions in the quality of life. Both private and public expenditures to improve the quality of life are subject to more misallocation than are health expenditures. Consider the expenditures on more attractive buildings or outdoor sculptures. Architects are beginning to realize that many possibilities in urban building are ruled out because of pollution: either the building will age at an extraordinary rate or else it will become so dirty that the effect is lost. I have no answers to how much these factors are worth, or even any suggestions for investigation. I merely note that the effects are real and that, as an affluent society, we are willing to expend much of our resources to improve the general quality of life.

Getting back to more concrete ground, air pollution increases cleaning costs, repainting and maintenance costs, and shortens the life of materials (Yocom 1962). These effects have received some investigation (Kneese 1967; Michelson and Tourin 1966; Ridker 1967) but the estimates are quite rudimentary.

One way of attempting to estimate all of these factors, including the health effect, is to look at differential rents for property. While one might not believe that people consciously calculate the trade-offs of cash for marginal improvements in health, visibility, cleaning, etc., one might believe that consumers have learned to act as if they knew these costs. They manifest their preferences in terms of purchasing air-conditioned cars, installing air conditioning with filtration devices in home and office, and in living in relatively unpolluted areas. Presumably, one might estimate the "pollution-rent gradient," as have Anderson and Crocker (1969); Nourse (1967); Ridker and Henning (1967); and Harris, Tolley, and Harrell (1968).

I find such studies of limited interest for two reasons. First, the estimated coefficient of pollution is extremely sensitive to other variables in the formulation. We know a great deal about the structure of cities: the value of land falls with distance from work and shopping centers, there are major pockets of high land values based on fashionable neighborhoods, and cities have been subject to rapid changes in the past two or three decades. It is difficult to specify a theoretically correct way to determine the effect of air pollution gradient—one would have to control for all of these other factors.

Failure to specify a complete model, controlling for other factors, is certain to lead to biased results. For example, pollution is positively related to population density. Thus, one could easily find that pollution makes land more valuable, if one ran a simple regression of land rents on measured pollution.

Second, there are also a host of measurement problems. Meteorological factors cause the pollution level in each part of the city to be a stochastic variable. The question is what measure of the distribution is most relevant for explaining land rents? Is it the worst day or the mean? The stochastic nature of pollution also means that establishing pollution isopleths for a city is very difficult. Major measurement errors are involved in any pollution map for an area.

There is also the problem of land rent data. Davis and Wertz (1969) showed that assessed land values are bad surrogates for market prices; but assessed values are virtually the only data available. Another difficulty is associated with using aggregates, such as census tracts, rather than individual parcel data. It is difficult to measure locational factors, quality of housing, and other relevant factors for an aggregate, just as it is difficult to get a measure of land rent for such an aggregate. I have real difficulties in interpreting the results of an analysis using such aggregates.

I doubt that anyone would seriously argue that land rents are going to embody all of the effects of air pollution. For example, major portions of time are spent outside the home at work, school, or shopping; moving to a clean suburb will have little effect on air pollution at work.

The pure pollution component of land rents represents some unknown percentage of the total effect and I do not see any way of estimating this percentage or using independent data to derive an estimate of the total effect from this rent gradient. Because of the two difficulties just discussed, there are important, unknown biases, both positive and negative, in estimating the pollution gradient.

Thus, if I knew the true pollution component of land rents, I would know that I have an underestimate of the true cost of air pollution. However, when I see a pollution component estimated from assessed values of census tracts, I have difficulty in interpreting the implied cost of pollution. I cannot decide whether such estimates are underestimates or overestimates of the true cost of pollution.

V. THE EVALUATION PROCESS IN THE PUBLIC ARENA

Regional Versus National Standards

One of the practical problems at the core of pollution regulation is whether emission standards should be regional or national. For example, in a current suit DuPont is arguing that a set of emission standards is unrealistically strict for a New Jersey plant, since that plant is located in a rural setting where there are no other polluters around to lower ambient air quality to a level which imposes costs on others.

Certainly the environment has a tremendous ability to absorb the pollution. A single plant need not exceed the capacity of the environment, even though it would do so if it were located alongside many similar plants. Such an observation argues for regional standards where either emissions are related to desired air quality and the number of possible polluters, or the tax rate for emission is a function of the demand to pollute. Such regional standards would encourage polluters to move to more remote locations and tend to spread the pollution more widely and more uniformly.[13]

The rub is that society has a tremendous investment in capital in our cities. It is also quite costly for individuals to emigrate; there is a capital loss on property, the cost of moving and job search, and the cost of adjusting to the new location. Insofar as these regulations would involve relocation of industry and impose large costs on society, it is worth reconsidering the matter. The problem is that the only investment that industry makes is in its own plant and equipment. Society as a whole invests in the houses, roads, schools, and the other capital of a community. There is probably an emission standard that would make it more profitable for industry to relocate its plants, but for which society as a whole would find it less costly to keep the industry in its current location and subsidize the cost of pollution control.

At the moment, there is no direct mechanism for control subsidization by the community, except possibly a reduction in some types of taxes.[14] In any case, the way that most communities have reacted is to bear the cost in terms of lower quality air. Thus, the cry for national emission standards, even though they make little sense economically, is a cry for obtaining clean air while forcing industry to remain in the same location.

We are faced with a series of choices. We can grant the national standards, and incur the reduced efficiency and higher cost associated with too strict standards in some places. We can impose regional standards, and incur the cost of making some social capital obsolete. Or, finally, we can try to minimize social cost by imposing regional standards, but working out mechanisms for subsidizing industry in some locations to keep them from moving.

---

[13] A series of studies calculating the proper "effluent charges" for firms that want to pollute a river are summarized in Kneese and Bower (1968).

[14] It is interesting to speculate as to whether tax reductions to specific industries to keep them might not be unconstitutional under the 14th amendment.

I would favor the first solution, except for the few largest cities, whose problems are more grave than those of the rest of the nation (these cities must be permitted to enact more stringent standards). I doubt that the misallocation of resources would be great under national standards that tended to be too strict. Since the minimum level of pollution seems to be most directly related to health, there seems to be some gain in keeping rural areas quite unpolluted. Finally, I do not see any good way for local government to intervene in the firm's affairs to determine the amount of subsidization that would minimize social cost.

Never Believe A Competent Benefit-Cost Analysis

A straightforward, statistically competent benefit-cost analysis will overstate the cost and understate the benefits. In general, the economist can estimate only short-run costs; i.e., the cost of abating pollution by putting on an additional device. It is always less expensive, and generally much less expensive to abate pollution in a plant designed to cope with the problem. Even here, the economist is likely to continue to overestimate cost substantially. There is currently a vast gap between knowledge of the basic principles of controlling pollution and their application in the form of production techniques and abatement devices. Were laws enacted, one would surely expect that R&D would respond quickly and one would find that costs were much less than expected.

On the benefit side, the analyst can estimate only a few of the effects of abatement. There are many benefits which cannot be quantified easily or for which there are no data. The analyst has no choice but to leave these out or toss in figures based on guesses. Even if we were to condone these guesses for projects we favored, we would be tempted to use them as a basis for dismissing the benefit analysis for projects we opposed. Indeed, where guesses formed a crucial component of the benefit analysis, I would hesitate to sell such an analysis as a "neutral, scientific" one that was an appropriate substitute for pork barrel practices of legislatures.

It is naive to believe that all benefits and costs can be quantified and reduced to dollar terms. Many effects benefit one group at the expense of another. Thus, these effects really involve interpersonal comparisons and general social judgements. There is no scientific basis for quantifying such effects, and so it is impossible to complete the benefit-cost analysis. In another paper (Lave 1970) I have argued that partial quantification is possible, with other effects being addenda to the quantification.

Consequently, costs will always be overestimated and benefits underestimated. These incorrect statements are likely to be of prime importance in rejecting many projects that should be justified. Indeed, some have defended unjustifiably low interest rates for government projects by claiming that they adjust for these misstatements. I cannot argue too strongly that using a low interest rate is not a reasonable way to adjust for these biases.

The Need To Do Something

The recent attention given to pollution has been beneficial in educating the public to the costs and problems. It has also led to demands for immediate action. Not only is the cost of bad laws likely to be enormous in this area, but the whole program can be discredited by bad laws.

Polluters will react to a new set of laws by installing equipment, relocating plants, and determining which processes are most profitable. Laws that fail to control all pollutants, or that are short-sighted in other ways, will lead to incorrect investments of enormous amounts. It is extremely important that laws be strict and comprehensive to begin with; it is far too costly to "inch up" on proper standards. These ideas are elaborated in the following section.

Emission Standards and Diffusion Models

The focus of our attention is the quality of the air. However, ambient air standards are useless. One has to get at the source of the pollution, not wishfully specify the end result. The difficulty is that there is no direct relation between emission standards and ambient air quality. To be able to set intelligent emission standards, we must have some idea of what the quality of the air will be for each possible standard.

The missing ingredient is a diffusion model. Knowing the quality of air entering an air basin, total emissions can be related to air quality by using a model of the diffusion of air throughout the basin. The model is complicated, since wind speed and direction vary, as do other critical factors. Thus, the quality of air will be a stochastic variable. Air quality is some characterization of the distribution (such as min, mean, or max) that results from a given emission standard.

Such diffusion models are extremely complicated to construct, but are crucial to setting standards. A given standard will require industry to invest in a vast array of abatement equipment, new plant, and utilization of new processes and fuels. If the standard is wrong, by being either too strict or too lax, the cost will be enormous. If the standard is too strict, inefficient processes will have been introduced, and too much money spent on abatement. The costs are even higher if the standard is too lenient. It is probable that the entire cost of abatement will have been wasted if the standard is too lenient.

The cheapest way to abate pollution by 50 per cent involves a simple process. If we desire to abate pollution by 90 per cent, an entirely different process is called for. If the first process were erroneously installed, it is probable that it would have to be removed before the second process could be installed. Given the nature of this equipment, it is likely that the entire cost of installing the first process would have been wasted. In this area errors are extremely costly.

VI. SUMMARY AND CONCLUSION

A vast number of problems associated with estimating the benefit of abating air pollution have been discussed. I have tried to suggest ways to handle them or to avoid them. A number of problems are still left to comfort doubters and decrease confidence in my point estimates.

Any reader patient enough to get this far deserves some compensation and so I will stop side-stepping and present a few numbers. As best I can tell, abating pollution by 50 per cent throughout the nation would add three to five years to the life expectancy of a child born in 1970. Another way of stating the effect is to estimate that a 50 per cent abatement would lower the economic cost of all ill health by just under 5 per cent.[15] The latter figure is almost certainly an underestimate of the true cost, since it is based on a mortality investigation in which morbidity and absence rates are underrepresented. However, it is a fairly robust figure in that it is insensitive to the particular values assumed for earnings and sick days.

A third way of stating the estimate is to note that abating pollution by 50 per cent would be worth about $2 billion per year in terms of the economic benefits of (a) increased work days, and (b) decreased direct health expenditures. This basic analysis comes from the work of Dorothy Rice (1966). Note that whenever I talk about economic costs, I am valuing life at the present discounted value of future earnings. Thus, most women are economically "worthless" in this analysis and anyone over 65 is an economic liability. Those readers who, as I am, are loathe to accept these implications, should regard the 5 per cent and $2 billion per year as gross underestimates of the correct figures.

Lest someone be deceived about the importance of a reduction of almost 5 per cent in the economic costs of ill health, some comparisons are relevant. Recent "miracles of medical care" have had a much smaller impact on the nation's health. For example, eradicating polio by vaccine is much less important than the 5 per cent reduction that would be gained by

---

[15] This estimate and the one following are calculated in Lave and Seskin (1970a).

abating pollution. As a final comparison, the total economic loss due to neoplasms (both benign and malignant cancers) is only slightly greater than the savings estimated to arise from a 50 per cent reduction in air pollution.[16]

REFERENCES

Anderson, R., Jr., and T. Crocker. 1969. Air pollution and residential property values. Paper read at the Econometric Society meetings, New York, 1969.

Arrow, K., and M. Kurz. 1970. *Public investment, the rate of return, and optimal fiscal policy*. Baltimore: Johns Hopkins Press for Resources for the Future.

Baumol, W. 1968. On the social rate of discount. *American Economic Review* 58:788–802.

Baumol, W., and D. Bradford. 1970. Optimal departures from marginal cost pricing. *American Economic Review* 60:265–83.

Brownlee, K. 1965. A review of smoking and health. *Journal of the American Statistical Association* 60:722–39.

Buell, P., and J. Dunn. 1967. Relative impact of smoking and air pollution on lung cancer. *Archives of Environmental Health* 15:291–97.

Buell, P., J. Dunn, Jr., and L. Breslow. 1967. Cancer of the lung and Los Angeles-type air pollution. *Cancer* 20:2139–47.

Cassell, E., D. Wolter, J. Mountain, J. Diamond, I. Mountain, and J. McCarroll. 1968. Reconsiderations of mortality as a useful index of the relationship of environmental factors to health. *American Journal of Public Health* 58:1653–57.

Davis, O., and K. Wertz. 1969. The consistency of assessment of property: Some empirical results and managerial suggestions. *Applied Economics* 2:151–57.

Davis, O., and A. Whinston. 1967. Piecemeal policy in the theory of second best. *Review of Economic Studies* 34:323–31.

Ferris, B. 1968. Epidemiological studies on air pollution and health. *Archives of Environmental Health*. 16:541–55.

Goldsmith, J. 1965. Epidemiology of bronchitis and emphysema. *Medicina Thoracalis* 22:1–23.

Harris, R., G. Tolley, and C. Harrell. 1968. The residence site choice. *Review of Economics and Statistics* 50:241–47.

Hechter, H., and J. Goldsmith. 1961. Air pollution and daily mortality. *American Journal of the Medical Sciences* 241:581–88.

Ipsen, J., F. Ingenito, and M. Deane. 1969. Episodic morbidity and mortality in relation to air pollution. *Archives of Environmental Health* 18:458–61.

Klarman, H. 1965. Syphillis control programs. In *Measuring the benefits of government investment*, ed. R. Dorfman. Baltimore: Johns Hopkins Press. p. 227.

Kneese, A. 1967. Economics and the quality of the environment—Some empirical experiences. In *Costs of Air Pollution*, ed. M. Garnsey and J. Hibbs. New York: Praeger.

---

[16] The total economic loss due to neoplasms in 1963 was $2.6 billion, according to Rice's figures (1966, p. 81). The economic benefit of a 50 per cent reduction in air pollution is estimated to be $2.1 billion (Lave and Seskin 1970a). Note that these two figures are comparable, since the latter was calculated from Rice's estimates.

Kneese, A., and B. Bower. 1968. *Managing water quality: Economics, technology, institutions.* Baltimore: Johns Hopkins Press for Resources for the Future.

Lave, L. 1968. Safety in transportation: The role of government. *Law and Contemporary Problems* 33:512–35.

———. 1970. Evaluating autos. In *Advanced Urban Transportation Systems*, ed. J. Romualdi and L. Hoel. Pittsburgh, Transportation Research Institute.

Lave, J., and L. Lave. Forthcoming. Medical care delivery: Some economic criticism. *Law and Contemporary Problems.*

Lave, L., S. Leinhardt, and M. Kaye. 1970. Low level radiation and U.S. mortality. Working paper, Carnegie-Mellon University.

Lave, L., and E. Seskin. 1970a. Air pollution and human health: The quantitative effect of air pollution on human health and an estimate of the dollar benefit of pollution abatement. *Science* 169 (1970):723–33.

———. 1970b. Air pollution and mortality: A statistical analysis of U.S. SMSAs. Draft paper, Carnegie-Mellon University.

Lerner, A. 1970. On optimal taxes with an untaxable sector. *American Economic Review* 60:284–94.

Lewis, R., M. Gilkeson, Jr., and R. McCamdin. 1962. Air pollution and New Orleans asthma. *Public Health Reports* 77:947–54.

McMahon, B., T. Pugh, and J. Ipsen. 1960. *Epidemiologic methods.* Boston: Little, Brown and Company.

Michelson, I., and B. Tourin. 1966. Comparative methods for studying the costs of controlling air pollution. *Public Health Reports* 81:505–11.

National Academy of Sciences and National Academy of Engineering. 1969. *Effects of chronic exposure to low levels of carbon monoxide on human health, behavior and performance.* Washington: U.S. Government Printing Office.

Nourse, H. 1967. The effect of air pollution on house values. *Land Economics* 43:181–89.

Prest, A., and R. Turvey. 1965. Cost-benefit analysis: A survey. *Economic Journal* 75:683–735.

Rice, D. 1966. *Estimating the cost of illness.* Washington, D.C.: U.S. Government Printing Office, PHS Publication No. 947-6.

Ridker, R. 1967. *Economic costs of air pollution.* New York: Praeger.

Ridker, R., and J. Henning. 1967. The determinants of residential property values with special reference to air pollution. *Review of Economics and Statistics* 49:246–57.

Rumford, J. 1961. Mortality studies in relation to air pollution. *American Journal of Public Health* 51:165–73.

Schelling, T. C. 1968. The life you save may be your own. In *Problems in public expenditure analysis*, ed. Samuel B. Chase. Washington, D.C.: The Brookings Institution, 1968.

Schoettlin, C., and E. Landau. 1961. Air pollution and asthmatic attacks in the Los Angeles area. *Public Health Reports* 76:545–48.

Sternglass, E. 1969. Infant mortality and nuclear tests. *Bulletin of the Atomic Scientists* 25:18–20.

Yocom, J. 1962. Effects of air pollution on materials. In *Air Pollution*, ed. A. Stern. New York: Academic Press.

Zeidberg, L., R. Prindle, and E. Landau. 1961. The Nashville air pollution study. I. Sulfur dioxide and bronchial asthma: A preliminary report. *American Review of Respiratory Diseases* 84:489–503.

7. *Distribution of Environmental Quality*

A. Myrick Freeman III

I. INTRODUCTION

This paper sets out to do three things: (a) find out what can be said now about the patterns of distribution of benefits and costs associated with environmental pollution and pollution abatement programs; (b) find out what can be said about the appropriate role of distribution considerations in environmental quality planning; and (c) in light of (a) and (b) examine research needs and priorities.

The first question is basically one of positive analysis. There are two elements, one analytical and one empirical. First we must understand the economic mechanisms by which environmental costs and benefits are distributed among individuals. This requires an analytical framework or model for discussing these economic mechanisms and predicting patterns of distribution. The elements of such a model will be sketched out in section III.

The fundamental empirical question is: What in fact are the actual patterns of distribution and incidence? In addition we would like to know how these patterns of differential environmental effects influence the distribution of human welfare. Does the degradation of environmental quality tend to increase or decrease the degree of inequality of welfare

This paper was prepared during my tenure as a visiting scholar at Resources for the Future, Inc. My colleagues there, especially Blair Bower, Charles Cicchetti, Robert Haveman, Allen Kneese, and Clifford Russell, were helpful and stimulating. Thomas Crocker made available socioeconomic and air quality data from his work on air quality and land values. Professor Crocker and Anthony Fisher read an earlier draft and made helpful comments. Iris Long wrote the programs for computations. To all of them I am indebted, and I absolve all of them from blame for any errors herein.

among individuals? Is pollution the great leveler? Or does it tend to increase the disparities among individuals caused by differences in money income or wealth?

We cannot answer this question conclusively for two reasons. The first is the problem of defining and measuring welfare where nonmarketed environmental services are central to the question at hand. Here in particular, money income is a totally inadequate surrogate for welfare. The second reason is that as yet we do not have sufficiently detailed information to present a comprehensive picture of the patterns of distribution of environmental services. However, some scattered fragments of evidence are available. In section IV the analytical framework will be applied to some of the distributional effects associated with the disposal of residuals in the air and water, and on land, and the resulting predictions will be compared, where possible, with the available evidence.

The second aim of the paper is to discuss the question: Should distribution considerations play a role in environmental quality planning and, if so, how? This question has two levels. At one level the question is whether equity considerations are appropriately in the domain of public policy, while the second concerns the relevance or importance of equity considerations specifically in environmental planning.

At the first level there is a wide range of opinion on this issue. At one extreme are those who assert that public investments and regulation of private enterprise have the purpose of correcting for market failures and only efficiency effects should be counted in planning and evaluation. Equity or distribution considerations should not enter (they carry a zero weight in the planner's objective function) either because they are nonobjective and therefore beyond the purview of the economist or because it is assumed that a perfectly functioning pure tax and transfer system adjusts the income distribution in an optimal fashion. The other extreme is characterized by such statements as, "Pollution abatement benefits the rich while the poor pay, therefore we should not abate pollution." Aside from the empirical question, this position implies a zero weight to efficiency considerations.

If equity is to be given some weight in public decision making, without being the sole criterion, then some consideration should be given to ways of incorporating equity in the decision process. Since I have discussed this question elsewhere I will not deal with it here.[1] However, I will consider both the ways in which equity concerns could affect environmental de-

---

[1] But see A. Myrick Freeman III, "Project Design and Evaluation with Multiple Objectives," in U.S. Congress Joint Economic Committee, *The Analysis and Evaluation of Public Expenditures: The PPB System*, A Compendium of Papers, 91st Cong., 1st sess., 1969, pp. 565–78, and references cited there.

cisions and the implications of equity concerns for environmental policy planning.

The third aim of this paper is to identify research needs. This can be done at two levels. The first is to ask what we need to find out in order to answer all the relevant questions about the distribution of the environment. Some possible studies will be suggested at several points. However, in this form the question implies too narrow a view. Given scarce resources and activities other than research into environmental distribution that make competing claims on these resources, what priorities should be established? The final section will conclude with some observations on this point.

Before turning to more specific issues, it is necessary to define the word "environment" more precisely. The usual dictionary definitions mention surroundings, conditions, and influences. A composite of these definitions would provide us with this: The environment is the totality of external conditions and influences that affect the way things live and develop. Although this definition is complete, it is unmanageable. In refining it we must first put the environment in the economist's usual frame of reference and then establish some limits on the nature and type of conditions and influences included.

As economists we are interested in the totality of conditions and influences only as they affect man directly or indirectly. This does not so much limit the range of environmental conditions that are relevant as establish the terms on which they are to be evaluated. It seems useful to view the environment as an asset or a kind of nonreproducible capital good that produces a vector of services for man. Some of these services are tangible, such as flows of water or minerals; or functional, such as the removal, dispersion, storage, and degradation of wastes or residuals; or intangible, such as a view. They are all economic goods in the sense that people are willing to pay to receive more or to avoid a reduction in the quantity or quality of a service. From this perspective, environmental quality means the level and composition of the stream of environmental services that people receive; and in principle at least the ultimate measure of quality is the value that people place on it. What these values are, who receives them, and who pays for them are interrelated questions, and they are the heart of the environmental quality management and distribution questions.

In the interests of manageability it is necessary to bound further the concept of the environment in terms of the nature of the services or influences considered. There are two bases for doing this. One is to limit our consideration to those aspects of environmental services that pose public policy problems. This would mean including only those environmental services that flow from the common property resources, are public goods, or act to connect the production or utility functions of firms and individuals through externalities.

The second basis for limiting the nature of the services considered is a practical one, the subject of this conference. Some parts of this paper can, I believe, be read without further narrowing this definition of the environment or specifying what characteristics or services are to be included. They are equally applicable to a discussion of air quality or to various measures of the housing environment or the political, social, or cultural environments. However, our main interest lies in that part of the environment that is related to and affected by the disposal of residuals from production and consumption activities. This means essentially the quality of the air, water, and land, and the composition and levels of services provided by these.

An environment can only be described relative to a point. In a given space there are as many environments as there are points in the space. To make the problem manageable, adjacent points must be aggregated into larger units within which the level of the relevant environmental quality characteristic can be taken to be uniform. The appropriate degree of aggregation depends on the nature of the service or characteristic as well as on the purposes of the study. For example, a study of the patterns of distribution of the environment must have more information on the differences in environmental quality between points within a region than must a study concerned with the relative seriousness of air pollution in different cities.

We now have a basis for describing what we mean by the "distribution of the environment." There may be some environmental quality attributes that are uniform or constant across space. But most vary considerably from place to place and over time, both because of natural causes and because of man's activities. For this reason the environment affects people differently according to where they live, work, and play. The services provided by the environment accrue to different people in different quantities and proportions. The purpose of this paper is to make a first step toward theoretical and empirical investigations of possible patterns in these differential effects.

II. SOME PROBLEMS CONCERNING MEASUREMENT AND DISTRIBUTION

In trying to assess the welfare effects of the environment, either in aggregate or with an eye to their distribution, one must ultimately be concerned with the valuation of environmental services or characteristics. Physical measures of quality, such as ppm of sulfur dioxides, cannot tell the whole story, even though the story can hardly be begun without them. Yet, as we know, there has been very little progress to date in valuing increments to air and water quality, etc. Most of the empirical evidence offered in this paper consists of measures of quantities or service use rather than of value. Hence most of the work of assessing distribution effects lies ahead.

While it is true that the study of the welfare effects of the distribution of the environment must logically await the successful valuation of environmental services, paradoxically it is also true that valuation cannot proceed without first settling two very important distribution issues. These are the assignment of property rights to the common property resource services of the environment and the question of the acceptability of the existing distribution of income and the market prices associated with it. The answer to the first question determines the appropriate conceptual foundation for measuring benefits, while the answer to the second determines whether or not the measures of benefits inferred from observed market-oriented behavior are acceptable.

It has long been accepted that the appropriate measure of the benefits of a new publicly built project is the aggregate willingness to pay for its services. Analytically, the willingness to pay is the sum of the price compensating variation measures of the individual consumer surpluses.[2] An alternative consumer surplus measure is the price equivalent variation that measures the amount individuals would have to receive to compensate them for the lack of or the loss of the new services. As long as the service is a normal good (income elasticity of demand greater than zero) over the relevant portions of indifference maps, the equivalent variation will always be larger than the compensating or willingness-to-pay measure.

The willingness-to-pay measure does not seem to do great violence to one's ethical judgments where the services of new public investments, such as electric power from a hydro project, are concerned. But it does have questionable distributional implications in the case of environmental services. Take the case of the benefits of improving air quality. Acceptance of the willingness-to-pay measure *implies* acceptance of the prior assignment of property rights to the atmosphere to those who are using it for waste disposal and causing degraded air quality. Conversely, use of the equivalent variation measure implie that property rights to the atmosphere reside in those who breathe it, and the costs of air pollution (benefits of abatement) are what these people would require in compensation for their degraded air. Just as any choice from among a set of alternatives implies a

[2] See John R. Hicks, "The Four Consumer's Surpluses," *Review of Economic Studies* 11, no. 1 (1943): 31–41.

relative valuation of the alternatives, the choice of a consumer surplus measure implies the acceptance of a particular assignment of property rights. Where property rights have been legally determined, the choice of a benefit measure must be consistent with the legal situation. But where property rights have not been determined or adjudicated, the analyst must recognize that his choice of a benefit measure is not value free.[3]

The problem of the acceptability of the existing distribution of income is fundamental to applied welfare economics. Since the values or shadow prices used in benefit and cost estimation are inferred in some way from observation of market-related behavior, their validity rests on the acceptability of the distribution of wealth and income that determined the market outcome. If the present distribution of income is judged to be not acceptable, the benefit and cost estimates derived from existing techniques will, in principle, be wrong. The case of the benefits of air quality improvement can be used to illustrate the very questionable ethical implications of basing benefit estimates on the existing distribution of income. It appears to be true that nonwhites and the poor have the highest exposure to air pollutants within an urban area. Whether they are measured by the compensating or equivalent variation consumer surplus measures, the measured benefits for a given improvement in air quality will be lower for a person with a low income than for one with a high income, assuming that preferences are similar and that air quality is a normal good. Where the low tail of the income distribution would receive the major share of the benefits of an improvement in air quality and where the present distribution of income is felt to be inequitable, benefits will be underestimated if based on actual consumer surplus measures. Similarly, if the high tail gets the benefits (e.g., wilderness preservation), benefit estimates based on observation may be found to be overstated when distributional judgments are introduced into the analysis.

In practice this kind of problem could be avoided by basing the benefit estimate and valuation on the willingness to pay (or required compensation) of people with incomes close to the mean. This would deflate values of benefits going to high-income groups and inflate those going to low-income groups. This technique would tend to correct for the presumed biases in benefit estimation. However, the implied ethical judgment on

[3] The assignment of property rights to environmental common property resources is also relevant to the choice of an environmental quality management strategy. Restructuring the incentive system faced by users of the environment by imposing residuals disposal charges necessarily implies that property rights to the environment are vested in the state or the people who benefit from the revenues collected. A system of bribes or public subsidies to private industry for construction of treatment facilities implies acceptance of the existing de facto assignment of property rights to waste dischargers.

which this is based would preclude the use of these benefit estimates to determine repayment obligations.[4]

When appropriate values for benefits and costs can be determined and their incidence traced to individuals, we still need a framework or terminology for describing the distribution effects. One possibility is to adopt a set of weights reflecting the relative value or importance to be given to dollars of benefits or costs going to people of different income levels.[5] Lacking both value figures and a widely accepted weighting function or a method for obtaining one, this suggestion is not operational.

The descriptive phrases "progressive" and "regressive" have traditionally been used to describe the distribution effects of tax schedules. But they are far less useful when applied to schedules of the distribution of benefits or expenditures or net benefit schedules with both positive and negative segments.[6] I propose instead to classify gross benefit and net benefit schedules in accordance with their elasticity with respect to income. If the benefits per person are a rising function of income, then the elasticity is greater than zero. If benefits are rising faster than income, the elasticity is greater than one and the distribution is strongly pro-rich; similarly, if benefits are a decreasing function of income, an elastic benefit schedule is *strongly* pro-poor. On the other hand, if benefits are rising at a rate slower than that of income, the elasticity is less than one and the distribution is mildly pro-rich; similarly, if benefits are a decreasing function of income, an inelastic benefit schedule is *mildly* pro-poor.

Where our concern is with the distribution of welfare, the individual's willingness to pay (or required compensation) for the goods received is the appropriate input into the elasticity measure. Where these are not known but market values are available, they could serve as an approximation. But where values are not known because markets are nonexistent, as in the case of environmental services, physical measures of the benefits must be used.

---

[4] This technique is actually an informal method of weighting benefits or real income changes according to the income levels of the recipients. It would be used in place of, rather than in addition to, an explicit set of welfare weights derived from an assumed social welfare function. See Freeman, "Project Design and Evaluation with Multiple Objectives" for further discussion of the use of weights to reflect equity values.

[5] See ibid.

[6] Gillespie proposed to extend the use of these terms to gross and net expenditure schedules. See W. Irwin Gillespie, "Effect of Public Expenditures on the Distribution of Income," in *Essays in Fiscal Federalism*, ed. Richard A. Musgrave (Washington, D.C.: The Brookings Institution, 1965), p. 132. In commenting on the version of this paper presented at the RFF Conference, Martin David convinced me that Gillespie's terminology was unsatisfactory.

III. SOME ELEMENTS OF A THEORY OF THE DISTRIBUTION OF THE ENVIRONMENT

Environmental Services Directly Consumed by Individuals

In this section I shall propose a way in which environmental quality considerations can be integrated into the framework of the conventional theory of individual choice and welfare. The environmental quality services to be considered are themselves "final products" that enter into utility functions directly, especially recreation and the amenity and life support aspects of air.[7] The first step is to make a different assumption about the form of individual utility functions and the way in which goods and services enter into them. Some consequences of this assumption will be discussed. Secondly, I shall attempt a general statement of the choice problem facing individuals where there are differences in the patterns of environmental quality across space.

In conventional economic analysis it has been assumed that goods are consumed as goods without any attention to what made some goods different from others. Until very recently, little or no attention has been given to the problem of the technology of consumption or how consumer goods produce utility. Lancaster has approached the question directly in an article in which he treats consumer goods as intermediate inputs into the consumption technology.[8] In his model, utility functions are defined in terms of characteristics. Goods produce characteristics. If a good produces only one characteristic upon being consumed, there is a one-to-one relationship between consumption of the good and consumption of the characteristic. Nothing new is added to our understanding of consumer behavior. However, if a good simultaneously produces two or more characteristics in some fixed proportion, or if the same characteristic can be obtained through the consumption of two or more different goods, the theory becomes much richer. For one thing, the concepts of substitute and complementary goods are made much clearer since they involve only properties of the consumption technology. For example, two goods are substitutes if they produce roughly similar sets of characteristics. Complementary relationships arise when two or more goods are required for the production of a single characteristic.

---

[7] In principle, this approach covers all aspects of the environment.

[8] Kelvin J. Lancaster, "A New Approach to Consumer Theory," *Journal of Political Economy* 74, no. 2 (April, 1966): 132–157. See also Richard E. Quandt and William J. Baumol, "The Demand for Abstract Transportation Modes: Theory and Measurement," *Journal of Regional Science* 6, no. 2 (1966): 13–26, for an apparently independent development and application of this approach.

Lancaster's distinction between goods and characteristics is analytically useful where an attribute of a good (e.g., land) varies continuously (e.g., distance from city center or air quality). In conventional analysis, each land site is different from every other, if in no other way than in location. This makes for a rather awkward kind of utility function if it must be defined across all possible sites. On the other hand, if each land site is seen as producing a different set of characteristics, and individual utility functions are defined in terms of these characteristics, differences among land sites, especially environmental quality differences, are manageable.

Now the individual's choice problem can be stated in its complete form. Assume that the individual's utility is a function of the characteristics consumed. Characteristics come from many sources. Some are associated with, or available from, both consumer goods and environmental sites, indicating a potential for substitution between sites and goods in satisfying the demands for these characteristics. For example, urban residence and air-conditioning may substitute for rural residence in shady areas.

The individual faces a set of opportunities for making economic transactions. The set of opportunities represents the constraints on his ability to maximize utility. These opportunities/constraints include:

1. his endowment of factors of production, including labor and capital;

2. the set of opportunities for selling his factor services, each of which can be described by a price and a set of nonprice characteristics (this is particularly relevant to the sale of labor where these characteristics describe working conditions, etc., that help to determine occupational choice and place of work);

3. the set of potential activities (e.g., going fishing) and consumer good purchase opportunities, each of which is described by a price and the vector of characteristics associated with it (the consumption technology);

4. the set of possible environmental sites available for residence, each of which is described by a price and a set of characteristics.

The individual is assumed to make choices that will maximize his utility given the opportunity set. He must choose a vector of consumer goods and activities, one or more environmental sites, and a factor supply vector. As for the latter, the individual must decide not only which of the set of opportunities he will avail himself of,[9] but also whether he will retain any of his factor endowment for his own use. In principle, this kind of choice encompasses the work/leisure choice, and the choice between owning and

[9] The choices of occupation and place of work are not independent of the residence choice. In addition, they both influence and are affected by the possible modes of transportation between work and home. See Quandt and Baumol, "The Demand for Abstract Transportation Modes."

251

renting a home, as well as a host of other rent/purchase possibilities. Also to the extent that some characteristics might be available either from the purchase of consumer goods or from the selection of certain occupations, factor sale choices and consumption choices may be substitutes. Since in principle a given characteristic may be available from the environment, from the sale of factor services under certain conditions, from the retention of factor services, or from the purchase of consumer goods, substitution possibilities in this model are completely general.

To the extent that the model represents reality, it describes how the environment gets distributed. Given the overall level and pattern of environmental quality in a region, an individual can obtain more of a desired environmental characteristic by (a) paying more money to rent or purchase a site with the desired attribute; (b) paying more money for the complementary inputs required to consume the desired characteristic; (c) changing jobs, place of work, or occupation; (d) substituting privately produced services for the missing environmental services; or (e) moving to a new, similarly priced site that has more of the desired attribute but less of some other, i.e., by trading off one attribute for another.

Choices (a) and (b) imply that persons with higher money income or wealth will tend also to experience higher overall levels of environmental quality. Opportunities for choice (c) depend upon the range of factor supply alternatives. Persons with more options are better off in this respect. Also changing jobs may involve some loss of income. Choice (d) shows that income or wealth enhances an individual's capacity to mitigate or avoid the effects of general environmental insults. Choice (e) is distributionally neutral. In fact, opportunities for "exchanges" of that sort raise the utility of all participants.

Environmental Services as Intermediate Inputs

Turning now to intermediate goods, I shall examine ways in which some economically relevant characteristics of common property resources (CPRs) affect the distribution of environmental quality.[10] The environmental quality management problem is concerned with the common property resource dimensions of the environment. The following characteristics can be used to define a common property resource:

1. A CPR is a stock-like thing that yields a flow of one or more services of economic value.

---

[10] This section owes a great deal to discussions with Robert Haveman, and to the chance to read a preliminary version of "Incentives in Common Property Resources Use and Management," by Haveman and Allen V. Kneese.

2. Ownership of this asset or stock is either lodged in some collectivity of individuals (e.g., the state) or has not been determined or defined by law. Appropriation or use of the service does not constitute ownership unless it has been sanctified by law.

3. Access to the services of the stock is, in principle, open to all of the members of the collectivity.

The air mantle and surface waters generally are CPRs. Land itself can be a CPR when it is in public ownership or "in commons"; and its visual characteristics constitute a CPR even when space is privately owned. Land can also overlay subterranean CPRs such as water-bearing aquifers and oil pools. The air, water, and CPR land provide a variety of services including residuals dispersal and assimilation, life sustenance, amenities, and recreation. But these services are generally scarce in the economic sense of the word. Since these services do not pass through markets, the scarcity manifests itself in ways other than a positive money price. One manifestation of scarcity is the congestion phenomenon where one individual's use of the service reduces the quantity or quality of the service available to another. Use of one type of service from a given CPR can reduce the flows of other services from that same CPR to that individual or others. Or the utilization of a service may require inputs of other scarce resources. For example, an ocean fishery yields a flow of fish only when an effort is made to fish. These three kinds of scarcity are not mutually exclusive.

The environmental quality management problem can be viewed as finding that mix of CPR services which, in conjunction with the outputs of the production sector of the economy, results in the highest level of welfare, however that is defined.[11] Knowledge of the values of these services is a prerequisite for effective management and for consideration of distribution effects. I now turn to some models of CPR services to see what determines these values in a market economy, and what the optimum and unregulated equilibrium values and levels of service use will be.

Assume an economic system with perfect competition and no externalities or common property resources except those explicitly introduced below. The analysis is partial equilibrium in nature and is limited to the case of a single CPR producing a single service. In other words, the interesting cases of the trade-offs among services from a single CPR and the interrelationships among CPRs are ignored.

Consider a single CPR service that is used as an input in a production

[11] See, for example, Allen V. Kneese and Ralph C. d'Arge, "Pervasive External Costs and the Response of Society," in U.S. Congress, Joint Economic Committee, *The Analysis and Evaluation of Public Expenditures: The PPB System.*

process. Further assume that in order to utilize the CPR service other inputs are required, and that an industry is established to exploit the CPR
and sell the service to the next-stage industry. This CPR-exploiting industry faces a demand curve that is a derived demand curve for the service
input on the part of the next-stage industry (see the bottom of figure 7.1).
An industry total revenue function can be derived from this demand curve
as in the top of figure 7.1. Further, assume constant marginal costs and
no fixed costs in the exploitation of the CPR service.

If the CPR service were monopolized, the monopolist would set output
at X_1 where marginal revenue equals marginal cost. He would earn a quasi
rent or monopoly profit equal to the vertical distance AB in the top part

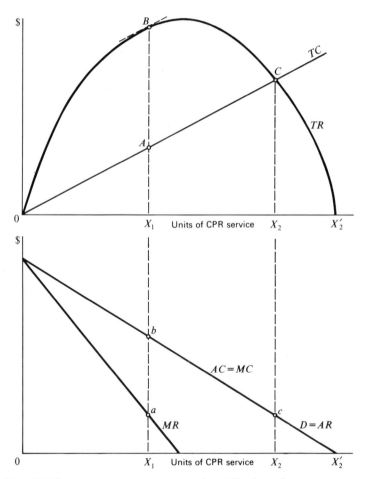

Figure 7.1. Common property resource services utilization—Constant cost case.

of figure 7.1. If entry into this industry were to become free, new entrants would result in expanding utilization of the service and falling price until all profits or quasi rents were eliminated. The equilibrium of the industry would be at X_2. This is also the socially optimal level of output since the price of the CPR service is equal to its marginal cost.[12]

At this social optimum, what is the total value of this CPR service? The value is obviously positive; but no profits or rents to indicate this value accrue to the firms who market this service. Under my assumptions the value is passed on to consumers and is a part of the consumer surplus associated with consumption of whatever final products utilize this CPR service in their production. To find this total value, we would have to postulate an increase in the price of the CPR service sufficient to drive its rate of utilization to zero. An increase in this, or any, factor price would shift the cost curves of the final product industries upward. This is analytically equivalent to the case of an excise tax on a factor input. Conventional incidence analysis can be applied to determine the distribution effects. The extent of the cost curves' shift would depend upon the technology, the ability to substitute other factors and intermediate inputs in production, and the elasticity of supply of other factors. The upward shift in firms' cost curves would ultimately result in an increase in the prices of the final products and decreases in quantities. Given the new prices and quantities, the reduction in consumer surplus associated with the elimination of this CPR service could be calculated. That reduction in consumer surplus would be the total value of the CPR service. Although the analysis has been partial, there are no formal problems in carrying it out in a general equilibrium framework.[13]

The case analyzed above was one of a concave total revenue function and linear total cost function. Another possible case would be linear total revenue and convex total cost[14] (see figure 7.2). In this case, free entry results in an equilibrium output of X_2. At any level of CPR service utilization below that, each producer finds average revenue exceeding average cost. Hence, there is an incentive to expand and/or for new firms to enter. In this case, the price-equals-marginal-cost optimal rule results in an output of X_1. In order to achieve this, the CPR would have to be regulated

---

[12] Here and below I am ignoring the necessity of specifying each firm's cost curves so that firm size is determinate.

[13] See E. J. Mishan, *Welfare Economics: Five Introductory Essays* (New York: Random House, 1964), pp. 67–78.

[14] This is the classical fisheries case. See H. Scott Gordon, "The Economic Theory of a Common Property Resource: The Fishery," *Journal of Political Economy* 62 (1954): 124–42. The total revenue function is linear under the assumption that this is but one of many such fisheries, and the output of this fishery is an insignificant proportion of total fish output.

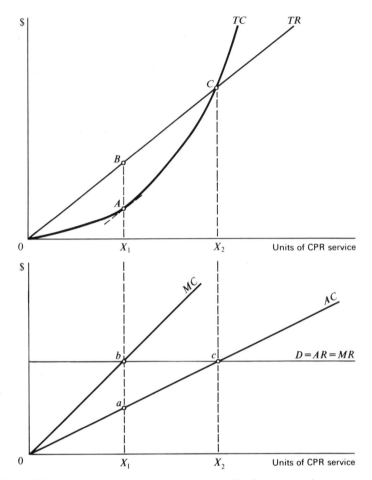

Figure 7.2. Common property resource services utilization—Increasing cost case.

or managed by some public authority, or monopolized. In either case, the CPR would yield a quasi rent equal to the distance AB in the upper part of figure 7.2.

What is the value of this CPR service at its optimal level of utilization, X_1? Again, to find the answer the change in consumer surplus associated with the withdrawal of this CPR service must be determined. The value so determined is in addition to the rent earned by optimal management, AB. To interpret the optimal management rent, we must determine why the total cost curve is convex. If its convexity is due to a rising supply curve for one or more of the complementary inputs, then AB is really a producer's surplus accruing to the inframarginal units of complementary

256

inputs.[15] If, on the other hand, the marginal cost curve is rising because superior units of the CPR are exploited first, then AB is a Ricardian inframarginal rent arising because of differential quality in units of the CPR. But these rents, if present, are in addition to the value of the CPR service that accrues to consumers of the final product.

Where the use of the air mantle for waste disposal does not cause third-party damages, the atmosphere can be considered a special case of the first model (see figure 7.1) where the total cost and marginal cost curves coincide with the horizontal axis. The value of this service of the atmosphere is passed on to consumers through lower prices. If external costs are present, a rising marginal and total cost curve would have to be added to reflect the diminished quality or quantity of other services (e.g., life sustenance) flowing from the atmosphere. The net distributive effect would depend on the combination of the positive waste disposal effect and the negative air quality effect on each individual.[16]

Summary

The major factor influencing the distribution of final product services of the environment from the supply side is whether associated inputs are required to utilize the service. For example, if fishing rods and boats are required to utilize the recreation services of a water body, the cost of associated inputs is a limiting factor in each individual's rate of utilization of the service. In the extreme the quality of the atmosphere is distributed in this way. Since air quality is not uniform across a city or region, those areas with higher air quality will be more popular as residence sites. They will be rationed by price to those with the highest willingness to pay for air quality. On the demand side the major factors are individual tastes and preferences and, where the services are marketed or require associated inputs, the distribution of wealth. Intermediate services are distributed according to the consumption patterns of the goods utilizing these environmental services as inputs. These, too, are determined by individual tastes and preferences and the distribution of wealth. In sum, the analysis of this

[15] But if this is the case, there is no incentive to expand output past X_1. The surplus of the inframarginal units cannot be captured by submarginal units, so entry ceases at X_1.

[16] When CPR services are final products, i.e., enter into utility functions directly, the factors governing the equilibrium use of the environment are somewhat different. The revenue function is replaced by a willingness-to-pay function. But since payment is not required, i.e., the actual benefits are not financial, they are not capturable by additional entrants. Each user equates marginal benefits and costs, and realizes a surplus. Unless each individual's use impairs the use of the service by others due to generic congestion, i.e., unless private and social costs diverge, the unregulated outcome is optimal given the conditions of the partial analysis.

section leads to the expectation that environmental quality, or more generally consumption of the services of the environment, will be positively associated with wealth or money income.

IV. THE DISTRIBUTION OF ENVIRONMENTAL SERVICES

The major managerial or resource allocation decision with regard to the air mantle is the choice of the correct mix of residuals disposal services and life support and amenity services. At least in the major urban areas, more of one means less of the other. The use of surface waters for residuals disposal competes with alternative service flows, principally water recreation. Land can also provide recreation services. In this section I shall examine the distributional patterns of these three principal environmental services, using the analytical framework discussed above and some bits and pieces of empirical evidence. I shall discuss both the patterns of distribution of the present flows of services and the probable incidence effects of an air and water quality improvement program.

Waste Receptor Services of the Air and Water

The distribution of the gross benefits associated with the use of the environment as a waste receptor is determined by consumption patterns, and these in turn are largely influenced by income. It would be possible to use budget studies to get a detailed picture of the extent to which the consumption activities of each income class impose direct and indirect residuals loads on the environment. Such a study would have to take into account differences in the consumption patterns of different households as well as the indirect residuals loads of consumer goods and services that may be large users of high-residual type goods. Two important examples are paper in government and industry, and energy and transportation in the production of consumer goods and services. Major imputation problems would be involved in trying to achieve a more detailed breakdown. Three kinds of waste loads would have to be traced to the consumption activity of the "typical" household at each income level. These are the wastes generated by the manufacturing and transport of consumer goods; wastes generated in producing intermediate products which are themselves inputs to consumer service provision—for example, government or finance; and the residual throughput from household "consumption" of goods and services, including transportation and home heating. If such a study were carried out, it would still not provide a picture of how the *values* of these environmental services were distributed, since it would deal only with the quantities or magnitudes of the services used by each household.

One would expect to find that the consumption of goods and services imposing residuals loads would increase with income, but at a decreasing rate. Table 7.1 shows expenditures as a percentage of income for total consumption and three categories of goods that are likely to impose above-average direct or indirect residuals loads on the environment. In all cases, while the absolute amount of the expenditure rises, the percentage falls with income.

The data suggest that for these broad aggregates the income elasticities of demand for the goods are less than one. If the residuals load per dollar of expenditure were constant over all income classes, then it could be concluded that the income elasticity of the derived demand for waste disposal services is less than one, and the distribution of the benefits associated with using the environment to dispose of wastes is mildly pro-rich.

This tentative conclusion must be interpreted with some caution. These figures are for rather crudely constructed aggregates. Within each group there are surely products with an income elasticity of demand greater than one that would indicate a strongly pro-rich distribution of the environmental services associated with their production. For example, it is possible that higher-income families spend a higher proportion of their food

Table 7.1. Consumption Expenditures as a Percentage of Income,
United States, 1960–61

Income class[a]	Total consumption[b]	Food	Energy[c]	Paper[d]
(dollars)	(------------------- per cent -------------------)			
0–999	178	49	13	3.0
1,000–1,999	112	33	8	1.7
2,000–2,999	105	30	7	1.6
3,000–3,999	104	27	8	1.5
4,000–4,999	97	25	7	1.4
5,000–5,999	94	23	7	1.4
6,000–7,499	92	22	7	1.4
7,500–9,999	88	21	6	1.3
10,000–14,999	83	18	5	1.3
15,000–over	66	13	3	0.9

[a] Money income after taxes plus other money receipts.
[b] Expenditures for current consumption.
[c] The sum of: coal and coke; wood, etc.; kerosene; fuel oil; other solid and petroleum fuels; gas; electricity; gas and electricity (combined bills); and transportation—gasoline.
[d] The sum of: household paper supplies; reading-matter total; education—books, supplies, and equipment.
Source: U.S. Department of Labor, Bureau of Labor Statistics, Survey of Consumer Statistics, Consumer Expenditures and Income, Supplement 3, Part A to BLS Report 237–238 (Washington, D.C.: Bureau of Labor Statistics, July 1964), table 29A.

budget on packaging, and this would impose a relatively high residuals burden per dollar of food expenditure both in production and in ultimate disposal. However, to take these considerations adequately into account would require a highly detailed household budget study associated with an input-output table disaggregated along product quality lines and with residuals coefficients for each product class. This would be a major undertaking.

Present rates and patterns of waste disposal in the environment are imposing uncompensated costs or damages on third parties. If these are to be avoided or reduced, waste disposal rates and patterns must change. These changes will impose costs on some individuals. There are three possible target groups for these costs. The costs can result in higher prices which shift them to consumers. If there are factors of production specific to the industry (supply elasticity less than infinite) the costs can be imposed on factors through lower quasi rents or monopoly profits. Or they can be shifted to third parties through government action. The incidence of these costs depends in part on the choice of environmental quality management tools. Three cases will be considered here: charges or standards, bribes, and tax incentives and subsidies.

Where an effluent or emission charge is levied or where environmental quality standards and residuals discharge standards are strictly enforced, production costs for private firms will rise.[17] This will lead to an increase in product price. In a competitive industry the cost will be at least in part passed on to the consumer. The income elasticity of this cost pattern would probably be positive but less than one since consumption as a percentage of income is a decreasing function of income. This would be like a regressive tax. Where firms have market power, conventional analysis suggests that some of the costs would be absorbed in lower profits. Reductions in other factor incomes (quasi rents) could be severe for small numbers of individuals.[18] In the case of a residuals charge, the situation is complicated by the need to take into account the disposition of the revenues collected.

[17] Total costs, including costs of treatment, process change, or whatever, must rise if the firm is originally on its production frontier. Those occasionally reported cases where firms report lower costs after adopting new processes as part of their production control efforts must result from failure to perceive or act upon existing opportunities for lowering costs prior to the new control program.

[18] Where high-residuals activities such as paper and textile mills are located in one industry town, and where they cut back operations or shut down in response to a residuals management program, these effects could be severe. Equity might best be served by adopting "adjustment assistance" programs such as those written into the Trade Expansion Act of 1962 and the U.S.–Canadian Automotive Agreement. After determining eligibility on the basis of unemployment or other economic loss in a locality substantially or in major part caused by the residuals management program, assistance would be available in the form of extended unemployment compensation, retaining relocation allowances, etc. See James Jonish, "Adjustment Assistance Experience

In the case of a charge or standard imposed against a municipality or other public discharger of municipal waste, the incidence of these costs depends on the set of taxes and charges used to cover the higher costs. As a general rule, one would expect the state and local taxes to be regressive in impact, while in the case of federal funding the incidence overall would be mildly progressive.[19] The net effect of pollution abatement where public services are involved would depend on the mix of federal, state, and local funding.

Another possible environmental quality management tool is a set of bribes to dischargers to induce reductions in residuals discharges. As is well known, bribes based upon the marginal damages caused by the dischargers are symmetrical in their efficiency or allocative effects, given certain assumptions about knowledge and restrictions on entry.[20] However, they are not symmetrical with charges in terms of their distributional impact. The money to pay the bribes must come from somewhere. While in the case of charges the incidence depends on the pattern of consumption of the goods utilizing the watercourse for waste disposal, in the case of bribes the incidence depends upon the mix of taxes chosen to raise the funds to pay the bribes.

Interregional as well as interpersonal income distribution effects may also be associated with bribes, charges, and standards. With charges or standards, if the industrial dischargers either serve a national market or have stockholders throughout the nation, the cost of pollution abatement will be borne largely by those outside the region. In addition, those outside the region compensate the region through the charges for the remaining uncorrected levels of pollution. In the case of bribes, the interregional impact depends on the tax mix, the extent of the market for the products, and the geographical distribution of ownership. With local taxes local residents incur the costs of achieving pollution abatement, but they also receive the benefits of abatement. In general, consumers pay and the stock-

---

Under the U.S.–Canadian Automotive Agreement" (Seminar Discussion Paper No. 13, Research Seminar in International Economics [Ann Arbor: University of Michigan, 1969]). Severe localized effects could be indirect as well as direct—for example, the impact of a shift away from high sulfur coal on employment of coal miners.

[19] See Gillespie, "Effect of Public Expenditures on the Distribution of Income," p. 136. His figures show some progressivity in total state and local taxes up to the $4,000–$5,000 income class, and steep regressivity beyond that. Effective federal tax rates are progressive up to $5,000 and beyond $10,000 but surprisingly regressive over that interval. This is because social security contributions, and excise taxes (including customs), are quite regressive over this range, while personal income taxes are only mildly progressive between $5,000 and $10,000.

[20] See Allen V. Kneese and Blair T. Bower, *Managing Water Quality: Economics, Technology, Institutions* (Baltimore: Johns Hopkins Press for Resources for the Future, 1968), pp. 175–79.

holders benefit from the implied definition of property rights in the favor of producers. If the good is nationally marketed but locally owned, the transfer is to the region.

A third means of achieving reduction in residuals discharges is to provide grants-in-aid, subsidies, or tax incentives to industrial dischargers. It can be argued that this approach is inefficient in that it does not achieve a given reduction in waste discharge at the least cost because it distorts the incentive system faced by firms.[21] The equity effects are not clear, but it seems likely that with multiplant firms and with oligopolistic industries it would be less likely that the subsidy or tax incentive would be passed on in the form of lower prices. To the extent that the subsidy is captured by the firm, this means of achieving environmental quality improvement would be accompanied by a transfer from taxpayers to stockholders.

At present, the federal law allows for subsidies to industry in the form of federal grant-in-aid funds to municipalities treating industrial wastes. Municipalities can obtain federal funds to cover up to 55 per cent of construction costs on plants that will treat both domestic and industrial wastes. The municipalities are required to recover only operating costs and the municipal share of construction costs from industry.

There are several possibilities for the direction of net transfer in these circumstances. If the firm is producing for a local market and is competitive, the net transfer would be from federal taxpayers in general to consumers in the locality. On the other hand, if the firm serves a national market and is competitive, national taxpayers would subsidize national consumers. In both cases the effect would be to make the cost schedule more progressive. To the extent that the subsidy accrues to profit for the firm, the federal share goes to benefit stockholders only. The federal government has not compiled detailed records of the use of this subsidy. However, as of 31 March 1969, federal grants to municipalities whose waste loads were at least 50 per cent industrial had reached a cumulative total of $83 million, or just under 8 per cent of all municipal grants.[22]

Air—Life Support and Amenities

A large body of evidence clearly supports the hypothesis that the value of air for life support and amenities goes down as the concentration of residuals/pollutants in the air goes up. The question is: Do existing patterns of air pollution impose absolutely or relatively greater burdens on low income households? There are two kinds of burdens. First, the effects, both chronic and acute, on health of exposure to polluted air. These effects

[21] Ibid.
[22] Private communication from Allen Hirsch, Federal Water Pollution Control Administration.

are to a large extent, but not completely, reflected in morbidity and mortality rates.[23]

These health effects may not be perceived. That is to say, an individual may not recognize the link between air pollutants and his poor health. This would be more likely where chronic pollution levels are below the level of perception or where odorless gases, such as carbon monoxide, are concerned. On the other hand, the increasing publicity being given to the "air pollution problem" is likely to lead to higher levels of awareness of possible health effects, at least among the better informed segments of the population, even though these people may not know when they are breathing unhealthy air.

The second kind of burden is the disutility and amenity loss and physical damages to structures, etc., that are in addition to the health effects. This burden is by definition perceived. To the extent that people perceive these adverse effects, whether to health, amenities, or nonhuman property, and whether or not they recognize that the cause is air pollution, they are motivated to avoid them. Since air quality is not generally homogeneous in an economic region, people are motivated to move to and occupy areas with higher air quality, but by the nature of things there is a scarcity of areas with the highest quality of air, and unit land rents or land values will tend to be higher, ceteris paribus, where air quality is higher. Thus, the land under the higher quality air will tend to be occupied by the households with the highest willingness to pay, and, if the effects of air quality are not an inferior good, with the highest incomes. An indirect test of this hypothesis is to see whether land values are correlated with air quality, ceteris paribus. The results of two multiple regression studies of urban areas tend to confirm this hypothesis.[24]

Since air quality is generally lower in city centers than in the suburbs, and there is a general pattern of center city/suburban segregation by income level for other reasons too, we would expect individuals with low incomes to reside in lower quality air. In other words, in terms of the life

[23] For a survey of the literature on the health effects of chronic levels of exposure to air pollutants and an attempt to place dollar values on these effects, see Lester B. Lave and Eugene P. Seskin, "Air Pollution and Human Health," *Science* 169, no. 3947 (August 1970): 723–33.

[24] Ronald G. Ridker and John A. Henning, "The Determinants of Residential Property Values with Special Reference to Air Pollution," *The Review of Economics and Statistics* 49, no. 2 (May 1967): 246–57. This study was of the St. Louis SMSA. See also Robert G. Anderson, Jr. and Thomas D. Crocker, "Air Pollution and Residential Property Values" (Paper presented at the Econometric Society meetings, New York City, December 1969). This study was of the Kansas City, St. Louis, and Washington SMSAs. In both studies, median property value, rather than unit land value, was the dependent variable. Property value captures size of lot effects and the value of improvements as well as differential site values.

sustenance and amenity services of the environment, the poor would bear an absolutely greater share of the burden of air pollution, both because of the inability to buy access to higher quality air and because of other social and economic forces that tend to exclude them from access to the higher quality suburban air. Of course, this conclusion is moderated somewhat, but not reversed, by the likelihood that the adult male member of the high-income suburban household must travel to, and work in, the low-air-quality city center.

I have examined evidence from three SMSAs in an attempt to determine whether the expected pattern of distribution is in fact observed. Using Census Tract data for 1960 on income, race, and housing tenure, I constructed indexes of pollution exposure per family. These indexes are necessarily based on the assumption that all members of the family spend their whole lives at their residence, thus being exposed to neither higher nor lower quality air in other parts of the city. Table 7.2 shows the exposure indexes by income level for suspended particulates, sulfation rates, and an unweighted index of the two normalized on a value of one. All data are for annual averages. Table 7.3 shows similar indexes for families classified by race and by whether they own or rent their home.

The systematic inverse variation of pollution exposure and income is obvious. These data show that air quality is distributed in a pro-rich manner. But whether the income elasticity of this distribution is greater or less than one cannot be determined because of the problem of units of measurement for air quality. There is also striking variation between cities in the overall pollution levels. As a result the lowest income class in Washington, D.C., is exposed on average to lower levels of suspended particulates than the highest income group in St. Louis. Similarly, the lowest income groups of Kansas City are exposed to lower sulfur oxide levels than the highest income residents of either St. Louis or Washington, D.C.

Even more striking are the differences in exposure between whites and blacks. In each city the average black family has a higher exposure to both air pollutants than does the average family (black or white) with an income under $3,000.

While the incidence patterns are clear enough in the cases studied, we must caution against hasty generalization. First, the data refer only to two pollutants. Second, the index does not take into account time spent exposed to air pollution away from home, both at work and in commuting. These two factors may lead to a reduction in the income-related exposure to air pollution generally. Third, these data cover only three cities. Fourth, the data used here obscure variation in socioeconomic variables within census tracts as well as variation in exposure within income and social

264

Table 7.2. Air Pollution Exposure Indexes by Income Size Class

Income size class	Suspended particulates	Sulfation	Mean
(dollars)	(μgms/ml)	(mg. SO₃/ 100 cm² per day)	
Kansas City			
0–2,999	76.7	0.22	1.16
3,000–4,999	72.4	0.20	1.09
5,000–6,999	66.5	0.18	0.98
7,000–9,999	63.5	0.17	0.93
10,000–14,999	60.1	0.15	0.86
15,000–24,999	57.6	0.14	0.80
25,000–over	58.1	0.12	0.76
St. Louis			
0–2,999	91.3	0.97	1.19
3,000–4,999	85.3	0.88	1.10
5,000–6,999	79.2	0.78	1.00
7,000–9,999	75.4	0.72	0.93
10,000–14,999	73.0	0.68	0.89
15,000–24,999	68.8	0.60	0.82
25,000–over	64.9	0.52	0.74
Washington, D.C.			
0–2,999	64.6	0.82	1.19
3,000–4,999	61.7	0.82	1.16
5,000–6,999	53.9	0.75	1.04
7,000–9,999	49.7	0.69	0.96
10,000–14,999	45.5	0.64	0.88
15,000–24,999	43.2	0.58	0.82
25,000–over	42.0	0.53	0.77

Sources: J. R. Farmer and J. D. Williams, *Interstate Air Pollution Study, Air Quality Measurements* (Cincinnati, Ohio: U.S. Department of Health, Education, and Welfare, Public Health Service, December 1966).

U.S. Bureau of the Census, *U.S. Censuses of Population and Housing: 1960*, Final Report PHC (1): no. 70, Kansas City, Kansas, Missouri; no. 131, St. Louis, Missouri, Illinois; and no. 166, Washington, D.C., Maryland, Virginia (Washington, D.C.: Government Printing Office, 1962).

U.S. Department of Health, Education, and Welfare, Public Health Service, *Kansas City, Kansas–Kansas City, Missouri, Air Pollution Abatement Activity, Phase II, Pre-Conference Investigations* (Cincinnati, Ohio: HEW, Public Health Service, 1968).

Cincinnati, Ohio: HEW, Public Health Service, November 1967, *Technical Report: Washington, D.C. Metropolitan Area Air Pollution Abatement Activity.*

classes. These variations may be, for example, due to occupation. Finally, the observed association does not prove causation. In fact, air pollution, measures of housing quality, age, race, income, and education are all highly intercorrelated among census tracts in the three cities studied.[25]

[25] Also canonical correlations between physical environment indicators (pollution and housing) and socioeconomic characteristics (age, race, income, and education) were highly significant (0.8–0.9).

Table 7.3. Air Pollution Exposure Indexes by Housing Tenure and Race

	Suspended particulates	Sulfation	Mean
	$(\mu gms/ml)$	(mg. SO_3/ 100 cm^2 per day)	
Kansas City			
Housing tenure:			
Owner-occupied	63.9	0.16	0.91
Rented	78.0	0.24	1.23
Race:			
White	64.3	0.17	0.94
Nonwhite	83.3	0.24	1.26
St. Louis			
Housing tenure:			
Owner-occupied	n.a.	n.a.	n.a.
Rented	n.a.	n.a.	n.a.
Race:			
White	78.2	0.80	1.00
Nonwhite	102.6	1.22	1.42
Washington, D.C.			
Housing tenure:			
Owner-occupied	48.4	0.63	0.90
Rented	57.5	0.79	1.10
Race:			
White	42.8	0.66	0.87
Nonwhite	78.4	0.95	1.42

n.a. = data not available.
Sources: See sources for table 7.2.

As in the section on "Waste Receptor Services of The Air and Water," the data presented deal only with physical measures of the flow of environmental services, or in this case with indirect measures of their impairment. Values have not been assigned. The problem of estimating these costs or values is symmetrical to the one of estimating the benefits of an improvement in air quality. We will deal with the problem in this latter context.

The literature recognizes two principal approaches to benefit estimation. The first utilizes health data to estimate effects on health, irrespective of whether or not they are perceived. The second uses changes in property values as a reflection of the perceived effects of changes in air quality.

In using health data the analyst attempts to establish statistical relationships between the levels of various air pollutants and morbidity and mortality rates for a particular disease classification.[26] The more disaggregated the morbidity and mortality data, the more fruitful this approach

[26] See also chap. 6.

266

is likely to be. One would want at least age-specific death rates and would prefer to have morbidity and mortality rates for various social/economic groupings. One would expect the mortality and morbidity experience of low-income people, for example, to be different from that of high-income people for reasons other than greater exposure to air pollution. Since low-income people as a group also experience greater exposure to air pollution, the use of aggregate morbidity and mortality rates could provide an inaccurate estimate of the relationship between air quality and health.

After establishing the pollution morbidity-mortality rate relationship, two very difficult conceptual steps are to be taken. These have not been successfully traversed as yet. The first is to translate mortality-morbidity rate changes caused by air quality into changes in healthy life expectancy. The second is to find a conceptually satisfactory basis for placing a value on the change in life expectancy.[27]

If land values are correlated with air quality, changes in air quality should be accompanied by changes in land values. The question is whether changes in land values can be used as the basis for estimating the value to individuals of the improvement in air quality. In an unpublished paper Strotz[28] has shown that, given certain simplifying assumptions, the difference in land values between two classes of land, alike in all respects save air quality, will equal the aggregate willingness to pay for the improvement in air quality. A crucial assumption in Strotz's model is that the two classes of land be perfect substitutes in all utility functions when they have the same air quality. It is only then that the differential in land value resulting from an improvement in air quality over one class of land will exactly equal the aggregate willingness to pay for better quality air. If the two classes of land are not perfect substitutes, then land value changes do not fully reflect willingness to pay, and an uncaptured consumer surplus accrues to residents of the improved area.

The rationale for this is fairly simple. The mechanism that gets land rents to change in response to air quality changes is the decisions of some households that were heretofore indifferent or actually preferred land in the other area to move into the improved area. This increase in the demand for a fixed supply of land results in land rents being bid up. If land in the

[27] See T. C. Schelling, "The Life You Save May be Your Own," in *Problems in Public Expenditure Analysis*, ed. Samuel B. Chase, Jr. (Washington, D.C.: The Brookings Institution, 1968), for an engaging discussion that raises but does not resolve most of the issues.

[28] Robert H. Strotz, "The Use of Land Rent Changes to Measure the Welfare Benefits of Land Improvement" (Resources for the Future, July 1966). It does not follow that cross-sectional studies of land values and air quality can be used to infer the demand for cleaner air or the benefits of pollution abatement. The rent-air quality relationship reflects an equilibrium given the demand for and supply of air quality. Cross-section data do not permit *identification* of a demand curve from this equilibrium relationship.

area is a perfect substitute for other land before the improvement in air quality, then all outsiders are on the margin of indifference between settling in one of the two areas. Any change in air quality causes them all to try to move into the improved area and bids up land rents. The system is fine-tuned to changes in air quality. When the two types of land are not perfect substitutes,[29] the magnitude of this desire for movement to the newly improved land is diminished and is eliminated by a smaller rental increase. Those who do live in the improved area experience the same air quality improvement, but have to pay less for it because rents do not rise as much. The difference is the uncaptured consumer surplus.

What is the relevance of this model for our analysis of the distribution of air quality? First, of course, it applies only to perceived differences among land sites in the effects of air pollution. Where there are unperceived health effects, improvements in air quality will accrue directly to those who live in the area. Also the analysis applies only to that portion of an individual's or family's total exposure that is related to his residence. To the extent that persons are exposed at work or in travel about the city, the benefits of reducing this exposure will not be reflected in any land rent changes but will accrue directly to the individuals.

The incidence of air quality improvements is partly determined by the land tenure situation. If homes are owner-occupied, the benefits accrue to the occupant whether or not land values rise. If land values rise, he can take his gain in the form of cleaner air or in a realized capital gain from the sale of his property. But if the occupant rents his home, the division of the benefits between the occupant and the landlord depends on the extent to which the benefits are captured in land values or in consumer surplus.

What can be said about the probable distribution of the benefits of an air pollution abatement program in an urban area? By the nature of atmospheric dispersion systems, any program to improve air quality will have its largest impact on those areas with the lowest air quality. As a first approximation we can say that the benefits of the program would go to the people with the highest exposure to air pollutants. As tables 7.2 and 7.3 show, these are largely people with low incomes, nonwhites, and renters rather than owners. The benefits of air quality improvements will accrue to the poor and nonwhites to the extent either that they are homeowners or that the Strotz mechanism for raising land values is not operative. For land values to rise, people must want to move back into the areas with newly improved air quality. Two factors will tend to retard this movement in urban areas. The first is the extent of sunk investment in housing, etc., which helps to determine the character of a neighborhood and makes

[29] Or when other goods are close substitutes for land in the Lancaster sense of also providing the desired characteristic.

changes in patterns of land use difficult and slow. The second is that urban and suburban land are imperfect substitutes with respect to characteristics other than air quality. For these reasons, I surmise that at least a significant portion of the benefits of improved urban air quality will escape capitalization into land values and accrue directly to the inhabitants of the inner city. If this is correct, the distribution of the benefits would have a negative elasticity with respect to income, i.e., be pro-poor.

Water Recreation

When surface waters are used for waste disposal, water-based recreation is the major alternative environmental service that is impaired. In addition, amenity losses may be caused by smell and unsightly films, scum, and other floating matter.[30] A priori reasoning suggests that utilization of water-based recreation services will be positively related to income, i.e., that people with higher incomes will make relatively more use of this environmental service. This is because boating and fishing, for example, require investments in complementary equipment. In addition, there are complementary travel costs to and from the recreation site and operating expenses for bait, gasoline, guides, etc.

The most comprehensive study of recreation participation has been carried out by Cicchetti, Seneca, and Davidson, based on data obtained by the U.S. Department of the Interior, Bureau of Outdoor Recreation's 1965 National Recreation Survey.[31] In this study multiple regression techniques were used to obtain estimates of the determinants of the probability of participation and the number of days of activity per participant for a number of outdoor recreation activities including six water-based activities. Family income was a significant variable in all of the equations for probability of participation (see table 7.4). The equation also showed that race was a significant variable for all cases except sailing. Race was a dummy variable with a 0/1 value for nonwhite/white. In the equations for number of days per participant, both variables were significant for swimming; and either race or family income was significant for all of the other activities except canoeing. These equations do not permit

---

[30] See U.S. Department of the Interior, Federal Water Pollution Control Administration, *Delaware Estuary Comprehensive Study* (Philadelphia: Federal Water Pollution Control Administration, 1966), pp. 71–81; Richard J. Frankel, "Water Quality Management: Engineering-Economic Factors in Municipal Waste Disposal," *Water Resources Research* 1, no. 2 (1965): 173–86; Kneese and Bower, *Managing Water Quality*, pp. 124–29; and Clifford S. Russell, "Municipal Evaluation of Regional Water Quality Management Proposals," in "Models for Managing Regional Water Quality," ed. R. Dorfman, H. Jacoby, and H. A. Thomas, Jr. (Harvard University Press, forthcoming).

[31] Charles J. Cicchetti, Joseph J. Seneca, and Paul Davidson, *The Demand and Supply of Outdoor Recreation* (New Brunswick: Rutgers-The State University, 1969).

Table 7.4. The Effects of Race and Income on Participation
in Water-Based Recreation Activities

Activity	Probability of participation		Number of days per participant	
	Race	Family income	Race	Family income
Swimming	+	+	+	+
Water skiing	+	+	+	0
Fishing	+	+	+	0
Sailing	0	+	0	+
Other boating	+	+	0	+
Canoeing	+	+	0	0

Note: + = Regression coefficient significantly greater than zero.
0 = Regression coefficient not significant.
Source: Charles J. Cicchetti, Joseph J. Seneca, and Paul Davidson, *The Demand and Supply of Outdoor Recreation* (New Brunswick: Rutgers–The State University, 1969), chap. 5.

one to draw conclusions about the causes of these differences in participation by race and income. For example, we cannot say whether there are systematic differences in tastes and preferences, or whether discrimination on the one hand and budgetary constraints on the other work to cause the observed relationships. However, the evidence seems conclusive that the opportunity for water-based recreation provided by the common property environmental resources is exploited more frequently by people with high incomes and by whites; i.e., the income elasticity of the distribution of these services is positive.

Turning to the incidence of recreation benefits associated with water quality improvement, the Cicchetti-Seneca-Davidson data would lead us to expect greater per capita increases in recreation activity on the part of people with high income. If the newly available recreation waters had the same characteristics and spatial distribution relative to population centers as the existing recreation waters, we would expect the incidence pattern of recreation benefits to follow existing patterns of recreational participation. However, this assumption almost certainly will not hold. The newly available recreation waters will almost certainly be different in nature as well as in location. To the extent that the newly available waters are closer to urban centers or to concentrations of people with lower incomes, the distribution of benefits will tend to be less pro-rich or more pro-poor.

To determine whether proximity would in fact result in a more pro-poor distribution of benefits, one would have to carry out an extensive survey of recreation participation along the lines of the 1965 National Recreation Survey, but include questions on distance traveled and correlate detailed supply/proximity data with each respondent. Then, with the resulting participation regressions, recreation days could be calculated by income class for the existing supply of recreation water and the projected supply after water quality improvement.[32]

Land-Based Rural Recreation

Land-based rural recreation is not, strictly speaking, residuals related. But the publicly owned recreation land is a common property resource; and there is considerable interest in the question of the adequacy of this stock of land for meeting present and future demands for recreation services.

As in the case of water-based recreation, a priori considerations suggest that this environmental service will be utilized relatively more by people with high incomes because of the necessity of obtaining complementary goods—transportation in particular. There is an offsetting factor which, however, is likely to be of limited significance. This is the opportunity for the substitution of private land-based recreation for recreation on public and. Private hunting preserves, vacation camps, and summer homes are private sector alternatives to participation in recreation activities on the public lands. And these opportunities are available only to the wealthy.

Again, the Cicchetti-Seneca-Davidson study is the most comprehensive source of information on this subject. Table 7.5 presents a summary of their findings concerning the effects of race and family income on eight land-based recreation activities. The National Recreation Survey on which the study is based did not distinguish between activities and participation on public vs. private lands. Thus, this information is not strictly applicable to our question. Nevertheless, it is suggestive. The general pattern is for either family income or race or both to have a positive impact on probability of participation and/or participation days.

Scattered information is also available on the incomes and educational characteristics of the users of wilderness areas. A 1960 survey of wilderness users in the Adirondacks, the Boundary Waters Canoe area, and the High Sierras showed that wilderness visitors had higher income levels on average than the U.S. population as a whole.[33] A number of other studies have

[32] This, in effect, is what Davidson, Adams, and Seneca did. See Paul Davidson, F. Gerard Adams, and Joseph J. Seneca, "The Social Value of Water Recreational Facilities Resulting from an Improvement in Water Quality: The Delaware Estuary," in *Water Research*, ed. Allen V. Kneese and Stephen C. Smith (Baltimore: The Johns Hopkins Press for Resources for the Future, 1966). Unfortunately, their supply/proximity variables were not sufficiently detailed to pick up the kind of differential supply effect hypothesized here. See especially p. 197.
[33] Outdoor Recreation Resources Review Commission, *Wilderness and Recreation: A Report on Resources, Values, and Problems*, Study Report No. 3 (Washington, D.C.: Government Printing Office, 1962), p. 132. I am indebted to Anthony Fisher for this and the next reference.

Table 7.5. The Effects of Race and Income on Participation
in Rural Land-Based Recreation Activities

	Probability of participation		Number of days per participant	
Activity	Race	Family income	Race	Family income
Hunting	+	0	0	–
Camping—remote	+	0	+	–
Hiking	+	0	0	0
Bird watching	0	0	–	0
Wildlife and bird photography	0	+	0	0
Picnicking	+	+	+	+
Sightseeing	0	+.	0	+
Camping—developed	+	0	+	+

Note: + = Regression coefficient significantly greater than zero.
    0 = Regression coefficient not significant.
    – = Regression coefficient significantly less than zero.
Source: Cicchetti, Seneca, and Davidson, *The Demand and Supply of Outdoor Recreation*, chap. 5.

found that wilderness users tend to have higher levels of educational attainment than the population as a whole.[34] Since higher educational attainment tends to be correlated with higher income levels, this evidence also suggests that the services of the wilderness environment tend to be utilized relatively more intensively by people with high incomes.

Shabman and Kalter have attempted to infer the distribution effects of public expenditures on recreation by making some admittedly crude simplifying assumptions.[35] They used the Bureau of Outdoor Recreation (BOR) 1965 National Recreation Survey to determine recreation activities by income level for New York State. The study included both land-based and water-based recreation and had two components. In the first, gross gains were defined as public sector recreation expenditures, and gross costs were defined as the taxes, fees, and user charges used to finance these expenditures. The gross benefits were allocated on the basis of the income data on users from the BOR survey. For each income class, a net gain or loss was computed. It was found that even though low-income families tended to use recreation less often, they also bore a smaller share of the total cost and tended to be net gainers. In fact, only those with income levels over $10,000 were net losers, because of the progressivity of the

[34] See U.S. Department of Agriculture, Forest Service, *Wilderness Users in the Pacific Northwest: Their Characteristics, Values, and Management Preferences*, Forest Service Research Paper PNW–61 (Portland, Oregon, 1968), p. 13.
[35] Leonard A. Shabman and Robert J. Kalter, "Effects of Public Programs for Outdoor Recreation on Personal Income Distribution," *American Journal of Agricultural Economics* 51, no. 5 (December 1969): 1516–19.

taxes used to finance recreation expenditures. The net gains were $5.82 per household for those with under $3,000 a year in income and $-$16.05 for those in the $15,000 a year plus category.

In the other component of the study, benefits were defined only for new investments in additional recreation capacity during the year studied. Recreation days were valued at $1.50 per day for all income levels. The BOR National Recreation Survey was used to project participation levels by income class. The costs of incremental projects were allocated in the same way as the first component of the study. Since all recreation projects undertaken had calculated benefit-cost ratios greater than one, aggregate net benefits were positive. Again, the net transfers tended to favor lower-income families relative to higher-income families. By this measure, all families with incomes under $15,000 tended to benefit at least in a small way by the incremental recreation investment.[36]

User Charges—Equity and Efficiency

It has been suggested that higher user charges might be appropriate to correct for the apparent net transfer to high-income users of wild areas, or to shift more of the cost of the preservation and maintenance of recreation areas to the actual beneficiaries. But user charges have both equity and efficiency implications that will be in conflict unless the existing distribution of income is the desired one. Furthermore, it is not always clear that user charges will have the desired redistribution effect.

The efficiency criterion for user charges would have the charge set equal to the marginal social cost where this includes congestion-type externalities in high-use areas. If the carrying capacity of a primitive area has not been reached and there are no marginal maintenance costs, the efficiency price is zero. As was pointed out, such areas are used predominantly by upper-income recreationists. A user charge imposed for equity reasons would have to equate the marginal welfare loss due to reduced participation by present users with the marginal welfare gains of the revenues.

Where there are some low-income users, the welfare effects of a charge are not clear. The charge would have the largest effect on the participation rates of the lowest income users. The more low-income users there are, and the higher the welfare weights attached to real transfers to them, the more likely it is that the net equity effects of a charge will be undesirable.

[36] This and the preceding section have focussed on rural recreation. For a discussion of urban recreation planning with particular attention to equity considerations, see Charles J. Cicchetti, "Some Economic Issues Involved in Planning Urban Recreation Facilities," *Land Economics* 47 (1971): 14–23.

If a social welfare function has been specified, it is a straightforward matter to establish the appropriate criterion and level of charge.

V. SOME CONCLUSIONS ABOUT PLANNING AND RESEARCH

Let us grant that distribution does matter in public decision making regarding the environment, perhaps because a political decision has been made to use transfers in kind rather than cash to achieve distributional goals. And let us assume that some means has been found to represent this equity concern—perhaps a set of weights reflecting social welfare judgments. In what ways could this equity concern affect or alter decisions about environmental quality management?

This equity concern could have three kinds of effects on the set of public decisions. First, it could result in some projects or programs being undertaken, even though their efficiency benefit-cost ratios were less than one, because the benefits were directed more toward a target group of "deserving" beneficiaries. Similarly, other projects, even with positive net efficiency benefits, could be rejected if their distributional effects were undesirable. Second, any project could be altered in some way to further distributional objectives. For example, financial aspects of the project such as repayment and cost sharing provisions can be changed to shift the burden away from target beneficiaries. Also, the physical or technical aspects of the project could be changed to redirect benefits to the desired beneficiaries. Finally, it must be realized that efficiency and equity objectives may be competitive in that to achieve greater equity in the distribution of benefits (or costs) it may be necessary to incur lower total benefits or higher costs. For example, the incidence of costs associated with an effluent charge system may be regressive, but the water quality management strategy with the most desired equity effects—perhaps federal subsidies to industrial and municipal dischargers—may mean higher total costs to society to achieve the desired water quality goals.

With this discussion of the ways in which distribution can affect planning, we can turn to the question of the appropriate role of distribution in environmental quality planning. There are two aspects to this question. The first is how important is the distribution of environmental quality relative to the overall distribution of income, wealth, or welfare? The second aspect is how important is environmental quality distribution relative to other aspects of the environmental quality management problem? With regard to the first, it has been argued in the course of this chapter that the distribution of environmental quality is largely the result of the interaction between the distribution of income and wealth and market incentives and market mechanisms. The distribution of the environment is largely a consequence of the broader distribution forces at work in the economic system. The evidence presented supports this conclusion. It does not appear that pollution is the great leveler. This may become true some day if continued environmental degradation results in global and massive ecological catastrophe. But at least so far, and in terms of those measures of environmental quality studied here, the rich have the opportunity and the means to protect themselves and/or avoid environmental insults to a much greater extent than the poor.

This suggests that the most effective way to improve the general distribution of the environment is to improve the basic distribution of wealth. Many economists would accept the proposition that this is a counsel of perfection, and would move on to argue that transfers in kind can be used to adjust the distribution of welfare in the desired direction. The second aspect of the question posed here really relates to the possibilities for accomplishing such transfers through environmental quality management. There are several considerations.

First, we must ask whether distributional considerations are likely to significantly alter the rankings of projects. For this to occur there must be differences among projects in the pattern of distribution of benefits and costs. Further, these differences in equity characteristics must be significant relative to the efficiency characteristics of the projects. It seems likely that the equity characteristics of projects *within* broad classifications—e.g., water quality, air quality, recreation—will be roughly similar. If this surmise is correct, then the ranking of projects within these classes is not likely to be significantly affected by equity considerations.[37] On the other hand, we would expect more marked differences in distribution patterns among classes of projects—e.g., rural recreation vs. urban air quality. In principle public expenditure decisions should be based on comparisons across all projects of all types. In practice it is much less likely that the political system will be able to make consistent comparisons on a systematic basis across dissimilar programs than it would be able to make them on similar projects within a single program. In other words, where equity considerations are most likely to have an impact on project rankings, they are least likely to play a systematic, coherent role in the decision process.[38]

A second consideration is the extent to which the physical or financial design of a given project can be altered to achieve equity goals. Given the constraints of the physical systems involved, there is probably very limited

275

flexibility for designing an air or water quality improvement project to achieve distribution goals. With the exception of the location of new recreation facilities,[39] the opportunities for using environmental quality programs to channel income in kind to specific target groups are extremely limited. The locations of sources and receptors of pollution and the dispersion and assimilation processes largely determine what can be done with the system. In principle the repayment/cost-sharing features of a program provide a high degree of flexibility in distributing project costs and influencing the net equity effects. However, it is impossible to alter the financial aspects of the project without altering the marginal price and cost signals governing the actions of private firms and individuals, both residuals generators and receptors. Alteration of these signals to achieve equity goals can be expected to be associated with inefficiency and high social cost.[40]

There is one respect in which the distribution question is ultimately unavoidable in environmental quality planning and decision making. Effective management of the environmental common property resources requires a clear delineation of property rights in the environment and the establishment of means to enforce these rights—whether through incentives such as bribes or charges or through standards. It probably matters less how this set of issues is decided than that it be decided clearly. The present strategies for water pollution abatement, which have been so effectively criticized by Allen Kneese among others,[41] could be interpreted as a set of stop-gap measures designed to avoid the fundamental issue. This may be why the effluent charge is so unattractive to bureaucrats and politicians. It would constitute a clear and obvious redefinition or redistribution of property rights in the waste disposal services of the waterways. And the political system does its best to avoid such basic issues.

Finally, it is appropriate at a conference on methodology and research to ask what more we need to know and to point the way for future research. First, let me assert that in broad terms the patterns of incidence and distribution can be fairly easily discerned. In the policy issues that we now face—for example, effluent charges vs. subsidies and tax incentives or the continued federal support of industrial waste treatment through grants to

[39] See Cicchetti, "Some Economic Issues."

[40] See A. Myrick Freeman III and Robert H. Haveman, "Water Pollution Control, River Basin Authorities, and Economic Incentives: Some Current Policy Issues," *Public Policy* XIX, no. 1 (Winter 1971): 53–74, for a discussion of this point in connection with water quality management. Also see Marc J. Roberts, "River Basin Authorities: A National Solution to the Water Pollution Problem," *Harvard Law Review* 83, no. 5 (May 1970): 1527–56; and Joseph J. Seneca, "The Welfare Effects of Zero Pricing of Public Goods," *Public Choice* 8 (Spring 1970): 101–11.

[41] See Allen V. Kneese, "Strategies for Environmental Management," *Public Policy* XIX, no. 1 (Winter 1971): 37–52.

municipalities—the equity implications are reasonably clear. There is a range of uncertainty and imprecision, but it is small in comparison with the questions we face. In the course of this paper several possible studies were mentioned that could, if carried out, reduce the range of this uncertainty. However, I do not propose that we rush to undertake these studies now. Rather, my own view of the priorities leads me to suggest a different allocation of scarce professional resources.

The first and most obvious point is that considerable progress must be made in measuring and valuing benefits and costs before we can say much more either about their distribution or about the optimality of a given level of environmental quality. Second, concerning the role of equity in environmental quality planning and public expenditure analysis in general, there are serious and unresolved questions concerning how decisions are actually made in the public sector, especially where equity and distribution effects are significant.

The question is whether the presumed public interest in equity can be or will be articulated and reflected in public expenditure choices made through the political process. Arthur Maass believes that they can be, and in fact are being articulated in community-oriented congressional choices.[42] An alternative view focusses on the role of special interest groups and a fragmented decision-making process which includes log rolling as a means of resolving conflicts.[43] The justification for gathering more detailed information on the distribution effects associated with environmental quality is that it can be used to improve (in terms of our own value judgments) policy decisions. But we need to have a better understanding of how these choices are made, or which description best characterizes the choice process, before we can safely predict the effect of more information on actual decisions.

It seems to me that the problem is not so much finding out more about the equity implications of possible policy alternatives, but getting the political system to come to grips with them and resolve them. It seems to me to be less important to trace the incidence of the cost of various pollution abatement strategies to various industrial groups (and beyond) than it is to establish an incentive system to actually impose these costs on re-

[42] Arthur Maass, "Benefit-Cost Analysis: Its Relevance to Public Investment Decisions," *Quarterly Journal of Economics* 80, no. 2 (May 1966): 208–26; and "Public Investment Planning in the United States: Analysis and Critique," *Public Policy* 18, no. 2 (Winter 1970): 211–43, but especially pp. 236–39.

[43] For example, Aaron Wildavsky, *The Politics of the Budgetary Process* (Boston: Little, Brown, 1964); Edwin T. Haefele, "A Utility Theory of Representative Government," *American Economic Review* 61, no. 3 (1971): 350–67 presents a formal discussion of the optimality of such a system under certain conditions. He warns that the relationship between his model and the American political system is similar to the relationship between the economist's model of perfect competition and the American economy.

siduals dischargers through bribes or charges. Although there is a very large gap between what we need to know about the environment and what we do know, and this is a spur to further research, there is also a very large gap between what we already know about coping with environmental problems and what we are doing now. I think that closing this gap should be given the highest priority, that researchers have very important contributions to make to this effort, and that these contributions should not necessarily be limited to doing more research.

PART III

DESIGNING POLITICAL AND LEGAL INSTITUTIONS

8.

Environmental Quality as a Problem of Social Choice

Edwin T. Haefele

I. INTRODUCTION

It was once generally true that environmental quality could be purchased in the private market. As my income rose, I could confidently look forward to enjoying cleaner air, a quieter neighborhood, and most other elements of what might have been (and was) called gracious living. Now, even though my income rises, I find the private market for environmental quality closed to all but multimillionaires, and even they are worried.

Were environmental quality still to be bought through individual transaction (like buying Cadillacs), we could ignore the social issue posed by bad environments by treating it (like 10-year-old Chevys) as an income distribution problem.

When, however, rich and poor alike suffer from an environmental quality problem (though perhaps not equally, as Freeman indicates in chapter 7 of this volume), we know that the invisible hand has deserted us. The effect of that desertion is to turn some economists into political philosophers,[1] some biologists into polemicists,[2] and may well drive historians to despair.

Aristotle said it first: "For that which is common to the greatest number has the least care bestowed upon it."[3] Since we have not been able, in general, to assign private property rights to all the air and water, we have owned them in common and cared for them least. Now that we have over-

---

[1] Kenneth E. Boulding, "The Network of Interdependence" (Paper presented at the Public Choice Society, Chicago, 1970).

[2] Garrett Hardin, "The Tragedy of the Commons," *Science* 162 (December 13, 1968): 1243–48.

[3] Aristotle, *Politics*, book II, chap. 3.

used them individually, we face the task of bringing these common property resources into some system of governance. We shall in the future have to make collective—that is, social—choices rather than individual choices about their uses.

Problems in Making Social Choices

Making social choices brings some special problems. It is often a case of "either-or" choices; e.g., this bundle of goods and services vs. that bundle. Since public monies, like private monies, are not unlimited, spending more for *A* means spending less for *B* or *C*. When "either-or" choices are faced by individuals, each man can choose. When these choices are faced by a number of people, some of them are not going to get what they would choose. That fact has been one of the main reasons for governments throughout human history. Dictatorial and administered states view this problem differently from states that try to determine social choices from individual preferences.

Other attributes of social choices are also bothersome. Besides being either-or, they are apt to involve conflicting or multiple objectives, with no generally accepted criterion for sorting them out. When an aggregate economic efficiency measure is either implicitly or explicitly accepted as the criterion for public investment, the indeterminacy is masked. As analysts begin to probe into the incidence of costs and benefits, including externalities, the indeterminacy is once again revealed.

Still other problems in social or collective choices relate to revealed preferences and the free-rider problem in pure public goods. If a public good is defined as a good or service, access to which cannot be denied and enjoyment of which does not diminish the quantity available to others, then it is easy to imagine situations in which it is to my profit not to state my preferences lest I be burdened with more of the cost.[4]

An equally troublesome problem closely allied to the free-rider problem is the problem of joint supply. Some common property resources—a river system, for example—serve multiple purposes. Although it is possible to charge users of the water, be they industries, municipalities, fishermen, or boaters, it is not altogether clear what each class of users should be charged. The problem is particularly vexing if public investments are made—dams, for example, that have multiple purposes. Any true joint cost is just that, and no allocation on cost principles is possible. Lacking a cost allocation formula, authorities may price on a willingness to pay (trying for a price discrimination regime which can bring financial self-sufficiency). These

---

[4] See Mancur Olsen, *The Logic of Collective Action: Public Goods and the Theory of Groups* (Cambridge: Harvard University Press, 1965).

schemes often run afoul of political realities—the users can influence the decision. In social choices, everyone can claim to be entitled to equity, and some to a little more equity than others.

All of the problems associated with social or collective choices have been known long before economists began to be interested in public finance, welfare economics, and public goods. It has been the economist, however, who has focused the issues in modern times and who has addressed the problem with most rigor, even if often with a total lack of historical insight.

Properties of a Social Choice Mechanism

The most famous modern statement describing the formal properties of a social choice mechanism is Kenneth Arrow's.[5] Arrow laid down five (reformulated then into four) seemingly reasonable conditions that a social choice mechanism should have and found that, in general, no mechanism could be devised that met these conditions. These conditions, taken from a recent restatement by Arrow[6] are:

1. Collective rationality: In any given set of individual preferences the social preferences are derivable from the individual preferences.
2. Pareto principle: If alternative A is preferred to alternative B by every single individual, then the social ordering ranks A above B.
3. Independence of irrelevant alternatives: The social choices made from any environment depend only on the preferences of individuals with respect to the alternatives in that environment.
4. Nondictatorship: There is no individual whose preferences are automatically society's preferences, independent of the preferences of other individuals.

Arrow, and others,[7] have devised restrictions on individual preferences that are sufficient to allow a social choice consistent with these conditions. The restrictions have been, however, so severe as to leave Arrow's essential theorem intact. Some have maintained that the conditions must be rejected

[5] Kenneth Arrow, *Social Choice and Individual Values*, 2nd ed. (New York: John Wiley, Inc., 1963).

[6] Kenneth Arrow, "Public and Private Values" in *Human Values and Economic Policy*, ed. Sidney Hook (New York: New York University Press, 1967), pp. 3–21.

[7] See Duncan Black, *The Theory of Committees and Elections* (Cambridge: The University Press, 1963) for the general case. See also C. R. Plott, "A Notion of Equilibrium and its Possibility Under Majority Rule," *American Economic Review* 57 (1967): 787–806; Gordon Tullock, "The General Irrelevance of the General Impossibility Theorem," *Quarterly Journal of Economics* 81 (1967): 256–70; and Gerald Kramer, "On a Class of Equilibrium Conditions for Majority Rule," mimeographed (New Haven: Cowles Foundation Paper No. 284, 1969).

as irrelevant to an understanding of how collective choices are actually made in a committee situation.[8]

The conditions remain, however, the clearest statement of what we might want in aggregating individual preferences into social choices. Moreover, they can be shown to be relevant when preference orderings are combined with voting stances. In another paper,[9] I have shown that representative government, with a two-party system, can provide a means of going from individual choices to social choices in a way that meets all of Arrow's conditions. The essence of the case is that the two-party system can function in a way that will bring out the two positions that, when voted upon, produce the same decision as is produced if the voters could have indulged in vote-trading on the issues involved. I emphasize that I say representative government *could* operate as an ideal social choice mechanism, not that it does in 1970. This is analogous to saying that a competitive price structure is ideal, not to saying that 1970 market prices are at that point.

The Present Environmental Quality Picture

The present governmental structure, which relates to environmental quality, bears little relationship either to representative government, the party system, or to social choices. Most of the choices made consciously by governments are made either by technicians who try to "balance" the interests of the affected parties or by a small group of politicians who hide their choices behind a "technical" but inadequate benefit-cost analysis. We thus have the worst of both worlds—technical analysis debased by political judgments, and political deals in which only a small number and perhaps the wrong people may play.

The criticism needs to be made explicit. I am saying two things about the technical analysis and two things about the political process. First, the technical analysis does not cover the full range of technical possibilities and, second, it is tempered by what the technician judges to be political reality. Both are grievous faults. The political process is faulty because, first, it is conducted by the wrong people (say, for example, the Public Works Committee) and, second, it is hidden behind technical surveys that purport to be objective.

It may well be that the technical and political processes now in operation served adequately in the past, perhaps in the not very distant past. Given a

[8] For example, Duncan Black, "On Arrow's Impossibility Theorem," *Journal of Law and Economics* 12 (1969): 227–48.

[9] Edwin T. Haefele, "A Utility Theory of Representative Government," *American Economic Review* vol. 61, no. 3 (June 1971): pp. 350–67.

rather broad consensus on objectives, the focus of a problem is the determinate issue of how best to reach the objective, so long as side effects are not perceived to be important. Certainly the early success of the Port of New York Authority (PNYA) is a case in point. Only recently, when it became clear that important social choices were being made (and others foreclosed) by PNYA, has the Authority ceased to enjoy its former approval. Only when the management of our water resources involves multiple-use problems do the work of the Corps of Engineers and the Bureau of Reclamation and the deliberations of water authorities lose their purely technical character in the eyes of the public. Only recently has the origin-destination survey ceased to be accepted as the sole criterion for determining highway investment need.

In the past, technical, administrative, and executive agencies, using the device of the public hearing and citizen or special interest advisory committees, may have been sufficient to solve the problems. We are moving now to a time when legislative government, using technical and administrative advisory committees, is needed. For when true social choices are at stake, nothing less than legislatures making these choices will suffice in our system of representative government. The spectacle of executive personnel attempting to assess the public interest through public hearings or to divine appropriate actions through committees "representing" all interests from housewives to steel mills is an outrage in the pure sense—it does violence to our system of government. In a technical sense it does not aggregate individual preferences correctly into social choices.

Paradoxically, an outrage of equal proportions is committed by the present workings of the legislative process in relation to water. With public investment in water management now largely the province of the federal government, and within Congress the province of the public works committees, something very different from a proper functioning of the legislative process occurs. The twentieth-century dominance of the seniority habit and of committee rule gives inordinate power to members from one-party states and breaks down the large-scale trading system, which Madison envisioned in *The Federalist*, Paper no. 10, into a number of small trading guilds. Even more specifically unfortunate for rational water policy is the unhappy fact that water projects are a major public currency in the Congress. As one of the most visible, tangible evidences of bringing money to a state or district, water projects have been in great demand by aspiring members of Congress. Again, it may well be true that in the past water was an appropriate specie, but with multiple and conflicting water uses it becomes a far less appropriate medium of exchange. Moreover, since the water is a local or regional resource, the national Congress becomes less and less the appropriate legislative body to be making the choices.

II. SOME TOOLS OF ANALYSIS

Americans were extraordinarily skilled at constructing social choice mechanisms in the seventeenth and eighteenth centuries, when the colonists used representative legislative bodies to wrest policy control from crown-appointed governors and executive councils. Later, their skill in this area seemed almost to die out. Instead, they perfected managerial and executive skills in both business and government. Faced now with value conflicts that call for social choices, we grope to relearn some of the more ancient arts. In doing so we are helped by a number of tools developed by men in economics and related fields as they turned their attention to problems of social choice. While the present discussion is not exhaustive, it does try to identify some of the important tools, show how they relate to each other, and demonstrate that we have progressed further than is generally recognized toward having a positivistic as well as normative basis for constructing new mechanisms for making social choices.

Nominal Voting Power—The Shapley Value

In any legislature, commission, or committee composed of a number of independent members, some coalitions or blocs have always been known to be more powerful than their numbers would indicate. Different subsets of the members could be designated as large city, small city, suburban, or rural or as industry, labor, or farm. More or less permanent protocoalitions often form around commonality of interest connoted by these designations.

Similarly, if in a two-house legislature one house has fewer members than the other, a member of the smaller house is more powerful than a member of the larger. Rousseau could thus say, with confidence, "that when the functions of government are shared by several tribunals, the less numerous [members] sooner or later acquire the greatest authority. . . ."[10]

Moreover, if weights are assigned to votes, and different entities have therefore more votes than others, the power of the different entities is not often proportional to the difference in votes. Thus, while small states have more power in the electoral college than their relative population (due to the constitutional formula of assigning electoral votes), their power is not as great as the numbers would indicate.

Sometimes the variation between the relative numbers and the real voting power is striking. While only intuitively felt in the past, the variation can now be calculated precisely, using Shapley values.[11]

[10] Jean Jacques Rousseau, *The Social Contract*, book III, chap. 4.
[11] The formal mathematics are in L. S. Shapley, "A Value for *N*-Person Games," *Annals of Mathematics Study* 28 (1953). Application to political bodies was first made

The Shapley value calculates how many times each (voter, bloc, unit, etc.) can appear in the "pivot" position by providing the winning margin for one side, assuming all possible permutations are equally likely. To give an example, assume an eleven-member group in which there are two voting blocs of three members, one two-vote bloc, and three voters who belong to no bloc. Assume also that a simple majority of six votes is needed to win on any issue. By proportion, the relative power of a three-vote bloc $(3/11)$ would be about 27 per cent, and that of a two-vote bloc and a single vote, 18 per cent and 9 per cent respectively. Instead, the relative strengths are more nearly 30, 20, and 7 per cent as shown in the following calculation:

A. Total arrangements possible of one two-vote bloc, two three-vote blocs, and three single votes

$$= c(6, 1) \times c(5, 3) \times c(2, 2)$$

$$= \frac{6!}{1!5!} \times \frac{5!}{2!3!} \times \frac{2!}{0!2!}$$

$$= 60 \text{ arrangements}$$

B. 1. Number of times a single vote is a pivot: (* designates pivot)

(a) 3 2 1 3 1 1
            *

(b) 3 1 1 1 3 2
               *

(i) 3 and 2 are predecessors

$c(2, 1) \times c(1, 1) =$

$\frac{2!}{1!1!} \times 1 \qquad = 2$

3 1 1 are successors
$c(3, 1) \times c(2, 2) =$

$\frac{3!}{1!2!} \times 1 \qquad = 3$

combine $= \frac{6}{60}$

(ii) 3 1 1 are predecessors $= 3$
   3 2 are successors $\quad = 2$ $\frac{6}{60}$

in L. S. Shapley and Martin Shubik, "A Method for Evaluating the Distribution of Power in a Committee System," *American Political Science Review* 48 (1954): 787–92. A method for exact calculation, by computer, for large bodies is in L. S. Shapley, "Values of Large Games VI: Evaluating the Electoral College Exactly," RAND–RM–3158 (Santa Monica: RAND Corporation, 1962). William Riker and L. S. Shapley explore the consequences of weighted voting in "Weighted Voting: A Mathematical Analysis for Instrumental Judgments," *Nomos* (1966).

therefore 1 is a pivot $\frac{6}{60} + \frac{6}{60}$ or $\frac{12}{60}$ of the time.

$\frac{12}{60}$ = 20 per cent or $6\frac{2}{3}$ per cent for each single vote.

2. Number of times a two-vote bloc is a pivot:

(a) 3 1 2 3 1 1
         *

(b) 3 1 1 2 3 1
            *

calculate as in 1: $\frac{6}{60} + \frac{6}{60}$ or $\frac{12}{60}$ of the time.

$\frac{12}{60}$ = 20 per cent for the two-vote bloc

3. Number of times a three-vote bloc is a pivot:

(a) 3 3 2 1 1 1
       *

(b) 3 2 3 1 1 1
          *

(c) 3 1 1 3 2 1
             *

(d) 3 1 3 2 1 1
          *

(e) 1 1 1 3 2 3
             *

(f) 2 1 1 3 3 1
             *

(g) 2 1 1 1 3 3
                *

(h) 2 1 3 3 1 1
          *

calculate as in 1:

$$\frac{4}{60} + \frac{2}{60} + \frac{6}{60} + \frac{6}{60} + \frac{2}{60} + \frac{6}{60} + \frac{4}{60} + \frac{6}{60} = \frac{36}{60} \text{ of the time.}$$

Check: $\frac{12}{60} + \frac{12}{60} + \frac{36}{60} = \frac{60}{60}.$ $\frac{36}{60} =$ 60 per cent or 30 per cent for each three-vote bloc.

Much more spectacular variations from proportionality are easy to construct and are present in the real world (for example, the Security Council of the United Nations). Some cases occur in which some voters have no power, i.e., can never be in a pivot position.[12]

The Shapley value is particularly useful in analyzing new institutions because of the "all permutations equally likely" assumption. In more localized situations, this assumption can be modified to reflect empirical evidence of different probabilities for coalition formation.

The Basis of Representation

Representation of people in a legislature is usually on a territorial basis, that is, people residing in one geographic area compose a representative unit. While this practice has a good deal of history behind it, it is not the only way, historically, that representation has been achieved. Classes of society can conceivably be represented and were during periods of English history. The House of Lords is perhaps the last lingering shadow of that practice.

Territorial representation was decisively chosen by the framers of the American government, however, and the decision has more than history to recommend it. Writing in the nineteenth century, Bagehot noted that a functional, or interest representation "would be a church with tenants; it would make its representative the messenger of its mandates and the delegate of its determinations."[13] A deliberate body composed of such inflexible (by definition) messengers has two options. Either nothing is agreed upon or side payments (trades) must be made on a far larger scale than would be necessary if representation were on a territorial basis. That this is necessarily so may be seen by considering two minimum winning coalitions, one territorial and one functional. To assemble a territorial coalition on a group of issues, some benefit must accrue to each member. The benefits may be in any functional area (e.g., a park in one area, better road maintenance in another, etc.). To assemble a functional coalition, some benefit must accrue to each function in the coalition (e.g., better road maintenance everywhere, more parks everywhere). The result is better described as a division of the spoils than as legitimate legislative trading related to intensities of preferences of citizens.[14]

[12] See John F. Banzhaf, "Weight Voting Doesn't Work: A Mathematical Analysis," *Rutgers Law Review* 19 (1965): 317–40; and Robert G. Dixon, Jr., *Democratic Representation: Reapportionment in Law and Politics*, New York: Oxford University Press (1968), pp. 537–43.

[13] W. Bagehot, *The English Constitution*, 2nd ed. (London: Kegan Paul, Trench, Trübner and Co., 1905), p. 156.

[14] Madison, unlike some of his modern interpreters, was not an advocate of representation of interests. What he said was that interests receive appropriate recognition through territorial representation. See *The Federalist*, Paper no. 10.

The foregoing discussion should be distinguished from the dissimilar case of "representation" in an executive or committee situation. In a company, for example, it is quite "correct" and efficient to have representatives of marketing, production, and accounting participate in making a decision. It is equally efficient to have spokesmen for industry, labor, and the consumer advising an executive or administrative agency of government on the most efficacious way of *implementing* a given policy. In the business example, the objective function (profit maximation) is not in dispute. In the executive agency example, policy is presumably already given by the legislative authority for the agency.

None of this is an assertion that "interests" do not dominate many existing legislatures; it is rather a statement that, if they do, representative government is not functioning as it was designed to function, and it is an indication that the failure is probably costly.

Assuming that we do not have to contend with functional representation, we still do have to contend with long-term confusion concerning the two-party system and proportional representation. This confusion essentially starts from the simplistic reasoning that, since 51 per cent of the electorate may elect, *therefore* 49 per cent of the electorate is unrepresented. If this premise is accepted, the next step is to devise schemes of multiple seats per district to allow a greater proportion of the electorate to be "represented." Lewis Carroll was preoccupied with this problem, as Duncan Black has shown us.[15]

It can be shown,[16] however, that a two-party system has the unique characteristic of being able to represent all the electorate. That is to say that for given issues, it throws up those two positions which, when voted upon, result in the same choice as would have been chosen if *all* the voters were assembled and capable of exploiting vote-trading possibilities. Let me illustrate by the following example.

Suppose three voters and two independent issues as:

Issue \ Voter	I	II	III
A	Y_2	Y_1	N_1
B	N_1	Y_2	Y_2

[15] Duncan Black, "Lewis Carroll and the Theory of Games," *American Economic Review* 59 (1969): 206–10 and Black, "The Central Argument in Lewis Carroll's 'The Principles of Parliamentary Representation,' " *Papers on Non-Market Decision Making*, vol. 3 (Charlottesville: University of Virginia, 1967).
[16] Haefele, "A Utility Theory of Representative Government."

where Y is a "yes" vote, N is a "no" vote, and the subscripts are the ordinal rankings of the issues by each man.[17] Were these men meeting in an assembly to decide (by majority vote) these two issues, issue A would pass and issue B would fail, even though the nominal outcome would appear to have both issues passing (two Y's on each row). But since it is in the interest of voters I and III to agree to a trade (Voter I voting N on issue A in exchange for Voter III voting N on issue B), the nominal outcome does not hold. The trade, however, is not stable, since voter II, rather than allow the trade to take place, agrees to give up his vote on issue B to keep voter I from trading. Hence, issue A passes, issue B fails.

Were we to suppose that the three men, not meeting in an assembly, simply vote for one or another candidate, we can see how a two-party system works to achieve the same result. In an election process, voters are faced with a set of mutually exclusive choices. Based on the above matrix, these outcomes can be displayed as follows:

Alternative Outcomes

Issue A	P	P	F	F
Issue B	P	F	P	F
Voter I wins	2nd	1st 2nd	none	1st
Voter II wins	1st 2nd	1st	2nd	none
Voter III wins	2nd	none	1st 2nd	1st

where P is pass, F is fail, and the numbers are the ordinal preferences won under each outcome by each voter. (Hence, under $\begin{bmatrix} P \\ P \end{bmatrix}$ Voter I wins his second choice, under $\begin{bmatrix} P \\ F \end{bmatrix}$ he wins both his first and second choices, etc.)

Knowing the nominal outcome (the typical information available to parties through opinion polls), the candidate of one party may, by testing which issues evoke most response, decide that he can win over $\begin{bmatrix} P \\ P \end{bmatrix}$ by attracting voters I and III on a $\begin{bmatrix} F \\ F \end{bmatrix}$ platform, this being the only outcome which dominates $\begin{bmatrix} P \\ P \end{bmatrix}$. Facing that platform, the second candidate finds that the outcome $\begin{bmatrix} P \\ F \end{bmatrix}$ can win over $\begin{bmatrix} F \\ F \end{bmatrix}$ and chooses it. As between the two, he is right. (Were a third candidate to appear, no clear dominant outcome is possible.)

---

[17] Thus, voter I prefers defeating issue B to winning on issue A; voter II prefers winning on issue A to winning on issue B; voter III prefers defeating issue A to winning on issue B.

Voter III will thus gain neither of his choices, no matter whether he is in the legislature himself or votes in a two-party election. His misery lies not in the fact that he is not represented, but in the fact that there is no way in which he can gain adherents to his positions on these issues.

In the paper cited,[18] I have shown that the congruence between the election results of a properly functioning two-party system and the decision of a legislature composed of the same voters extends at least through all nontrivial permutations of the two-issue–three-voter cases (eight examples) and the three-issue–three-voter cases (432 examples).

The Decision Rule for Legislative Bodies

The long history of simple majority rule for legislative bodies leads one to speculate that its roots go back to primitive days when physical force was the decision principle. However, Douglas Rae and Michael Taylor have recently explicated the logic of simple majority and special majority decision rules.[19] Their contribution is especially noteworthy since economists, following Wicksell, have had nothing to say on this matter other than to agree that unanimity is a sufficient condition for optimality while admitting that it suffers a little in practical application. Rae shows that, if an individual is equally interested in minimizing the summed frequency of rejection of proposals he favors and passage of proposals he is against, then simple "majority rule corresponds uniquely to the minimum summed frequency [of these events] in committees with an odd number of members, and shares the minimum with $n/2$ in committees with an even number of members." This is shown in table 8.1.

Rae's analysis also allows us to value differently the possibility of losing on a supported proposal and winning on an opposed proposal. In other words, in some cases we may be more interested in keeping "bad" actions by others from occurring than we are in getting an action we approve of passed. An example is amendments to the Constitution. We require two-thirds majorities rather than simple majorities. Why? Because we are minimizing the possibilities of bad actions; i.e., actions which are disapproved by even one-third of the voters. In effect, we are assigning double weight to bad actions when we use a two-thirds majority rule. Rae shows this for $n = 7$ as follows:

[18] Haefele, "A Utility Theory of Representative Government."
[19] Douglas Rae, "Decision Rules and Individual Values in Constitutional Choice," *American Political Science Review* 58 (1969): 40–56. Michael Taylor, "Proof of a Theorem on Majority Rule," *Behavioral Science* 14 (1969): 228–31.

EDWIN T. HAEFELE

k \\ n	7
1	1.00
2	.91
3	.72
4	.51
5	*.45*
6	.47
7	.50

Here the expected frequencies are unequally weighted (one for ability to pass legislation, two for ability to defeat legislation). Contrast this column, in which $k = 5$ at the minimum, with the corresponding column in the following table where $k = 4$ at the minimum. Should we want to attach different weights, we can find the appropriate decision rule by Rae's formula.

Decision-Process Models

One way to look at a decision process is to posit, or assume, a structure (government) and then look at the way in which men and interest groups move, coalesce, or lobby, to get what they want. The emphasis is on personality, social groupings, and power. Much insight is gained about the particular circumstances of a case in this way.

Table 8.1. Expected Summed Frequencies

k^b \\ n^a	3	4	5	6	7	8	9	10	11	12
1	.43	.47	.48	.49	.50	.50	.50	.50	.50	.50
2	*.28*	.34	.39	.43	.46	.47	.48	.49	.50	.50
3	.43	*.34*	.32	.35	.39	.38	.45	.47	.48	.48
4		.47	.39	*.35*	*.34*	.36	.39	.42	.44	.46
5			.48	.43	.39	*.36*	*.36*	.38	.40	.42
6				.49	.46	.38	.39	*.38*	*.38*	.39
7					.50	.47	.45	.42	.40	*.39*
8						.50	.48	.47	.44	.42
9							.50	.49	.48	.46
10								.50	.50	.48
11									.50	.50
12										.50

Note: Italicized probabilities show minimum in each row. Read for values of k in relation to n.

[a] n = number of members.

[b] k = number of members necessary to impose a policy on the group.

Source: Douglas Rae, "Decision Rules and Individual Values in Constitutional Choice," *American Political Science Review* 58 (1969): 40–56.

293

Another way is to posit, or assume, that men and groups try to attain their goals (at all times and in all societies) and then look at the way a particular structure, or set of rules, shapes the way that men and groups must act to get what they want. Much insight is gained about the general influence of the institutional arrangements in this way. The decision models we shall be looking at are all of the latter kind. Institutions are easier to change than is human nature.

We have so far been dealing with rather static concepts. They were appropriately static, however, because they pertained to the construction of the basic building blocks of a process. Increasingly, we are gaining insight into the process itself and it will be useful to examine how various people have done that.

Regression Analysis. Several writers, notably Birdsall, Kramer, and Jackson, have made use of multiple regression analysis to explain voting behavior.[20] While no explicit use will be made of regression analysis in this paper, it is fundamental to many decision models. Jackson's work, an analysis of the voting behavior of U.S. senators in general and on specific bills, is a good example of what may be learned from such analyses.

Using such independent variables as constituency, party position, majority and minority leadership, and committee position, Jackson was able to explain up to two-thirds of the variation in senatorial voting behavior. Different senators require, of course, different variable specification, but much variation turns out to be regional (particularly among the Democrats). Jackson extended the analysis by examining the residuals from the specified models explaining senators' votes in order to find differences among specific bills. Since log-rolling (vote-trading) was not a part of the regression equations, this technique can reveal whether vote-trading might have played a role on some bills but not on others. In particular, if the regression equation explains a great deal of a senator's voting behavior on bills known to be of high interest to him, while explaining little of his voting behavior on bills known to be of less interest to him, one can surmise that he may be trading off his votes on the latter cases. Jackson found four bills in the Eighty-seventh Congress with relatively large unexplained variance, all of which were "bills which evoke an image of special interest, vote-trading, and bargaining." They were the Sugar Act Amendments of

[20] W. C. Birdsall, "Public Finance Allocation Decisions and the Preferences of Citizens: Some Theoretical and Empirical Considerations" (Ph.D. diss., Johns Hopkins University, 1963). Gerald Kramer, "Short Term Fluctuation in U.S. Voting Behavior: An Econometric Model" mimeographed (Yale University, 1967). John E. Jackson, "A Statistical Model of United States Senators' Voting Behavior" (Ph.D. diss., Harvard University, 1968).

1962, elimination of the West Coast Maritime Subsidy Preference, establishment of a National Wilderness Preservation, and the Public Works bill.

While cautioning that there may be other explanations for these results, Jackson concludes that vote-trading may have accounted for at least a part of the poor performance of the regression equations in these cases. There is the further possibility that some of the vote-trading is masked by the specification of the models themselves.

Regression analysis and its more complicated relatives (factor analysis and principal components analysis) will obviously play an increasing role in analyzing past actions and in giving some insight into possible future actions.

The Significance of the Mean. Since Black[21] demonstrated that the median position can win over any other position under majority vote and single-peaked preference conditions (analogous to Hotelling's location theorem for stores along a single street), there have been explorations of the significance of the median and mean positions for political strategy. In a series of articles, Davis, Hinich, and Ordeshook expanded this theme into multidimensional space.[22] The work proceeded along two lines. First, following Arrow, they expanded the set of individual utility functions (beyond single-dimensional ones), for which necessary and sufficient conditions for transitive, social preference ordering could be determined. This work will not be discussed in this chapter. Second, they showed that in a variety of multivariate distributions of preference, that position (a multivariate mean) which minimizes the Euclidean distance from all individual positions is a social welfare maximization (weighting all individuals equally). Where median and mean diverge, therefore, a candidate can achieve a dominant position at the median on all issues, while a social welfare "solution" would be at the mean.

While the Davis, Hinich, and Ordeshook theorems are undoubtedly correct, the assumption of independence between issues and intensities of

---

[21] Black, *Theory of Committees*, p. 18.

[22] Otto Davis and Melvin Hinich, "A Mathematical Model of Policy Formation in a Democratic Society," in *Mathematical Applications in Political Science*, vol. 2, ed. Joseph Bernd (Dallas: SMU Press, 1966); Davis and Hinich, "Some Results Related to a Mathematical Model of Policy Formulation in a Democratic Society," in *Mathematical Applications in Political Science*, vol. 3, ed. Joseph Bernd (Charlottesville: University Press of Virginia, 1967); Davis and Hinich, "On the Power and Importance of the Mean Preference in a Mathematical Model of Democratic Choice," *Public Choice* 5 (1968): 59–72. Melvin Hinich and Peter Ordeshook, "Social Welfare and Electoral Competition in Democratic Societies" (Paper presented at Public Choice Society, Chicago, 1970).

interest suppresses an important feature of politics, as Jackson's critique[23] of the Davis and Hinich works makes clear.

It may be helpful to explain this point in words and with the aid of a diagram.[24] Imagine, for purposes of exposition, a two-dimensional situation (two issues) and only two voters. Suppose that one voter feels very strongly about one of the issues but not about the other while the other voter has a similar set of preferences but about the opposite issues. Thus in figure 8.1 the preferred or ideal points of the two voters are indicated by x_1 and x_2 respectively. The above assumption means that the indifference curves (with increasing loss indicated by curves further from the ideal points) of one voter are elongated in the east-west directions while the other's indifference surfaces are elongated along the north-south dimensions. The mean x_1 and x_2 falls along the dotted line connecting the two points and is indicated by the point μ. Clearly, however, point μ is inferior from the viewpoints of both of the voters to some other point, such as the point y, which allows each to have something closer to the ideal amount of the more desired item at the expense of the unimportant one. Hence, in this example the mean μ is neither a dominant point nor a welfare maximum (loss minimum). This point obviously is important whenever there is an "opposition" of the kind shown in this example.

Since neither preference positions nor preference intensities of voters are known, in most practical cases, perhaps we should not concern ourselves with the problem at all. In fact, of course, most politicians realize that discovering such information is crucial to being elected. Moreover, "defining" issues so as to change voters' preferences and intensities in one's favor is at the heart of the matter.

This point may better be grasped by illustration. Pollution may be regarded as a current problem of intense interest, but the way in which issues are formed about the problem will greatly affect the distribution of intensities of interest. A proposal to institute a system of effluent charges will evoke one set of intensities; a proposal to subsidize treatment plants will evoke another; a proposal combining both approaches will evoke a third. Varying the amounts and incidence of either charges or subsidies will affect intensities further. These are not the same as the position means brought forth by different ways of forming the issue around the pollution problem. The man or group who is successful in forming the issue determines the relative (ordinal) ranking that the problem will take, not

---

[23] John E. Jackson, "An Exception to the Power and Importance of the Mean in Models of the Democratic Electoral Process," Working Paper 705-72 (Washington, D.C.: The Urban Institute, October 1970).

[24] I am indebted to Otto Davis for this illustration, which I have taken from his written comments on my paper.

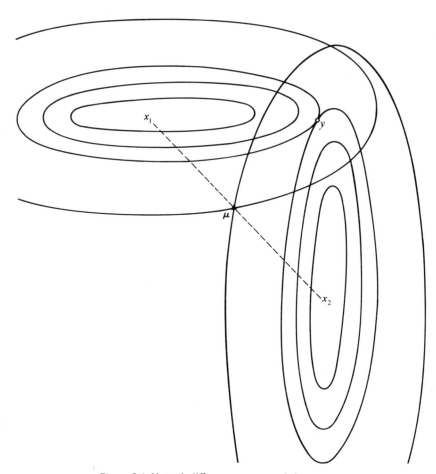

Figure 8.1. Voter indifference curves and the mean.

only in his preference orderings *but also in everyone else's.* This is why the committees that determine which bills reach the floor are so powerful and why the process of issue formation among the electorate is so important. If I, as a candidate, can define an issue so that it divides your supporters while uniting and adding to mine, then making such definitions has high payoff. Examples are numerous. One of recent years was the deliberate linking of the church-state separation issue with federal aid-to-school proposals. The linkage split off some support for the school aid proposal. The point here, it must be emphasized, is that the bill's position on school aid was no farther from the former supporters' position than it had been, but intensity of interest in supporting the bill had fallen because the religious issue had been linked to it. Since intensities of interest around the general church-state problem and around the school-aid problem were not distributed independently of the issue position on each, finding a multi-variant mean (loss function) on the two-issue space serves, not to specify a preferred candidate position, but to respecify the issue. Candidate positions will be taken in response to intensities of interest for and against each such redefined issue. (See Appendix B for further discussion of issue formation.)

The Role of the Party in Issue Formation. The two-party system in twentieth century America has played less than its appropriate role in issue formation, even though the utility theory of representative government depends upon a two-party system that is able to formulate the issues appropriately. American government depends much more on parties than we suppose. We neglect parties at the peril of having to contend increasingly with intransigent, nonnegotiable demands made by one or another faction within our society. A government can "cope" with demands, but such actions should not be confused with the process of self-government under any definition. In Burke's words, "Men of intemperate minds cannot be free. Their passions forge their fetters."[25]

Issue formation will reflect individual utilities if there is a functioning party structure. No other group or organization in society has this task. The press has no warrant to do more than raise cries of alarm and argue points of view. Special interest groupings have no interest beyond their own. Neither has any responsibility for decisions and cannot be made responsible. The executive branch of any government cannot be expected to form issues correctly because it is controlled by one party at a time.

While all of these groups and many others contribute to the formation of issues, only the party system that runs candidates and, when elected, is identified as responsible for programs has the task and the incentive for defining the area of battle over time. Parties can, moreover, operate in time horizons longer than one term, unlike individual candidates with no strong party backing. In the United States parties have the role held in Bagehot's England by the House of Commons,[26] and perform the following functions:

1. The expressive function—reflecting what is on the public mind.
2. The informing function—informing us (and the government) of what we would not otherwise hear (since there are many publics and we know only a few of them at first hand).

[25] Edmund Burke, *A Letter to a Member of the National Assembly in Answer to Some Objections to his Book on French Affairs* (1971).
[26] Bagehot, *The English Constitution*, p. 132–75 *et passim*.

3. The teaching function—restating the crude and formless worries, prejudices, and off-hand opinions of the public into reasonable, defensible proposals.
4. Coalescing function—forming proto-coalitions around each proposal.
5. The elective function—presenting final positions from which individual choices must be made by the voter.

This deliberately chosen "old-fashioned" statement of moderate men engaged in moderate action stands in sharp conflict with the politics of the 1960s, a time of growing estrangement from traditional party politics.

It is worth a moment to dismiss the claim (frequently made by some professionals) that the role of the professional expert preparing unbiased plans is a surrogate for party positions. This modern variant of the "there is no Republican way to collect the garbage" fallacy can best be illustrated by the failure of the Brandywine Plan[27] in which it was found (again) that planning plus public relations is not the same thing as self-government·

The point is a simple one. If we do not use the party system to insure that moderate men will take moderate action, what other recourse do we have?

Minority Interests and the Dominant Majority.   Closely allied to the role of parties in forming the issues is the role of general purpose legislatures as a device that protects against a dominant majority. In a recent paper,[28] I have shown how Madison's defense of representative government as a way to avoid "the tyranny of the majority" is justified in general-purpose legislatures far more than in special-purpose commissions. Essentially, with more independent issues to consider it is less likely that any one coalition will agree on all issues (see figure 8.2). If they do not, then vote-trading can allow minority interests to achieve (or block) legislation of greatest concern to them. The two-party system does not interfere with this vote-trading, since by definition a two-party system is composed of nondoctrinaire, rather loose associations of many interests. (With doctrinaire parties, as in proportional representation, such trades are greatly inhibited.)

As the number of independent issues is reduced, trading is inhibited and thus many commissions may show records of all issues being decided by the same majority for long periods. Minority "representation," in these cases, is a sham.

[27] See Peter Thompson, "Brandywine Basin: Defeat of an Almost Perfect Plan," *Science* 163 (March 1969): 1180–82.
[28] Edwin T. Haefele, "Coalitions, Minority Representation and Vote-Trading Probabilities," *Public Choice* 8 (Spring 1970): 75–90.

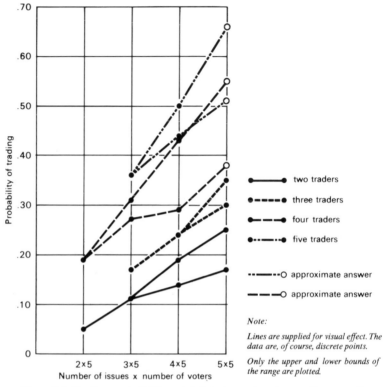

Figure 8.2. Trading probabilities related to issues (random preference set).

Source: E. T. Haefele, "Coalitions, Minority Representation, and Vote-Trading Probabilities," *Public Choice* 8 (Spring 1970).

The same frustrated minority issue can easily arise in a city in which the council is elected at large rather than by wards. A minority may not be able to get into the council at all under such circumstances. If, in addition, the city functions on a "non-partisan" basis, a minority may have no way to bring pressure on officials other than by violence.

Variation on the Utility Maximizing Theme. So far all of the discussions on the decision process have implicitly assumed that there are utility maximizing individuals and groups. Standing somewhere between this approach, common to economics, and the full-scale bargaining models applied to international relations (in which threats and outright irrationality may play a larger role) are some attempts to make explicit what a political philosopher would recognize as a theory of the state. Kenneth Boulding has become increasingly concerned with distinguishing selfishness and selflessness.[29] While at first blush his malevolence-benevolence distinction seems to be only a fruitless inquiry into the *motivation* of behavior and thus falls under the criticism that the utility maximizer's motivation is not at issue, Boulding's analysis is not to be so dismissed. His concern is with showing that the consequences for social choice are different depending on how benevolence or malevolence influences individual utility functions.

This general area has been explored by Rufus Browning.[30] By simulation, he examines the consequences of positing different rules by which collective decisions are made; i.e., "selfish" utility by each individual, maximizing overall welfare (summing cardinal utilities) and competitive utility (maximizing the difference between one's own and others' utility). Different probabilities of being in the minority are assigned to each actor in each process. Strikingly different results are obtained. For example, table 8.2 relates the effects on total payoffs (summed over all actors) of three collective decision processes for three utility distributions. Consequences for individuals are also quite different under the three choice processes.

The relevance of this work is in its ability to guide the design of a flexible decision structure. For example, if an economically efficient charge is com-

Table 8.2. Payoffs of Collective Decision Processes

Distribution			Sum of payoffs before decision	Increment in sum of actors' payoff due to collective decision		
				Social welfare	Individual bargaining	Competitive bargaining
0.9	0.1	0.0	496	332	52	−140
0.6	0.3	0.1	682	10	62	−88
0.5	0.3	0.2	688	10	88	37

Effects on Inequality (average deviations)

Distribution			Inequality before collective decision	Decreases in inequality		
				Social welfare	Individualistic	Competitive
0.9	0.1	0.0	443	250	288	363
0.6	0.3	0.1	252	50	11	83
0.5	0.3	0.2	199	56	−59	46

Source: Rufus R. Browning, "Quality of Collective Decisions: Some Theory and Computer Simulations," mimeographed (Michigan State University, 1969).

[29] Boulding, "The Network of Interdependence."
[30] Rufus P. Browning, "Quality of Collective Decisions: Some Theory and Computer Simulations," mimeographed (Michigan State University, 1969).

bined with a receipts distribution on a per capita basis, there will be a different response than there would be if the receipts were not so distributed. The receipts distribution formula gives a "social welfare" or maximum sum rationality. An example of the perverse workings of this approach is found in the "per capita" component of highway fund disbursements.

Another possibility along the lines Browning suggests is consideration of using a competitive bargaining scheme (maximizing difference between an actor's and others' utility) regarding the amount of effluent any one firm can discharge into a watercourse at a particular point. Converting the effluent to some standard unit, a zero-sum game is involved (assuming some water quality standard) that the firms may play given an appropriate set of rules. The incentive would be somewhat different from that which results from allowing bids for the available assimilative capacity (which implies no interest in capacity beyond one's own need). Under Browning's "competitive" rules, each firm would have an equal interest in denying the capacity to others as it has in garnering the capacity for itself. Hence, in some situations a firm's interest would be precisely consonant with that of a conservation group! Likewise, the incentives in a cooperative (as is the German *Genossenschaften* system of river management in the Ruhr) are different from the individualistic approach.

III. SOME SPECIFIC CRITIQUES

Using the theory and tools of analysis from the preceding section, I shall now examine some specific examples of institutions that have as their primary purpose the making of environmental choices.

The Potomac River Basin Commission

Governmental jurisdictions at local, state, and federal levels are now in the process of designing an institution to make environmental choices regarding the uses of Potomac River Basin water. The proposed federal-interstate compact would establish a river basin commission, composed of the governors (or their representatives) of West Virginia, Virginia, Pennsylvania, and Maryland as well as appointed representatives for the federal government and the District of Columbia.[31] The compact is patterned closely after the Delaware River Basin Compact despite the substantial differences between the two basins and their problems. The commission

---

[31] For a general survey see Alvin C. Watson "A Proposed Partnership Compact for our Nation's Rivers," *Journal of Soil and Water Conservation* 24, no. 3 (1969): 89–93.

302

would, in Alvin Watson's words ". . . by its very existence provide a mechanism to weigh alternative values associated with different plans or components of plans when conflicts in values, uses, or components arise."[32] There is no doubt that this is the case. The question is, is it the appropriate mechanism?

The case for coordinated or unified management of the river is compelling. Kneese and Bower have investigated the economic efficiency gains from systemwide management and Davis has applied these principles to the Potomac.[33] Were efficiency gains the only issue, river basins could well be turned over to any efficient organizational form—a public corporation, a franchised monopoly, or a cooperative.

The actual situation is, of course, reversed. We have a long, involved, and *in-place* system for dealing with equities, and government investment has traditionally been at least as concerned with distribution of the public investment portfolio as it has with economic efficiency, which is a newcomer to the public calculus and finds some difficulty in dislodging older interests and procedures. In table 8.3 Davis illustrates a part of the problem in the context of the alternative technological possibilities for achieving a given level of dissolved oxygen in the Potomac. Such a distribution of costs might suggest that system *H* would be an overwhelming favorite of area residents. Were the costs listed the only ones incurred, this would no doubt be the case. However, system *H*, essentially a series of dams and reservoirs, would have a widely differential effect on residents. Some would be flooded out, others overrun by tourists and vacationers, and still others assured of

Table 8.3. Cost of Alternative Systems for Improving Dissolved Oxygen in the Potomac Estuary

System alternative	Cost	Cost to area
	(million dollars)	*(million dollars)*
A	22	14
C	29	29
D	38	26
H	115	0

Source: Robert K. Davis, *The Range of Choice in Water Management: A Study of Dissolved Oxygen in the Potomac Estuary* (Baltimore: The Johns Hopkins Press for Resources for the Future, 1968), table 24.

[32] Ibid., p. 92.
[33] Allen V. Kneese and Blair T. Bower, *Managing Water Quality: Economics, Technology, Institutions* (Baltimore: The Johns Hopkins Press for Resources for the Future, 1968). Robert K. Davis, *The Range of Choice in Water Management: A Study of Dissolved Oxygen in the Potomac Estuary* (Baltimore: The Johns Hopkins Press for Resources for the Future, 1968).

a more reliable water supply. There was, in fact, such substantial opposition to the plan that the incidence of its effects is being radically shifted.

It is worth noting, in passing, that the agency responsible—through formal public hearing—for generating, recording, and "assessing" public reaction to plan *H* was the Corps of Engineers of the Department of the Army. While such tasks may teach humility to the Corps (as it would to any body of men on the receiving end), the rationale for putting such a requirement on the Corps can only be justified by the absence of any representative government to which citizens might turn. Substituting an appointive board for the Corps does not lessen the sham that consists of using the form of representative government to deny the substance of it. Officials are either directly responsible to the electorate over whose hearings they preside or they are not. Appointed officials and executive branch personnel are not.

Distributional effects of public policy and equity considerations are important aspects of river basin policy. Such considerations are not necessarily consonant with economic efficiency considerations. To these three elements we should add a fourth—reallocation of resources for some public policy objective. To keep the distinction between this element and redistribution of income, think of the difference between the objectives of the space program and the objectives of the Appalachia program.

Thus the four major objectives for river basin investment are:

1. economic efficiency or efficient allocation of resources—where the criterion is to put investment where the aggregate pay-off is greatest in economic terms *or* where the aggregate economic cost is least if some other objective function is externally imposed;
2. equity—redressing the balance on the incidence of benefits and costs on programs taken in pursuit of economic efficiency;
3. income distribution—where the criterion is some specified redistribution of income through programs having a differential impact of costs and benefits;
4. reallocation of resources—where resources are deliberately forced into noneconomic patterns for a specific public policy purpose; e.g., to increase public recreation facilities, which, while it has a general welfare orientation, is focused on the provision of the good rather than on any particular redistribution effects for specific groups of people.

While there is some substantial, operational overlapping of objectives 3 and 4, the conceptual distinction may be useful. Only the first of the four is a management issue, the other three are clearly social choice questions where conflicts in values will certainly occur. Consequently, the interstate compact, in its present form, is suspect as a political mechanism for making social choices.

Some 4 million people live in the Potomac River Basin. Disregarding, for the moment, the 800,000 District of Columbia residents who have no political representation anywhere, the other basin residents do not dominate any state government of the area. Unlike some other river basins, where nearly everyone in the basin states are in the basin, Potomac Basin residents make up, at most, 27 per cent of a single state's population and 36 per cent of its area, as shown in table 8.4.

Table 8.4. State Areas vs. State Populations in the Potomac Basin

State	Per cent of state area in basin	Per cent of state population in basin
Maryland	36	27
Pennsylvania	4	2
Virginia	14	23
West Virginia	15	8

Source: Potomac River Basin Advisory Committee.

The basin residents do not nominally control either house of any of the legislatures (see appendix A). When one adds the fact that the voters of each state who live in the basin are by no means unanimous on what they want in terms of water choices for the Potomac, and thus will not function as a bloc, it is obvious that the state legislatures do not have a clear a priori claim as the appropriate bodies to resolve the issues.

Even less appropriate is the typical interstate agreement among sovereigns. While the proposed compact would give each state one vote, along with one vote each for the District of Columbia and the federal representative, the population figures (basin-wide) show a far different proportionality (see table 8.5).

Table 8.5. Potomac Basin Population

Within	Total	Proportion of total population in basin
District of Columbia	811,000	22.6%
Maryland	1,339,000	37.4
Pennsylvania	185,000	5.2
Virginia	1,103,000	30.7
West Virginia	148,000	4.1

Source: Potomac River Basin Advisory Committee, 1969 estimates of population.

The fact that the river basin is not coterminous with state boundaries (and nowhere dominates any of the states) lends weight to the thought that the interstate compact in its usual form is not wholly appropriate to the case. It is, of course, necessary that state power be brought into the picture. The compact could be made to safeguard the interests of basin residents through a requirement that the states delegate power to basin residents, who then would elect the members of the commission. They would vote on the basis of equal population districts (congressional districts furnish a suitable, ready-made structure closely coinciding with basin boundaries). In addition to the one federally appointed member, representation on the commission would then be on the basis of about 400,000 people per vote for the other ten members. Maryland (Cong. Dist. 5, 6, and 8) and Virginia (Cong. Dist. 7, 8, and 10) would have three votes each; Pennsylvania (Cong. Dist. 12) and West Virginia (Cong. Dist. 2), one each; and the District of Columbia, two votes.

There is no legal reason why the states could not negotiate a compact that would include such a representative pattern nor is there any legal reason barring the Congress from approving it. Were this to be done, the compact would undoubtedly also provide that any state funding would come from assessment of basin residents only, rather than from general state revenues. Such a provision would not only be essential for equity but fundamental to fiscal responsibility. A well-known defect in federal grant-in-aid programs is that the money is usually available only for specific technical remedies, thereby reducing the incentives of states and localities to use any other remedies, even though they might be more efficient. Thus, federal monies are available for dams but not for reaeration treatment. What state would give serious consideration to the latter under such circumstances? Likewise, if basin residents receive funds from their state's general revenues, their choices will be biased in the direction of those features funded by the state. Moreover, to the extent that costs of any sort can be transferred to the general state or federal taxpayer, these costs will not be fully considered by basin residents.

An interstate compact setting up a basin representative commission would not, of course, solve problems created by grants-in-aid tied to particular solutions. Moreover, a basin-based commission could create some administrative problems within each state. Which of the three Virginia representatives on the proposed commission would be responsible to deal with the governor in Richmond? How is basin water policy to be "coordinated" with the state official responsible for water matters?

Answers to these questions lie in the interstate compact itself. If a representative basin commission were established, it would have to have a clear delegation of state authority regarding water policy and a sharing of state authority in the recreation area. In the water management field, the state would cease to act administratively within the basin (having delegated its authority to do so to the basin commission). In the recreation area, the role of the state (like that of the federal government), would be limited to funding facilities over and above those desired by the commission (to take account of nonbasin needs). This latter issue, while providing a planning problem, is no different in principle from any federal park in a state or a state park in a particular county. Such administrative problems are minor compared with the larger problem created by the present interstate compact proposal which ignores real basin representation.

Attempts to provide for basin representation by advisory committees dealing with recreation, land-use planning, and other special interests do not serve as surrogates for representative government in weighing values. Any citizen has many interests. He may be an avid fisherman *and* a pinch-penny taxpayer. He may be a land speculator *and* a supporter of free recreation. If citizens are represented only by their special interest groupings (either by committees or by associations and clubs), the resulting pressures do not necessarily converge toward any real public choice. It is when each citizen must resolve, within his own mind, how he feels about all aspects of the river basin that choices begin to converge, extreme positions fall, and public choice become realistic. But the citizen, speaking as a whole man, can do so only if he can vote. Since he cannot vote on all the technical issues (not because they are technical but because there is no way to set up an efficient vote-trading mechanism), he should vote on his choice for a representative. If representatives are to throw up the correct choices for him, then the two political parties should be sponsoring the candidates.[34] It is sometimes argued that voters respond very poorly to special districts, both by allowing political machines to capture all nominations and by ignoring the elections in droves. Such arguments cut both ways, however. Many special districts are poorly conceived and deal with very narrow issues that give the voter no clue as to their relevance to his interests. If a basin commission is given broad authority to act, the many citizen interests which are now frustrated in the "public hearing" charade will not be reluctant to make very live election issues out of the real alternatives and candidates offering themselves for election.

If we assume the existence of such an elected commission (10 elected officials and an appointed federal representative), then we can make some judgments about the decision rules under which the commission might operate. First, using Shapley values, we can test the bloc power by states

[34] It should go without saying that technical analysis must underlie these party positions. To argue that political choice processes are paramount is not to argue that the choices must be based on ignorance of the consequences of alternative actions.

(see table 8.6). The interesting feature revealed here is that attempts to help "one-vote blocs" by increasing the majority required for approving decisions does do so, but at the primary expense of the District voting power rather than of that of the three-vote blocs.

Table 8.6. Nominal Voting Power, by State, under Different Decision Rules

Area	Number of votes	Shapley values in per cent		
		Votes needed to pass = 6	Votes needed to pass = 7	Votes needed to pass = 8
Maryland	3[a]	30.00	28.33	28.33
Virginia	3[a]	30.00	28.33	28.33
District of Columbia	2	20.00	18.33	13.33
Pennsylvania	1	6.66	8.33	10.00
West Virginia	1	6.66	8.33	10.00
Federal representative	1	6.66	8.33	10.00
Total voting power	11	100.00	100.00	100.00

[a] Assuming a bloc vote in order to test dominance possibilities.
Note: Totals do not add due to rounding.

A more realistic Shapley value relates to upstream-downstream differences. Table 8.7 makes three separate assumptions about how the upstream-downstream coalitions would shape up and then tests the voting power under each.

Here the voting power values fluctuate sharply; some changes in the decision rule cause dramatic shifts in relative power and others have no effect at all. Other bloc assumptions might be considered in the process of

Table 8.7. Upstream-Downstream Nominal Voting Power
Under Different Decision Rules

Number and size of blocs	Shapley values in per cent		
	Votes needed to pass = 6	Votes needed to pass = 7	Votes needed to pass = 8
Case I			
1 five-vote bloc	50.00	58.33	50.00
1 four-vote bloc	16.67	25.00	50.00
2 one-vote blocs	16.67	8.33	0.00
Case II			
2 five-vote blocs	33.00	50.00	50.00
1 one-vote bloc	33.00	0.00	0.00
Case III			
2 four-vote blocs	30.00	35.00	50.00
3 three-vote blocs	13.00	10.00	0.00

Note: The power listed in the "one-vote" bloc cases is for *each* such vote.

308

deciding upon the decision rule which has greatest general acceptance (i.e., can pass all relevant legislative bodies).

In the case of the Potomac at the time of this writing (March 1970), the issue of control of land along the river has become a major divisive problem. The work of Rae[35] concerning special majorities may be useful here. Assuming that land-use issues will not become a bloc issue (i.e., that each representative's interest will diverge in some important respects from that of every other representative), then we might give the commission power on land use but require a larger (say two-thirds) majority for the enactment of any restriction on land use. Since the two-thirds rule gives double weight to blocking unwanted actions, those opposed to the commission having authority to control land use would have far less to fear.

Alternatively, a less than simple majority could be made sufficient to approve certain uses. Thus, being able to affect in a positive way what is done could also bring agreement among those who at present are reluctant to approve the compact.

There is some merit in including land use powers (and indeed other environmental issues) in the proposed commission, since a greater variety of independent issues *about which all parties have an interest* is conducive to greater trading potential. It is also the only defense against the problem of the dominant majority. A counsel of perfection would maintain that perfectly functioning general legislatures could make Potomac Basin choices, appropriately coordinated with other legislatures, without needing the compact at all. Without falling into that error, it should remind us that the necessity to devise any mechanism for making choices in a river basin is, to some degree, the recognition of failure at the state and national legislative (not executive)[36] level. What a properly shaped elective Potomac River Basin Commission could do is to remove the currency of Potomac water projects from the halls of Congress and put it into circulation as the legal tender of an institution appropriate to its reach.

The San Francisco Bay Commission[37]

The social choice problems confronted by persons living around a bay may take on different characteristics from those confronted by those living

---

[35] Rae, "Decision Rules and Individual Values."

[36] The use of the state governor as the representative of the state on interstate matters is essentially an executive idea. Under no utility theory can this be associated with the aggregation of individual preferences into social choices. It is doubtless political, since the governor is an elected official, but the politics are far removed from the issues at hand.

[37] I am indebted to Joseph E. Bodovitz, executive director of the Bay Commission, and his staff for help in preparing this section and correcting some errors of fact. Mr. Bodovitz is not, of course, responsible for my interpretations or conclusions.

in a river basin. Taking the three utility classifications of Browning,[38] for example, we may distinguish the two cases. The classic river problem is the upstream-downstream conflict. The utility framework of the upstream users is most like Browning's "selfish" or individualistic utility; i.e., the upstream user is concerned with maximizing his own satisfactions. The downstream user, however, is closer to Browning's "competitive" utility maximizer; i.e., one who is forced to maximize the difference between his utility and that of the upstream user. I do not make the distinction to deprecate one side or the other, but to show what roles each is allowed, or forced, to play by the lack of a riverwide platform in which policy may be set.

If we were to imagine that each river basin user were in a compulsory cooperative regarding the uses of the water, we could see that an additional utility concept—overall maximization—would be added to the picture. This is because increasing the total uses of the river will enable both up-stream and downstream users to increase their utilities (using their own principles of maximization). River basin commissions have as their under-lying motivation the same addition to the utility calculations.

The users of a bay quickly run to the limits of selfish or individualistic utility maximization and become, even without formal machinery, aware that everyone plays a zero sum game on use and that everyone could be better off (a bigger pie) by cooperating. The interdependence of utilities is perceived more easily, and this is particularly true when the bay is a great scenic resource.

San Francisco Bay is such a scenic resource that it is not surprising that there have been increasingly strict rules regarding its use; despite the large number of governmental jurisdictions and levels of government involved.

The San Francisco Bay Conservation and Development Commission (BCDC) was created in 1965 by the California legislature (the McAteer-Petris Act) and was made a permanent agency by the 1969 legislature. The BCDC has three major responsibilities:

1. To regulate (by issuance or denial of permits) all filling and dredging in San Francisco Bay in accordance with law and the BCDC Bay Plan.
2. To have limited jurisdiction over substantial developments within a 100-foot strip inland from the bay. Within this strip, the commission's responsibility is twofold; to require public access to the bay to the maxi-mum extent possible consistent with the nature of new shoreline develop-ments, and to ensure that existing shoreline property suitable for high-priority purposes such as ports, water-related industry, and water-related

---

[38] Browning, "Quality of Collective Decisions."

310

recreation, is reserved for these purposes, thus minimizing pressures to fill the bay.

3. To have limited jurisdiction over any proposed filling of salt ponds or managed wetlands (areas diked off from the bay and used for salt production, duck-hunting preserves, or similar purposes). These areas, though not subject to the tides of the bay, provide wildlife habitat and water surface important to the climate of the bay area. If filling of these areas is proposed, the commission is to encourage dedication or public purchase to retain the water area. If development is authorized, the commission is to ensure that such development provides public access to the bay and retains the maximum amount of water surface consistent with the nature of the development.[39]

These responsibilities evoke the range of social choices under consideration in the area. The objectives, according to the bay plan, are to maintain and enhance the bay as a "magnificent body of water that helps sustain the economy of the western United States, provides great opportunities for recreation, moderates the climate, combats air pollution, nourishes fish and wildfowl, affords scenic enjoyment, and in countless other ways helps to enrich man's life."[40]

It will be noted that while water quality is of concern to the commission, it does not have legal responsibility for regulation of waste discharges into the bay.

Membership on the Bay Commission reflects a complex pattern of local, state, and federal concerns. The twenty-seven members are appointed as follows:

Federal level executive officials
1. One member by the Division Engineer, U.S. Army Engineers, South Pacific Division, from his staff [does not vote on permits].
2. One member by the U.S. Secretary of Health, Education, and Welfare, from his staff [does not vote on permits].

State level executive officials
3. One member by the Secretary of Business and Transportation, from his staff.
4. One member by the Director of Finance, from his staff.
5. One member by the Secretary of Resources, from his staff.
6. One member by the State Lands Commission, from its staff.

[39] Taken from various publications of the San Francisco Bay Conservation and Development Commission.
[40] San Francisco Bay Conservation and Development Commission, *San Francisco Bay: What Will It Be Like in 50 Years?* (January 1969).

7. One member by the San Francisco Bay Regional Water Quality Control Board, who shall be a member of such board.

Local level executive officials

8. Nine county representatives consisting of one member of the board of supervisors representative of each of the nine San Francisco Bay area counties, appointed by the board of supervisors in each county. Each county representative must be a supervisor representing a supervisional district which includes within its boundaries lands lying within San Francisco Bay.

9. Four city representatives appointed by the Association of Bay Area Governments from among the residents of the bayside cities in each of the following areas:
   (a) North Bay—Marin County, Sonoma, Napa, and Solano.
   (b) East Bay—Contra Costa County (west of Pittsburg) and Alameda County north of the southern boundary of Hayward.
   (c) South Bay—Alameda County south of the southern boundary of Hayward, Santa Clara County and San Mateo County south of the northern boundary of Redwood City.
   (d) West Bay—San Mateo County north of the northern boundary of Redwood City and the city and county of San Francisco.
   (Each city representative must be an elected city official.)

"Public" members

10. Seven representatives of the public, who shall be residents of the San Francisco Bay area and whose appointments shall be subject to confirmation by the Senate. Five of such representatives shall be appointed by the Governor, one by the Committee on Rules of the Senate and one by the Speaker of the Assembly.[41]

At first blush, the membership may remind one that fascism (or state syndicalism), in the nonpejorative sense, is not dead but is alive and well in California. Such a body could even make the trains run on time.

This judgment may be modified by a closer examination. There is an absolute majority of elected officials on the commission, though their election is not primarily, or even importantly, predicated on service on the commission. There is also an absolute majority of local government members, although it is rare that all local members' interests would coincide·

A more compelling reason for approval of the commission membership is that it is serving an executive function. Basic policy for development and conservation of the bay is spelled out in the McAteer-Petris Act by the

[41] Government Code of California, Title 7.2, chap. 3, 66620.

state legislature. While set in broad terms, the policy does specify priorities on uses of the bay shoreline, sets guidelines in some detail, and specifically endorses and adopts the bay plan. Thus, the representation of executive agencies and, in effect, of interest groups can be considered a legitimate device to ease implementation of basic state policy. It would be far different, and less desirable, to set up such a body of men *and* give them authority to write their own basic policy or, worse yet, to allow them to operate without one. As it is, the statutory policy may be amended by the state legislature and appeals to the law can act as a restraint on commission decisions. In effect, the major social choices about the bay are made in the state legislature and the commission is an implementing or executive agency.

The commission is nonetheless interesting on that account, as an examination of its minutes will reveal. With twenty-five members allowed to vote on permit applications (thirteen votes needed to grant a permit), the voting records do not show cases of local officials ranged against other members. As one would expect, they show instead voting patterns based more on geographical and interest lines. Taking a number of permit cases over the last three years in which the vote margin was only one (therefore a minimum winning coalition existed), it was observed that: (a) no dominant majority problem exists, i.e., the members of the minimum winning coalition change; (b) there is a small pro-permit bloc; (c) there is a small anti-permit bloc; (d) there are two larger blocs that normally vote together and in opposition to each other.

Tables 8.8 through 8.10 do not reflect these blocs as such, but rather explore a larger range of Shapley values for blocs operating in this system.

Contrast the values in table 8.8 with the power of the same blocs when all voting members are present, as shown in table 8.9. If nothing else, such a contrast should increase attendance at commission meetings.

Using some alternative bloc sizes, and assuming full attendance, table 8.10 explores some of the variations in voting power that are possible. As shown in table 8.10, adding one member to a bloc of four actually may double the bloc's power, while adding a sixth member does nothing.

Table 8.8. San Francisco Bay Commission—Bloc Voting Power
(with 19 present, 13 needed to pass)

Bloc size	Number of such blocs	Voting power (per cent)[a]
6	1	30
5	1	22
4	1	22
3	1	22
1	1	5

[a] Does not add up to 100 per cent due to rounding.

Table 8.9. San Francisco Bay Commission—Bloc Voting Power
(with 25 present, 13 needed to pass)

Bloc size	Number of such blocs	Voting power (per cent)
6	1	27
5	1	20
4	1	15
3	1	10
1	7	4 each

Table 8.10. San Francisco Bay Commission—Possible Variations in Voting Power

	Bloc size	Number of such blocs	Voting power (per cent)
I	11	1	48
	9	1	14
	1	5	7.6 each
II	6	1	25
	4	3	16
	3	1	13
	1	4	3
III	9	1	50
	6	1	17
	4	2	17
	1	2	0
IV	9	1	50
	5	1	17
	4	2	17
	1	3	0
V	8	1	43
	6	1	20
	5	1	20
	4	1	10
	1	2	3

One feature of the picture inhibits the whole process of vote trading, and adds to the feeling that the commission is essentially an executive (non-policy) agency. Since permit applications are not decided on simultaneously there are continual and nondirected changes in the issue space. Since there is judgment about each permit, there is also a record. Quite clearly, consistency has a necessary part to play here unless the courts are to get many of the cases on appeal.

The record of the last three years supports the view that consistency (the executive virtue) has been achieved. Court appeals have not been numerous. Some cases involving many interests have been drawn out over time until a compromise acceptable to many was worked out. The Oakland Airport permit is a case in point.

Having reinforced the case for designating the commission as an executive agency, one may properly ask why fourteen elected officials are on it and whether or not the state legislature was the appropriate policy body to define policy for this "land management" agency for San Francisco Bay. Knowing nothing about the practical politics of the case, I would still venture the opinion that, in the absence of any policy mechanism at the metropolitan level, the state legislature was the only legitimate device that could have been used. Since the legislature endorsed the Bay Plan as developed by the commission, policy was at least initiated locally and the presence of fourteen elected officials on the commission is an indication that policy may well be changed incrementally by commission decision in the future.

If that is true, the commission's structure and operations should be seen as a response to the present realities of the California situation. In particular, the successes and failures of the commission will be sui generis and the commission form and structure should not be considered a general solution that other areas could copy with profit.

The Penjerdel Air Pollution Case

Making environmental choices about air quality in particular places is even more difficult than making choices about water. Not only are many governmental jurisdictions involved, as in water problems, but also the airshed is not well defined, unlike the watershed.

Nevertheless, the growing problem of air pollution in urbanized areas makes it essential that the problem become subject to governance by someone, and federal, state, and local governments are beginning to try to cope with the peculiarities of the problem.

Unfortunately, the standard formula of the interstate compact among sovereign states is the primary mechanism now being considered. The Air Quality Act of 1967, authorizing the Department of Health, Education, and Welfare (HEW) to establish air quality control regions, also looks to the establishment of traditional interstate compacts to provide the mechanism for control.

In the area that encompasses Philadelphia, Camden, Trenton, and Wilmington, known as the Penjerdel (from Pennsylvania, New Jersey, and Delaware) Region,[42] some preliminary studies of possible government organization to manage air quality for the region has been made by the Fels

[42] Area of about 4,454 square miles with about 5 million people.

Institute of the University of Pennsylvania. The adaptions of the interstate compact devised by the Fels Institute study team are worth some attention, as they represent one of the first attempts to face the problem on an interstate basis.

The study team suggests an interstate agency, created by interstate compact but containing a regional constituency representation, to "plan, manage, and control" the Penjerdel airshed. The power and duties of the compact agency would include:

1. undertaking research;
2. establishing, promulgating, and enforcing regulations, including air quality standards and emission standards;
3. designating control districts;
4. issuing and enforcing orders against offending emissions;
5. establishing warning systems and exercising emergency powers;
6. requiring the registration and reporting of emissions;
7. requiring and issuing licenses and permits to emission sources.[43]

These are seen to be a mixture of executive and policy powers. In particular, the quality and emission standards by districts constitute the heart of the policy on social choice issues involved.

Recognizing the deficiencies of the one state–one vote principle as applied to this kind of problem, the study group suggested that the compact agency (commission) be composed of two members from each state (Pennsylvania, New Jersey, and Delaware), one representing the government of the state and the other that part of the state located in the Penjerdel region. They further suggested that the local representative in each state be elected by the people comprising the counties concerned. Thus, local political parties could have become involved.

One provision sets up a dual voting structure somewhat similar to that of the Security Council of the United Nations; i.e., that "no action . . . shall be taken . . . unless a majority of the membership, including . . . a majority of the State representatives shall vote in favor thereof."

This provision practically weights the states' votes double those of the local representatives, although nominally it is a three to two weighting. (That weighting which ensures that no majority exists unless at least two states concur, *and* ensures that at least one locality concurs—three states cannot pass bills alone—is a three to two weighting with a two-thirds

---

[43] Taken from "Governmental Organization for a Regional Air Resource Management and Control System" (Fels Institute, University of Pennsylvania, 1968). It should be noted that the study, done under contract from HEW, was responsive to the HEW definition of the problem, as it should have been. My critique is somewhat unfair since I am suggesting a course of action beyond the scope of their study.

majority decision rule.) The nominal voting power may hence be calculated as if each state had three votes and each local representative had two, with ten votes needed to pass:

Votes	Number of voters	Total number of votes	Shapley value (per cent)
3	3	9	21.67 (each)
2	3	6	11.67 (each)
	6	15	

⅔ majority = 10

Table 8.11 shows the power of different bloc arrangements. Thus, the best that the people involved can have is one-half the voting power and that only under the highly improbable assumption that the region is totally united and the states totally fragmented.

The voting arrangements are, however, a minor matter in this case, since there are more serious flaws in the proposal. The right to control air quality and emission standards over the area, were it to be given to the proposed agency, would have great leverage over the industrial development decisions for the area and for land use generally. The framework for making these decisions (or more precisely, for placing restrictions on the decisions of others) should obviously not be that of an air quality control commis-

Table 8.11. The Power of Penjerdel Voting Blocs Measured in Shapley Values

State and local representations	Votes	Number of voters	Shapley value (per cent)
$S_1 + L_1 + L_2$	7	1	67
$S_2 + L_3$	5	1	17
S_3	3	1	17
$S_1 + L_1$	5	1	33
$S_2 + L_2$	5	1	33
$S_3 + L_3$	5	1	33
$S_1 + S_2$	6	1	60
S_3	3	1	10
$L_1 + L_2 + L_3$	2	3	10 (each)
$S_1 + S_2 + S_3$	9	1	75
$L_1 + L_2 + L_3$	2	3	08 (each)
$L_1 + L_2 + L_3$	6	1	50
S_1	3	1	17
S_2	3	1	17
S_3	3	1	17

Majority = 10
S = State representatives
L = Local representatives

317

sion: allowing it to decide these issues is analogous to letting the Port of New York Authority continue to make transport policy.

Some attention to the necessity for coordination with the water authority in a region was given by the study team. The issue, however, is not just coordination of residuals management policy, but rather the question of who is authorized to make decisions about the size, shape, land uses, and relative economic as well as physical health of the Penjerdel region. The precision with which an interstate compact on air management is drawn pales beside the social choice issues involved. These are better discussed in the framework of a metropolitan area government of general jurisdiction, rather than in a special-purpose agency with a very limited pattern of representation and little scope for party politics.

Minneapolis-St. Paul Metropolitan Council

In 1967, the state legislature of Minnesota created "an administrative agency" for the purpose of coordinating the planning and development of the metropolitan area comprising the counties of Anoka, Carver, Dakota, Hennepin, Ramsey, Scott, and Washington.[44] The agency, the Metropolitan Council, has as its members fifteen appointees by the governor, fourteen of whom come from equal population districts (see figure 8.3) comprising the area, and the fifteenth designated as chairman. The motion to have the fourteen elected lost by the narrowest of margins, for, though deemed an administrative agency, the council is, and increasingly will be considered, the policy making body for the area, making the environmental choices for the region.

The council's present powers include:

1. preparation and adoption of a development guide for the metropolitan area;
2. review of all long-term plans of each independent commission, board, or agency and government unit in the metropolitan area if the plans have area-wide or multicommunity effect, or have a substantial impact on metropolitan development;
3. review of applications of all governmental units, independent commissions, boards, or agencies operating in the metropolitan area for loans or grants from the United States or any of its agencies, which require review by a regional agency;
4. right to levy a tax not to exceed $7/10$ mill of assessed valuation of taxable property in the area to provide funds for its operation (estimated to yield over $1 million in 1970);[45]

[44] Area of about 3,000 square miles with approximately 2 million people.
[45] The council may also issue general obligation bonds for the acquisition and betterment of sewer and treatment works.

318

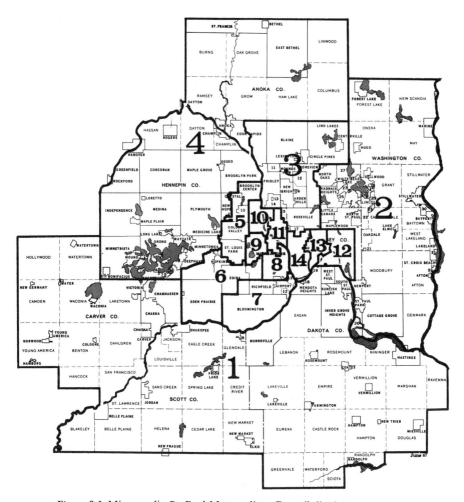

Figure 8.3. Minneapolis–St. Paul Metropolitan Council districts.

5. development of a data center;
6. research on area-wide problems including air pollution, parks and open space, water pollution, solid waste, and tax structure of the area and consolidation of common services.[46]

Some of the independent agencies over which the Council exercises policy control (for review in most instances means power to reject) are the Minneapolis-St. Paul Sanitary District; the Minneapolis-St. Paul Metropolitan Airports Commission; the Metropolitan Mosquito Control Dis-

[46] Taken from "Referral Manual" (Metropolitan Council of the Twin Cities Area, March 1968), and other official statements of the Metropolitan Council.

trict; the Metropolitan Transit Commission; the Hennepin County Park Reserve District; the North Suburban Sanitary Sewer District; hospital districts (North Suburban and Forest Lake); the Dakota-Scott Library District; the Lake Minnetonka Conservation District; soil conservation districts in six of the seven counties; four watershed districts; Metropolitan Park Board; Metropolitan Zoo Board.

These are, of course, in addition to the regular municipal governments in the area. The reality of the review process is evoked by the fact that the council denied the Airports Commission's choice of a new airport site on the grounds that it might interfere with the recharge of reservoirs that supply part of the area's water supply.[47]

It was after considerable discussion inside the legislature and through the very active and prominent Citizen's League that the unusual step of subordinating (but not abolishing) the independent boards was taken. It was clearly recognized that the independent boards are mostly operating agencies. Rather than replace them with professional staffs, it was decided to allow them to be intermediate lay boards between the professional staffs of their own special purpose agencies and the multipurpose Metropolitan Council. In most, but not all cases, the independent board members are appointed by the chairman of the Metropolitan Council.

The practical and useful result is that the council is relieved of the multitude of operating decisions in many special fields, but retains policy control over the special-purpose agencies. At the same time, the kind of executive agency accommodation of interests *at the implementation level* can be effectively handled by the appointed special-purpose boards. In practice, there are some problems in sorting out the roles of general purpose council *staff* vs. special-purpose board *members*. These will not be solved, as the participants tend to believe, by "working it out"; there is an inevitable conflict here which the council members, particularly the chairman, will have to contain and channel to productive purpose.

The council represents the first real innovation on the metropolitan government problem since World War II. Its chief virtue is that it has broken out of the Council of Governments (COG) mold, which suffered not only from its one-town, one-vote (implicit) principle, but also from its total lack of authority to act in most instances. The council is not attempting to supplant municipal governments in the area, nor does it draw its strength from, or depend upon, them. It enjoys widespread support of municipalities. It is at the state level that some unease is felt about the council and that un-

[47] I am indebted to Ted Kolderie, executive director of the Minneapolis–St. Paul Citizen's League, and his staff for information on this point and for their help on this section. Neither Mr. Kolderie nor the league is, of course, responsible for my analysis or conclusions.

ease, plus some second thoughts of state legislators, represents the only potential danger to the eventual consolidation of the council as an elected, multipurpose government.

It can be seen that a Bay Commission or an Air Pollution Commission could fit easily under such an area-wide governmental unit. It is also clear that, were a multistate area involved, the concerned states could combine powers to create a multistate metropolitan council. The interstate compact device is not limited to setting up one kind of organizational structure.

The Metropolitan Council of the Twin Cities area, unlike the Bay Commission or the Air Pollution Commission, does offer a general pattern worthy of emulation. It fits into the system of government both in terms of law and of utility. It will offer an excellent opportunity for the two political parties to contest for seats when (if) the commissioners become elected. It has taxing and limited bonding power and the potential of getting more. It provides, most importantly, that metropolitan stage essential to creative action. Norton Long has put it most eloquently:

> To provide a leadership that can appreciate the desirability of a rich community life, a significant theatre of action and the means to significant action are requisite. Such a theatre of action exists in potentiality in our metropolitan areas if they can be given the political form requisite to the recruitment and functioning of a metropolitan leadership. Such a leadership is essential if local self-government is not to atrophy in the decline of the central city, the triviality of the suburb, and the growth of *ad hoc* and upstream agencies for the administrative, piecemeal handling of urgent problems. There is still no substitute for territorial representation as a means to coordinate and integrate the functional organizations that share a territorial field. Unless the means of electing and instrumenting such a territorial leadership can be found, local self-government will give way to the administration of people rather than the self-direction of citizens.[48]

There are many ways in which a multipurpose government can operate to change the rules under which people and municipalities compete. The movement toward sharing of some part of the property tax is well underway in the Twin Cities area. The issue here is not to pry some of the local revenue away from municipalities, but to share new tax revenues resulting from new business and industrial investments, relieving every municipality from the necessity of competing for new industry.

As industry is attracted to the economic area, not usually to a particular site within it, an area-wide approach can increase benefits for all without reducing local options for differentiation on municipal services. While it is true that the more densely populated areas will dominate the council, and

---

[48] Norton E. Long, "Citizenship on Consumership in Metropolitan Areas," *Journal of the American Institute of Planners* 31, no. 1 (1965): 6.

thus sparsely settled, outlying areas will come more under the control of the center, it is wholly appropriate that this should happen. The existing practice, wherein windfall gains are reaped by landowners outside the taxing power of the city whose economic base is responsible for the gain is, while common, quite intolerable on any grounds of equity or efficiency.

The creation of the council may enable some intermediate levels of government, e.g., the county, to reduce their functions and in some cases to disappear. In other contexts than that of the Twin Cities, the central city may gradually disappear as a unit, no longer appropriate for decision making, leaving smaller units to handle purely local affairs and an area-wide unit to handle metropolitan problems.[49]

The lesson here is simply that the appropriate size for general purpose governments may change and has changed over time. When this happens, the governments become ineffective, not because they are general purpose governments composed of elected officials, but because they no longer provide a stage on which leadership can play. Because that stage is at two levels in urban areas today—the neighborhood level and the metropolitan level—this is where general purpose governments can be useful.

At the risk of belaboring the point, it is useful to recall here that with a number of independent issues to consider, the council members can make trade-offs over the whole spectrum of issues. They do not have to compromise each special issue to the median position in order to resolve it, neither do they have to let every area have *some* transit, *some* parks, or whatever. The systems can each be designed more efficiently overall and the trades serve intensity of interest concerns. In other words, the utility mechanism can work.

IV. CONCLUSION

Viewing environmental quality as a social choice problem and representative government as the utility mechanism that has unique capabilities for aggregating individual preferences into social choices enables me to make a number of general conclusions about the present state of institutions in the environmental field. These may be summarized as follows:

1. There is a need to redress the balance between the legislative and the executive role in environmental choices at all levels of government. Historically, we may be in a period akin to the early eighteenth century in

---

[49] This is consistent with the recommendations of two recent studies of metropolitan government. See Committee for Economic Development, *Reshaping Government in Metropolitan Areas* (New York: CED, February 1970); and Alan K. Campbell, ed., *The States and the Urban Crisis* (Englewood Cliffs, N.J.: Prentice Hall, 1970).

North America, at which time the states and commonwealths wrested policy control away from Crown-appointed governors and executive councils. The supremacy of the legislature for policy determination (the old Whig position), which was firmly established at that time, has gradually eroded over the centuries. We now face, again, the need for strong legislatures. Reestablishing them will require sweeping out many twentieth-century habits of legislatures, among them the excessive dependence on seniority and the abuses of the committee system, and creation of some twentieth-century research capabilities within the legislatures.

2. There is a need to force environmental issues into partisan politics at every level of government. Fortunately, this seems to be happening, as Senator Muskie has made environmental quality a prime issue and President Nixon, in response not only to Muskie but also to the concerns of the young, has moved to reinforce the image of the Republican party on this issue. If the parties are to function effectively, however, many citizen groups, special interests, and professional pressures will be needed to keep the parties from equating environmental quality with motherhood and refusing to take stands on particular issues.

3. There is a need to focus directly on institutional design. In doing so, we must recognize that making social choices between hard alternatives requires technical expertise and political expertise. Both are necessary; neither is sufficient by itself. So long as we have our present system of government, we must recognize that it was designed to make social choices through legislative action. We must, therefore, disenthrall ourselves from the habit of applying interstate compacts on the rigid one state–one vote principle and of copying business organization and forms.

Using the tools of utility analysis, we can examine the political processes and outcomes of present and proposed political institutions, judging them in terms of:

(a) the territorial reach of their representation and of the problems they face;
(b) the number of independent issues under their control;
(c) the decision rules
    (i) relative to passing and blocking measures that come before them,
    (ii) relative to what utility "game" the situation forces the interested parties to play;
(d) the viability of party politics in the institution.

4. Environmental issues, while they have local, state, and federal aspects, are often primarily regional in nature. Sometimes the region is in one state, sometimes in more than one. There is therefore a need for rep-

resentative governmental structures at the regional level. These may either be created by one state, or by several acting through the compact route. In either case, both the legislative and executive dimensions must be attended to. Both dimensions need not be in the same agency. In the Minneapolis–St. Paul case, for example, they are not.

5. While not a major subject in this paper, the utility framework used leads inescapably to the conclusion that the public works committees in Congress have become almost wholly inappropriate mechanisms for making project decisions on water and other environmental issues. The point here is not that pork-barrel politics is bad or that the men on these committees are wicked. It is simply that the physical environment is now too important to be used as the principal, or even a major, currency of Congress. The need is not, therefore, to reform the public works committees but to remove water projects and other regional project investment concerns from Congress. This process has, in fact, already started. It will be hastened as congressmen learn of their constituents' resistance to certain projects in their districts. Dams, army bases, and all the other "prizes" awarded are no longer greeted with unmitigated joy. This is a healthy trend in utility terms as it will hasten the move to let local citizens make local decisions. In passing, it should be noted that the widest possible scope for trading would still remain with the national Congress. Many of these trades are regional in nature and can take the place of water as a medium of exchange. Moreover, the executive side of the federal government, in particular the Corps of Engineers, could easily put its expertise to the service of, and under the policy direction of, regional or state agencies on a project-by-project basis.

The federal role would then emphasize, on the legislative side, the questions of how much money should be appropriated for environmental purposes and what regional distribution should be made. On the executive side, the federal role would emphasize the availability of technical expertise in many areas on which regions and states could call.

The states, regions, and localities would, on the other hand, be making environmental choices (in a few cases being limited by nationwide minimum standards), and deciding how to allocate federally disbursed monies, what additional monies were needed, and how best to implement these decisions.

The picture this presents is far different from the one that now exists, but it is far closer to the process of self-government envisioned for the country two centuries ago.

Appendix A

POTOMAC RIVER BASIN COUNTIES AND THEIR NOMINAL REPRESENTATION IN STATE LEGISLATURES

Maryland   Population (1960): 3,100,689

Congressional district	County	Population (1960)	Representation on basis of population	
			House of Delegates	State Senate
5th	Charles	32,572	2	0.46
	Prince George's	357,395	16	5.00
6th	Allegheny	84,169	4	3.00[a]
	Carroll	52,785	2	2.00[b]
	Frederick	71,930	3	[b]
	Garrett	20,420	1	[a]
	Washington	91,219	4	[a]
8th	Howard	36,152	2	5.00[c]
	Montgomery	340,928	16	[c]
Total representation			50	15.46
Total for state			142	43

Note: Throughout appendix matching letters in parentheses indicate shared representatives.

Source for apportionment: National Municipal League, *Apportionment in the Nineteen Sixties* (New York, 1967).

Pennsylvania   Population (1960): 11,319,366

County	Population (1960)	Representation on basis of population	
		House of Delegates	State Senate
Bedford	42,451	1	1.00[a]
Blair	137,270	2	[a]
Somerset	77,450	1	[a]
Fulton	10,597	[b]	1.00[c]
Franklin	88,172	2[b]	[c]
Huntingdon	39,457	1	[c]
Juniata	15,874	1[d]	0.25[e]
Mifflin	44,348	1	[e]
Perry	26,582	[d]	[e]
Total representation		9	2.25
Total for state		203	50

325

Virginia Population (1960): 3,966,949

		Representation on basis of population	
County	Population (1960)	House of Delegates	State Senate (per cent)
Albemarle*	60,396	2.00[a]	0.86[b]
Greene	4,715	[a]	[b]
Augusta*	75,289	2.00[c]	1.00[d]
Highland	3,221	[c]	[d]
Bath	5,335	1.00[e]	0.05
Rockbridge*	30,339	[e]	[b]
Clarke	7,942	1.00[f]	0.73[g]
Frederick*	37,051	[f]	[g]
Culpeper	15,088	1.00[h]	0.29[j]
Madison	8,187	[h]	[b]
Orange	12,900	[h]	[j]
Fluvanna	7,227	0.20	[b]
Page	15,572	2.00[k]	1.00[l]
Rockingham*	52,401	[k]	[l]
Shenandoah	21,825	[k]	[l]
Rappahannock	5,368	0.45[m]	[l]
Warren	14,655	[m]	[l]
7th Cong. Dist. Subtotal		9.65	3.93
Caroline	12,725	1.00[n]	0.71[o]
Essex	6,690	[n]	0.79[p]
King & Queen	5,889	[n]	[p]
King George	7,243	[n]	[o]
Fairfax	376,217	9.00	5.00[r]
Arlington	163,401	4.00	[r]
Fauquier	24,066	0.55	1.00[s]
Goochland	9,206	0.61[t]	[o]
Hanover	27,550	1.00[u]	[p]
King William	7,563	[u]	[p]
Lancaster	9,174	1.00[v]	[p]
Loudoun	24,549	2.00[u]	0.27
Louisa	12,959	[t]	[o]
New Kent	4,504	0.28[x]	0.10[y]
Charles City	5,492	[x]	[y]
Northumberland	10,185	[v]	[p]
Prince William	50,164	[w]	[s]
Richmond	6,375	[v]	[p]
Spotsylvania	27,458	1.00[z]	[o]
Stafford	16,876	[z]	[s]
Westmoreland	11,042	[v]	[p]
8th & 10th Cong. Dist. subtotal		20.44	7.87
Add 7th Cong. Dist. subtotal		9.65	3.93
Total representation		30.09	11.80
Total for state		100	40

* Includes independent city in county.

West Virginia Population (1960): 1,860,421

County	Population (1960)	Representation on basis of population	
		House of Delegates	State Senate
Barbour	15,474	1	2.00[b]
Berkeley	33,791	2[a]	2.00[c]
Morgan	8,376	[a]	[c]
Grant	8,304	1[d]	[b]
Tucker	7,750	[d]	[b]
Greenbriar	34,446	2[e]	0.7
Pocahontas	10,136	[e]	2.00[f]
Hardy	9,308	1[g]	[e]
Pendleton	8,093	[g]	[f]
Hampshire	11,705	1	[f]
Jefferson	18,665	1	[f]
Mineral	22,354	1	[f]
Monongalia	55,617	3	1.00
Preston	27,233	1	[b]
Randolph	26,349	1	[f]
Upshur	18,292	1	[b]
Webster	13,719	1	[f]
Total representation		17	7.7
Total for state		100	34

Appendix B

ISSUE FORMATION

If trading on independent issues and selection of candidates by their stand on issues are to proceed along optimal lines, then the issues must be "correctly" specified. Any issue—say, federal aid to education—may be framed in hundreds of different ways. How it is framed determines not only which people are for it and which against (specifying the vote matrix), but also the intensities of feeling pro and con (thus providing an input to the ordinal matrix). Control over how issues are to be framed is a powerful lever; one that is almost analogous to controlling the initial distribution of income in a market setting.

Let us illustrate this problem by first examining an ordinal matrix in which a legislature of five members is considering issue A. Each member has his own bill on this issue, as follows (subscripts identify each member's bill):

Members	1	2	3	4	5
A_1	1	2	3	5	4
A_2	2	1	2	4	5
A_3	3	3	1	3	3
A_4	5	4	5	1	2
A_5	4	5	4	2	1

It is not possible to solve this matrix without implicitly assuming some vote matrix. Before specifying the vote matrix, however, let me call attention to the possibility of partitioning this matrix on affinity lines (which could correspond to party lines, liberal-conservative lines, urban-rural lines):

Members	1	2	3	4	5
A_1	1	2	3	5	4
A_2	2	1	2	4	5
A_3	3	3	1	3	3
A_4	5	4	5	1	2
A_5	4	5	4	2	1

328

Members 1, 2, and 3 show an affinity to each other's bills and an aversion to the bills of members 4 and 5. The affinity and aversion in this case are reciprocated. Now, to solve this matrix, we must ask only whether the vote matrix of the upper left side has one or more rows of Ys. If it has only one such row (say, A_2), then this version of the bill will dominate the matrix. Suppose, however, the vote matrix of this partition to be (where the Y subscripts indicate ordinal ranking):

	Members		
	1	2	3
A_1	Y_1	Y_2	Y_3
A_2	Y_2	Y_1	Y_2
A_3	Y_3	Y_3	Y_1

Pure bargaining appears to be indicated here, unless these three members belong to one party, and a party caucus under established rules of selection (majority vote, for example) is used to determine the outcome.

We cannot ignore members 4 and 5, however. If they are prepared to vote Y on their third choice, then the game is up and A_3 will dominate the matrix in the absence of pressures external to our consideration (party loyalty, for example). Is A_3 the "right" choice?

To examine that question, look at the total combined vote and ordinal matrix as specified by our assumptions on voting:

	Members				
	1	2	3	4	5
A_1	Y_1	Y_2	Y_3	N_5	N_4
A_2	Y_2	Y_1	Y_2	N_4	N_5
A_3	Y_3	Y_3	Y_1	Y_3	Y_3
A_4	N_5	N_4	N_5	Y_1	Y_2
A_5	N_4	N_5	N_4	Y_2	Y_1

First, although A_3 is unique in having a unanimous Y vote, that fact is not significant. Suppose members 1 and 2 vote N on their third choice. A_3 still dominates the matrix. The crux of the matter is that only member 3 is in all minimum winning coalitions and he chooses A_3.

Still delaying an answer to the question of whether A_3 is the "right" choice, let us explore how general the specification for solution of these matrices with mutually exclusive alternatives can be through a series of logical statements:

1. Any ordinal matrix of n voters which displays different versions of one bill (A) can be reduced to an $n \times n$ matrix if there are n different first choices.

2. If there are fewer than n first choices, the matrix can be reduced to a $k \times n$ matrix where $k < n$, $k = 1, \ldots, n - 1$.

3. Any such $n \times n$ and $k \times n$ ordinal matrix will have vote matrices which can be combined with it. Using majority vote as the decision rule, only rows containing at least $(n + 1)/2$ (if n is odd) or $(n/2) + 1$ (if n is even) Y votes need be considered.

(If no row has a majority of Y votes, no version of a bill on the issue (A) can be passed by the legislature.)

(If only one row has a majority of Y votes, then this is the only version which can be passed.)

4. If two or more rows have (at least) a majority of Y votes, selection among them takes the following form:

  (a) for $k \times n$ matrices (every row passing),
      (i) Any minimum winning coalition (MWC) composed *only* of first choices is dominant (there can be no more than one such coalition in any ordinal matrix).
     (ii) If no dominant row exists, then any rows with one or more first choices in an MWC should be compared. If there are common members of these coalitions, the common members will determine the solution. If the ordinal matrix of such common members, when reordered so as to put those members' highest preference on the main diagonal, results in a symmetrical matrix, the solution may be indeterminate.

  (b) for $n \times n$ matrices (every row passing),
      (i) Partition the ordinal matrix to include only members who are in two or more MWCs. If only one such member exists, his choice dominates.
     (ii) If two or more such members exist, reorder their ordinal matrix to put their highest preference on the main diagonal. If the resulting ordinal matrix is symmetrical, the solution may be indeterminate.
    (iii) If the resulting matrix is not symmetrical, the common members (by bargaining, caucus vote, or whatever) dominate the $n \times n$ matrix.

It is worth noting that ordinal symmetry in either the $k \times n$ or $n \times n$ matrix denotes a cyclical (indeterminate) case. Here, however, the meaning of the cycle is clear and its lack of decision benign. It denotes a lack of minimum agreement on an issue and hence chooses, correctly, to pass nothing. The issue is excluded from resolution pending a new set of legislators or a reformulation of the issue that can attract a better clustering of interests.

The same four logical statements can be used to describe the actions of a majority party in a legislature (if one assumed a high degree of party discipline) or of a committee system or dominant coalition of any kind. To take any number smaller than n, however, upsets the notion of majority rule; a notion which both Rae and Taylor have shown to have a strong claim on our rational interests. Thus, such decisions have some claim to be the "right" ones, and the presence of restrictions that exclude (at the outset) some members from the decision of how an issue is framed can be suspected of turning up with "wrong" decisions even though such exclusion is a way to mask indeterminate (cyclical) matrices.

A separate case posed with issue formation is considered in an election process. Here the candidates frame the issues in response to their reading of public interest and response. Since that reading cannot be as precise as that which the close interaction of men in a legislature can develop, the candidates must perforce cast the issues in broader and less precise terms. The ambition and hope is, however, the same—to frame the issue in such a way that a majority is for it in comparison to any counterformulation by an opponent. That statement is not equivalent to saying, being at *the* median on the issue; it is equivalent to saying, being at *a* median on the issue, and at that median which dominates all other medians.

Appendix C

I am indebted to Otto Davis and Rufus Browning for written comments on the paper and have, in at least one instance, incorporated material directly from the comments.

Other of their comments, equally important, could not be incorporated but should be noted. Both commentators emphasized, quite rightly, that models are models, and reality is something else. In particular, both were aware that I am pushing strongly for certain institutional forms on the basis of their theoretical strengths, and ignoring the weaknesses which such forms have, in practice, developed. Davis notes that I am ignoring the problem of voter information and motivation. Browning raises the very relevant criticism that the appropriate size for regional legislatures is no easy question, and that to err on either side of this appropriate size is to bring on both practical and theoretical problems of not inconsequential proportions.

Finally, both men point out, correctly, that the theory on which I base my analysis is far from complete; is, in fact, in its infancy. With this I must regretfully concur.

9. *Legal Strategies Applicable to Environmental Quality Management Decisions*

Joseph L. Sax

To most nonlawyers, legal research seems to consist principally of two species of work. Either lawyers are collecting and organizing old precedents, so that judges can accurately perpetuate the follies of their predecessors; or they are engaged in a priori debate over such questions as how much free speech, or how much privacy, is good for you. Certainly many attorneys busy themselves with such tasks, but to a substantial extent the public confuses the way in which lawyers talk to each other with the substance of what they are doing.

Because lawyers work largely with official decision makers, they have learned to cloak bold thoughts in cautious rhetoric. While novelty is welcome in scholarly debate, those who have responsibility for public decisions are very eager to have the comfort of precedent, example, and analogy to support their actions. It is not that they are unwilling to act in new ways, or that they do not welcome the possibility that history will see their decisions as forward-looking departures; it is rather that they feel compelled to accommodate progressive policies to the essential conservatism which characterizes public attitudes.

The style of lawyers reflects these facts. I note this by way of introduction because the need for communication among scholars across traditional disciplinary lines is going to be impeded unnecessarily unless we distinguish between form (the language we use among ourselves) and substance (the issues we are seeking to illuminate).

Let me give you an illustrative example, taken (as you might expect) from a recent court precedent. A utility company condemned a pipeline right-of-way across privately owned land. The landowner, an association

333

which maintained the tract as a wildlife preserve and nature study area, objected. It felt the proposed pipeline would be inordinately damaging to the natural habitat it had preserved—against considerable odds—in a rapidly urbanizing area.

Unfortunately, there was no easy way to make this objection effective. No law prohibited environmentally damaging condemnations for pipelines; indeed, except as to disputes over money damages due, the law permitted very little room to challenge condemnation actions at all.

The landowner hired a lawyer, who was immediately presented with a dilemma. He had a case to win for a client in the real world; and he had against him a long-standing tradition of precedent which suggested that such cases could not be won. The lawyer on the other side had an easy job. He could simply cite established rules and precedents. But the landowner's attorney had to think through the question of *why* all the existing rules of law prevented his client from prevailing; what, if anything, was wrong with those rules; and how an ordinary trial judge could be persuaded to begin reversing the course of decades—or perhaps centuries—of legal history. Challenges such as this make it fun to be a lawyer.

I am first going to tell you what the lawyer did in the overt sense; that is, what you would see if you read the formal public record of the case. Then I will call to your attention the real significance and meaning of his strategy.

While it is generally true, the lawyer agreed, that a landowner cannot challenge the need for a right-of-way condemnation, there is historically one circumstance in which such challenges are allowed. If the land sought to be condemned is already devoted to a public purpose (that is, typically, if it is held in public ownership, as a park or for school use), then the courts are compelled to decide whether the existing use or the proposed use is paramount. Because *this* land—though privately owned—is held open for public use, he said, it should be treated like public lands devoted to a public use; thus the merits of the proposed condemnation ought to be examined. The court accepted this argument and sent the case back for a trial on the merits, with the result that an accommodation was worked out that minimized disruption of the land's use as a wildlife preserve.

What is the meaning of such a decision? Was it simply a routine matter of getting a judge to apply the proper rule to an unusual set of facts? Certainly it was more than this, for the traditional rule had been devised to prevent unseemly struggles between two public entities, both holding condemnation power. In such circumstances, unless a court intervened to resolve the conflict, the two agencies might interminably condemn the disputed tract back and forth.

Plainly this problem was not presented by the wildlife preserve case, for the private landowner had no eminent domain power. And plainly the

334

court knew this; it was not tricked by a clever lawyer into doing something it did not wish to do, or did not understand.

Rather the court had decided that it ought to turn its attention to a problem that has significantly engaged the attention of all those who are concerned with problems of environmental quality. How do we evaluate the public interest in resources that are relatively scarce, not easily renewed, and have no easily available substitutes, whose services have been traditionally supplied as free goods and have that peculiar character of common property resources—that they are not readily marketable to any limited class of beneficiaries?

Traditionally the common property values of resources like a wildlife preserve have simply been preempted by enterprisers, much as clean air and water have been, for the simple reason that ordinary market transactions have imperfectly (or not at all) taken them into account. When the court in the wildlife preserve case agreed to hold a trial on the merits of condemnation, it thereby—significantly—undertook to cope with this troublesome problem. This is the real meaning of a case which, on its surface, appears to be a technical disputation about the technical rules of condemnation law.

If this is what the case is really all about, why did the lawyers and the judge not say so directly, rather than doing their formalistic little dance? The reasons, if one thinks about it for a moment, are good ones. First, since the court is undertaking a rather unusual function with great implications, it is reluctant to commit itself too much until it has had a chance to see, by experience, whether it is equal to the task it would like to perform and believes ought to be performed. Thus it states, at the outset, a narrow rule from which it can easily withdraw if the experiment appears to be unsuccessful. In addition, the lawyer, by calling attention to a traditional line of cases in which the courts have performed a similar function in the past (that is, disputes between two public agencies), suggests to the court that it has the competence to do this sort of job, and also gives the court a suggestion about some historical precedents to which it can turn for guidance. Finally, by cloaking itself in precedent, the court takes on some protective coloration which helps to insulate it from political attack, thus maintaining a larger degree of freedom within which it can innovate new solutions to newly recognized problems. These are the factors that lead lawyers to describe the common law process as evolutionary.

Having noted these tactical elements in the case, I turn to the substantive task before the court. Three basic choices were available to the judge. He could try to evaluate the costs incurred by impairing the use of the land as a wildlife sanctuary, and to charge those costs to the pipeline company as the "just compensation" it must pay for having exercised its condemnation power. In legal theory, this would be the easiest solution, but its practical difficulties are great. How does one go about measuring the losses in such a situation, where the services afforded by the sanctuary are not marketed in ordinary transactions, where the losses are spread over an extremely diffuse and unidentifiable group of beneficiaries, are also likely to be diffused over a great period of time, and where the potential losses from this sanctuary can only meaningfully be calculated in respect to what is occurring with other similar lands (a question that is hardly litigable within the confines of a particular lawsuit)? Money compensation, based on a calculation of dollar losses, is a remedy difficult to enforce.

A second choice is to require the condemnor to provide equivalent substitute land or, in the alternative, money with which an equivalent tract of land can be purchased. This solution has sometimes been adopted. There are laws, for example, requiring that when publicly owned parkland is converted to other uses, the government must make available equal acreage for a substitute park. Similarly, an administrative rule was adopted in Maryland a few years ago providing that when publicly owned wetlands were conveyed to private developers, the developers must pay the state by acquiring and deeding to it other wetlands, on a basis of two acres for every one conveyed to the developers. Notably, this rule has died aborning in some instances, and in others created considerable controversy over the true equivalence, in natural values, of the exchanged lands.

In any event, the effort to provide a substitute in kind for a resource that is generally in short supply may be somewhat self-defeating. For if the totality of such lands is at stake, a formal change of ownership of one such tract would still appear to produce a net loss. Moreover, even if it were technologically possible to create a substitute—as, for example, by excavation, construction and cultivation—the dollar cost of such an enterprise would probably be enormous. Rarely would such a technique be the lowest-cost method of achieving the desired result.

In practice, then, the optimal solution is likely to be a search for methods that allow the pipeline company to build its facility, but in a manner—and under conditions—which reduce toward the zero point diminution of the benefits provided by the existing resource as a wildlife preserve. This was exactly what the court attempted to do, working out in the course of the trial a detailed set of construction stipulations so that the tract would be left essentially unimpaired. These stipulations, of course, imposed costs on the pipeline company, which costs reflected, within practical limits, the price of preserving the benefits formerly enjoyed by the beneficiaries of the preserve. In other words, the court adopted a scheme which internalized the negative externalities of the pipeline business.

I have detailed this example both to suggest that lawyers are struggling with the same problems that engage economists and other professionals working with problems of environmental quality, and that lawyers worry particularly about formulating solutions that seem practically adaptable to pending problems. If there is a single issue that specially engages the lawyer's attention, it is effective translation of theory into practice. Let me turn now to that question.

I recently read testimony given by Allen Kneese before a congressional committee in which he pointed out that economists are not surprised at the heavy toll taken by industrial development in the quality of resources such as water, air, and open space.[1] Conventional market transactions usually assign these resources a very low price (sometimes a zero price) and thus, naturally, there is a tendency to use them in an extravagant fashion. If we can begin to price these resources, we can at least force a careful reexamination of the true costs and benefits of certain activities. The example most often given is the imposition of effluent charges on waste water discharges.

The lawyer understands and appreciates this point, but the first question he asks is how well the mechanism we adopt to implement this principle is going to work. Who is going to fix the charges, and how great are the chances that charges will be set higher or lower than some optimal level to satisfy the self-interest of particular interest groups? It is, of course, possible to legislate standards that seek to reduce the exercise of discretion; but lawyers are properly suspicious of the notion of iron-clad legislation. Like novel door locks or military weaponry, legislative constraints have to a substantial degree proven to be incentives to the ingenuity of those with an interest in devising countermeasures. I need only point to the example of real estate assessment and the Internal Revenue Code to suggest the difficulty of the problem.

The dilemma of effective implementation has begun to dominate the attention of lawyers concerned with environmental quality. For in asking why certain environmental resources have been priced so low, one important answer seems to be that the voices speaking in support of some of the values represented by those resources have been too muted; as a consequence the benefits are "underpriced." The point is important. While it may be true that certain resources—like clean air and water—are not priced effectively by ordinary market transactions, or while it may be true that we have tended too long to treat them as free goods (which may be to say the same thing), I think it is also true that simply to impose a price on them by fiat (as by enacting effluent charge laws) will by no means necessarily make a substantial difference in result. If those who administer

[1] U.S. Congress, House of Representatives, Subcommittee on Government Operations, *The Environmental Decade* (*Action Proposals for the 1970's*), 91st Cong., 2d sess. (Washington: U.S. Government Printing Office, 1970), pp. 190–97.

effluent tax laws are too compliant, nothing much is likely to change except our theory.

It thus becomes very important indeed *who* speaks for the beneficiaries of the benefits provided by common property resources, and whether those who speak have a position of power. Environmental lawyers have begun to discover that if the beneficiaries themselves speak, rather than working through traditional intermediaries, such as government regulatory agencies, the benefits provided by common property resources seem to get a higher valuation. And that valuation is enhanced when they speak from a position of power, such as a lawsuit in which they may be able to enjoin proposed activity until certain conditions are met or certain alternative courses taken.

I suppose the typical highway location lawsuit is the clearest example of this proposition. In highway law, a number of provisions have been enacted requiring that potential negative externalities (on open space, or on fish and wildlife) be avoided; in this respect the law has already "priced" these values, by declaring that every effort should be taken to preserve them by adopting alternatives, even at greater cost in immediate dollar outlay for the road. It is fair to observe that these mandates were not exactly seized upon by highway departments as an opportunity for building less environmentally destructive roads; indeed it has not always been easy to see any significant relationship between such enactments and policy changes by administrative agencies. A barrage of citizen lawsuits, however, initiated by members of the public who would bear the adverse impacts of traditional highway building practices, and some decisions in which courts enjoined proposals that presented such potential harms, seem at last to have begun to get highway builders to put some value on threatened environmental benefits (formerly treated as free), because those values have been presented to them as costs to be borne in delay, litigation, and political unpopularity.

Litigation, as in a highway location or industrial plant siting case, is in practical effect quite similar to an effluent charge system. It is a device to force enterprisers to face up to the external costs of their operations, and to bear them. Sometimes that job can be done by the imposition of a formal charge or compensation system (and, as noted earlier, it may be done more or less effectively; so at times even such a formal system may have to be pushed by various legal or political pressures). In other circumstances, as with the highway case or the pipeline location, the difficulty of determining and managing a charges system may require a proceeding in which the goal is to find a way of reducing negative externalities, or, if possible, eliminating them.

I have already commented that lawyers spend a good deal of their time worrying about how to assure that these theories are implemented as work-able realities. Putting legal power directly into the hands of the people who have a direct self-interest in maintaining threatened benefits seems to be one quite effective device for getting this job done. Indeed, it seems to be a useful substitute for ordinary market transactions in a situation of market failure, just as litigation is often a substitute for market forces—as in land-lord and tenant law, where protective legal rules displace certain disparities in market power.

This observation has some interesting implications for legal theory. For example, one reason amenities like clean air have not been given a price in the marketplace is that the air has not been the subject of ownership, like other properties. In addition, no private individual or group was in a posi-tion to withhold access to the air, a sine qua non of ordinary forms of private property. Yet if we want to have the values of clean air considered by industry in its activities, we have to provide some sort of substitute for traditional ownership, so that enterprisers must bear the cost of using that resource.

In this context, the ancient legal notion that the ambient air is *res nullius*, the property of no one, is deterimental to rational policy making. So one job that lawyers have is to find a substitute concept. One effort in this direc-tion has been to try to define resources like air as a commodity that is held in trust for the benefit of the entire community of citizens. If the citizenry is the beneficiary of the trust, its representatives should have the right to protect the values in air for themselves and their fellows. And government, which stands in the position of trustee to implement the trust for the public benefit, has an obligation to prevent uses of the air that impair the in-terests of the beneficiaries.

Put in concrete terms, this approach suggests that there is someone who can speak for the interests ordinarily represented by a property owner; and access to the "property" *can* in practice be controlled by the issuance of court orders enjoining the discharge of deleterious substances into the air. Thus, by building a legal construct, such as public trust doctrine, we can provide a workable substitute for market forces. Judicial protection of resource values against destruction or impairment is the price that must be paid, usually in the form of a nondestructive alternative. By having a doctrine suggestive of traditional property law approaches, we encourage courts to implement for the benefit of the general public (the beneficiaries of the trust) the standard legal principle, *sic utere tuo ut alienum non laedas* —use your own property in such a manner as not to injure that of another. The result is decisions of the kind made in the pipeline case noted earlier, a result analogous to that produced by an effluent charge.

I mention this doctrinal concept not because any label or concept in itself has particular value or importance, but only because it helps to create a frame of reference for thinking about, and identifying, the results that are sought to be achieved. It is helpful to courts, for example, in that it gives them a handle for coping with the rather unfamiliar notion of legally enforceable rights claimed on behalf of the public at large.

Recent developments in environmental law have also dramatically brought to the surface another problem that is going to demand a great deal of the attention of lawyers in the next few years. I have already adverted to this issue in mentioning that it has been found very useful to give a strong voice to the people who will be directly affected by changes in the quality of common property resources, rather than working through traditional intermediaries, such as public regulatory agencies. The basic question is, who shall represent the public interest? To an extraordinary degree, the direction of American law and institutions has been to minimize the role of private citizens and to create presumably professional and expert regulatory officials who—with a single voice—spoke for the public. The tremendous proliferation of public agencies, from the old Interstate Commerce Commission to the relatively new Federal Water Quality Administration,[2] with all their counterparts in state and local government, denotes the extent to which this development has flowered. Not only have these agencies been created to speak for the public, but in the process ordinary citizens have been largely excluded. Many legal doctrines have essentially held that jurisdiction was exclusively vested in public agencies and that citizens had no right to participate. While these rules are beginning to break down, their very existence indicates the direction in which we had been moving for quite a long time.

One of the particularly interesting aspects of environmental law is that it is in the forefront of the attack on this traditional development. The coming changes portend two very significant modifications in our fundamental assumptions about how government should work. First, and obviously, we are beginning to see in operative terms—and not merely political rhetoric—that the notion of participatory democracy has great significance for our ability to cope with grave environmental problems. We are now beginning to ask quite seriously whether it is possible to deal with environmental issues unless we let the ordinary citizen—call him the victim, or the beneficiary of the trust, or whatever you will—play a central role in the decision-making process.

In addition, we see the demerits of a system of government that is tightly structured along jurisdictional lines so that certain people or agencies, and only they, have authority to make certain kinds of decisions. We begin to

[2] Now the Office of Water Quality in the Environmental Protection Agency.

JOSEPH L. SAX

see that flexibility and leverage in the process of government is a very valuable tool; that instead of putting exclusive responsibility in a certain regulatory agency, making their determinations essentially unchallengeable, and excluding most persons from participation in their processes, we seem to gain ability to deal intelligently with problems if we let more groups (with their diverse interests) into the process, and if we give those interests a variety of avenues of recourse, including the agencies themselves, the legislature, and the courts. In some very interesting ways, we are finding that a loosely structured, somewhat fragmented process of government has considerable advantages.

Let me give you just two examples to indicate how what I have called a "loose" system of government provides advantages over a "tight" system. Not many months ago, it was announced that a large German chemical company was planning to build a factory along the water near Hilton Head, South Carolina. As frequently happens in such cases, the company had carefully prepared the groundwork with local officials, obtaining from them written statements to the effect that no objections would be interposed to the building of the plant.

Some time later, when the plans were made public, an unusual coalition of well-to-do local citizens, recreational developers, and poor fishermen, objected because of potential damage to the fisheries and to the area's scenic amenities. They found, however, that state and local officials seemed to be essentially committed to the project. Thus, they sought to pull some other levers, where commitments might be less firm, or nonexistent. They hired lawyers and filed a case to challenge the environmental protection procedures planned for the factory; they also sought the intervention of federal administrative officials concerned with fish and wildlife. In the latter forum they were met with a sympathetic hearing; in the former (the court) they began to take depositions to get some hard evidence about the proposed facility. They also worked diligently (and successfully) to get widespread newspaper and magazine coverage of their dispute. The combination of these factors brought results; evidence produced in the discovery process arising out of the lawsuit fed information to federal officials upon which they could develop a position; and the publicity encouraged those officials to take a stand. As this paper was being written, the newspapers reported that construction plans for the plant had been suspended.[3] Whether the battle is over is not yet clear, but a major victory for the environmentalists has been won largely because the objectors were able to work in a diffuse,

[3] The company has since announced the abandonment of its plans to build at the site. To what extent this reflects the objections raised, or the current (1970–71), relatively depressed state of the chemical processing industries, or both, is not known. [Editor's note.]

341

open-ended, "loose" system, in which various elements were able to strengthen and support each other. Had this matter been dealt with in traditional fashion, along strict jurisdictional lines, the plant would probably have been built already. Here is a significant case study for lawyers who are trying to think about the administrative, regulatory, and legislative schemes we should build to deal with our ever-expanding environmental problems.

My second example involves an issue with which everyone is at least somewhat familiar; the proposed Alaska pipeline to carry oil some 750 miles from the North Slope to the southern coast of the state. The land involved is almost all owned by the United States, and a consortium of oil companies had applied to the Department of the Interior for a permit to build the pipeline and a construction road. Fears of damage to the arctic tundra and wildlife activity from a pipeline carrying heated oil were widely debated. Around the first of April 1970, it appeared that the permit for the beginning of construction was about to be granted. Several conservation organizations filed a lawsuit and sought temporarily to enjoin the grant of the permit. Among their claims, the details of which are not important here, was the combined allegation that the matter had been insufficiently studied, and that proper study would show the prospect of unacceptable damage. At this early stage the relief they sought had not been refined, but they might have desired either to stop the pipeline entirely, or at the least to obtain detailed and specific protective construction specifications along the lines of those that were adopted in the much simpler wildlife preserve pipeline case. Incidentally, while the government had already issued a set of protective stipulations, they were essentially in the form of general "thou shalt nots"—such as a prohibition on pollution—rather than being phrased in specific standards to govern construction.

In any event, when the case came on for a hearing, while the government lawyer suggested that some details relating to environmental protection remained to be ironed out, he strongly implied that they could be settled quite soon. There was no basis, he emphasized, for judicial intervention. The Department of the Interior was scrupulously protecting the public interest. He even showed the court a report, in compliance with the detailed provisions of the new National Environmental Policy Act, to emphasize that the government had been more than careful in fulfilling its obligations to protect the environment.[4]

[4] The official document is dated January 1971 and entitled "Draft Environmental Impact Statement for the Trans-Alaska Pipeline Section 102 (2) (C) of The National Environmental Policy Act of 1969," prepared by the Department of Interior. Several government agencies, including the Corps of Engineers, have questioned the adequacy of the report. [Editor's note.]

JOSEPH L. SAX

At exactly the same time as this hearing was under way, the *New York Times* carried an article with the headline "Arctic Pipeline Test Promises Wide Boon."[5] The story beneath the headline was fascinating. In essence it said that Canada had vast arctic oil reserves, and that the Canadian government was exploring ways and means of getting that oil to market. And one thing it had done was to spend about 3 million dollars to hire an American engineering firm to build an experimental 48-inch oil pipeline in a loop in the tundra "to determine how much a pipeline carrying hot oil would melt the permanently frozen ground of the Arctic and sub-Arctic region and what consequences thawing of the permafrost might have." The experiment had begun in February, and according to the *New York Times*, would probably continue for a year.

Of course I was astonished. First, this experimental pipeline was the same size as the proposed Alaska pipeline, and was built to test the very questions that had been raised about the Alaska pipeline proposal. Obvious questions jumped into my head. Had the American government run any such experiment prior to declaring itself satisfied that construction could begin in Alaska? If so, no one had mentioned it, and presumably no one had informed the Canadians. If not, why not? If the Canadians, who, according to the paper, are most eager to see the pipeline experiment succeed, can wait at least twelve months, why are we in such a hurry?

It seems plain enough that the mere enactment of laws stating that these problems must be considered is not self-enforcing. Nor is the mere presence of a scheme for calculating benefits and costs going to assure that the calculation is adequately made or applied. The need is for a "market" in which, as a practical matter, there is a seller with power to restrain the sale unless his interest is adequately compensated. It is toward the development of such "markets" that environmental lawyers are turning their attention. The job is difficult and it requires, among other things, a willingness to abandon the faith we have so long put in traditional administrative processes.[6] It requires a renewal of confidence in the ordinary citizen and in his ability to take initiatives for the protection of those values which inure to him simply as a member of the public. The job of lawyers is to fashion tools that will make the public interest into public rights.

[5] *New York Times*, 6 April 1970, p. 57.
[6] In response to discussion, the author stated that his comments should not be construed as indicating that litigation is a complete substitute for administration and administrative agencies. [Editor's note.]

343

10. Power Structure Studies and Environmental Management: The Study of Powerful Urban Problem-Oriented Leaders in Northeastern Megalopolis

Delbert C. Miller

Community-power research has progressed through three identifiable stages. The first stage was characterized by case studies of American communities and the various uses of positional, reputational, and issue-decisional methods of identifying influential leaders and decision-making processes. Stage two began with the appearance of comparative studies, both intranational and international. In both stages, emphasis was upon the structure and functioning of the community *qua community*. It was marked especially in stage two by the combined use of two or more methods of identifying influential leaders and associations. Usually, the reputational and issue-decisional methods were selected. The issues were those considered by community judges to be the most important. It mattered little what the issues were. The researcher simply wanted salient issues in order to identify community leaders and the contours of community decision-making processes.

Stage three has emerged in recent years and is characterized by a focus on power relations as centered on a specific problem, issue, or community decision organization. The issue is now one that arrests the specific attention of the researcher because of the *nature* of the issue or problem. Stage three can be illustrated by the work of some current researchers. Terry N. Clark of the University of Chicago has published his study of the relation among community structure, decision making, budget expenditures, and urban renewal in fifty-one American communities. Roland L. Warren of Brandeis University is conducting research on community decision organizations (urban renewal authority, health and welfare council, board of education, antipoverty organization, mental health planning board, and the city demonstration agency of the Model Cities Program) in nine cities extending from Oakland, California, to Boston, Massachusetts. Peter Rossi, Robert Crain, James Venecho, and Laura Horlock, all of Johns Hopkins University, are studying school desegregation and power in ninety-one cities of the United States. Robert Alford and Michael Aiken of the University of Wisconsin have investigated political orientation and public policy on urban renewal, poverty, and public housing programs based on their statistical archive of 200 American cities. Harold Wolman of the University of Pennsylvania, in his study of how federal housing policy is made, interviewed sixty-eight top influentials in Congress, the White House, Housing and Urban Redevelopment, the Bureau of the Budget, and various professional organizations and lobbies representing housing. Ray Johnston of Wayne State University has sought to define the relationship between holders of reputed power or influence and the political demand-articulation processes by which priorities and allocation of resources are determined for urban problems.[1]

This inventory could be extended at length and a fuller list may indeed be examined in the Newsletters of the Committee for Comparability in Community Research.[2] The list of current studies underway reveals a number of characteristics in the emergent stage of community research· The distinctive emphasis on a specific problem can be noted and also the inclusion of large samples of communities. There is often a search for statistical relationships between community factors and the problem investigated. Path analysis, factor analysis, as well as simple, multiple, and partial correlation analysis are making their appearances. It can probably be said that interest in structural relationships is dominating concern for processes and qualitative analysis.

Certainly many researchers active on urban problems are using community power methodologies, but there is a dearth of research effort focused on regional analysis and on such an urban problem as environmental quality. When I and my associates, James Barfoot and Paul Planchon, began work on the study reported in this paper, there was almost nothing in the literature to serve as a guide.

A regional power structure had never been undertaken and we faced the

[1] Clark, "Community Structure, Decision-Making, Budget Expenditures, and Urban Renewal in 51 American Communities," *American Sociological Review* 33, no. 4 (August 1968): 576–93. Warren, "Interorganizational Study Project" (Working Paper of the Project, Brandeis University, April 18, 1968). Wolman, "How Federal Housing Policy is Made," *Journal of Housing* 26, no. 4 (April 1969): 188–91. Johnston, "Levels of Community Demand—Articulation and Indices of Power," *Proceedings, Indiana Academy of Sciences* 78, pt. 2 (April 1968), pp. 74–98.

[2] *Newsletter of the Committee for Comparability in Community Research* (April 1969 and October 1969). Obtainable from Terry N. Clark, University of Chicago.

known fact that a large macroscopic system of power is especially difficult
to deal with. C. Wright Mills has been criticized severely for his description
in *The Power Elite* of the power structure of the United States, although
the book still sells in the thousands of copies.[3] Sociologists and political
scientists reject the methodology but use the book because they say that
there is nothing better. Floyd Hunter studied the power structure of the
United States with the same techniques used in his community power
studies.[4] Yet *Top Leadership, U.S.A.* is seldom read or referred to. It has
been dismissed as biased toward business dominance and not getting at the
complex web of decision making.

In regard to environmental quality research, there were only two studies
on power relations centered on problems of air quality, water quality, and
solid wastes. Roscoe Martin, Guthrie S. Birkhead, Jesse Birkhead, and
Frank Munger had made a useful start in identifying working relations
between organizations active in the Delaware Basin.[5] This was suggestive
for much of the organizational analysis that we were to carry out. However, Martin and his associates stopped with a simple tally of mentions
given to organizations that each respondent said were those with which his
organization most often cooperated. Matthew Crenson of Johns Hopkins
University recently made a pioneer study of power relations and air pollution problems.[6] However, this study was not available when our studies
were designed.

DIVERSITY IN THE SCIENTIFIC COMMUNITY

The research review in this section highlights two features of the background of the study: (a) the trend away from macroscopic analysis of
power structures toward more concern with specific problems and (b) the
extremely limited knowledge about power relations around environmental
quality issues.

[3] C. Wright Mills, *The Power Elite* (New York: Oxford University Press, 1956).
Arnold M. Rose tried to strike a more balanced treatment in *The Power Structure,
Political Process in American Society* (New York: Oxford University Press, 1967) but
it is not as widely read.

[4] Floyd Hunter, *Top Leadership, U.S.A.* (Chapel Hill: University of North Carolina
Press, 1959).

[5] Martin *et al.*, *River Basin Administration and the Delaware* (Syracuse: Syracuse
University Press, 1960).

[6] Crenson found that perceived influence of industry in a community tends to thwart
the rise of air pollution as an issue. Even where industry enjoys no reputation for power
in the pollution field, it may affect the course of pollution politics through power repu-
tations that it has established in other issue areas. See his "Non Issues in City Politics:
The Case of Air Pollution," in *An End to Political Science*, ed. Marvin Surkin and Alan
Wolfe (New York: Basic Books, 1970).

To proceed upon a study of power structures across a region and espe-cially to an attack on environmental quality was to compound difficulty. The situation became especially troublesome because of the lack of con-sensus on the Northeastern Megalopolis as a region,[7] on the nature of the power structures within a region, on methodological techniques, and on the outcomes desired from the study. The researcher finds himself in the center of the schema shown as figure 10.1.

Concepts of Megalopolis

| 1. Regional community | 2. Congeries of subregions | 3. Functional regional groups | 4. Part of national network | 5. Separate metropolitan centers |

Concepts of Power Structure and Decision Making

1. Power is a generalized poten-tial for action; decision-mak-ing mechanisms are im-portant.
2. Power is an influence system derived from issue resolu-tion; decision-making pro-cesses are unimportant.

Researcher

Concepts of Methodology

1. Positional analysis desired.
2. Reputational analysis desired.
3. Issue analysis desired.
4. Combined analysis desired.

Expected Outcomes

1. Clients' pragmatic expectations for useable knowledge about decision-making processes.
2. Scientists' interest in greater understanding of underlying structural patterns and opportunities to extend methodology in regional analysis.

Figure 10.1. Schema showing four principal areas of disagreement with the competing varieties of concepts attached to each area.

This schema tries to convey how competing varieties of concepts sur-round the researcher. To understand this diversity thoroughly one must experience it as pulls from fellow scientists, clients, and respondents of the study. Each shares in some of the areas of diversity and the researcher can-not duck and run. He must make operating choices. In designing the re-search program the budget provided for one year's work for one senior investigator (myself) and two graduate assistants. Our client expected us to come up with useful knowledge about decision-making processes cen-

---

[7] The most comprehensive work on the Northeastern Megalopolis—Boston to Washington—is Jean Gottman, *The Megalopolis, Urbanized Northeastern Seaboard of the United States* (New York: 20th Century Fund, 1961). When region "in the large" or Megalopolis is referred to herein, it is this Northeastern Megalopolis. It is also referred to as the Atlantic urban region.

tering around roles of decision makers engaged in environmental quality management. Problems of interest included the setting of air and water quality standards; the decision-making orientations of commissions charged with air, water, and solid wastes management; the forces impinging upon authorities in establishing and maintaining standards; and the power struggles centered around the securing of new legislation and regulations. Attention was directed toward decision-making processes within the region, and focused on urban problems generally and environmental quality problems specially. It was believed that the true priority given to environmental quality problems could not be ascertained except as they were examined within the competing claims of other urban problems.

The most difficult area of diversity is that introduced by various concepts of power and their corresponding validation. The major division of opinion centers around the difference between a power structure and a decision-making structure. Terry Clark has pointed out these distinctions with clarity. *Power is the potential ability* of an actor or actors to select, to change, and to attain the goals of a social system. *Influence is the exercise of power* that brings about change in a social system. It follows then that a *power structure* is a patterned distribution of power in a social system and is distinguished from a *decision-making structure*, which is the patterned distribution of influence in a social system. Clark continues, "To study a power structure it is necessary to measure the distribution of resources and the potential ability of actors to bring about change in the system. Implied is a strategy for analyzing the system at one point in time. A decision-making structure, on the other hand, is best analyzed by studying actual processes of influence as exercised over time." [8]

In our research program we found it useful to study both power structures and decision-making structures. In studies made with the region as the geographic entity, our major focus was on power structures. In studies made within a subregion such as the Delaware River Basin, the decision-making structure has been the principal focus. It is important to be aware of these differences, because the differing concepts of method relate directly to whether a power structure or a decision-making structure is under study. Generally positional and reputational analysis is utilized for power structure study and issue analysis for the study of decision-making structures.

A combination of these types of analysis is often possible and is desirable for checking the validity of findings. Positional and reputational leaders and organizations can be asked what issues they have participated in and

[8] Terry N. Clark, *Community Structure and Decision Making: Comparative Analysis* (San Francisco: Chandler, 1968), p. 47.

what stands they took. Issue leaders can be ranked for their reputed standing and their official positions can be analyzed for the potential authority they may wield.

Both decision-making mechanisms and decision-making processes can be analyzed. A decision-making mechanism refers to modes and patterns of decision making, such as working through powerful persons on an informal basis or working through organizations in formal channels. A decision-making process refers to the actual progress of issue resolution from inception to decision. The roles of actors and decision-making mechanisms are described as they actually occur in time.

Research versatility requires an ability to move through the range of technical skills available and make applications to appropriate situations. James Barfoot and Paul Planchon used reputational methods to identify the most powerful environmental quality leaders and organizations in the Northeastern Megalopolis and establish working relationships between environment quality organizations. Miller, Barfoot, and Planchon studied the linkage between the most powerful urban-oriented leaders and organizations and the environmental quality leaders and organizations of Megalopolis. In a supplementary study Planchon identified the most influential environmental quality leaders and organizations engaged in the Delaware River Basin on water management problems and issues. Barfoot studied decision-making processes among sixty "parties at interest" who expressed positions on the issue of water quality standards for the Delaware Estuary.

The work to be described was based on a search for the most powerful urban problem–oriented leaders of Megalopolis (Boston to Washington). One of six structures of power within Megalopolis that the research program investigated will be described.[9] Seven months were required to assemble a listing of over 2,200 active leaders and then to reduce this list to 400 key and top leaders by using the voting consensus of some forty-eight judges from the major centers. Responses to the questionnaire sent to these leaders provided data on urban problem interest and activity patterns, acquaintance and working relations of the key leaders, and some decision-making mechanisms. A number of hypotheses dealing with contact and interaction between leaders in different occupational groupings and different cities within the region were then tested. A limited report on the findings is made in this chapter. To see how this single study relates to the

---

[9] The six structures are: (a) powerful representative urban-oriented leaders in Megalopolis; (b) powerful urban-oriented organizations in Megalopolis; (c) powerful environmental quality leaders in Megalopolis; (d) powerful environmental quality organizations in Megalopolis; (e) powerful environmental quality leaders in the Delaware River Basin; (f) powerful environmental quality organizations in the Delaware River Basin.

overall design of the research program, it is necessary to explain some
theoretical positions and guiding assumptions.

THEORETICAL POSITIONS

*The Linkage of Urban-Oriented and Environmental
Quality Leaders and Organizations*

The first major decision involved the theoretical assumption that the
urban-oriented leaders and associations were influential in the initiation,
support, or vetoing of actions taken by environmental quality leaders and
organizations. It was believed that a high degree of supportive relationship
was necessary to increase the attention, resources, and personnel directed
to environmental quality problems and that such maximum support would
originate with powerful urban-oriented leaders and associations. Little
was known about the ties between the two groupings. Theoretical leaps
were taken to bring these parts into an integrated study design. Some guiding assumptions were elaborated to do this.

Guiding Assumptions

1. A network of economic and social concerns ties the region together
and regional (or national) leaders emerge and can be identified. On this
proposition rests the premise that a number of power structures exist in
this region and that decisions with respect to policy, programs, and institutional organization are influenced by these structures. Within a generalized
urban problem–oriented structure there may be substructures relating to
particular problems, such as environmental quality, transportation, and
housing. For example, the birth of the Delaware River Basin Commission
would have been impossible without the support of top influentials in
Pennsylvania, New York, New Jersey, and Delaware.

2. An informal network of top regional influentials and organizations
is essential for support of governmental action agencies dealing with problems of environmental quality and this network can be identified. Political
power is mobilized by common working relations and coalition formations.

3. Regional power structures can be delineated by techniques of sociological research. Although these techniques have been used most often
with respect to urban communities, there appears to be no reason why they
are not just as relevant to a wider area and to the special cluster of problems encompassed by the term "environmental quality." The application
of these techniques to a region for the first time provided a pioneering
opportunity for basic and applied social science.

351

THEORETICAL BASE: COALITION DECISION MODEL
OF A COMPLEX SOCIAL SYSTEM

A region such as the Northeastern Megalopolis or a subregion such as a river basin is a complex social system. It encloses a decision-making network composed of persons and groups in interrelated governments and public agencies woven in a net of influence generated by persons and organizations in the private sector. This decision-making network functions in formal and informal channels. The units composing the complex social system are heterogeneous and interdependent. The power base is wide and large and diverse coalitions arise to make policies. In spite of wide distribution of power in the coalitions, central figures frequently hold considerable power.

DESIGN FOR A RESEARCH PROGRAM

These theoretical positions point to a design that envisages three networks of influence: A (general) urban influence network of leaders and organizations in Megalopolis; an environmental quality (technological) network of leaders and organizations in Megalopolis; and a Delaware River Basin (subregional) influence network of leaders and organizations. These three networks are believed to interlock and interact in policy-making and other decision-making processes affecting environmental quality problems. Key concepts for analysis are power elements, linkage, and coalition. *Power elements* refer to the identifiable units regarded as important: influential leaders and influential organizations. Each requires equal attention so that both collective structure and individual leadership will be carefully considered. *Linkage* refers to those bonds that tie the urban, environmental quality, and subregional networks together in policy and decision making. Such bonds may be discovered through shared problem interests, acquaintanceship and contact, and working relationships on committees, programs, and commissions. *Coalition* refers to the uniting of interest and shared support of issues. Such coalitions can be observed when parties at interest appear at various public and governmental hearings.

A heuristic model of the three networks is shown as figure 10.2. Some fifteen intralinkage and interlinkage patterns are denoted. The central connections are: (a) the intralinkages between leaders in an influence network; (b) the intralinkages between organizations in such a network; (c) the intralinkages between leaders and organizations in the network and the interlinkages to all similar connections in the other influence networks. The model depicts the complexity of the interactional web that exists in the macrocosmic patterns elected for study. It also demonstrates the importance of identifying the structure of relationships before attempting

Megalopolis generalized influence network

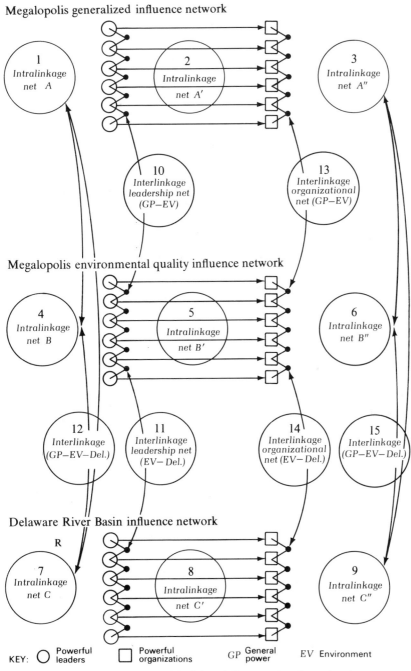

Megalopolis environmental quality influence network

Delaware River Basin influence network

KEY: ○ Powerful leaders   ▢ Powerful organizations   GP General power   EV Environment

Figure 10.2. A heuristic model of three influence networks centered on environmental quality problems.

intensive study of decision-making processes. Obviously, no one-year study could map all of these interactions. However, selection of appropriate linkages is possible. The first task is to identify the power elements and intralinkages between leaders and organizations in each influence network. The second is to seek interlinkages between the general influence network and the environmental quality network. This can only be accomplished after the identifications are made in each of the constituent networks in Megalopolis. Still later in order of procedure is the task of identifying the subregional Delaware River Basin Network.

Each of these methodological strategy elements is requisite to any comprehensive study of decision-making processes. Each of the most important power elements must be identified and understood in detail. For organizations this means their own internal organization, objectives, and policies, and also their working relationships and coalitions with other organizations. Similar determinations must be made for leaders.

The overall study identified the leaders and organizations of principal influence in initiating, supporting, or vetoing action on urban problems generally within the northeastern area of the United States; ascertained current working relationships of leaders and organizations in environmental quality problems; described the interaction of formal private, state, interstate, and federal policy-making networks; and described the decision-making network and processes within the Delaware River Basin as certain environmental quality issues and operating decisions are made.

It has been stated that the nature of Megalopolis does not provide us with many common points of regional decision making. Rather we have posited that Megalopolis is an integrated economic and functional unit in which powerful leaders and organizations wield influence on national, state, interstate, and local problems as representatives within the region. No single power structure presents itself, but many interactional networks can be found. The concept of a plurality of structures dominated our search. Thus, the research program became not one but many separate studies.[10]

[10] The outlined tasks were undertaken and the total report, "Power and Decision Making in the Crisis of Megalopolis: A Special Focus on Environmental Quality Problems," was mimeographed (Resources for the Future, 1970). The six parts of the report include: Part I: Urban Organizational and Leadership Influence Pattern in Megalopolis, by Delbert C. Miller; Part II: Environmental Quality Pattern of Organizational and Leadership Influence in Megalopolis, by James L. Barfoot and Paul Planchon; Part III: Linkage Structure of Urban and Environmental Quality Organizations and Leaders in Megalopolis, by Miller, Barfoot and Planchon; Part IV: The Delaware River Basin as a Water Quality Management Region, by Barfoot and Planchon; Part V: Leadership Perceptions and Behavior Focused on Water Resources Problems in the Delaware River Basin, by Planchon; Part VI: Decision-Making Processes Among Parties at Interest in a Water Pollution Issue Within the Delaware River Basin, by Barfoot.

END PRODUCTS

It was not believed that this would be the definitive sociological study of Megalopolis.[11] It was to be a first—a probe in which, as oil geologists might say, six holes were to be drilled in a wildcat field. The sociological probes are the six regional and subregional power structures and their linkage patterns (as described in footnote 9). The expected payoff is not a tangible product, but a showing that power interrelationships within a region constitute the base for social action. Among the possible goals for such social knowledge might be a better establishment of representative boards and commissions to study and administer social problem areas within Megalopolis, the use of more efficient channels to secure legislation or needed regulation, and finally an awakening of a community consciousness in Megalopolis. If regional problems are ever to be administered on a regional basis, the citizens of Megalopolis must become aware that they live in a region. They do not now have that sense of regional community. Gottman demonstrated that the economic base exists; this study should show that an embryonic social base is in being.

At first it was not recognized that the search for interactional patterns among organizations was to lead into a new field of study—associational interaction. Nor did we recognize that the sociometric data found in acquaintance and working relations among leaders would offer an opportunity to apply new computer programs and enable us to find clique relations and intercity ties among a large sampling of leaders. These discoveries have added some happy by-products.

THE IDENTIFICATION AND LINKAGE OF KEY AND TOP INFLUENTIAL URBAN-ORIENTED LEADERS OF MEGALOPOLIS WHOSE CONCERN IS WITH URBAN AND ENVIRONMENTAL QUALITY PROBLEMS

It was assumed that a network of interaction would be found among leaders oriented toward urban problems from Boston to Washington; that they would know each other; and that they would manifest a pattern of contact and working relationships both in their professional lives and in their civic activities.

The first task was to identify the influential leaders and then to discover those aspects of behavior that would reveal the extent to which a linkage pattern might exist. A number of questions presented themselves:

[11] Gottman reports that he spent twenty years of study on his investigation of the economic and geographic character of Megalopolis. See Gottman, *The Megalopolis.*

What are the urban problem interests of the influential leaders? What problems are they actually working on? What priority do problems of environmental quality receive?

Do leaders know one another in their own cities and in various major cities of the region?

Are leaders working together on urban problems from Boston to New York to Philadelphia, Baltimore, and Washington, D.C.?

Who are the key sociometric leaders that top leaders of Megalopolis nominate as those who could best represent the Boston to Washington urban region in the shaping of urban policy and programming for the region?

How do top and key leaders function in decision-making processes? These kinds of questions led to the construction of test hypotheses.

Test Hypotheses

Three test hypotheses have been chosen for presentation from the seven hypotheses in the study. They provide a good view of the efforts made to find an influence network in Megalopolis.

1. Influential urban-oriented leaders will place their highest priorities of personal interest and activity on unemployment, housing, and education and their lowest priority on environmental problems of air pollution, water pollution, and solid wastes.

This hypothesis rests on the belief that there is vigorous competition among urban problems for the attention, funds, time, and energy of leaders. Influential leaders must choose among demands upon time for their allocation of effort to the many problems of public life. Even a minimal list must include such problems as air pollution, control of lawlessness and crime, improvement of public education, water pollution, transport, traffic and parking, solid wastes, housing and urban renewal, roads and streets, land use planning and preservation of open spaces, unemployment and poverty, and race relations. Many leaders are busy with additional problems such as improvement of local government and governmental relations generally, family welfare, drug addiction, student protests, juvenile delinquency, and mental health. The interest and activity given to environmental quality by influential leaders is important for this study since it is assumed that the interest and support of these generalized influential leaders is vital to making progress toward the improvement of environmental quality. Roughly the equation may be: The higher the interest and activity of key influentials, the greater the legislation, funding, and activity given to environmental quality efforts.

2. Business, labor, government, religious, and civic leaders will differ significantly in their acquaintance and contact, with the greatest to least acquaintance and contact ranging from business, civic, political, religious, to labor leaders.

This hypothesis is derived from observation of participation in organizations and the character of leader behavior in communities. Business leaders have more personal wealth, corporate expense accounts, policy support for time spent in civic affairs, and freedom of movement away from their offices. These facts predispose those business leaders who wish for civic participation to engage in it more actively than all other leaders. It is believed that civic leaders rank second because the broad scope of their contacts is encouraged by the nature of democratic participation in community organizations. Political, religious, and labor leaders are believed to be restricted to limited areas of movement because of many factors related to their jobs and the cultural definitions of their roles.

The acquaintance and contact pattern has a number of dimensions. There is the extent to which a leader's acquaintance extends across the local community through business, labor, political-governmental, religious, and civic leaders. This may be thought of as the lateral dimension of acquaintance. A vertical dimension is represented by a leader's acquaintance and contact in his own occupational group from Boston to Washington, D.C. An oblique dimension may be seen as the residual: i.e., all other contacts that he has with leaders outside his own community and his own occupational group. If he is truly a citizen of Megalopolis, the most convincing dimension is this residual gradient. These dimensions may be pictured for a Boston business leader as shown in figure 10.3. It is believed that all three dimensions are intercorrelated.

Contacts can be classified as general, i.e., any contacts occurring in occupational and social life, or they can be specifically denoted as those con-

Cities \ Leaders	Business	Labor	Political-governmental	Clergy and religious	Civic and civil rights
Boston	Lateral *A* (Communal)				
New York	Vertical *B* (Occupational)	Oblique Residual *C* (Megalopolis)			
Philadelphia					
Baltimore					
Washington					

Figure 10.3. The three dimensions of leader acquaintance and contact in Megalopolis (a heuristic diagram drawn to represent a Boston business leader).

tacts resulting from work on urban problems. In the following study both types of contact are analyzed. However, to simplify the analysis, a single acquaintance and contact score has been derived for each respondent according to the manner in which he checks each of the 200 key leaders on the list. Similarly, the dimensions of his response have been reduced to two by combining his vertical or occupational score with his oblique residual score so that one "Megalopolis acquaintance-contact score" is found and one "local community acquaintance-contact score" may be isolated and the two compared.

3. There is a significant variation in acquaintance and contact among leaders in the major urban areas, with the greatest to least acquaintance and contact ranging from New York, Washington, Philadelphia, Boston, to Baltimore. New York, the largest city with high remunerative opportunities, has a selective influence in drawing key leaders to it. Moreover, leaders from other cities frequently visit these leaders in New York. Washington, D.C., as the political capital, is the center in which political and labor leaders of high repute are located. Philadelphia is in third position because of its size and its nearness to both New York and Washington. Boston is believed to be in fourth rank as a contact point because of its relative isolation. It lies to the north, about 230 miles from any other major city in Megalopolis. Baltimore, whose position is advantageous, simply does not have the historic, political, cultural, or even economic attractions which enable it to attract or develop key leaders.[12]

Research Design Decisions

The Decision to Study Business, Labor, Government, Religious, and Civic Leaders. A number of decisions were made in arriving at the final research design for a test of the hypotheses. Perhaps the most important was a decision to use the National Urban Coalition as a model in selecting leaders from the five groupings—business, labor, government, religion, civic and

---

[12] Other hypotheses tested were: the degree of acquaintance and contact of a leader with other leaders is directly related to his nomination ranking as a potential regional policy maker; the policy making ranking of leaders chosen for their ability and influence in shaping urban policy will reflect a patterned institutional power ranking with business, government, labor, civic, and religious sectors exhibited in the order named; there is a relationship between the degree of acquaintance and contact of leaders and their perception of decision making as monolithic or pluralistic; business, labor, government, religious, and civic leaders will differ significantly in their contact patterns with governmental and voluntary organizations on the local, state, and national levels of activity which they regard as most rewarding, and in their ranking of leaders with whom they have established contact and who they regard as most valuable for their own contacts, and finally in modes of contact for civic policy making.

DELBERT C. MILLER

civil rights.[13] This decision established the range and focal points of attention. It also promised to make available immediately an excellent list of
leaders from the rosters of newly formed or forming urban coalitions in
Washington, Baltimore, New York, Philadelphia, and Boston. In the
decision to select leaders in these five groupings, it was decided again to
follow the model of the National Urban Coalition and to omit all federal
officeholders in the cabinet, all senators, and all congressmen. These were
omitted by the Urban Coalition because the leaders of the organization
saw their task as one of marshaling influence that would be brought to
bear on these government leaders. Similarly, it seemed that the same purpose underlay this study, that is, to find the leaders who were influential in
marshaling influence to press for remediation of urban problems. The
omission of the federal legislative and cabinet officials did not extend to
other government officers. Mayors, governors, city, and county officials
(and federal officers in Washington, D.C.) were eligible for nomination as
influential leaders in the various cities.

*The Decision to Focus on the Metropolitan Areas of Boston, New York,
Philadelphia, Baltimore, and Washington, D.C.* The decision to focus on
the metropolitan areas around the five major cities gave attention to the
centers in which most respondents identified activity. This produced some
problems because outstanding leaders were often not mentioned if they
came from Hartford, Camden, Wilmington, New Haven, Providence, and
other similar smaller but significant cities of Megalopolis. Respondents
would say, "But he's not in the city." In selected cases, I have included some
leaders who suffered from such lack of identity in order to represent the
"area."[14]

The Decision to Study Leadership Interaction, Linkage, and Goals. Another important decision was made gradually but definitely. It became
obvious that this study of leadership interaction should not be considered
as sharply defining "a single regional power structure." As the research
progressed and the more it became clear that Megalopolis was regarded by
respondents rather as a geographic and social place than as a viable community, the less a regional power structure seemed possible. Perhaps an
embryonic structure, one that could be marshaled, would be feasible.
At any rate, in the beginning stage it was decided to focus attention on

[13] This decision was made on two counts: (a) to provide a representative range of
leaders considered vital to full community support of policy and programs; and (b) to
avoid the excessive overrepresentation of business leaders that often develops in the
use of the reputational technique (at least in the United States).
[14] Notably Crawford Greenawalt of Wilmington, Delaware; Kingman Brewster of
New Haven, Connecticut; and Frank Licht, governor of Rhode Island.

359

leadership interaction, linkage, and leadership goals. If a pattern emerged, and respondents could agree on key leaders for regional programming and policy making, a regional power structure prototype could be considered.

The Decision to Construct an Urban Influential Leader Matrix. A decision to construct a matrix of urban influential leaders was an outcome of the earlier decisions. Once the five leadership groupings of the five major metropolitan areas were established, a matrix of twenty-five cells was envisioned. This matrix, table 10.1, shows the numbers of leaders chosen to occupy each cell. These numbers are chosen on the basis of a number of arbitrary decisions. First, a minimum of thirty key leaders was considered necessary to represent a metropolitan area.

As size of metropolitan area was considered an important variable, the New York area was given a maximum representation. Philadelphia, roughly one-half the size of New York, was given one-half as many leader spaces as New York. Washington, although small compared with these two giants, was given a number of spaces equal to Philadelphia because of its concentration of labor leaders. Boston and Baltimore were each given the minimum of thirty spaces because of their smaller sizes.

The largest total representation of leaders in any grouping was given to civic and civil rights leaders because their grouping is very broad, encompassing educators, civil rights leaders, association and foundation leaders, and social welfare leaders. In New York, business leaders were given a larger representation because of its high concentration of powerful business leaders. These decisions yielded a total of 200 leader spaces. The plan then was to locate those urban oriented leaders in Megalopolis who would be characterized by ability: (a) to work with other business, labor, governmental, religious, and civic leaders; (b) to commit themselves to the work required; and (c) to be able and willing to influence others. A brief description of this search for leaders will be made after a final design decision is reported.

Table 10.1. Urban Influential Leader Matrix

Metropolitan areas	Business	Labor	Political-govern-mental	Clergy and religious	Civic and civil rights	Total
New York	20	10	10	10	20	70
Philadelphia	10	5	5	5	10	35
Boston	5	5	5	5	10	30
Baltimore	5	5	5	5	10	30
Washington	5	10	5	5	10	35
N =	45	35	30	30	60	200

The Decision to Provide a Replicated Population of Leaders. The cost
and effort needed to provide a replicated population of leaders appeared
relatively small. In the search for the most influential leaders it was obvious
that many leaders would be named and those who received a lower number
of nominations could easily be included in the research inquiries of the
study. The plan was to fill the same influential leader matrix with its 200
places with leaders who received fewer votes. These leaders would in all
probability be of great influence because they would be drawn from large
reservoirs of leadership. In order to maintain a proper perspective on the
leader populations, the first group winning the greater consensus was called
key leaders; the second group, top leaders. These names will be used
throughout to designate the two influential leader populations.
   Altogether 400 leaders were sought and similar research inquiries made
of them. The two populations of key and top leaders taken separately provided opportunities for a replication in the tests of the hypotheses. The
possibility of combining both groups into a single population of influential
leaders was also available. This advantage of directing a future questionnaire to 400 rather than only 200 was considered an important asset. If the
rate of questionnaire returns were very low, every case would be especially
important.

*The Decision to Interview Judges in the Major Cities and to Search for
Consensus on Influential Leaders.* A long documentary search for leaders
was carried out. However, a fundamental demand placed on the design was
that interviewing would be conducted in the five major urban areas to obtain data best secured by this method. The senior investigator lived successively in Washington, D.C. (3 months), New York (3 months), Philadelphia (2 months), and Boston (1 month). Only Baltimore was omitted
as a place of residence. It was reached from Washington, D.C.

The Decision to Use a Questionnaire to Collect Leadership Data. The
decision to use a questionnaire was made with great trepidation. The rate
of return from such busy and influential leaders could not be predicted as
high. On the contrary, the safest prediction was that it would be low—
perhaps as low as 15 per cent. On the basis of 400 questionnaires, this
would furnish 60 replies. Such a sample of the population might be biased
and the results subject to considerable sample error, but the data would
still be valuable for ascertaining the existence of communication and contact networks.
   In the first stage of the study design it was hoped that the influential
leaders might all be reached by interview. Later, it was hoped that some
might be reached by interview and others by questionnaire. When the re-

search study was under way, experience showed that the interview had some marked disadvantages, particularly with regard to time consumption. It soon became obvious that one researcher could not carry out the study in the available time by interviewing all of the influential leaders. The effort to secure consensus on a list of leaders by interviewing judges was a demanding effort in and of itself. Hence the decision was made to use a mail questionnaire procedure.

The use of the questionnaire mailed to top influentials proved to be a very happy decision and the results will be recorded in the following section. Suffice it to say here that the questionnaire fits the habits of these busy leaders. They can fill it out when they can fit it in to their workday, week, or month. It can be reported that it is easier to get a questionnaire in and out of the office door of a top influential than it is for a researcher to get in and out of that same door.

Execution of the Research Design

The major steps in execution of the research design were: (a) the identification of 400 most influential urban oriented leaders in the five major metropolitan areas; (b) the preparation and mailing of the questionnaire, and subsequently obtaining returns; and (c) the analysis of results. Each of these steps will be discussed.

The Identification of 400 Top Influential Leaders: The Acquisition of Nominees. The identification of leaders began at the very beginning of the study by a documentary search supplemented by interviewing. These operations included:

1. Reviewing and evaluating Easterners who were nominated as top national leaders in 1953 in Floyd Hunter's study.[15] The eastern leaders were checked and those alive in 1968 were listed. These were then rated by selected judges for their current influence. Those nominated as most influential leaders were set out as the Hunter follow-up list.

2. Securing lists of eastern members, especially board members, of the National Industrial Conference Board, the Committee for Economic Development, and the Business Advisory Council. Hunter wrote:

> After concluding the more extensive study, I feel that the membership lists of the National Industrial Conference Board, the Committee for Economic Development, and the Business Advisory Council provide good starting points for anyone interested in a quick and partial rundown of national leadership. These boards are highly selective in recruiting members and

[15] Hunter, *Top Leadership, U.S.A.*, pp. 196–198.

they represent a stable cross-section of top business leadership. They are made up of persons who have access to each other and who have channels to persons in other power networks of civic, professional, political, and religious leadership.[16]

3. Securing lists of board members of the National Urban Coalition, Urban America, and the National Alliance of Businessmen. These leaders were known to have been selected by other top leaders because of both their influence and willingness to work on urban problems. An operating list was compiled of eastern leaders of these organizations.

4. Listing of leaders on U.S. government commissions such as those on urban problems, civil rights, civil disorders, sources of violence, equal opportunity, and intergovernmental relations. It was known that these commissions had been staffed by many top influentials and by their service had committed themselves to urban oriented activities. Eastern members were identified and separated for an operating list.

5. Securing a list of the richest persons in the United States. Eastern members were identified.

6. Securing a list of the leaders of the twenty-five top corporations. Most of these were found to be in New York City.

7. Examining a list of the largest political contributors and identifying eastern members.

8. Listing eastern trustees of the major foundations (Ford, Carnegie, and Rockefeller).

9. Evaluating a list of national labor leaders. Three judges evaluated all labor leaders with the Executive Council and staff of AFL-CIO for their influence and activity with urban problems. Most of them were in Washington, D.C.

10. Evaluating, by three judges, a list of influential eastern educators. Initial lists were derived from writings by Theodore White and Daniel S. Greenberg.[17]

11. Evaluating, by three judges, a list of influential civil rights leaders.

12. Assembling a list of leaders in social welfare.

13. Listing mayors of all the major cities of Megalopolis and governors of all constituent states for subsequent evaluation.

14. By November 1968 lists of members in the Urban Coalitions of Washington, D.C., Baltimore, Philadelphia, and New York were available. A committee for the formation of the Boston Coalition was in existence. Members of these organizations were regarded as having the kind of leadership influence sought by the study, and so were added.

[16] Ibid., p. 33.
[17] White, "The Action Intellectuals," *Life*, vol. 62, no. 23 (June 9, 1967), pp. 43–78; Greenberg, *The Politics of Pure Science* (New York: New American Library, 1967).

These combined operations produced a large number of names. Persons listed in two or more connections were given weight in preparing a starter list for judges. Leaders were then grouped into five classifications: business, labor, political-government, religious, civic and civil rights, for each of the five metropolitan areas. Thus, step by step, names were assembled to correspond to each of the twenty-five cells in the Influential Leadership Matrix.

Final Evaluation of Leaders by Selected Judges. Judges were selected on the basis of knowledge and range of contact. An ideal judge was one who knew all of the persons he was asked to judge and could add names of influential leaders who were not yet on the list. Judges were drawn from the following sources: national and local Urban Coalition officers, association and foundation officers in labor, civil rights, education, business, government, and religion, company public relations and urban affairs officials, and retired influentials. In each city a panel of eight to ten judges was asked to evaluate the most influential civic leaders. Each judge used an adaptation of the influential leader matrix. Figure 10.4 is an Acquaintance Check List of Leaders in Megalopolis. This figure has been checked by an active civic leader of Philadelphia who is a top influential in the study. He was asked to "check boxes in which you feel you can recognize some of the most important leaders who are active in urban affairs," and was told that lists of leaders had been prepared and that he might be asked to evaluate the influence of leaders in any of the boxes that he checked.

The checking of this matrix gave some valuable information about each judge. It indicated his scope of acquaintance and contact. The instrument has now been titled an Acquaintanceship Scope. It provided the first data about the leadership nets existing from Boston to Washington. The pat-

---

Please check boxes in which you feel you can recognize some of the most important leaders who are active in urban affairs.

Metropolitan region of:	Business leaders	Labor leaders	Political-governmental leaders	Clergy and religious leaders	Civic and civil rights leaders
Washington	✓	✓	✓		✓
Baltimore			✓		✓
Philadelphia	✓	✓	✓	✓	✓
New York	✓		✓		✓
Boston	✓		✓		✓

Figure 10.4. Acquaintanceship Scope for Megalopolis of a Philadelphia civic leader.

terned interactions of leaders in Megalopolis became more apparent as various judges marked the Acquaintanceship Scope. Diversity of pattern was also revealed. The responses indicate that some judges become acquainted only with leaders in their own communities. This is no small chore in the large cities under study. If there is an extension of acquaintance outside the community, it occurs generally in the occupational grouping shared by the respondent, and last in various categories outside his occupation.

The Acquaintanceship Scope can be scored: if one point is given for each box, a maximum score of twenty-five is possible. Thirty-five judges received scores ranging from three to twenty-five, with an average score of thirteen. This means that the average judge had considerable acquaintance outside his own community.[18]

Figure 10.4 indicates that the judge regards *himself as able* to evaluate seventeen groups of leaders in various cities. The researcher has prepared lists for all twenty-five cells and can decide in which of the seventeen groups he wishes this judge to make his evaluation. The aim is to find out if there is consensus on names and the researcher will ask the judge to help where a growing consensus has not yet been achieved. He may ask him to rate categories outside his own community if he wishes to have a regional perspective on certain leaders. To illustrate, let us suppose the Philadelphia civic leader were asked to name five political and governmental leaders of Philadelphia who could best represent Megalopolis in the shaping of urban policy and programs for the region. He would be handed a list similar to that in Table 10.2 and asked to evaluate the names he finds and to add others if he wished. He is given a very specific criterion: "Ideally a leader should be able: (a) to work with other business, labor, governmental, religious, and civic leaders; (b) to commit himself to the work required; and (c) to be able and willing to influence others." He is urged to add names if he feels the ablest persons are not on the list. If he does add names these will be carried on all subsequent lists put before other judges. Thus, the list is refined and evaluated. The civic leader may be given the sixteen other lists of leaders with whom he has marked himself as being acquainted. What is actually done depends on time available to the judge and the needs of the research at this stage.

In this study two months of documentary search and six months of interviewing brought a rough consensus on the 400 names that became the re-

[18] The instrument could add the dimension of contact. The range of acquaintance and contact is an important factor in the efficiency of the personnel of many corporations, government organizations, etc. Some respondents told me that their own scope was limited but that the staff reporting to him could easily pool a collective score of twenty-five.

Table 10.2. List of Political and Governmental Leaders
(Metropolitan Region of Philadelphia)

If you were asked to nominate the leaders who could best represent the Atlantic urban region (Megalopolis: Boston–New York–Philadelphia–Baltimore–Washington, D.C.) in the shaping of urban policy and program for the region, which persons on the list would you choose? Ideally, a leader should be able (a) to work with other business, labor, governmental, religious, and civic leaders; (b) to commit himself to the work required; and (c) be able and willing to influence others. Add other names if you wish.

Vote for Five:
Circle Numbers of Your Choices

1. MARK SHEDD
2. ED BACON
3. JAMES H. J. TATE
4. JOSEPH CLARK
5. RAYMOND P. SHAFER
6. RICHARDSON DILWORTH
7. RUSSELL W. PETERSON
8. PAUL D'ORTONA
9. THOMAS MCINTOSH
10. THE REV. HENRY NICHOLS
11. WILLIAM GREEN
12. WILLIAM BARRATT
13. ARLEN SPECTER
14. FRANK RIZZO
15. RAYMOND BRODERICK
16. HERBERT FINEMAN
17. THATCHER LONGSTRETH
18. PAT PATTERSON

search population. The first 200 names have the highest consensus and have been called key leaders; the second 200 names have good consensus, but not the highest, and are called top leaders.

The Preparation and Mailing of the Questionnaire. The questionnaire was designed so that systematic data could be collected to test the seven hypotheses previously stated. The questionnaire and accompanying letter are attached as Appendix A. The cover sheet on the questionnaire is a map of Megalopolis showing the major urban axis that runs in a straight line through Boston, New York, Philadelphia, Baltimore, and Washington. Note that four questions are posed in order to provide interest and motivation to the respondent.

The questionnaire itself is constructed in five parts: part 1 seeks the urban problem interest and activity pattern of each leader; part 2 is a leadership acquaintance and contact index in which each of the 200 key leaders is listed and all respondents (key and top leaders) are asked to check each name according to their own acquaintance and contact with the key leaders; part 3 is a nomination roster in which each respondent lists twenty-five leaders "who could best represent the Boston to Washington urban region in the shaping of urban policy and programming for the region"; part 4 is a survey of contacts as each respondent checks the occupational groupings and cities in rank order of contact; part 5 contains items relative to patterns of policy making.

The questionnaire was mailed to the 400 leaders in mid-April, 1969, with the covering letter. A follow-up letter was sent two weeks later. A second follow-up was sent in mid-May with a second questionnaire. One hundred of the 200 key leaders responded (a 50 per cent return) with the last return arriving July 2. Seventy-eight of the 200 top leaders responded (a 39 per cent return). The final response of 44.5 per cent for all leaders (key and top) is a very good return for a mail questionnaire and is especially gratifying since the people involved are among those with the heaviest responsibilities. Some leaders were out of the country. Some had retired and refused to reply because they no longer held the position or were at the address to which the questionnaire had been sent. Some mailing addresses could not be found. Twenty-five letters explaining why they could not or would not respond were received from persons who did not respond to the questionnaire. In this group, most said they had a standing prohibition against answering any questionnaires because of the press of duties. Furthermore, in interpreting the returns of these leaders it must be remembered that it was necessary for them to provide the information personally. No secretary or assistant could do an accurate job and there is evidence that each respondent checked the questionnaire personally.

There is every indication that the significant features of the questionnaire which facilitated return were: first, the sponsorship listed as Eastern Leadership Study directed by Delbert C. Miller, Professor of Sociology and Business Administration, Indiana University and funded by Resources for the Future, Inc., Washington, D.C.; second, the format using an interesting map, introductory research questions, and a carefully constructed letter explaining the purpose; and third, the listing of the names (in the questionnaire) of all key leaders. This last feature provides an interesting exhibit, because very rarely does a questionnaire recipient know the names of other persons in the sample. In this case each of the 200 key leaders saw his name and the names of others who were regarded as his influential peers. The 50 per cent response of key leaders can be compared to the 39 per cent response of top leaders whose names were not listed and who responded only to listed key leaders.[19]

---

[19] I now believe that listing the names of respondents may be a valuable adjunct to questionnaires, perhaps adding as much as 15 per cent to the returns.

Ranking of the 178 returns to the questionnaire by occupational groups and by the five major cities was as follows:

Ranking hierarchy of questionnaire returns by occupational grouping	Ranking hierarchy of questionnaire returns by city
Clergy and religious leaders 57 per cent	Baltimore 70 per cent
Labor leaders 51 per cent	Philadelphia 57 per cent
Civic and civil rights leaders 44 per cent	Boston 42 per cent
Business leaders 39 per cent	Washington 40 per cent
Political-governmental leaders 33 per cent	New York 28 per cent

The data were tested in numerous ways to check for possible bias that might have been introduced by nonreturns. The three successive waves of return following each of the three mailings to both key leaders and top leaders were analyzed for significance of differences on such items as urban interest and activity patterns and acquaintance and contact scores. No differences of statistical significance (5 per cent level) were found between the first and second wave or between the first and third wave for either the key leaders or top leaders. This finding of no difference is plausible since the sample is a highly selective one. Only the most influential leaders survived the ratings of judges on the criterion presented and these were the ones who received the questionnaire. Nonrespondents compare with respondents on types of positions held, with the exception that many of the most powerful governmental leaders did not respond. I received many letters from such persons (or their secretaries) telling me that they never answered any questionnaire as a standing policy.

A resurvey of the urban problem interest and activity of all key and top leaders, made in the summer of 1970, will provide yet another opportunity to check for bias. Each successive wave will again be submitted to careful examination for possible bias. Based on all results to date, bias can be regarded as minimal.[20]

Test of Hypotheses—Findings. Hypothesis 1. Influential urban-oriented leaders will place their highest priorities of personal interest and activity on unemployment, housing, and education and their lowest priority on environmental problems of air pollution, water pollution, and solid wastes.

[20] An analysis of a new sample taken from the returned responses by random selection and ordered according to the rates assembled in the original urban influential leader matrix (figure 10.3) is being undertaken to provide an additional test of bias.

DELBERT C. MILLER

The 100 key leaders and the 78 top leaders who responded to the questionnaire were presented with the urban problem interest and activity patterns check list (see table 10.3 and Appendix, page 387). The interest check requested listing of multiple interests if the respondent wished to record more than one interest; the activity record asked for the one problem on which he was currently working most intensively. These instructions were generally followed although sometimes more than one problem was marked. The list of problems itself usually was comprehensive, but some respondents did write in their interest and activity as:

> Reduction of drug abuse
> Family planning
> Economic development of ghetto
> Private university education
> Child welfare
> Creation of a new value system
> Labor problems
> Developing a new city
> Black participation in decisions that affect them.

Table 10.3. Urban Problem Interest and Activity Patterns of Civic Leaders in the Boston to Washington Urban Region

I have most interest in		I am currently working hardest on		
Num- ber	Per cent	Num- ber	Per cent	Urban problems
27	5	4	1	1. Air pollution
49	9	14	5	2. Control of lawlessness and crime
82	14	42	14	3. Improvement of public education
15	3	4	1	4. Water pollution
28	5	12	4	5. Improvement of transport, traffic movement, and parking
14	3	2	1	6. Solid wastes (garbage, litter, and dumps)
98	17	47	16	7. Improvement or elimination of poor housing; rebuilding of cities
12	2	3	1	8. Improvement and maintenance of roads and streets
22	4	10	3	9. Planning and zoning of land; preservation (or improvement) of park and other natural areas; beautification
93	16	65	22	10. Unemployment and poverty
100	18	64	22	11. Race relations
21	4	30	10	12. Other (please specify)
561	100	277	100	Totals

369

Table 10.3 reports on the frequency and percentages of response for all 178 key and top leaders on urban problem interest and activity patterns. The complete questionnaire is shown in Appendix A. Leader interest is centered on race relations (18 per cent); improvement or elimination of poor housing, rebuilding of cities (17 per cent); unemployment and poverty (16 per cent); improvement of public education (14 per cent); and control of lawlessness and crime (9 per cent). These five interests account for 74 per cent of all urban problem interests. Activity patterns parallel these interests. Environmental quality interests as represented by air pollution (5 per cent), water pollution (3 per cent), and solid wastes (3 per cent) rank relatively low in the scale of interests. Although the total interest in environmental quality is 11 per cent, much of this is duplication of interest by a relatively few leaders. The activity pattern reveals this since only 3 per cent of the work on problems is divided among the major environmental quality interests (1 per cent to air pollution, 1 per cent to water pollution, and 1 per cent to solid wastes).

The question arises as to possible differences among types of leaders. Table 10.4 shows the frequency and percentage response of the key and top leaders who indicated interest in environmental quality problems: air pollution, water pollution, and solid wastes. Both groups of leaders are reported according to their affiliation as business, labor, political-governmental, religious, and civic. The final tally combines the frequencies of both the key and top leaders.

There is wide variation between the key and top leaders in some of the cells, but with such low frequencies sampling error is very high. It would be unwarranted to draw conclusions on differences shown between key and top leaders. It is almost as risky to search for a pattern among the occupational groupings. Yet the data do suggest that political-governmental, business, and labor leaders have the highest interest in environmental quality problems and religious and civic leaders the lowest. Moreover, interest ranks highest for air pollution, followed by water pollution and solid wastes as we compare all occupational groups. When it comes to working hardest on the problems, activity drops to a 1 per cent level for each of the three problems.

Hypothesis 2. Business, labor, government, religious, and civic leaders will differ significantly in their acquaintance and contact, with the greatest to least acquaintance ranging from business, civic, political, religious, to labor leaders.

This hypothesis may be tested by the scores received by key leaders from both key and top leaders as respondents checked the leadership acquaintance and working relationship index. Figure 10.5 shows a part of the questionnaire with the instructions given to the respondent. The part shown

370

Table 10.4. Environmental Quality Interest of 100 Key and 78 Top Leaders
(Problems of air pollution, water pollution, solid wastes)

Problem interest		Business leaders		Labor leaders		Political-governmental leaders		Clergy and religious leaders		Civic and civil rights leaders	
		f	Per cent	f	Per cent	f	Per cent	f	Per cent	f	Per cent
Air pollution	Key	4/23	17.4	3/18	16.7	4/13	30.8	4/20	20.0	4/26	15.4
	Top	2/12	16.7	3/18	16.7	0/7	0.0	0/14	0.0	3/27	11.1
	Both	6/35	17.1	6/36	16.7	4/20	20.0	4/34	11.8	7/53	13.2
								All totals		27/178	15.2
Water pollution	Key	1/23	4.3	3/18	16.7	3/13	23.1	2/20	10.0	1/26	3.8
	Top	1/12	8.3	3/18	16.7	0/7	0.0	0/14	0.0	1/27	3.7
	Both	2/35	5.7	6/36	16.7	3/20	15.0	2/34	5.9	2/53	3.8
								All totals		15/178	8.4
Solid wastes	Key	1/23	4.3	2/18	11.1	4/13	30.8	1/20	5.0	0/26	0.0
	Top	3/12	25.0	1/18	5.6	0/7	0.0	0/14	0.0	2/27	7.4
	Both	4/35	11.4	3/36	8.3	4/20	20.0	1/34	2.9	2/53	3.8
								All totals		16/178	9.0

Please look at the leaders listed. All live and work in the Boston to Washington urban region. Please indicate by (√) your acquaintance and civic activity with each. All information is confidential and each person will be recorded by code number.

(Note: The researcher is trying to discover the degree of acquaintance and contact within and between such leadership groups as business, labor, political, religious, and civic leaders in the metropolitan area and the Atlantic urban region.)

						Contact
		Acquaintance				Worked with him on a committee or project dealing with urban problems during the past 3 years
Name of leader	0 Don't know	1 Have heard of	2 Know little (reading or con-tact)	3 Know well (reading or con-tact)	4 Know socially (visit at home or personal contact)	I have had business, civic, or social contacts during past 3 years	
Boston leaders (business)							
1. Robert Slater							
2. Paul C. Cabot							
3. Eli Goldstone							
4. John M. Fox							
5. Roger P. Sonnabend							

Figure 10.5. Leadership acquaintance and working relationship index.

includes five business leaders in the Boston area. Respondents are asked to check their degree of acquaintance and whether they had business, civic, or social contacts during the past three years, and/or had worked with the leader on a committee or project dealing with urban problems during the past three years. An acquaintance score is derived from weights of zero to four as shown, ranging respectively from "don't know" to "know socially." A contact score is similarly derived, with business, social, or civic contact given a score of three, and an urban committee or project contact also given a score of three. The index is the sum of the two scores. Thus, a given leader may secure a maximum score of ten from any leader who knows him well and has both types of contact with him.[21]

[21] It is recognized that the most rigorous criteria are probably "know socially," "had contacts," and "worked with him on a committee or project." Current computer analysis is being made with newly devised sociometric programs to identify possible clique relations and intercity ties using these "hard" criteria. The results to date show patterns existing in depth across Megalopolis.

The total score will show the activity pattern of different occupational groups of leaders. It is assumed that leaders with high scores have a better chance and those with lower scores less chance to participate in decision making.

It is also assumed, as explained earlier, that three dimensions of acquaintance and contact may be located: the local community dimension; the occupational dimension; and the residual dimension (other Megalopolis contacts outside one's occupational group and outside the local community). In the following analysis the occupational and residual dimensions have been combined to simplify the analysis. Occupational groups will be compared for their mean acquaintance and contact scores in their local community and in the rest of Megalopolis. Thus, the two scores separate the "localite" and the "Megalopolite" dimensions.

An analysis of the relationship between the two dimensions shows that for key leaders a correlation of 0.33 exists. This indicates that their Megalopolis acquaintance-contact score bears a low but definite relationship to their local score. For top leaders a lower correlation of 0.17 indicates a very slight relationship between their local and Megalopolis acquaintance-contact scores. These two correlations provide the first real indication that the two populations do vary in their interactional attributes. Table 10.5 shows more clearly the difference in local and Megalopolis acquaintance-contact scores of the key and top leaders. Key leaders consistently outscore top leaders in both local community and Megalopolis acquaintance-contact (with one exception). The key leader population will be regarded as a more accurate determination of the interactions being examined. The top leaders constitute a control sample to ascertain if similar patterns are replicated by the two samples. The combined sample presents a further possibility of checking results, as sample size is increased by combining the two populations.

Table 10.5. Mean Local Community and Megalopolis Acquaintance and Contact Scores for Business, Political, Religious, and Civic Leaders as Reported by the Key Leaders, the Top Leaders, and the Combined Key and Top Leaders

Leaders' scores on local and Megalopolis acquaintance and contact	Mean local community acquaintance-contact scores			Mean Megalopolis acquaintance-contact scores		
	Key leaders	Top leaders	Key and top	Key leaders	Top leaders	Key and top
Civic	174	158	166	177	158	165
Political	170	155	164	160	83	133
Business	169	159	165	129	112	123
Labor	163	147	132	137	150	148
Religious	138	114	128	125	83	109

Table 10.5 demonstrates that the original hypothesis on the rank ordering of leaders from business, civic, political, religious, and labor is not
appropriate. On the contrary, the new ranking of key leaders for local and
Megalopolis dimensions of acquaintance and contact show two different
orders, as is shown below.

Ranking by local community acquaintance-contact	Ranking by Megalopolis acquaintance-contact
1. Civic and civil rights leaders (174)	1. Civic and civil rights leaders (177)
2. Political-governmental leaders (170)	2. Political-governmental leaders (160)
3. Business leaders (169)	3. Labor leaders (137)
4. Labor leaders (163)	4. Business leaders (128)
5. Clergy and religious leaders (138)	5. Clergy and religious leaders (125)

The top and bottom rankings—civic and religious leaders—are presented
with strong support for their positions in both local and Megalopolis
dimensions. Business, political, and labor leaders occupy intermediate
positions on both dimensions. If there is a "problem" group in terms of
community and regional perspective it is made up of the religious leaders
who consistently occupy the bottom rung in all the tests. (The top religious
leaders show means of 114 for local community acquaintance-contact and
83 for their Megalopolis score. They are the lowest scores registered by any
leadership group.) A surprising finding is the uneven ranking of business
leaders who have very high scores for local community acquaintance and
contacts but who drop to fourth rank in Megalopolis acquaintance-contact. Civic, political, and labor leaders exhibit higher average scores. This
suggests that key and top business leaders are more closely tied to their
local urban areas than might be imagined.

Hypothesis 3. There is a significant variation in acquaintance and contact
among leaders in the major urban areas, with the greatest to least acquaintance and contact ranging from New York, Washington, Philadelphia, Boston, to Baltimore.

This hypothesis focuses attention on the acquaintance and contact of
leaders between cities. The nature and extent of these ties is crucial to the
determination of bonds by which we can affirm or reject the existence of an
influence network. The questionnaire sought to discover the ties among 200
key leaders and the ties between 200 top leaders with these 200 key leaders.
Each of the 178 respondents had an individual net of connections. For
example, figure 10.6 depicts a net of acquaintance and contact of a Boston

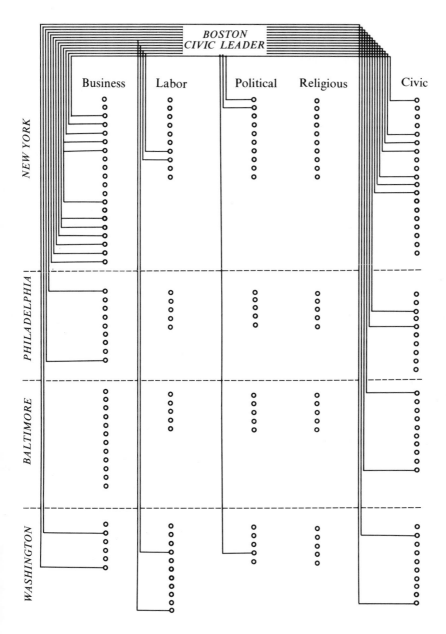

Key: o   A key leader
──────── Contacts with key leaders whether known well or known socially

Figure 10.6. Net of acquaintance and contact of a Boston civic leader with other key leaders in New York, Philadelphia, Baltimore, and Washington.

375

civic leader with other key leaders in New York, Philadelphia, Baltimore, and Washington. The various lines refer to a record made by the respondent indicating key leaders he knew well or socially and with whom he has had business, social, or civic contacts. His local community contacts, although extensive (acquaintance and contact score = 169), are not shown. What is set forth are his ties with business, labor, political, religious, and civic leaders in the cities outside his local community. The Boston civic leader had sixteen contacts with business leaders, twelve with civic leaders, four with labor leaders, and three with political leaders. No outside ties with the key religious leaders are recorded.

There is no question that this leader, with his thirty-five ties to other key leaders in Megalopolis, is coupled to the network that is our major object of study. His total Megalopolis acquaintance and contact score of 302 is an outstanding record, but not unique. One New York civic leader has a Megalopolis acquaintance and contact score of 473. These individual networks demonstrate that there are true citizens of a "Megalopolis," leaders who move in and through the leadership net of other major urban areas which constitute the North Atlantic urban region.

Since it is not feasible to draw and study each individual network, acquaintance and contact scores may best be used for further analysis. These scores do not reveal what kind of acquaintance and contact with leaders is recorded nor from what cities these scores are derived. What they do show is the outreach of leaders from each city to the other four urban areas in Megalopolis. Table 10.6 is a report of mean Megalopolis acquaintance-contact scores for the five major urban areas, first combining the key and top leaders and then separating key leaders only to see how that population compares with the total population of leaders. The order of mean scores for key and top leaders is surprising: Washington, Boston, Philadelphia, New York, Baltimore, from highest to lowest. This order is maintained for key leaders only, except that New York drops to fifth position and Baltimore moves up to fourth. Before accepting these as true means for the

Table 10.6. Mean and Standard Deviations of Megalopolis Acquaintance and Contact Scores for Leaders in the Major Metropolitan Areas

Metropolitan area	Key and top leaders combined			Key leaders only		
	Number	Mean score	Standard deviation	Number	Mean score	Standard deviation
Washington	27	170	68	12	171	75
Boston	28	151	86	20	152	69
Philadelphia	40	132	84	21	149	103
Baltimore	42	114	71	20	147	77
New York	40	115	82	26	129	93

populations, it should be observed that the standard deviations around the means are very high and sample size is relatively small. Tests of significance were carried out on the assumption of heterogeneous variance and allowing for the unequal sample sizes. For the combined sample of key and top leaders, significant differences between means were detected for the leaders in Washington compared with those in Baltimore[22] and New York,[23] with Washington in the highest mean position. When the key leaders only are examined for significant differences, none of the differences reaches the .05 level of significance. In proclaiming a significance to the order of the means, an observer must tread warily. The sampling errors are large and it would be easy to say that no order has been established. However, the rankings between Washington and New York and Washington and Baltimore demand some careful questioning. Why should Washington leaders have the highest Megalopolis acquaintance-contact scores? Is it because Megalopolis leaders come to Washington and become acquainted with Washington area leaders there? This implies a directionality to contact. But Megalopolis leaders do go to New York. Why should the mean score for New York be so low? One possibility is that the very size of New York and its leadership reservoir absorb the energies of its leaders locally. It does lead all other areas in the means for local community acquaintance and contact. And what of Baltimore? Why is it so low? Why are its leaders not drawn into Megalopolis more intensively? The findings and their tentative interpretations invite more research, especially directed at the nature of movement of leaders, their points of contact, and the special influence of a leader's occupation and residence. This cluster of variables awaits further research before a meaningful explanation can be given for each urban area·

An insight can be had from a quite different approach, based on asking the leaders to make a general response to the following statement:

My best to poorest knowledge of leaders and organizations *in the major cities* of the Atlantic urban region can be ranked from 1 through 5 as:

___Boston   ___New York   ___Philadelphia   ___Baltimore
___Washington, D.C.

It should be noted that this statement directs the leader to think about his knowledge of all leaders and organizations in the five major cities. It differs from his own acquaintance-contact scores because they were based on 200 designated leaders. Here he is asked to respond more widely to leaders and organizations as he defines them.

[22] Washington compared with Baltimore gives a value (heterogeneous) of 3.157 (T at .05 = 2.006).
[23] Washington compared with New York gives a value (heterogeneous) of 2.589 (T at .05 = 1.996).

The ranking by respondents of their own knowledge of leaders in the major cities can be seen in table 10.7, which records judgments by key and top business, labor, political, religious, and civic leaders. An observer can begin with Boston and examine the number of leaders who recorded their knowledge of Boston leaders from "know best" to "know least." In the case of Boston, 158 of the 178 leaders responded with 19.6 per cent marking "know best" and 23.4 per cent marking "know least." Since twenty-eight of all the leaders (15.8 per cent) are from Boston, the "know best" is not a surprising figure since in general they are responding to their local acquaintance. What becomes significant is that 23.4 per cent of all responding leaders say they know Boston leaders least. This figure becomes meaningful in comparison with those of other cities. Only 2.5 per cent responded that they know New York leaders least. In Washington it is 10.7 per cent, in Philadelphia the figure rises to 17.4 per cent, in Baltimore to 37.6 per cent. A ranking of leader knowledge by cities can now be established. Cities in which leaders are known least were in the following order:

Baltimore	37.6 per cent
Boston	23.4 per cent
Philadelphia	17.4 per cent
Washington	10.7 per cent
New York	2.5 per cent

If the fourth and fifth rankings are combined to provide a large number who mark "know least," the ranking shifts slightly with the following order and percentages:

Baltimore	61.1 per cent
Philadelphia	56.5 per cent
Boston	43.7 per cent
Washington	24.0 per cent
New York	7.5 per cent

What explains this order? New York and Washington have a prominence that overshadows the other three urban areas. We believe that Boston suffers from isolation because of its distance from the other four major areas. Baltimore seems not to have developed an equivalent economic, social, and cultural position, and this lack perhaps gives it less prominence. Philadelphia is overshadowed and perhaps even cowed by the awesome size and dominance of its near neighbor, New York.

These findings now move understanding one step forward. Directionality of focus is pretty well established. New York and Washington leaders and organizations are better known. Baltimore is least known. Boston and Philadelphia are in intermediate positions with Boston having some physi-

Table 10.7. Frequencies and Percentages of Response by Key and Top Leaders to a Ranking of Leaders and Organizations in the Major Cities of Megalopolis from Best (= 1) to Least (= 5) Knowledge

Key and top leaders (N = 178)	Boston Know best 1	2	3	4	Know least 5	New York Know best 1	2	3	4	Know least 5	Philadelphia Know best 1	2	3	4	Know least 5	Baltimore Know best 1	2	3	4	Know least 5	Washington, D.C. Know best 1	2	3	4	Know least 5
Business (N = 35)	7	8	7	5	5	9	19	2	1	1	10	0	10	12	1	6	1	2	5	19	2	4	11	9	6
Labor (N = 36)	5	0	8	5	8	7	14	4	1	1	3	1	3	12	7	7	3	3	5	9	6	9	10	2	0
Political-governmental (N = 20)	4	2	7	3	3	3	12	1	3	0	4	4	3	7	5	5	1	2	3	8	4	3	6	3	3
Religious (N = 34)	8	2	8	7	5	11	12	6	2	0	4	0	6	7	10	5	3	2	9	10	3	9	10	4	3
Civic (N = 53)	7	5	11	12	16	8	25	15	1	2	13	0	6	21	11	14	2	2	13	20	9	18	16	3	5
Totals	31	17	41	32	37	38	82	28	8	4	34	6	25	59	26	37	10	11	35	56	24	43	53	21	17
Final totals of responses	.......158.......					.......160.......					.......150.......					.......149.......					.......158.......				
Per cent of response	19.6				23.4	23.7				2.5	22.6				17.4	24.8				37.6	15.2				10.7

	Boston Number	Per cent	New York Number	Per cent	Philadelphia Number	Per cent	Baltimore Number	Per cent	Washington, D.C. Number	Per cent
Number and percent of leaders from each city	28	15.8	40	22.4	40	22.4	42	23.6	28	15.8

cal isolation to combat, and Philadelphia is overshadowed by its big neighbor.

Other Findings Relevant to Linkage Among Leaders

1. Key and top leaders say that in civic activity their least frequent contacts are with labor and religious leaders. Their most frequent contacts are inside their own occupational grouping. The next most frequent contacts are with political and civic leaders. Business leaders are in an intermediate position.

2. Key and top leaders say that in civic activity their most valuable contacts are in their own occupational group. Political leaders are generally named as the most valuable group outside their own. Labor leaders are most often placed in the lowest position.

3. The largest number of key and top leaders (42.4 per cent) find it most rewarding in civic activity to work at the local level; another large group (39.2 per cent) says they like all three levels—local, state, and national; the national level with all its prestige only secures a 7.6 per cent response as the single choice. The state level as a single choice is still lower—2 per cent.

4. Leaders show a positive correlation between their Megalopolis acquaintance-contact scores and the number of nominations received for regional representative. An r of .33 was secured between key leaders' Megalopolis acquaintance-contact scores and nominations received from other key leaders. An r of .45 was secured between key leaders' Megalopolis acquaintance-contact scores and nominations received from top leaders.

5. Key and top leaders nominated twenty-five leaders who could best represent the Boston to Washington urban region in the shaping of urban policy and programming for the region. Those persons receiving the highest number of votes are listed on the following page.

The composition of this hypothetical regional board shows that the order of occupational representation is: civic leadership, 42 per cent; political-governmental, 27 per cent; business, 15 per cent; labor and religious, 8 per cent each. New York, by virtue of its civic, political, business, and to some extent, labor and religious leaders, offers a high concentration of policy making leaders—61 per cent. The other cities seem like satellites revolving around this urban sun.

CONCLUSIONS AND FUTURE RESEARCH

Megalopolis is best conceptualized as a distinctive highly urbanized locale containing a network of leaders and organizations that are usually concerned with local, state, or national, but not regional, policy.

380

Leader Nominated[a]	Type of leader	Metropolitan area
John V. Lindsay	Political	New York
Nelson A. Rockefeller	Political	New York
Bayard Rustin	Civic	New York
Whitney Young	Civic	New York
Arthur J. Goldberg	Civic	New York
David Rockefeller	Business	New York
Richard J. Hughes	Political	New York–New Jersey
A. Philip Randolph	Labor	New York
Kenneth B. Clark	Civic	New York
John K. Galbraith	Civic	Boston
Roy Wilkins	Civic	New York
Rev. Leon Sullivan	Religious	Philadelphia
Walter E. Washington	Political	Washington
McGeorge Bundy	Civic	New York
Paul N. Ylvisaker	Political	New York–New Jersey
James Rouse	Business	Baltimore
Richardson Dilworth	Political	Philadelphia
George Meany	Labor	Washington
Joseph Clark	Political	Philadelphia
Kingman Brewster	Civic	Boston–New York
John Collins	Political	Boston
Cardinal Terrence Cooke	Religious	New York
Cornelius W. Owens	Business	New York
Robert C. Weaver	Civic	New York
Andrew Heiskell	Business	New York
Milton Eisenhower	Civic	Baltimore

[a] The 178 key and top leaders who voted show the following distribution: Boston, 28; New York, 40; Philadelphia, 40; Baltimore, 42; Washington, 28.

However, the trend toward closer regional integration is clearly affirmed by a multitude of metropolitan and subregional planning agencies and a growing number of regional administrative agencies. These include the Boston, New York, Philadelphia, and Washington metropolitan regional councils; the New England Regional Commission; the Port Authority of New York; the Delaware River Basin Commission; the Tri-State Transportation Agency; the regional headquarters in Boston, New York, and Philadelphia for Regional Councils of U.S. Department of Health, Education, and Welfare, U.S. Office of Economic Opportunity, U.S. Labor Department, U.S. Housing and Urban Development, and U.S. Small Business

Administration; and various interstate air and water quality-control agencies.

Regional power structures within Megalopolis can be delineated by community power techniques. However, this study has attempted only a rudimentary first step. It has searched for leadership interaction and has tried to ascertain acquaintance and contact for those leaders of Megalopolis who are active in urban problems. At this stage, the possibility of these leaders coming together to work on common problems of Megalopolis is not likely. There is neither the psychological or social definition of a community nor appropriate governmental machinery. However, our data provide evidence of extensive linkage among leaders interested in urban problems, including environmental quality problems, and affirm that contacts are achieved both by leaders within and between the five principal metropolitan areas of Megalopolis. As representatives from Megalopolis they are found in abundance working together in organizations, on committees, and on commissions. The consciousness of community is now extending to metropolitan areas and to such interstate concerns as water supply and water quality, air pollution, solid wastes, highways, airport location, and recreational areas. Increasingly, governmental machinery is being set up in the wake of appropriate legislation.

An embryonic power structure does exist and there is rather high consensus about the key leaders who would have the most influence in regional planning and policy making for urban problems in Megalopolis. To this extent, sociological techniques have delineated one "regional power structure" appropriate for attacks on urban problems within Megalopolis. If regional integration increases, as seems likely, and if the sense of regional community grows, the social base will be ready to support the new governmental machinery. Only future development can provide the answer as to whether Megalopolis will become a community and treat its problems as common to it. I believe that the possibility is high and that this research will be a forerunner of similar efforts.

Immediate Future Research

The data collected provide unusual opportunities to study communication networks of powerful key and top urban-oriented leaders. Many new areas are now open for analyses.[24] These include:

1. Determination of group cohesion and cleavage of key and top business, labor, political, religious, and civic leaders. This will require analysis

[24] Sociograms developed by computer programs (July 1970) now show true Megalopolis cliques, intercity cliques, intercity ties, and Megalopolis "brokers" who make contacts across the major metropolitan areas.

382

of reciprocated and nonreciprocated acquaintance and contact. This can be analyzed by occupation and city.

2. Analyses of urban problem activity, and especially of environmental quality problem activity, to determine network of leaders by occupation and by city and show reciprocal chains of acquaintance and contact.

3. Determination of power rating of individual leader and occupational group networks, using nominations for a regional board as weights to establish power rating.

4. Establishment of profiles of ten highest key leaders by total acquaintance and contact to determine their network of communication in each city with each occupational group.

5. Establishment of profiles of ten highest key leaders by total acquaintance and contact to determine their acquaintance and contact with twenty-six regional nominees.

All of these efforts should prove fruitful in understanding problems of building coalitions for social action.

The Challenge of Long-Range Sociological Research in Megalopolis

The search for decision-making structures is probably the most important long-range research objective. To understand thoroughly an area like Megalopolis, a large research team should be assembled and many years should be given to the task. The location of the arenas of decision making would be an important consideration. Informal groups, committees, caucuses, societies, organizations, governmental bodies, lobbies—all are potentially important for the study of decision-making processes. It would be necessary to identify the issues which concern citizens of Megalopolis. Some of the current issues include community control of schools; the dividing of federal funds between and among cities and states; the demands for representative coalitions on public policy–making boards and community service organizations; and the demands of blacks for employment quotas, open housing, and free admission to colleges and universities. Decision-making processes centered on common social problems could provide a useful comparative analysis as the great metropolitan centers struggle with such problems as unemployment and poverty, housing, education, crime, pollution, and race relations. In each instance where larger units, such as interstate compact agencies, are engaged in problem solving, the researcher could get a clearer notion of decision making and its difficulties as various political sovereignties contest for power. Activity within the many regional professional and business societies would provide another set of processes for analysis.

This brief sketch of the possible points of entry only begins to open the possibilities. Our research commitment has been to give equal weight to powerful persons and powerful organizations. Regrettably, it is not possible to present here the completed studies of the powerful urban-oriented and environmental quality organizations. These studies show program interests and working relations. The manner in which powerful persons work in and through organizations has not been examined and remains a very important question. The research tasks are as monumental as Megalopolis. But two underlying sociological problems loom large. These are first, how power arises and is mobilized, and second, how group consciousness grows and extends to larger geographic units. If Megalopolae are the wave of the future, eventually these problems must be addressed, and the longer-range research task cannot be avoided.

Appendix to Chapter 10

AN EXHIBIT OF THE EASTERN LEADERSHIP QUESTIONNAIRE AND THE ACCOMPANYING LETTER

EASTERN LEADERSHIP AND ENVIRONMENTAL QUALITY STUDY

DEPARTMENT OF SOCIOLOGY — INDIANA UNIVERSITY

BLOOMINGTON, INDIANA 47401

Sponsored by:
RESOURCES FOR THE FUTURE
1755 Massachusetts Avenue, N. W.
Washington, D. C. 20036

I and my teamworkers have just completed eight months of intensive interviewing leaders and organizations in the cities of Boston, New York, Philadelphia, Baltimore and Washington, D.C. We have sought to identify influential leaders and organizations that are active in urban problems. The list shown in the questionnaire contains 200 leaders; another 200 could have been added.

The purpose has been to find out if there is any regional identity—a viable community of interest stretching from Boston to Washington. A partial answer would be forthcoming if the acquaintance and contacts of leaders in this highly urbanized area could be known.

Many leaders say that many segments of American life have been out of touch with one another—and, in many cities, are still out of touch. Is this true? I would like to contribute to social science research more adequate information about leadership communication and the human boundaries of Megalopolis.

I am completely dependent upon your help. Your answers to the questions enclosed will make it possible to ASSESS LEADERSHIP IN THE EAST AS IT HAS NEVER BEEN DONE BEFORE. You are a leader identified by the panels of knowledgeable persons of very high importance in the life of your city and of the Eastern region. Your knowledge (and contacts with other leaders) is basic for this study.

The search is for knowledge to solve problems better. Behind the effort is a critical question. Can Americans develop the capacity to organize and work through coalitions and interstate or regional compacts if urban problems demand them? My research sponsor, Resources for the Future, would like an answer as it pertains to problems of water quality and air pollution. And other urban problems pose the same question.

The questionnaire can be completed in less than 15 minutes. All data will be held in strict confidence. Each person will be recorded by a code number and any publication will list only an anonymous number. The analysis is carried out on a university campus and no access will be permitted to the data—not even to our sponsor.

Please take time to fill out the questionnaire. This could be the most effective contribution you could make to urban problems in a brief allocation of time. We need your experience and each missing name will weaken the research. A stamped addressed envelope is enclosed for your use. A report will be made to you of the results in mid-summer, 1969.

Yours truly,

Delbert C. Miller

Delbert C. Miller
Professor of Sociology
and Business Administration

385

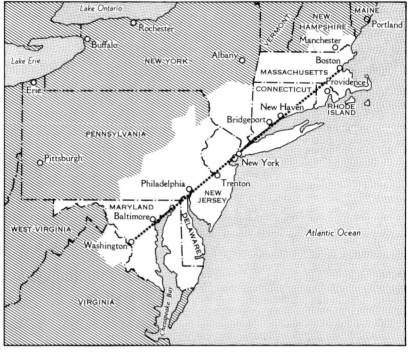

From drawing by Wolf von Eckardt, "Megalopolis: A Very
Special Region," in *The Challenge of Megalopolis* (Macmillan, 1964).

MEGALOPOLIS
A VERY SPECIAL REGION

WITH SOME VERY SPECIAL QUESTIONS

Who are the business, labor, political, religious, and civic leaders of this region?

What are the urban problem interests of these leaders?

Do leaders know one another—in their own cities? in the various major cities of the region?

Are leaders working together on urban problems—from Boston to New York to Philadelphia to Baltimore to Washington, D.C.?

EASTERN LEADERSHIP STUDY directed by Delbert C. Miller, Professor of Sociology and Business Administration, Indiana University, and funded by Resources for the Future, Inc., Washington, D.C.

386

DELBERT C. MILLER

URBAN PROBLEM INTEREST AND ACTIVITY PATTERN OF CIVIC LEADERS IN THE BOSTON TO WASHINGTON URBAN REGION

(1) Check problems in which you have the highest personal interest.
(2) Mark the one problem on which you are currently working most intensively.

(Note: The researcher is seeking to estimate the degree of interest and current activity pattern of civic leaders engaged in urban problems. All information is confidential and each person will be recorded by code number.)

I Have Most Interest In	I Am Currently Working Hardest On	URBAN PROBLEMS
		1. AIR POLLUTION
		2. CONTROL OF LAWLESSNESS AND CRIME
		3. IMPROVEMENT OF PUBLIC EDUCATION
		4. WATER POLLUTION
		5. IMPROVEMENT OF TRANSPORT, TRAFFIC MOVEMENT, AND PARKING
		6. WASTE (GARBAGE, LITTER, AND DUMPS)
		7. IMPROVEMENT OR ELIMINATION OF POOR HOUSING: REBUILDING OF CITIES
		8. IMPROVEMENT AND MAINTENANCE OF ROADS AND STREETS
		9. PLANNING AND ZONING OF LAND; PRESERVATION (OR IMPROVEMENT) OF PARK AND OTHER NATURAL AREAS; BEAUTIFICATION
		10. UNEMPLOYMENT AND POVERTY
		11. RACE RELATIONS
		12. OTHER (PLEASE SPECIFY)

In your civic activity on urban problems do you work mainly with leaders associated with (Rank in order of the amount of activity):

_____Private voluntary organizations
_____City government agencies
_____State government agencies
_____National government agencies
_____Business organizations
_____Your own firm or organization
_____Universities
_____Independent professionals

387

POWER STRUCTURE STUDIES

LEADERSHIP ACQUAINTANCE AND WORKING RELATIONSHIP INDEX

Please look at the leaders listed. All live and work in the Boston to Washington urban region. Please indicate by (your acquaintance and civic activity with each. All information is confidential and each person will be recorded by code number.

(Note: The researcher is trying to discover the degree of acquaintance and contact within and between such leadersh groups as business, labor, political, religious, and civic leaders in the metropolitan area and the Atlantic urban regio

	ACQUAINTANCE					CONTACTS	
Name of Leader	0 Don't Know	1 Have Heard Of	2 Know Little (Reading or Con- tact)	3 Know Well (Reading or Con- tact)	4 Know Socially (Visit at Home or Personal Contact)	I Have Had Business, Civic or Social Con- tacts During Past 3 Years	Worked Wi Him on a Committee Project Dea ing With Urban Prob lems Durin Past 3 Yea
BOSTON LEADERS (business)							
1. Robert Slater							
2. Paul C. Cabot							
3. Eli Goldstone							
4. John M. Fox							
5. Roger P. Sonnabend							
BOSTON LEADERS (labor)							
6. Vince Murphy							
7. Paul Flynn							
8. James P. Loughlin							
9. Larry Sullivan							
10. Salvatore Camilio							
BOSTON LEADERS (political & Government) U.S. Senators, Congressmen & Cabinet Mem- bers have been omitted.							
11. John Collins							
12. Kevin White							
13. Tom Atkins							
14. Frank Licht							
15. John Winthrop Sears							
BOSTON LEADERS (civic & civil rights)							
16. Melvin King							
17. Kenneth Guscott							
18. Edward Mason							
19. Paul Parks							
20. Howard W. Johnson							
21. Arthur Schlesinger							
22. Nathan Pusey							
23. John K. Galbraith							
24. James Killian							
25. Kingman Brewster							
BOSTON LEADERS (religious)							
26. Bishop Anson Stokes							
27. Rev. James Breeden							
28. Rev. James Mathews							
29. Rev. Robert Drinan							
30. Cardinal Richard Cushing							

DELBERT C. MILLER

Name of Leader	ACQUAINTANCE					CONTACTS	
	0 Don't Know	1 Have Heard Of	2 Know Little (Reading or Con- tact)	3 Know Well (Reading or Con- tact)	4 Know Socially (Visit at Home or Personal Contact)	I Have Had Business, Civic or Social Con- tacts During Past 3 Years	Worked With Him on a Committee or Project Deal- ing With Urban Prob- lems During Past 3 Years
EW YORK LEADERS (business)							
1. Roswell B. Perkins							
2. Gustave L. Levy							
3. Cornelius W. Owens							
4. Thomas S. Gates, Jr.							
5. Emilio G. Collado							
6. H. I. Romnes							
7. Roger M. Blough							
8. Albert L. Nickerson							
9. Charles F. Luce							
0. Floyd D. Hall							
1. Gilbert W. Fitzhugh							
2. Christian A. Herter, Jr.							
3. James F. Oates, Jr.							
4. Fred J. Borch							
5. Thomas J. Watson, Jr.							
6. C. Douglas Dillon							
7. Andrew Heiskell							
8. George Champion							
9. Frank Stanton							
50. David Rockefeller							
EW YORK LEADERS (labor)							
51. Albert Shanker							
52. Peter Brennan							
53. Gus Tyler							
54. Victor Gotbaum							
55. Howard Coughlin							
56. Max Greenberg							
57. Matthew Guinan							
58. Jacob S. Potofsky							
59. Harry VanArsdale, Jr.							
60. A. Philip Randolph							
EW YORK LEADERS (political and government)							
61. Nelson A. Rockefeller							
62. John V. Lindsay							
63. Stanley Steingut							
64. Eugene Nickerson							
65. Herman Badillo							
66. Richard J. Hughes							
67. Percy Sutton							
68. Francis X. Smith							
69. Paul N. Ylvisaker							
70. Paul O'Dwyer							

POWER STRUCTURE STUDIES

Name of Leader	ACQUAINTANCE					CONTACTS	
	0 Don't Know	1 Have Heard Of	2 Know Little (Reading or Con- tact)	3 Know Well (Reading or Con- tact)	4 Know Socially (Visit at Home or Personal Contact)	I Have Had Business, Civic or Social Con- tacts During Past 3 Years	Worked With Him on a Committee or Project Deal- ing With Urban Prob- lems During Past 3 Years
NEW YORK LEADERS (religious)							
71. Cardinal Terrence J. Cooke							
72. Rev. Edler Hawkins							
73. Rev. Milton A. Galamison							
74. Rabbi Marc Tannenbaum							
75. Algernon Black							
76. Msgr. Fox							
77. Rev. L. P. McLaughlin							
78. Rev. Calvin Marshall							
79. Rev. George Younger							
80. Rev. Lucius Walker							
NEW YORK LEADERS (civic and civil rights)							
81. Laurance S. Rockefeller							
82. Arthur J. Goldberg							
83. Bayard Rustin							
84. Whitney Young							
85. Kenneth B. Clark							
86. Roy Wilkins							
87. McGeorge Bundy							
88. Theodore Kheel							
89. Robert C. Weaver							
90. Francis Keppel							
91. Hector Vazquez							
92. I. Ted Velez							
93. Alan Pifer							
94. Charles Abrams							
95. John Doar							
96. T. George Silcott							
97. Franklin A. Thomas							
98. Arthur Ochs Sulzberger							
99. Wallace S. Sayre							
100. Roy Innis							
PHILADELPHIA LEADERS (business)							
101. Crawford H. Greenwalt							
102. John R. Bunting							
103. William L. Day							
104. R. Stewart Rauch, Jr.							
105. John P. Bracken							
106. Gustave G. Amsterdam							
107. Richard C. Bond							
108. Stuart T. Saunders							
109. Robert M. Wachob							
110. Thomas B. McCabe							

DELBERT C. MILLER

Name of Leader	ACQUAINTANCE					CONTACTS	
	0 Don't Know	1 Have Heard Of	2 Know Little (Reading or Con- tact)	3 Know Well (Reading or Con- tact)	4 Know Socially (Visit at Home or Personal Contact)	I Have Had Business, Civic or Social Con- tacts During Past 3 Years	Worked With Him on a Committee or Project Deal- ing With Urban Prob- lems During Past 3 Years
PHILADELPHIA LEADERS (labor)							
1. William Ross							
2. James Jones							
3. Edward F. Toohey							
4. Anthony Cortigene							
5. James J. Loughlin							
PHILADELPHIA LEADERS (politics and government)							
6. Richardson Dilworth							
7. James H. J. Tate							
8. Arlen Specter							
9. Paul D'Ortona							
10. Joseph Clark							
PHILADELPHIA LEADERS (religious)							
11. Paul M. Washington							
12. Bishop John Bright							
13. Rev. Leon Sullivan							
14. Rev. Robert L. DeWitt							
15. Cardinal John J. Krol							
PHILADELPHIA LEADERS (civic and civil rights)							
16. William L. Rafsky							
17. Herman Wrice							
18. Gaylord P. Harnwell							
19. Maurice B. Fagan							
20. Millard E. Gladfelter							
21. Clarence Farmer							
22. Samuel Evans							
23. Mrs. Albert M. Greenfield							
24. Raymond Pace Alexander							
25. Walter Phillips							
BALTIMORE LEADERS (business)							
36. Robert Levi							
37. Nicholas V. Petrou							
38. William Boucher III							
39. Walter Sondheim, Jr.							
40. James Rouse							
BALTIMORE LEADERS (labor)							
41. Dominic Fornaro							
42. Jacob J. Edleman							
43. Edward Gutman							
44. Jacob Blum							
45. Charles A. Della							

391

POWER STRUCTURE STUDIES

Name of Leader	ACQUAINTANCE					CONTACTS	
	0 Don't Know	1 Have Heard Of	2 Know Little (Reading or Con- tact)	3 Know Well (Reading or Con- tact)	4 Know Socially (Visit at Home or Personal Contact)	I Have Had Business, Civic or Social Con- tacts During Past 3 Years	Worked With Him on a Committee or Project Deal- ing With Urban Prob- lems During Past 3 Years
BALTIMORE LEADERS (politics & government)							
146. Samuel Daniels							
147. Robert Embry							
148. Edgar Ewing							
149. Thomas J. D'Alesandro, Jr.							
150. Theodore R. McKeldin							
BALTIMORE LEADERS (religious)							
151. Frederick J. Hanne							
152. Vernon N. Dobson							
153. Marion C. Bascom							
154. Rabbi Morris Lieberman							
155. Cardinal Lawrence J. Shehan							
BALTIMORE LEADERS (civic & civil rights)							
156. Milton Eisenhower							
157. Parren Mitchell							
158. Homer Favor							
159. Mrs. Joseph Levi							
160. Furman Templeton							
161. George Gelston							
162. Mrs. Juanita Mitchell							
163. Eugene M. Feinblatt							
164. Walter Lively							
165. Lincoln Gordon							
WASHINGTON LEADERS (business)							
166. George Olmsted							
167. Thornton W. Owen							
168. L. A. Jennings							
169. William Calomiris							
170. Stephen Ailes							
WASHINGTON LEADERS (labor)							
171. P. I. Siemiller							
172. Jacob Clayman							
173. Joseph D. Keenan							
174. Paul Jennings							
175. George Meany							
176. James A. Suffridge							
177. David Sullivan							
178. Andrew J. Biemiller							
179. Jerry Wurf							
180. Joseph A. Beirne							

Name of Leader	ACQUAINTANCE					CONTACTS	
	0 Don't Know	1 Have Heard Of	2 Know Little (Reading or Con- tact)	3 Know Well (Reading or Con- tact)	4 Know Socially (Visit at Home or Personal Contact)	I Have Had Business, Civic or Social Con- tacts During Past 3 Years	Worked With Him on a Committee or Project Deal- ing With Urban Prob- lems During Past 3 Years
WASHINGTON LEADERS (politics and government)							
81. Channing Phillips							
82. Flaxie Pinkett							
83. Walter E. Washington							
84. John W. Macy, Jr.							
85. Frederick A. Babson							
WASHINGTON LEADERS (religious)							
86. Bishop Paul Moore, Jr.							
87. Rev. Philip R. Newell, Jr.							
88. Rabbi Richard G. Hirsch							
89. Bishop Smallwood Williams							
90. Rev. Walter E. Fauntroy							
WASHINGTON LEADERS (civic & civil rights)							
91. Carl Shipley							
92. Kermit Gordon							
93. H. Carl Moultrie							
94. Mrs. David Scull							
95. G. Franklin Edwards							
96. Carl T. Rowan							
97. Clarence Mitchell, Jr.							
98. Sterling Tucker							
99. Marion Barry							
00. John W. Gardner							

POWER STRUCTURE STUDIES

NOW PLEASE LOOK OVER THE LIST AND NOMINATE 25 LEADERS
WHO COULD BEST REPRESENT THE BOSTON TO WASHINGTON
URBAN REGION IN THE SHAPING OF URBAN POLICY AND PRO-
GRAMMING FOR THE REGION.

Simply put the NUMBER of your nominee here. See list. The order is not
important. (All information is confidential and each person will be recorded by
code number only. This information is for research purposes only.)

—— —— —— —— —— —— —— —— —— —— —— ——

—— —— —— —— —— —— —— —— —— —— —— ——

Other names, not on the list that you would give higher priority. (Please do not
name U.S. Senators, Congressmen, or Cabinet members. These have been
omitted.)

_____   _____

_____   _____

In my choices I have given most weight to the criterion which states:

___1. A leader should be able to work with other business, labor, govern-
mental, religious, and civic leaders.
___2. A leader should commit himself to the work required.
___3. A leader should be able and willing to influence others.

For me, the most valuable contacts in civic work and policy making dealing
with urban problems have generally been with leaders from: (Rank 1 through 5)

___BUSINESS   ___LABOR   ___POLITICAL-GOVT.

——RELIGIOUS   ——CIVIC

In regard to contact I have established with leaders, my most frequent to
least frequent contacts with *various groups of leaders* can be ranked 1 through 5
as: (1 equals most frequent)

___BUSINESS   ___LABOR   ___POLITICAL-GOVT.

___RELIGIOUS   ___CIVIC

My best to poorest knowledge of leaders and organizations *in the major cities*
of the Atlantic urban region can be ranked from 1 through 5 as:

___BOSTON   ___NEW YORK   ___PHILADELPHIA

___BALTIMORE   ___WASHINGTON, D.C.

In civic activity, do you personally find it most rewarding to work at the:

___LOCAL LEVEL   ___STATE LEVEL

___NATIONAL LEVEL   ___ALL THREE

394

I find that I can be most effective in civic policy making through:

____Face to face contact with another person
____Telephone calls
____Letters
____Committee activity
____Talking to large groups
____Talking with small groups of leaders meeting informally

As you watch different issues of high importance arise in urban life, would you say that leaders generally change according to the issue or that the same crowd generally makes the decisions regardless of the issue.

____Leaders generally change with the issue at stake.
____Same crowd of leaders generally makes the decisions regardless of the issue.

COMMENTS:

_____

Thank you for your assistance. A report will be mailed to you as soon as a summary is possible. Reference to persons will be made only by a confidential code number.   Delbert C. Miller

Index

Abatement: benefits of, 213–41, 247, 248–49, 261, 266, 268–69, 274, 275, 277; costs and expenditures of, 234, 239; devices and methods for, 161; estimating demand for, 231–32; estimating value of, 213–41; and health, 213–14, 231, 238, 240, 268; and life expectancy, 240; subsidization and tax relief for, 237; willingness to pay for, 213, 214, 215, 231, 233, 247
Adams, F. Gerard, 152n, 271n
Agriculture: policy on pesticides, 191–93, 210–11; productivity and use of chemicals, 187–91. *See also* Pesticides
Aiken, Michael, 346
Air: clean, value of, 339; concept of ownership, 339; equity of distribution, 262; life support and amenities, 262–68; as waste receptor service, 258–62. *See also* Air pollution
Air pollution, 116, 117, 154, 163; ambient concentrations, 173t; control mechanism, 237; data observation errors, 218–19; diffusion models, 239–40; effect in dollar terms, 231–34; emission standards, 236–38, 239–40; estimating damage, 215–31; exposure indexes, 264, 265t, 266t; formula for increase of emissions tonnages, 12; and health, 122, 124, 152, 215–31, 262–63; and land value, 214, 215, 235, 236; legal construct to prevent, 339; links with meteorology and economic activity, 227, 236; major episodes, 167; measurement, 219, 224–26, 231; nonhealth damages, 234–36; Penjerdel case, 315–18; policy implications, 223; power relations studies centering on, 347; and quality of life, 235; and smoking interaction, 217–18; social cost, 237, 238; top leader interest in, 370, 371t; value added (or lost) of, 215, 216. *See also* Abatement
Alaska pipeline, 342–43
Alford, Robert, 346
Allen, R. G. D., 191n
Amenities, 262–68
America, 363
Anaximander of Miletus, 33
Anderson, Robert G., Jr., 235, 263n

Note: n = note; *t* = table; *f* = figure.

397

Animals, pesticide damage to, 198, 201, 202, 204*t*
Anticyclones, 167*n*
Antiquities, 71
Arey, D. G., 153*n*
Aristotle, 281*n*
Arrow, Kenneth, 213*n*, 283, 295
Art, 70
Ayres, R. U., 11, 13, 15, 18, 37, 38, 42

Bagehot, Walter, 289*n*, 298
Baltimore, Md., 356–63 *passim*, 374–38 *passim*, 379*t*
Banker, R. F., 152*n*
Banzhaf, John F., 289*n*
Barfoot, James, 346, 350, 354*n*
Barnett, H. J., 12, 69*n*
Baumol, William J., 213*n*, 250*n*, 251*n*
Bees, damage to, 199
Beet sugar, 163–64; input-output matrix, 56, 62*t*, 63–65; materials flow, 59*f*; production alternatives, 163; residuals, 56, 62*t*, 63–65, 165*t*
Beverton, R. J., 25*n*
Biochemical oxygen demand (BOD), 128, 149, 150, 151, 160, 163, 166, 167, 172*t*
Biologists, view of pesticide damage, 204
Birds, damage to, 199, 205
Birdsall, W. C., 294
Birkhead, Guthrie S., 347
Birkhead, Jesse, 347
Black, Duncan, 283*n*, 284*n*, 290*n*, 295
Bodovitz, Joseph E., 309*n*
Boston, Mass., 355–61 *passim*, 364, 374, 378; leadership acquaintance and contacts in, 372*f*, 375*f*, 376, 377, 379*t*
Boswell, Thomas O., 202
Boulding, K., 11, 281*n*, 300, 301*n*
Bower, Blair T., 119*n*, 159*n*, 160*n*, 237*n*, 243*n*, 261*n*, 262*n*, 269*n*, 303
Bradford, D., 213*n*
Bram, J., 134*n*

Brandywine Plan, 299
Breslow, L., 217
Brewster, Kingman, 359*n*
Brook, E., 11*n*
Brown, Gardner, 23, 69*n*, 97
Browning, Rufus P., 301*n*, 302, 310, 332
Brownlee, K., 217*n*
Buchanan, James M., 198
Buell, P., 217
Burke, Edmund, 298
Burt, O. R., 23
Business Advisory Council, 362

Camp, T. R., 149*n*
Campbell, Alan K., 322*n*
Canada, experimental pipeline in, 343
Cancer, 217–18
Carbon monoxide, 15, 32, 263
Carroll, Lewis, 290
Chant, Donald, 207
Charges or bribes, 248*n*, 260–62, 276, 278, 282, 337, 338; equity and efficiency implications of, 273–74; and receipts distribution, 301–2. *See also* Effluent, charges
Chavez, I. Paul, 88
Chemicals, farm, 188*t*, 189. *See also* Pesticides; *and specific chemical*
Chenery, H. G., 43
Chlorinated hydrocarbons, 196, 197, 202, 203, 207–10 *passim*
Chura, Nicholas J., 202
Cicchetti, Charles J., 82, 90, 243*n*, 269, 270, 271, 273*n*, 276*n*
Clark, P. G., 43
Clark, Terry N., 345, 346*n*, 349
Clawson, M., 152*n*
Cleary, E. J., 159*n*
Clement, Roland C., 205
Committee for Comparability in Community Research, 346
Committee for Economic Development, 322*n*, 362
Common property resources (CPR): characteristics, effect on distribu-

tion, 252–53; choices about use of, 281–83; citizen role in protection, 339–40, 341–43; concept of, 3–4, 5, 339; evaluation of public interest in, 335, 337–39; management, 5; multiple purposes of, 282, 285; and property rights, 3, 247–48, 276, 281; as public trust, 339–40; publicly owned recreation land as, 271; role of legal processes in allocation, 333–43; substitution for, in condemnation cases, 336; tradeoffs among services from, 253; value, 337–39. *See also* Services, environmental

Compacts, interstate, 302, 304–9, 315, 316, 323

Consumer surplus, measures and option value of, 95–96, 97*f*, 98*f*, 99–106, 107*f*, 108, 247

Consumers: cost to, of achieving quality environment, 260; and individual choice problem, 250, 251–52; value of abatement to health, 232. *See also* "Willingness to pay"

Consumption: expenditures and residual loads, 259–60; residuals from, 119, 120*f*, 139, 146, 147, 148; technology of, 147

Coontz, C., 14

Cootner, P. H., 161*n*, 170*n*

Copeland, Frank, 202

Crain, Robert, 346

Crenson, Matthew, 347

Crocker, Thomas, 235, 243*n*, 263*n*

Cumberland, J. H., 38

Cummings, R. G., 23

Daly, H., 11

Damage, 12, 13, 26, 31, 118*n*; actions to modify, 119; to animals, 198, 201–2, 204*t*; costs, 16, 17, 260; functions for, 124–25, 130, 151–56, 170, 171; to health, 152, 154, 198–200, 203, 204*t*, 215–31; marginal, 126, 130, 136, 148, 156–60, 174*t*; to structures, 263

d'Arge, Ralph C., 15, 25*n*, 119*n*, 125*n*, 253*n*

Dasgupta, P. S., 21*n*, 31

David, Martin, 249*n*

Davidson, Paul, 82, 90, 152*n*, 269, 270, 271*n*

Davies, John E., 203

Davis, Otto, 213*n*, 236, 295, 296, 332

Davis, Robert K., 303*n*

Deane, M., 215*n*, 227*n*

Death rate. *See* Mortality

Decision making, 20*n*; citizen role in, 340; coalition model for, 352, 353*f*; in community organizations, research on, 345; equity concerns in, 244, 274, 276; legal strategies in, 333–43; mechanisms for, 349, 350; models for, 293–302, 352, 353*f*; payoffs of, 301*t*; principle of, in legislatures, 292–93; in regional environmental quality management, 349, 352, 353*f*, 354; utility maximizing in, 300–302

Delaware River Basin, 349, 350, 352–54

Dexter, Edwin, 5

DDD, 205

DDT, 15, 205

Dissolved oxygen, 148*n*, 149, 150, 151, 154, 159, 160, 166, 176*f*; cost of improving, 303*t*

Distribution of environment, 243–78; application of a model to, 258–73; and characteristics of CPR, 252–57; costs and benefits of, 274, 275, 277; elements of a model for analyzing, 250–58; equity considerations in, 244, 274, 276, 277; and final product services, 253, 257, 258–73; and individual choice, 250, 251–52, 257; measurement problems associated with, 246–49; research into, 276–78; role of, in quality planning, 274

Dixon, Robert G., Jr., 289*n*

Dobbins, W. E., 149*n*

Dorfman, R., 11*n*, 23, 27, 118*n*, 160*n*

Dunbar, C., 19n
Dunn, J., Jr., 217
Durable goods, and waste generation, 28, 32

Earley, J. S., 11n
Eckstein, O., 89
Ecological catastrophe, 275
Economy: extraction-consumption-waste process of model, 18–24; growth forecasts, 37; interaction with natural environment, 11–33; material and waste flows in, 13–14, 15–24 *passim*, 32, 33
Edwards, W. F., 193n, 200
Effluent: allowable discharge, 302; charges, 61, 118, 119, 260–62, 274, 276, 337, 339
Eichers, Theodore, 190n
Emissions: charges, 260–62; standards, 236–38, 239
Environment, definition of, 245–46
Environmental Protection Agency, Office of Water Quality, 340n

Farmer Cooperative Service, 187
Feedback loops, man-environment interaction, 183f
Fels Institute, University of Pennsylvania, 315–16
Ferris, B., 215n, 217n
Fertilizer, 188t, 189
Fiacco, F. A., 129n
Firey, Walter, 5
Fish, damage to, 199
Fisher, Anthony, 83, 84n, 243n
Flint, R. F., 19n
Florida, Dade County: insurance claims for pesticide injury, 200–201; use of pesticides, costs and benefits, 194–96, 198–204, 205, 208
Florida Department of Public Health, 203
Florida Industrial Commission, 200
Fly ash, 142, 144, 145, 163, 164
Frankel, Richard J., 152n, 269n

Freeman, A. Myrick, III, 244n, 249n, 275, 276
"Generic congestion," 17
Gifts of nature, 71, 72, 90
Gilkeson, M., Jr., 234
Gillespie, W. Irwin, 249n, 261n
Glacial age, 18n
Goldsmith, J., 215n, 227n
Goods: characteristics, 250–52; intermediate, and distribution of environmental quality, 253. *See also* Durable goods
Gordon, H. Scott, 255n
Gottman, Jean, 348n, 355n
Government: area-wide approach to, 321; and basis of representation, 289–92; impact of policies on environment, 33; limitations on, in representation and protection of public interest, 338, 340–41; "loose system," 341, 342; metropolitan, innovation in, 320–21; and participatory democracy, 340, 341–43; role of, in decision making, 430–41; self-, 299, 321, 324; and social choice, 284–85, 289–92, 322–34; as trustee of CPR, 339
Grants-in-aid, 262, 306
Greenawalt, Crawford, 359n
Greenberg, Daniel S., 363

Haefele, Edwin T., 118n, 124n, 277n, 284n, 290n, 292n, 299n
Harberger, A., 89
Hardin, Garrett, 281n
Harner, E. H., 152n, 154n
Harrell, C., 235
Harris, R., 235
Haveman, Robert H., 243n, 252n, 276n
Headley, J. C., 187, 188, 193
Health, 15, 17n; and abatement of pollution, 213–14, 231, 238, 240, 268; damage to, 152, 154, 198–200, 203, 204t, 215–31; economic cost of, 240–41; income and pollution effects on, 224, 227–28, 267; nonlinear rela-

tion of pollution to, 219–23; problems of measuring damage to, 154; urban factor in, 216–17; value of improvement in, 232–34. *See also* Life expectancy; Morbidity; Mortality; *and under* Air pollution; Pesticides

Heat, 118*n*, 163, 176*f*
Heath, Milton, 116*n*
Hechter, H., 227*n*
Hells Canyon, 71, 95, 106; benefits from existing uses of, 91, 92*f*; development alternative for, 72–76, 83; preservation alternative for, 76–88; as resource allocation problem, 88–95

Henderson, A., 97, 98
Henderson, James M., 194*n*
Henning, John A., 235, 263*n*
Herbicides, 188*t*, 189, 190
Hetch Hetchy Valley, 71
Hibbs, J. R., 38
Hickey, R. J., 152*n*, 154*n*
Hicks, John R., 96, 98, 247*n*
Highway law suit, 338
Hilton Head, S.C., factory location case in, 341–42
Hinich, Melvin, 295, 296
Hirsch, Allen, 262
Holt, S. V., 25*n*
Horlock, Laura, 346
Households, consumption patterns and waste loads of, 146, 147, 148, 258
Housing, and pollution exposure, 264, 266*t*
Housing development (hypothetical), effects of pollution on, 153–54
Hunter, Floyd, 347, 362, 363*n*
Hydrocarbons, 15
Hydroelectric development, 72–76, 89*t*

Igenito, F., 215*n*, 227*n*
Incentives, 118, 248*n*, 261–62, 276, 277–78
Incineration, 164

Income: and distribution of the environment, 248, 249, 252, 257–58, 262–67, 275; and irreplaceable asset demand and price, 79, 81; and participation in recreation activities, 269, 270*t*, 271–72, 273; and pollution exposure, 262, 264, 265*t*, 267; relation to consumption expenditures and residual loads, 258–59, 260
Industry, linear programming model, 122, 137, 138–41, 142–48. *See also* Beet sugar; Production, industrial; Wool
Influence, networks of, 352, 353*f*, 354
Insecticides, 189, 190, 192
Institutions: designs for, 5–6, 118, 281–324, 333–43; legal, 333–43; for making environmental choices, examples and critiques of, 302–24; political, 302–22; for residuals management, 116, 119; and social choice problems, 282–85; tools for analysis of, 286–302. *See also* Government; Legislatures; Political parties
Interstate compacts. *See* Compacts, interstate
In-stream aeration, 128*n*, 156, 159, 166
Ipsen, J., 215*n*, 217*n*, 227*n*
Irreplaceable assets: analytical model, 77–82; classes of, 70–71; "composite" benefit computational model, 82–88, 89; and consumer incomes, 79, 81; consumer surplus and option values, 95–108; development alternative, 72–76; effects of demand shifts, 78, 79*f*, 81, 82*f*; and population increases and preferences, 78–79; preservation alternative, 76–88; preservation benefits, 76, 77, 83–88, 90*t*, 91*t*, 94*t*, 95; substitution for, 70; and technical change model, 74–75, 88; trade-offs between producible goods and, 80*f*
Isard, Walter, 121*n*

Jackson, John E., 294, 295, 296

Jacoby, H. D., 160n
Japan, damage to, 115n
Jessell, Joseph J. A., 88
Johnston, Ray, 346
Jonish, James, 260n
Judy, Richard, 69n

Kalter, Robert J., 272
Kansas City, 264
Kates, R. W., 153n
Kaye, M., 217n
Keith, J. A., 202
Keynes, John M., 77
Kimball, Thomas L., 202
Klarman, H., 233
Kneese, A. V., 11, 12, 13, 15, 18, 25n, 37, 38, 42, 119n, 125n, 152n, 161n, 163n, 170n, 215n, 235, 237n, 243n, 252n, 253n, 261n, 262n, 269n, 276, 303, 337
Knetsch, J., 152n
Koenig, L., 152n
Kogiku, K. C., 11n
Kohn, Robert E., 138n
Kolderie, Ted, 320n
Korshover, Julius, 167n
Kramer, Gerald, 283n, 294
Krutilla, J. V., 83, 89n
Kurz, M., 213n

Lancaster, Kelvin J., 250n, 268n
Land: substitution of, for farm chemicals, 191–93; value of, and air quality, 214, 215, 235, 236, 263, 267–69
Landau, E., 234
Langham, R., 193n
Lave, Lester B., 217n, 226n, 227n, 230, 231, 233n, 234, 238, 240n, 241n, 263n
Law: and concept of CPR ownership, 339, 340; condemnation, 333–35; highway, 338; pollution control, 239. *See also* Legal strategies
Leaders: acquaintance and contacts, 357f, 358, 364–65, 370, 372f, 373t, 374, 375f, 376t, 378–79t, 380; acquaintance check list, 364–66; en-

vironmental quality interest of, 370, 371t; evaluation of, 364–66; identification and linkages of, 350, 351, 355–80; influence network, 352, 353f, 354; key and top categories, 361, 362–64, 365–66; in Northeast Megalopolis, list of, 381; in Philadelphia, 366t; priorities of interest and activity, 356, 368, 369t; questionnaire directed to, 361–62, 366–68, 387–95
Legal strategies, 333–43
Legislatures: decision rule for, 292–93; majority rule and summed frequencies in, 292, 293t; and protection of minority interests, 299; research capabilities of, 323; role in policy determination, 323; and social choice, 285; vote-trading in, 299, 300f; voting power in, 286–89
Lehner, Philip M., 202
Leighton, P., 12
Leinhardt, S., 217n
Leontief, W., 38
Lerner, A., 213n
Lewis, R., 234
Licht, Frank, 359n
Life expectancy, 228–30, 233, 240, 267
Lindsay, Cotton, 96n, 101
Locke, Louis N., 202
Löf, G. O. G., 161n, 163n, 170n
Long, Millard, 72, 96n, 101
Long, Norton E., 321
Longwell, C. R., 19n
Los Angeles, Calif., 12, 17n
Los Angeles County Health Association, 17n
Lotka, A. J., 18, 25n
Loucks, D. P., 160n
Low-flow augmentation, 128, 148, 151, 156, 160, 166
Low probability events, evaluation of, 232–33

Maass, Arthur, 277n
McCamdin, R., 234

McCormick, G. P., 129n
MacMahon, B., 217n
Madison, James, 285, 289n, 299
Man-environment interactions, 182–87; feedback loops, 183f
Management, 5, 24; alternatives for environmental, 35–36, 138, 147, 159–60; computer program, 169–70; decision-making process of, 349; delineation and enforcement of property rights for effective, 276; designing a program for, 36; and equity concerns in decision making, 274; major decisions of, 253; problems of, 116–17; quality planning model for, 123f; regional, 118; of residuals, 115–79; strategy for, 35, 248n, 274, 333–43; tools of, 261; water, 274, 303, 307. *See also* Charges; Incentives; Legal strategies; Management methodology; Management model
Management methodology, 127–60; ambient concentration of residuals, 148–51; constraint set, 127–28; damage functions, 124–25, 130, 151–56, 170, 171; marginal costs and damages, 126, 130, 136, 148, 156–61; model development, 126–37; nonlinear programming technique, 130–35; objective function, 121–22, 126–28, 135–37, 171f; optimization scheme, 128–30. *See also* Management model
Management model: assumptions, 125; components, 121, 122, 123f, 124; development, 126–37; didactic version, 161–76; diffusion model, 122; externalities, 125–26; goals, 120–21, 138–39; linear programming model, 122, 138–41, 142–48; quality planning model, 123f; receptor-damage functions, 122–26, 129, 130; as staff tool, 118–19
Martin, Roscoe, 347
Marx, Carl, 14n
Materials: in beet sugar production,

59f, 62t; changes in characteristics, 58; classification, 42–45, 46t, 47t; electro-chemical, 44–45, 46t, 47t; flow of, between natural environment and economy, 13–18, 19–23 *passim*, 37, 55f; microprocesses affecting, 52t, 53t; and quantity of residuals generated, 37–47. *See also* Materials balance approach; Materials-process-product model
Materials balance approach, 13–18
Materials-process-product model, 35–37; application, 55–67; classification of materials and processes, 42–55; theory, 36–42
Meade, J. E., 32
Megalopolis: concepts of, 348f; issues that concern citizens of, 383; regional power structures within, 382; and sense of regional community, 355. *See also* Northeastern Megalopolis; Power structure
Michelson, I., 235
Miller, Delbert C., 350, 354n, 367
Mills, C. Wright, 347
Minneapolis–St. Paul Metropolitan Council, 318–22
Mishan, E. J., 255n
Modification of environment: costs and benefits, 159–61; management alternatives, 156
Morbidity, 154; and air pollution, 216, 224, 227, 228, 240, 266–67
Morse, C., 12, 69n
Mortality, 154; age specific, 226, 228–30; and air pollution, 216–25, 226–31, 266–67; and population density, 222, 226; problems in analyzing rates, 216; rates, 216, 218, 219, 220t, 225t, 226, 228–30; urban factor in, 216–17
Munger, Frank, 347
Muskie, Edmund, 323

National Academy of Sciences, 202n, 234

National Alliance of Businessmen, 363
National Environmental Policy Act, 342
National Industrial Conference Board, 362
National Urban Coalition, 358, 359, 363
Nelsen, Darwin, 69n
New York City, 358–63 passim, 374, 376, 377, 378, 379t
New York Times, 343
Nitrogen oxides, 12, 32, 154
Nixon, Richard M., 115, 323
Noise, 118, 154
Northeastern Megalopolis: acquaintanceship check list of leaders within, 364f; areas of disagreement concerning, 348; Boston leader's acquaintances and contacts, 375f, 376; decision making and influence network, 352, 353f, 354; identification of leaders, 350, 351; leaders' interest and activity priorities, 369t; leadership acquaintance and contact, 370–80; list of leaders, 381; six power structures within, 350n
Nourse, H., 235

Oakland, Calif., airport case, 315
Obsolescence and decay, 28, 29, 33
O'Connor, Donald J., 149n
Oil depletion allowances, 32
Olsen, Mancur, 282n
Option price, 100–104 passim
Option value: and consumer surplus, 95–102, 103–8; definition of, 98–108; game tree for analysis of, 99f, 100, 105, 106; and probability of demand, 109f; and risk aversion, 105f
Ordeshook, Peter, 295
Oregon State University, Natural Resources Institute, 69n
Organic phosphates, 196, 197f, 198f, 202, 208, 209
Organizations: influence networks, 352, 353f, 354; interaction, 355; and

power structure, 384; urban-oriented and environmental, linkages of, 351
Ortolano, Leonard, 159n
Outdoor Recreation Resources Review Commission, 272n

Packaging, 147
Panofsky, H. A., 167n
Parlante, R., 152n
Particulates: exposure to, 264, 265t, 266t; and morbidity and mortality, 219–25 passim, 226, 228
Patinkin, D., 97
Patterson, W. L., 152n
Patuxent Wildlife Research Center, 205
Penjerdel: air pollution case, 315–18; proposal for agency to manage airshed, 316–17
Pest control, biological, 210n. See also Pesticides
Pesticides, 116; animal damage from, 198, 201–2, 204t; brain and egg residue levels, 205–6; community studies on, 202–3; constraints on use, 205–7; costs and benefits, 186, 187–91, 193–209; definition of, 187; drift of, 199–200, 204; exposure levels, 205–7; externality function and measurement of use, 195–97, 198–205; and health, 198, 200, 203, 204t; insurance claims arising from use, 200–201; marginal contributions, 188–89; models for analyzing usage, 184–86, 194–95, 205–9; monitoring, 206–7; policy for use, 186, 202, 205–10 passim; and productivity, 187–93; research in progress, 202; social costs, 193–94; substitutions for, 191–92, 193, 208; technological advance in, 210; veterinarians' records as source of data, 201
Pesticides Monitoring Journal, 207
Phelps, E. B., 149
Philadelphia, Pa., 356–64 passim, 374,

376, 378, 379*t*, 380; list of leaders, 366*t*

Phosphates. *See* Organic phosphates

Pipelines, 142, 342–43; case involving, 333–37, 339

Planchon, Paul, 346, 350, 354

Planning, environmental: equity considerations, 244, 274–77; model, 123; role of distribution in, 243, 274–75

Plott, C. R., 283*n*

Policy: deterent to national, 339; economic and fiscal, 31, 32, 33; effect of equity concerns on, 274–76; pollution, 186, 202, 205–10 *passim*; role of legislatures in determination of, 323; for utilizing the environment, 31

Political parties, 284, 290–92, 298–99, 323

Political process: and issue formation, 296–99, 323, 328–31; and social choice, 284–85, 290–92; tools for analyzing, 323

Population: aged, nonwhite, and poor, 222, 226, 229, 230; decimation of, 17–18, 20, 31; density of, and pollution, 12, 19, 221, 226; and material and waste flow, 16, 17, 18, 31, 183–84; program for curbing growth, 31–32

Port of New York Authority, 285

Potomac Estuary: cost of improving dissolved oxygen in, 303*t*; land control issue along, 309

Potomac River Basin: population, 305*t*; representation in legislature, 325–27

Potomac River Basin Commission, 302–9

Power generation: alternatives, 161, 163; discharges, 165*t*; technological advances, 73–75

Power structure studies: areas of diversity within scientific community concerning, 347–50; coalition deci-

sion model, 352, 353*f*; findings, 355, 368–80; goals, 355; guiding assumptions, 351; linkage patterns, 351; methodology, 347–68; research design and execution, 352–54, 358–80; review of research, 345–47, 382–84; tests of hypotheses, 356–58; theoretical positions and base, 351–52. *See also* Leaders; Megalopolis; Northeastern Megalopolis

President's Science Advisory Council, 182

Prest, A., 213*n*

Prindle, R., 234

Production, industrial: costs, 260; effect of product demand changes, 58; facilities design or modification, 161; models, 36–42, 122, 138–41, 142–48. *See also* Production processes; Residuals

Production processes: alternatives, 61, 67, 138, 147, 162–63; analysis of unpriced externalities in, 37, 38; classification, 42, 43, 44, 48–55; efficiency measures, 66*t*; flow diagrams, 54*f*, 55*f*, 56*f*, 57*f*, 58*f*, 59*f*; microprocesses, 48*t*–50*t*, 51, 52*t*, 53*t*; and quantity of residuals, 48–60; technology and material flow relationships in, 37–42, 57–58; unit costs, 66*t*

Projects: design of, and equity considerations, 274, 275–76; publicly built, measure of benefit from, 247; and social choice mechanism, 285

Property rights. *See under* Common property resources

Public, the: issues of concern to, in Megalopolis, 383; and protection of CPR, 339–40, 341–43; role in decision-making process, 340

Public trust doctrine, 339

Pugh, T., 217*n*

Quality of life, 235

Quandt, Richard E., 250*n*, 251

Quint, Arnold, 69*n*

Race: mortality rates and life expectancy, 222, 226, 229; participation in recreation, 269, 270*t*, 272*t*; pollution exposure, 264, 265*n*, 266*t*
Radiation, 217
Rae, Douglas, 292, 293, 309
Recreation: land-based, rural, 271–73; and river basin commission, 307; social costs, 153; water-based, 152, 153, 257, 269–73
Recycling, 2, 14, 25*n*, 28, 29, 30, 33, 119
Region: hypothetical, for testing quantitative procedures, 161, 162*f*, 164–66, 167; management authority for, 118; and social choice, 324; trend toward closer integration within, 381
Reproductive process, damage to, 202, 204–5
Research: future, 109–11, 152, 178–79, 208, 245, 276–78, 382–84; previous, 4–6, 345–47; in progress, 202, 210, 368*n*
Residuals: ambient concentrations, 122, 127–30, 148–51, 167, 173*t*, 175; from beet sugar production, 56, 62*t*; biodegradable, 145; costs, 121, 122, 124*n*, 144, 145; damages from, 121, 124, 151–58, 174*t*, 260; definition, 117*n*; density, as measure of, 15–24 *passim*, 31; discharge levels, 172*t*; dispersion models, use of, 166; external diseconomies of emissions, 12–13; flows, 13, 14–16, 18–33 *passim*, 119, 120*f*; forecasting, 36–42, 55–67; forms of, 164, 165*t*; gaseous, 122, 168*f*; generation of, 2, 13, 18–24, 32, 37–47, 141*f*, 142, 146; household, 146, 147, 148; and income, 258–59; inducements to reduce, 118, 261–62; interaction in natural environment, 128, 129; management of, 115–79; in man-environment system, 183*f*; models, 36–42, 122, 138–41, 142–48; nontreatment alternatives, 138; prices of discharge activities, comparison, 175*t*; from

production and consumption, 13, 14–16, 119, 120*f*, 139, 141*f*, 146, 147, 148; quantity, and nature of production processes, 35–67; secondary, 142; trade-offs among, 118, 161; transport of, 121, 122, 138, 140, 142, 143, 144; treatment of, 118, 122, 138–48 *passim*, 164. *See also* Particulates; Pesticides; Solid wastes
Resource system, closed, 11, 31; materials-balance view, 13–18
Resources, natural, 70; extractive, 24–30 *passim*; nonrenewable, 69; optimum flow rate, 183; rate of use, 24–33; social costs of extraction, 26. *See also* Irreplaceable assets
Resources for the Future, Inc., 1, 2, 12*n*, 69*n*, 119, 181, 243*n*, 354*n*, 367
Rice, Dorothy, 240, 241*n*
Ridker, Ronald G., 152*n*, 214*n*, 231, 235, 263*n*
Riker, William, 287*n*
River: ambient concentrations of discharges, 173*t*; BOD-DO relationship, 148*n*, 149, 151, 170; major objectives for basin investment, 304; temperature and DO Profile, 176*f*
Roberts, Marc J., 276*n*
Rogers, P. P., 131*n*
Rose, Arnold M., 347*n*
Rossi, Peter, 346
Rothenberg, J., 17
Rousseau, Jean Jacques, 286*n*
Rumford, J., 227*n*
Russell, Clifford S., 140*n*, 153*n*, 159*n*, 243*n*, 269*n*

Saaty, T., 134*n*
St. Louis, Mo., 264
San Francisco Bay Conservation and Development Commission: major responsibilities, 310–11; membership, 311–13; social choice problems confronted by, 309–10; voting blocs within, 313–14
Sander, Donald, 69*n*

INDEX

Schelling, T. C., 232, 267
Schoettlin, C., 234
Schushert, C., 19*n*
Scitovsky, T., 12
Seagraves, J. A., 89
Seneca, Joseph J., 78*n*, 82, 90, 152*n*,
269, 270, 271*n*, 276*n*
Services, environmental, 12, 262–69;
directly consumed by individuals,
250–52; distribution of, 243–49, 253,
257, 258–73; as intermediate inputs,
252–57; models, 253–57; and prop-
erty rights, 3, 247–48, 276, 281; use
of, for waste reception, 258–62;
utilization of, 254*f*, 255*f*; value de-
terminants of, 253–57
Seskin, Eugene, 224, 226*n*, 227*n*, 230,
231, 240*n*, 241*n*, 263*n*
Shabman, Leonard A., 272*n*
Shadow prices, 22, 27, 30, 126, 137,
156, 158, 207, 248
Shapley, L. S., 286*n*, 287*n*, 289, 307,
308, 313, 317
Shapley value, 286–89, 307, 308
Shell, K., 19
Shepherd, Godfrey, 78*n*
Shubik, Martin, 387*n*
Sludge, 138, 164, 165*n*
Smith, S. C., 152*n*
Smith, V. Kerry, 69*n*
Smog, 128
Smoking, 216, 217, 230, 231
Social choice: examples of institutions
making, 302–22; mechanisms of,
283–84, 286; problems in making,
281–83; tools for analyzing, 286–302
Social costs, 26, 32
Social welfare, 193–94, 209, 210, 243–
49
Solid wastes, 116, 117, 138, 154, 163,
164; top leader interest in, 370, 371*t*
Soviet Union, 115*n*
Spofford, Walter O., Jr., 159*n*
Stack gases, 161, 163, 164
Standard Industrial Classification (SIC
code), 37, 38, 43, 44

Standard Metropolitan Statistical Areas
(SMSA), 218, 224, 225*t*, 230
Standards: quality, 124*n*, 239, 260,
261, 276; regional versus national,
236–38
Steiner, Peter O., 73
Sternglass, E., 217*n*
Stevens, J. B., 152*n*
Stewart, Paul A., 202
Stickel, Lucille F., 205
Stickel, William H., 205
Streeter, H. W., 149
Strotz, Robert H., 11*n*, 23*n*, 267*n*, 268
Stubblebine, William Craig, 198
Subsidies, 12, 61, 237, 248*n*, 262, 274
Sulfates and sulfation, 222, 223, 225*t*,
226, 228, 229, 264, 265*t*, 266*t*
Sulfur dioxide, 153, 154, 163, 164; dis-
tribution of concentrations, 176,
177*f*

Taxes, 13, 24, 32, 61, 237, 249, 261,
262, 321
Taylor, Michael, 292
Technological change model, 74–75;
quantitative results of application,
88
Technology: and alternative uses of
Hells Canyon, 72–88, 89*t*, 94; impli-
cations of, for uses of irreplaceable
assets, 70, 72–75; and production
processes, 37–42, 57–58; and re-
sources flow rate, 183–84; and stand-
ard of living, 186; and substitution,
70; taxation of waste-generating, 24;
thermal generation as advance in,
73–75
Thomas, H. A., Jr., 160*n*
Thompson, Peter, 299
Thomsen, F. L., 78*n*
Tolley, G., 235
Tourin, B., 235
Trade-offs, 80*f*, 118, 161, 253, 322
Tullock, Gordon, 283*n*
Turvey, R., 213*n*
Typology, basic criteria for, 42

407

United States government: Bureau of the Census, 39, 43; Bureau of Mines, 39; Bureau of Outdoor Recreation, 269; Bureau of Reclamation, 285; Congress, 187, 191, 207, 285, 294, 306, 309, 324, 337n; Corps of Engineers, 285, 304, 324, 342; Department of Agriculture, 39, 182, 191, 192, 202, 207; Department of Health, Education and Welfare, 315, 316n; Department of the Interior, 269n, 342; Federal Power Commission, 73n, 98n; Forest Service, 272n; Public Health Service, 203; Supreme Court, 98n; Weather Bureau, 167

Urban areas: air pollution and mortality in, 217–18; benefits of abatement in, 268–69; leader interest and activity priorities in, 369t

Urban coalitions, 359, 363

Vanek, J., 32

Venecho, James, 346

Voting: majority vote and significance of the mean, 295–97, 298; power of blocs, 286–89, 308t, 317t; regression analysis of, 294–95; structure of, in Penjerdel, 316; trading in, 284, 290–91, 299, 300f, 314, 322

Walras-Cassel model, 38, 42

Warren, Roland L., 345, 346n

Washington, D.C., 264, 355–64 passim, 374–79 passim

Waste receptors: benefit and cost distribution of, 258–62; damage to, 122–26, 129, 130

Wastes. See Residuals; Solid wastes

Water: costs and benefits of modifying, 159; legislative process in relation to, 285; management of, 274, 303, 307; multiple-use problems, 285; policy for use, 285, 304, 306; and politics, 324; predicting quality of, 149; as waste receptor service, 258–62. See also Water pollution

Water pollution, 116, 117, 142, 145, 154; ambient concentrations, 173t; effect of wastewater treatment on, 163, 164; pesticide residue, 199; top leader interest in, 370, 371t

Water supply, treatment of, 152

Watson, Alvin G., 302n, 303

Weisbrod, B., 72, 95, 96, 99, 100, 101, 109

Welfare. See Social welfare

Wertz, K., 236

Whinston, A., 213n

Whipple, William, Jr., 159n

White, Gilbert, 5

White, Theodore, 363

Wildavsky, Aaron, 277n

Wilderness, 271

Wildlife, damage to, 198, 199, 202, 342

Wildlife preserve case, 334–37

"Willingness to pay," 80, 81, 95, 121n, 126, 139, 213, 214, 215, 231, 233, 247, 248, 249, 257, 263, 282

Wolman, Harold, 346

Woodwell, George M., 202

Wool processing, 56, 66t

Yocum, J., 215n, 235

Yosemite National Park, 71

Zeckhauser, R., 96n

Zeidberg, L., 234